O9-AIE-330

MOUNTAIN BIKE!
Southern California

THIRD EDITION

MOUNTAIN BIKE!

Southern California

A GUIDE TO THE CLASSIC TRAILS

THIRD EDITION

DAVID STORY
LAURIE & CHRIS LEMAN

Menasha
Ridge
Press

To Tracy, Katherine, and Fiona—my three muses for the third edition.—D.S.

© 2001 by David Story, Laurie Leman, and Chris Leman
All rights reserved
Printed in the United States of America
Published by Menasha Ridge Press
Distributed by The Globe Pequot Press
Third edition, first printing

Library of Congress Catololging-in-Publication Data
Story, David, 1962-
Mountain bike! Southern California / David Story. –3rd ed.
p. cm.
Includes index
ISBN 0-89732-393-9 (alk. paper)
1. All terrain cycling–California, Southern–Guidebooks.
2. Bicycle trails–California, Southern–Guidebooks.
3. California, Southern–Guidebooks. I. Title.

GV1055.5.C22 S687 2001
796.6'3'097949–dc21

2001034281

Photos by the author unless otherwise credited
Maps by Steven Jones and Jeff Goodwin
Cover and text design by Suzanne Holt
Cover photo by David Reddick

Menasha Ridge Press
P.O. Box 43673
Birmingham, Alabama 35243
www.menasharidge.com

All trails described in this book are legal for mountain bikes. But rules can change—especially for off-road bicycles, the new kid on the outdoor recreation block. Land access issues and conflicts between bicyclists, hikers, equestrians, and other users can cause the rewriting of recreation regulations on public lands, sometimes resulting in a ban of mountain bike use on specific trails. That's why it's the responsibility of each rider to check and make sure that he or she rides only on trails where mountain biking is permitted.

CAUTION

Outdoor recreational activities are by their very nature potentially hazardous. All participants in such activities must assume the responsibility for their own actions and safety. The information contained in this guidebook cannot replace sound judgment and good decision-making skills, which help reduce risk exposure, nor does the scope of this book allow for disclosure of all the potential hazards and risks involved in such activities.

Learn as much as possible about the outdoor recreational activities in which you participate, prepare for the unexpected, and be cautious. The reward will be a safer and more enjoyable experience.

CONTENTS

AMERICA BY MOUNTAIN BIKE! MAP LEGEND

Ride trailhead	Steep grade	Optional trailhead		
Primary bike trail	Direction of travel	(arrows point downhill)	Optional bike trail	Restricted area	Hiking trail

Interstate highways (with exit no.)	US routes	State routes	Other paved roads	Unpaved, gravel, or dirt roads (may be 4WD only)

Covell Blvd.

US Forest Service roads	Cities	Towns or settlements	Lake	Dam	River, stream, or canal

Asheville ◉   Linville ◉

0 1/2 1 MILES			
Approximate scale in miles	True north	Public Lands*	International border	State border

TOPANGA ST. PK.

✈ Airport

🎿 Ski Area

🌳 Orchard

▲ Campground (CG)

≡ Cattle guard

⬛ Spring

⬆ Park

〰 Cliff, escarpment, or outcropping

🔥 Drinking water

🏭 Power Plant

Fire tower or lookout

🔟 Food

✉ Gate

🏠 House, shelter, or cabin

🛏 Lodging

☀ Mountain or butte

🏃 Mountain pass

△ Mountain summit
3312 (elevation in feet)

👫 Rest room

✕ Mine

♨ Museum

🔭 Observatory

♟ Park office or ranger station

⊼ Picnic area

❄ Sno-Park

╱ Power line or pipeline

🐎 Ranch or stable

🏊 Swimming Area

⚡ Transmission towers

⌒ Tunnel or bridge

*Remember, private property exists in and around our national forests.

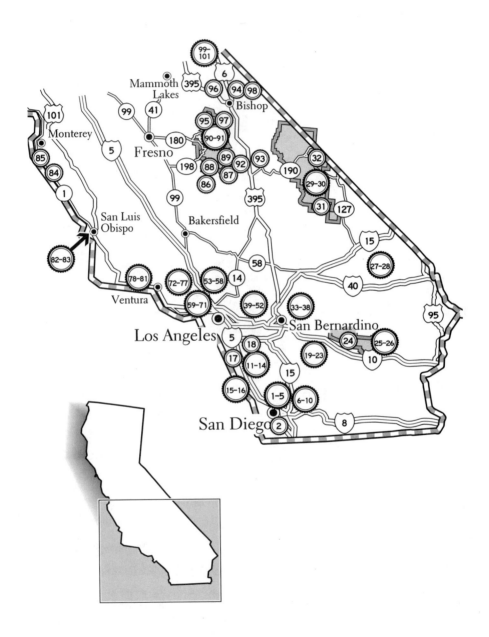

ACKNOWLEDGMENTS

The toughest thing about writing guidebooks is that you can't simply make stuff up. It's a lot of work getting to the truth, and it's work that I couldn't have done on my own. I had a lot of help.

I am especially grateful to Laurie and Chris Leman for writing the first edition of this title back in 1992. Though the rides and information have changed significantly over the last three editions, the spirit and form of the Lemans' original work remain.

I also would like to thank all the land managers who have contributed their time, information, and guidance. I'm amazed at the energy and diligence of rangers and managers in Southern California's national parks; national forests; Bureau of Land Management (BLM) lands; and state, county, and municipal parks. I'd like to especially thank those managers who helped fact check the second edition as my editors and I prepared this update. Please keep up the good work.

Series editor Dennis Coello was a major catalyst for my involvement in this series, and all the people at Menasha Ridge Press have mirrored Dennis' extraordinary patience while accommodating me during the long process of updating this book.

Bike shops all over California's southland helped keep my wheels and trail choices in line. In particular, I'm grateful to Helen's Cycles in Santa Monica for restoring my bike to working order despite my best attempts to destroy it. Likewise, I could not have completed this book without the support of Cannondale Corporation. You've made a thrilling sport even "thrillinger." Burley Design Cooperative has also made it possible for me to research this book and be a good father at the same time, and that's a miracle worth mentioning.

My parents and siblings have always encouraged the love of words and the outdoors, and I hope this book reflects that. At home, my wife and daughters put a smile on my face when even mountain biking could not. Finally, I would like to simultaneously give thanks and apologize to my riding buddies who posed for interminable pictures and suffered through endless note-taking. You're off the clock for a while—until the fourth edition, that is.

—David Story, Santa Monica, CA, Spring 2001

FOREWORD

Welcome to *America by Mountain Bike*, a series designed to provide all-terrain bikers with the information they need to find and ride the very best trails around. Whether you're new to the sport and don't know where to pedal or an experienced mountain biker who wants to learn the classic trails in another region, this series is for you. Drop a few bucks for the book, spend an hour with the detailed maps and route descriptions, and you're prepared for the finest in off-road cycling.

My role as editor of this series is simple: First, find a mountain biker who knows the area and loves to ride. Second, ask that person to spend a year researching the most popular and very best rides around. And third, have that rider describe each trail in terms of difficulty, scenery, condition, elevation change, and all other categories of information that are important to trail riders. "Pretend you've just completed a ride and met up with fellow mountain bikers at the trailhead," I told each author. "Imagine their questions, be clear in your answers."

As I said, the *editorial* process—that of sending out riders and reading the submitted chapters—is a snap. But the work involved in finding, riding, and writing about each trail is enormous. In some instances, our authors' tasks are made easier by the information contributed by local bike shops or cycling clubs, or even by the writers of local "where-to" guides. Credit for these contributions is provided, when appropriate, in each chapter, and our sincere thanks goes to all who have helped.

But the overwhelming majority of trails are discovered and pedaled by our authors themselves, then compared with dozens of other routes to determine if they qualify as "classic"—that area's best in scenery and cycling fun. If you've ever had the experience of pioneering a route from outdated topographic maps, or entering a bike shop to request information from local riders who would much prefer to keep their favorite trails secret, or if you know how it is to double- and triple-check data to be positive your trail info is correct, then you have an idea of how each of our authors has labored to bring about these books. You and I, and all the mountain bikers of America, are the richer for their efforts.

You'll get more out of this book if you take a moment to read the Introduction explaining how to read the trail listings. The "Topographic Maps" section will help you understand how useful topos will be on a ride and will also tell you where to get them. And though this is a "where-to," not a "how-to" guide, those of you who have not traveled the backcountry might find "Hitting the Trail" of particular value.

In addition to the material above, newcomers to mountain biking might want to spend a minute with the glossary, page 365, so that terms like *hardpack, single-track,* and *waterbars* won't throw you when you come across them in the text.

All the best.

Dennis Coello
St. Louis

PREFACE

When my publishers asked me to revise and update this book to better reflect the landscape of Southern California mountain biking, I jumped at the chance. In my mind, I envisioned riding a lot and writing just a little. The true ratio was somewhat reversed. Though my inner sloth kept urging me to make quick work of this update, I persistently found different ways to enrich the book, from listing websites so readers can better access trail information, to rewriting route descriptions to make sure you don't get lost, to double-checking mileages and phone numbers until I felt like an IRS auditor.

All in all, compared to the second edition, this third edition contains 26 new or significantly modified rides; hours of fact-checking; and countless instances of text-tweaking. Though in previous editions this book has always proved its worthiness by selling better than many of its competitors, I believe it is now significantly improved. I like to think it offers all the resources you need as either a native or visiting Southern California mountain biker.

But while researching this third edition, I discovered something strange. To investigate potential new rides, I frequently accessed the Internet, especially those sites that encourage users to post reviews of their favorite trails. As part of these reviews, bikers note the day they last rode the trail. I was astonished to find that some riders rode the same trail every day—weekday and weekend. Even when they lived just a few miles from other great routes, they stuck to the familiar. These riders rightly consider themselves active bikers, but in many ways they're as weighed down by inertia as the couch potatoes they probably scorn.

As a guidebook author, inertia is my enemy. I wrote this new edition to help you break the shackles of inertia. I want you to explore paths and places you might not have considered. There are thirteen regions in this book; sample all of them. You'll be surprised by how different your riding experience can be if you simply travel an hour or two in a different direction in Southern California. The next time you wonder what the biking is like one mountain range over from your home turf, actually go over and ride it—and use this book as your guide. After all, ruts are bad—in trails and in life.

Sharing the trail–and another perfect day–in Southern California.

This book features legal routes (primarily on public lands) suitable for all abilities, from beginner to expert. The rides range all over Southern California—from Big Sur south to San Diego, and from Mammoth Lakes down to Mexico. It's a vast area, and I don't pretend that this book covers every trail in it. The major SoCal biking destinations are accounted for, but there are probably some regions whose full potential is still open to discovery. You might notice a bit of an emphasis on rides in the more populous southern part of Southern California, and that's intentional: not only is the riding superb, but there are more trails and trail users there. Still, I like to think I've covered most of the prime routes throughout the area. If in fact I've missed a (legal) "don't miss" ride, please drop me a line, care of the publisher. It'll likely show up in the next edition.

In the meantime, I've tried to make this book work for you by introducing routes that you might otherwise overlook. Therefore, I often don't dwell too long in any one place. For instance, the superb Chino Hills State Park has a vast network of trails, from which any number of rides can be created. If I were to examine every ride there, I'd probably have to leave out the entire Sequoia National Forest region to save pages. Instead, I've simply profiled one particular ride at Chino Hills so that you gain a better knowledge of the area. Further explorations are up to you.

Likewise, I don't spend valuable space on places where you don't need a guidebook, such as ski areas that offer lift-serviced mountain biking. Mammoth Mountain, Mt. Baldy, and Snow Summit all provide access to wonderful trails and offer guides and maps that will prevent you from getting lost. I realize that

Contrary to rumor, commutes in southern California really aren't that bad.

some other guidebooks feature chapters on commercial mountain biking areas, but I see no sense in taking up pages that could be devoted to helping you discover other, lesser-known, legal trails.

Please keep all the trails in this book legal by riding responsibly. Fortunately, it seems that the relationship between bikers and other trail users is improving. Except for a few gonzo downhillers, most bikers seem to be aware of trail-use courtesy. But even as awareness has increased, so has the technology that tempts you into forgetting that courtesy. Though you may be technically able to bomb a hill that might have scared you back in the early days, please ride in control, obey speed limits, slow down near hikers, and call out to equestrians before passing them on the trail.

If you're new to Southern California, be aware that we seem to experience more than our share of floods, droughts, fires, and earthquakes. All of these elements can greatly affect trails. It's always a good idea to ask a ranger or land manager for an update before cycling in an unknown area. You'll find the necessary "Sources of Additional Information" listed for each ride.

Finally, please note that the United States Forest Service/Pacific Southwest Region has implemented the National Forest Adventure Pass program. All visitors using the Angeles, Cleveland, Los Padres, or San Bernardino National Forests—in which many of this book's rides are located—will be required to display either a daily (cost: $5) or yearly ($30) pass on the rearview mirror of their vehicles. I've attempted to list all trailhead parking areas that require the Forest Adventure Pass. You can purchase a pass at Forest Service offices, local vendors, and by mail. Call the following national forests for more information: Angeles (626) 574-5200, Cleveland (858) 673-6180, Los Padres (805) 683-6711, or San Bernardino (909) 383-5588.

It's worth noting that there's an ongoing controversy behind the Adventure Pass program. Some say taxpayers shouldn't have to fork over additional money to use public lands, others counter that the forests are underfunded and that those who use them should pay the small fee for improvements and upkeep. Whatever your position on this controversy, there's no arguing that the biking routes in these forests and throughout California are priceless in value. I hope this book allows you to enjoy them to their fullest.

Happy Trails.

Family

3 Los Penasquitos Canyon
16 Dripping Cave/Hollow Oak
26 Queen Valley
37 Keller Peak/National Children's
    Forest
43 West Fork Road/Red Box Rincon
    Road (beginner option)
59 Betty B. Dearing Trail
66 Malibu Creek Loop (beginner

    option)
68 Paramount Ranch
69 Cheeseboro/Palo Comado
    Canyons
82 Bluff Trail/Montana de Oro
    State Park
88 Unal Trail
91 River Road Loop
100 Horseshoe Lake Loop

Novice and Beginner

3 Los Penasquitos Canyon
6 Green Valley Loop
16 Dripping Cave/Hollow Oak
26 Queen Valley
37 Keller Peak/National Children's
    Forest
43 West Fork Road/Red Box Rincon
    Road (beginner option)
59 Betty B. Dearing Trail
66 Malibu Creek Loop (beginner
    option)

68 Paramount Ranch
76 Gridley/ Trail Loop (novice
    option)
82 Bluff Trail/Montana de Oro State
    Park
84 Central Coast Ridge Road
88 Unal Trail
91 River Road Loop
100 Horseshoe Lake Loop

Intermediate and Advanced (Short Rides)

1 Mission Trails Regional Park
2 San Clemente/Rose Canyons
4 Lake Hodges
5 Daley Ranch
6 Green Valley Loop
9 Big Laguna Trail
11 Bell Canyon
13 Trabuco Canyon/West Horsethief
14 Whiting Ranch/The Luge
15 Wood Canyon
17 Moro Canyon
23 The Goat Trails
35 Delamar Mountain
40 Manzanita Trail
41 Marshall Canyon
52 La Tuna Canyon
53 Sierra Pelona/Five Deer Trail
57 South Ridge/North Ridge
60 Kenter Fire Road/
    Whoop-De-Doos
61 Westridge/Sullivan Canyon

63 Eagle Rock/Eagle Springs
65 Red Rock Canyon/Calabasas
    Motorway
67 Backbone Trail/Castro Crest
69 Cheeseboro/Palo Comado
    Canyons
73 Lynnmere/Wildwood Regional
    Park
74 Butte Trail/Santa Rosa Trail
77 Pine Mountain
83 Islay Creek Trail/Montana de
    Oro State Park
84 Central Coast Ridge Road
85 Ridge Trail/Andrew Molera
    State Park
86 Black Gulch Rabbit
    Ramble/Keysville Road
90 Converse Basin
98 Knolls Trail
101 San Joaquin Ridge Trails/
    Mountain View

Intermediate and Advanced (Long Rides)

Loops

Loops *(continued)*

73 Lynnmere/Wildwood
  Regional Park
74 Butte Trail/Santa Rosa Trail
76 Gridley/Pratt Trail Loop
  (novice option)
82 Bluff Trail/Montana de Oro
  State Park
83 Islay Creek Trail/Montana
  de Oro State Park

86 Black Gulch Rabbit Ramble/
  Keysville Road
87 Shirley Meadows Shebang
91 River Road Loop
95 Buttermilk Country Loop
97 Lower Rock Creek
98 Knolls Trail
100 Horseshoe Lake Loop

Out-and-Backs

3 Los Penasquitos Canyon
4 Lake Hodges
9 Big Laguna Trail
16 Dripping Cave/Hollow Oak
24 Pinkham Canyon Road
31 Aguereberry Point
33 Santa Ana River Trail
42 Mount Baldy
43 West Fork Road/Red Box Rincon
  Road (beginner option)
66 Malibu Creek Loop (beginner
  option)

75 Sulphur Mountain Road
77 Pine Mountain
78 Romero Canyon
79 Little Pine Mountain
80 Wildhorse/Zaca Peak
81 Bates Canyon Road/Sierra Madre
  Road
84 Central Coast Ridge Road
94 Ancient Bristlecone
96 Red Canyon/Chidago Canyon

Point-to-Points

10 Coyote Canyon
21 Palm Canyon
32 Titus Canyon

46 Mt. Wilson/Big Santa Anita
  Canyon
47 Mt. Wilson/Gabrielino Trail
89 Cannell Trail

Combinations

2 San Clemente/Rose Canyons
5 Daley Ranch
6 Green Valley Loop
7 Cuyamaca Peak
11 Bell Canyon
12 San Juan/Old San Juan Trail
13 Trabuco Canyon/West Horsethief
15 Wood Canyon
17 Moro Canyon
23 The Goat Trails
26 Queen Valley
29 Greenwater Valley
38 Mr. Toad's Wild Ride
39 Blue Ridge "d"
48 Inspiration Point

50 Brown Mountain/Ken Burton
  & El Prieto Options
51 Mendenhall Ridge/
  Pacoima Canyon
53 Sierra Pelona/Five Deer Trail
54 Elderberry Forebay/
  Cienaga Loop
55 Burnt Peak/Upper Shake
57 South Ridge/North Ridge
58 Mt. Pinos Loop
60 Kenter Fire Road/Whoop-De-
  Doos
63 Eagle Rock/Eagle Springs
67 Backbone Trail/Castro Crest
68 Paramount Ranch

Combinations *(continued)*

Technical Heaven

High-Speed Cruising

Wildlife Viewing

Great Scenery

Great Scenery (*continued*)

54 Elderberry Forebay/
       Cienaga Loop
56 Liebre Mountain/Golden
       Eagle Trail
58 Mt. Pinos Loop
61 Westridge/Sullivan Canyon
62 Sullivan Ridge/Backbone Trail
64 Paseo Miramar/Topanga Loop
65 Red Rock Canyon/Calabasas
       Motorway
66 Malibu Creek Loop (beginner
       option)
67 Backbone Trail/Castro Crest
68 Paramount Ranch
69 Cheeseboro/Palo Comado
       Canyons
73 Lynnmere/Wildwood
       Regional Park
74 Butte Trail/Santa Rosa Trail
76 Gridley/Pratt Trail Loop (novice
       option)
77 Pine Mountain
78 Romero Canyon

80 Wildhorse/Zaca Peak
81 Bates Canyon Road/Sierra
       Madre Road
82 Bluff Trail/Montana de Oro
       State Park
83 Islay Creek Trail/Montana
       de Oro State Park
84 Central Coast Ridge Road
85 Ridge Trail/Andrew Molera
       State Park
86 Black Gulch Rabbit Ramble/
       Keysville Road
87 Shirley Meadows Shebang
88 Unal Trail
89 Cannell Trail
91 River Road Loop
94 Ancient Bristlecone
95 Buttermilk Country Loop
97 Lower Rock Creek
98 Knolls Trail
99 Inyo Craters
101 San Joaqui Ridge/Mountain View
       Trails

Single Track

2 San Clemente/Rose Canyons
4 Lake Hodges
8 Noble Canyon
9 Big Laguna Trail
12 San Juan/Old San Juan Trail
13 Trabuco Canyon/West Horsethief
14 Whiting Ranch/The Luge
15 Wood Canyon
17 Moro Canyon
19 Thomas Mountain Road/
       Ramona Trail
20 Santa Rosa Mountain/
       Sawmill Trail
21 Palm Canyon
22 Art Smith Trail
23 The Goat Trails
33 Santa Ana River Trail
34 Skyline Drive
36 Arctic Canyon Overlook
39 Blue Ridge "d"
40 Manzanita Trail

41 Marshall Canyon
44 Chilao Flat Figure 8½
46 Mt. Wilson/Big Santa Anita
       Canyon
47 Mt. Wilson/Gabrielino Trail
48 Inspiration Point
50 Brown Mountain/Ken
       Burton & El Prieto Options
52 La Tuna Canyon
53 Sierra Pelona/Five Deer Trail
56 Liebre Mountain/Golden
       Eagle Trail
58 Mt. Pinos Loop
60 Kenter Fire Road/
       Whoop-De-Doos
67 Backbone Trail/Castro Crest
71 Big Sycamore Canyon/Point
       Mugu State Park
73 Lynnmere/Wildwood
       Regional Park
74 Butte Trail/Santa Rosa Trail

Single Track *(continued)*

INTRODUCTION

Each trail in this book begins with key information that includes length, configuration, aerobic and technical difficulty, trail conditions, scenery, and special comments. Additional description is contained in 11 individual categories. The following will help you understand all of the information provided.

Trail name: Trail names are as designated on United States Geological Survey (USGS) or Forest Service or other maps, and/or by local custom.

At a Glance Information

Length/configuration: The overall length of a trail is described in miles, unless stated otherwise. The configuration is a description of the shape of each trail — whether the trail is a loop, out-and-back (that is, along the same route), figure eight, trapezoid, isosceles triangle, decahedron . . . (just kidding), or if it connects with another trail described in the book. See the Glossary for definitions of *point-to-point* and *combination*.

Aerobic difficulty: This provides a description of the degree of physical exertion required to complete the ride.

Technical difficulty: This provides a description of the technical skill required to pedal a ride. Trails are often described here in terms of being paved, unpaved, sandy, hard-packed, washboarded, two- or four-wheel-drive, single-track or double-track. All terms that might be unfamiliar to the first-time mountain biker are defined in the Glossary.

Note: For both the aerobic and technical difficulty categories, authors were asked to keep in mind the fact that all riders are not equal, and thus to gauge the trail in terms of how the middle-of-the-road rider — someone between the newcomer and Ned Overend—could handle the route. Comments about the trail's length, condition, and elevation change will also assist you in determining the difficulty of any trail relative to your own abilities.

Scenery: Here you will find a general description of the natural surroundings during the seasons most riders pedal the trail and a suggestion of what is to be found at special times (like great fall foliage or cactus in bloom).

Special comments: Unique elements of the ride are mentioned.

Category Information

General location: This category describes where the trail is located in reference to a nearby town or other landmark.

Elevation change: Unless stated otherwise, the figure provided is the total gain and loss of elevation along the trail. In regions where the elevation variation is not extreme, the route is simply described as flat, rolling, or possessing short steep climbs or descents.

Season: This is the best time of year to pedal the route, taking into account trail conditions (for example, when it will not be muddy), riding comfort (when the weather is too hot, cold, or wet), and local hunting seasons.

   Note: Because the exact opening and closing dates of wild game seasons often change from year to year, riders should check with the local fish and game department or call a sporting goods store (or any place that sells hunting licenses) in a nearby town before heading out. Wear bright clothes in fall, and don't wear suede jackets while in the saddle. Hunter's-orange tape on the helmet is also a good idea.

Services: This category is of primary importance in guides for paved-road tourers, but is far less crucial to most mountain bike trail descriptions because there are usually no services whatsoever to be found. Authors have noted when water is available on desert or long mountain routes and have listed the availability of food, lodging, campgrounds, and bike shops. If all these services are present, you will find only the words "All services available in . . ."

Hazards: Special hazards like steep cliffs, great amounts of deadfall, or barbed-wire fences very close to the trail are noted here.

Rescue index: Determining how far one is from help on any particular trail can be difficult due to the backcountry nature of most mountain bike rides. Authors therefore state the proximity of homes or Forest Service outposts, nearby roads where one might hitch a ride, or the likelihood of other bikers being encountered on the trail. Phone numbers of local sheriff departments or hospitals are hardly ever provided because phones are usually not available. If you are able to reach a phone, the local operator will connect you with emergency services.

Land status: This category provides information regarding whether the trail crosses land operated by the Forest Service, Bureau of Land Management, or a city, state, or national park; whether it crosses private land whose owner (at the time the author did the research) has allowed mountain bikers right of passage; and so on.

Note: Authors have been extremely careful to offer only those routes that are open to bikers and are legal to ride. However, because land ownership changes over time, and because the land-use controversy created by mountain bikes still has not completely subsided, it is the duty of each cyclist to look for and heed signs warning against trail use. Don't expect this book to get you off the hook when you're facing some small-town judge for pedaling past a Biking Prohibited sign erected the day before you arrived. Look for these signs, read them, and heed their advice. And remember there's always another trail.

Maps: The maps in this book have been produced with great care, and in conjunction with the trail-following suggestions, they will help you stay on course. But as every experienced mountain biker knows, things can get tricky in the backcountry. It is therefore strongly suggested that you avail yourself of the detailed information found in the 7.5-minute series USGS (U.S. Geological Survey) topographic maps. In some cases, authors have found that specific Forest Service or other maps may be more useful than the USGS quads and tell how to obtain them.

Finding the trail: Detailed information on how to reach the trailhead and where to park your car is provided here.

Sources of additional information: Here you will find the address and/or phone number of a bike shop, governmental agency, or other source from which trail information can be obtained.

Notes on the trail: This is where you are guided carefully through any portions of the trail that are particularly difficult to follow. The author also may add information about the route that does not fit easily in the other categories. This category will not be present for those rides where the route is easy to follow.

ABBREVIATIONS

The following road-designation abbreviations are used in *Mountain Bike! The Southern Appalachian and Smoky Mountains:*

CR	County Road	I-	Interstate
FR	Farm Route	IR	Indian Route
FS	Forest Service Road	US	United States highway

State highways are designated with the appropriate two-letter state abbreviation, followed by the road number. Example: CA 1 = California State Highway 1.

RIDE CONFIGURATIONS

Combination: This type of route may combine two or more configurations. For example, a point-to-point route may integrate a scenic loop or an out-and-back spur midway through the ride. Likewise, an out-and-back may have a loop at its farthest point (this configuration looks like a cherry with a stem attached;

the stem is the out-and-back, the fruit is the terminus loop). Or a loop route may have multiple out-and-back spurs and/or loops to the side. Mileage for a combination route is for the total distance to complete the ride.

Loop: This route configuration is characterized by riding from the designated trailhead to a distant point, then returning to the trailhead via a different route (or simply continuing on the same in a circle route) without doubling back. You always move forward across new terrain but return to the starting point when finished. Mileage is for the entire loop from the trailhead back to trailhead.

Out-and-back: A ride where you will return on the same trail you pedaled out. Although this might sound far more boring than a loop route, many trails look very different when pedaled in the opposite direction.

Point-to-point: A vehicle shuttle (or similar assistance) is required for this type of route, which is ridden from the designated trailhead to a distant location, or endpoint, where the route ends. Total mileage is for the one-way trip from the trailhead to endpoint.

Spur: A road or trail that intersects the main trail you're following.

Ride Configurations contributed by Gregg Bromka

TOPOGRAPHIC MAPS

The maps in this book, when used in conjunction with the route directions present in each chapter, will in most instances be sufficient to get you to the trail and keep you on it. However, you will find superior detail and valuable information in the 7.5-minute series USGS topographic maps. Recognizing how indispensable these are to bikers and hikers alike, many bike shops and sporting goods stores now carry topos of the local area.

But if you're brand new to mountain biking, you might be wondering "What's a topographic map?" In short, these differ from standard "flat" maps in that they indicate not only linear distance but elevation as well. One glance at a topo will show you the difference, for "contour lines" are spread across the map like dozens of intricate spider webs. Each contour line represents a particular elevation, and at the base of each topo a particular "contour interval" designation is given. Yes, it sounds confusing if you're new to the lingo, but it truly is a simple and wonderfully helpful system. Keep reading.

Let's assume that the 7.5 minute series topo before us says "Contour Interval 40 feet," that the short trail we'll be pedaling is two inches in length on the map, and that it crosses five contour lines from its beginning to end. What do we know? Well, because the linear scale of this series is 2,000 feet to the inch (roughly 2 3/4 inches representing 1 mile), we know our trail is approximately 4/5 of a mile long (2 inches × 2,000 feet). But we also know we'll be climbing or descending 200 vertical feet (5 contour lines × 40 feet each) over that distance. And the elevation designations written on occasional contour lines will tell us if we're heading up or down.

The authors of this series warn their readers of upcoming terrain, but only a detailed topo gives you the information you need to pinpoint your position exactly on a map, steer yourself toward optional trails and roads nearby, plus let you know at a glance if you'll be pedaling hard to take them. It's a lot of information for a very low cost. In fact, the only drawback with topos is their size — several feet square. I've tried rolling them into tubes, folding them carefully, even cutting them into blocks and photocopying the pieces. Any of these systems is a pain, but no matter how you pack the maps you'll be happy they're along. And you'll be even happier if you pack a compass as well.

In addition to local bike shops and sporting goods stores, you'll find topos at major universities and some public libraries where you might try photocopying the ones you need to avoid the cost of buying them. But if you want your own and can't find them locally, contact:

USGS Map Sales
Box 25286
Denver, CO 80225
(800) HELP MAP (435-7627)

VISA and MasterCard are accepted. Ask for an index while you're at it, plus a price list and a copy of the booklet *Topographic Maps*. In minutes, you'll be reading them like a pro.

A second excellent series of maps available to mountain bikers is that put out by the U.S. Forest Service. If your trail runs through an area designated as a national forest, look in the phone book (white pages) under the United States Government listings, find the Department of Agriculture heading, and then run your finger down that section until you find the Forest Service. Give them a call and they'll provide the address of the regional Forest Service office, from which you can obtain the appropriate map.

TRAIL ETIQUETTE

Pick up almost any mountain bike magazine these days and you'll find articles and letters to the editor about trail conflict. For example, you'll find hikers' tales of being blindsided by speeding mountain bikers, complaints from mountain bikers about being blamed for trail damage that was really caused by horse or cattle traffic, and cries from bikers about those "kamikaze" riders who through their antics threaten to close even more trails to all of us.

The authors of this series have been very careful to guide you to only those trails that are open to mountain biking (or at least were open at the time of their research), and without exception have warned of the damage done to our sport through injudicious riding. All of us can benefit from glancing over the following International Mountain Bicycling Association (IMBA) Rules of the Trail before saddling up.

1. *Ride on open trails only.* Respect trail and road closures (ask if not sure), avoid possible trespass on private land, obtain permits and authorization as may be required. Federal and state wilderness areas are closed to cycling.

2. *Leave no trace.* Be sensitive to the dirt beneath you. Even on open trails, you should not ride under conditions where you will leave evidence of your passing, such as on certain soils shortly after rain. Observe the different types of soils and trail construction; practice low-impact cycling. This also means staying on the trail and not creating any new ones. Be sure to pack out at least as much as you pack in.

3. *Control your bicycle!* Inattention for even a second can cause disaster. Excessive speed can maim and threaten people; there is no excuse for it!

4. *Always yield the trail.* Make known your approach well in advance. A friendly greeting (or a bell) is considerate and works well; startling someone may cause loss of trail access. Show your respect when passing others by slowing to a walk or even stopping. Anticipate that other trail users may be around corners or in blind spots.

5. *Never spook animals.* All animals are startled by an unannounced approach, a sudden movement, or a loud noise. This can be dangerous for you, for others, and for the animals. Give animals extra room and time to adjust to you. In passing, use special care and follow the directions of horseback riders (ask if uncertain). Running cattle and disturbing wild animals is a serious offense. Leave gates as you found them, or as marked.

6. *Plan ahead.* Know your equipment, your ability, and the area in which you are riding—and prepare accordingly. Be self-sufficient at all times. Wear a helmet, keep your machine in good condition, and carry necessary supplies for changes in weather or other conditions. A well-executed trip is a satisfaction to you and not a burden or offense to others.

For more information, contact IMBA, P.O. Box 7578, Boulder, CO 80306; (303) 545-9011.

HITTING THE TRAIL

Once again, because this is a "where-to," not a "how-to" guide, the following will be brief. If you're a veteran trail rider these suggestions might serve to remind you of something you've forgotten to pack. If you're a newcomer, they might convince you to think twice before hitting the backcountry unprepared.

Water: I've heard the questions dozens of times. "How much is enough? One bottle? Two? Three?! But think of all that extra weight!" Well, one simple physiological fact should convince you to err on the side of excess when it comes to deciding how much water to pack: a human working hard in 90-degree temperature needs approximately ten quarts of fluids every day. Ten quarts. That's two and a half gallons—12 large water bottles, or 16 small ones. And, with water weighing in at approximately 8 pounds per gallon, a one-day supply comes to a whopping 20 pounds.

In other words, pack along two or three bottles even for short rides. And make sure you can purify the water found along the trail on longer routes. When writing of those routes where this could be of critical importance, each author has provided information on where water can be found near the trail—if it can be found at all. But drink it untreated and you run the risk of disease. (See *Giardia* in the Glossary.)

One sure way to kill the protozoans, bacteria, and viruses in water is to boil it. Right. That's just how you want to spend your time on a bike ride. Besides, who wants to carry a stove or denude the countryside stoking bonfires to boil water?

Luckily, there is a better way. Many riders pack along the inexpensive and only slightly distasteful tetraglycine hydroperiodide tablets (sold under the names Potable Aqua, Globaline, and Coughlan's, among others). Some invest in portable, lightweight purifiers that filter out the crud. Unfortunately, both iodine *and* filtering are now required to be absolutely sure you've killed all the nasties you can't see. Tablets or iodine drops by themselves will knock off the well-known *Giardia*, once called "beaver fever" for its transmission to the water through the feces of infected beavers. One to four weeks after ingestion, *Giardia* will have you bloated, vomiting, shivering with chills, and living in the bathroom. (Though you won't care while you're suffering, beavers are getting a bum rap, for other animals are carriers also.)

But now there's another parasite we must worry about—*Cryptosporidium*. "Crypto" brings on symptoms very similar to *Giardia*, but unlike that fellow protozoan it's equipped with a shell sufficiently strong to protect it against the chemical killers that stop *Giardia* cold. This means we're either back to boiling or on to using a water filter to screen out both *Giardia* and crypto, plus the iodine to knock off viruses. All of which sounds like a time-consuming pain but really isn't. Some water filters come equipped with an iodine chamber, to guarantee full protection. Or you can simply add a pill or drops to the water you've just filtered (if you aren't allergic to iodine, of course). The pleasures of backcountry biking—and the displeasure of getting sick—make this relatively minor effort worth every one of the few minutes involved.

Tools: Ever since my first cross-country tour in 1965 I've been kidded about the number of tools I pack on the trail. And so I will exit entirely from this discussion by providing a list compiled by two mechanic (and mountain biker) friends of mine. After all, since they make their livings fixing bikes, and get their kicks by riding them, who could be a better source?

These two suggest the following as an absolute minimum:

tire levers
spare tube and patch kit
air pump
Allen wrenches (3, 4, 5, and 6 mm)
six-inch crescent (adjustable-end) wrench
small flat-blade screwdriver
chain rivet tool
spoke wrench

But, while they're on the trail, their personal tool pouches contain these additional items:

channel locks (small)
air gauge
tire valve cap (the metal kind, with a valve-stem remover)
baling wire (ten or so inches, for temporary repairs)
duct tape (small roll for temporary repairs or tire boot)
boot material (small piece of old tire or a large tube patch)
spare chain link
rear derailleur pulley
spare nuts and bolts
paper towel and tube of waterless hand cleaner

First-aid kit: My personal kit contains the following, sealed inside double Ziploc bags:

sunscreen
aspirin
butterfly-closure bandages
Band-Aids
gauze compress pads (a half-dozen 4" × 4")
gauze (one roll)
ace bandages or Spenco joint wraps
Benadryl (an antihistamine, in case of allergic reactions)
water purification tablets / water filter (on long rides)
moleskin / Spenco "Second Skin"
hydrogen peroxide, iodine, or Mercurochrome (some kind of antiseptic)
snakebite kit

Final considerations: The authors of this series have done a good job in suggesting that specific items be packed for certain trails—raingear in particular seasons, a hat and gloves for mountain passes, or shades for desert jaunts. Heed their warnings, and think ahead. Good luck.

Dennis Coello

AND NOW, A WORD ABOUT CELLULAR PHONES . . .

Thinking of bringing the Flip-Fone along on your next off-road ride? Before you do, ask yourself the following questions:

- Do I know where I'm going? Do I have an adequate map? Can I use a compass effectively? Do I know the shortest way to civilization if I need to bail out early and find some help?

- If I'm on the trail for longer than planned, am I ready for it? Do I have adequate water? Have I packed something to eat? Will I be warm enough if I'm still out there after dark?

- Am I prepared for possible injuries? Do I have a first-aid kit? Do I know what to do in case of a cut, fracture, snakebite, or heat exhaustion?

- Is my tool kit adequate for likely mechanical problems? Can I fix a flat? Can I untangle a chain? Am I prepared to walk out if the bike is unrideable?

If you answered "yes" to *every* question above, you may pack the phone, but consider a good whistle instead. It's lighter, cheaper, and nearly as effective.

If you answered "no" to *any* of these questions, be aware that your cellular phone does little to reduce your risks in the wilderness. Sure, being able to dial 911 in the farthest corner of the White Mountains sounds like a great idea, but this ain't downtown, friend. If disaster strikes, and your call is routed to some emergency operator in Manchester or Bangor, and it takes a while to figure out which ranger, sheriff, or search-and-rescue crew to connect you with, and you can't tell the authorities where you are because you're really not sure, and the closest they can come to pinpointing your location is a cellular tower that serves 62 square miles of dense woods, and they start searching for you but dusk is only two hours away, and you have no signaling device and your throat is too dry to shout, and meanwhile you can't get the bleeding stopped, you are out of luck. I mean *really* out of luck.

And when the battery goes dead, you're on your own again. Enough said.

Jeff Faust
Author of Mountain Bike! New Hampshire

SAN DIEGO COUNTY

Some time ago, *Sports Illustrated* magazine dubbed the city of San Diego as America's most athletic metropolis. Today, the label still fits. Having fun in the great outdoors is the county's favorite pastime, which is why local governments, environmental activists, and bikers have teamed up to create an impressive number of mountain biking opportunities here. If there's another place in California or North America where municipal, county, and state parks (along with a national forest) all try to outdo each other in welcoming mountain bikers, I'd like to hear about it.

And what a place to ride! San Diego County perhaps epitomizes the image of California better than anywhere else. Sunnier, drier, and much more casual than Los Angeles, San Diego has both the meteorological and social climate for mountain biking. It doesn't hurt that the terrain is amazingly diverse, either. For instance, San Diego County's arid deserts make up some of the hottest, driest regions on earth. Yet they butt up against mountains with upper elevations that receive more yearly precipitation than Puget Sound. And you get to ride in both.

So whether it's an after-work spin around Daley Ranch, an alpine loop at Cuyamaca Peak, or a desert descent through Coyote Canyon, you're sure to find some favorite trails. After riding here, you'll likely feel a kinship with Juan Cabrillo, who, upon landing in San Diego County in 1542, immediately declared that the land belonged to the Spanish Crown. Ride in San Diego, and you too might want to claim it all for yourself.

RIDE 1 · Mission Trails Regional Park

AT A GLANCE

Length/configuration: 8.1-mile loop on fire road, single-track, and pavement

Aerobic difficulty: Strenuous during two major climbs, but mostly moderate

Technical difficulty: Moderate to difficult; very rideable except for some rocky sections near Fortuna Mountain

Scenery: Diverse, ranging from scrubland to shady riverbeds

Special comments: This is a fun in-town ride, easily accessible from most of San Diego

Situated in Mission Trails Regional Park, this ride allows cyclists to experience both San Diego's past and future in a fun 8.1-mile loop. The past is represented by the Old Mission Dam, an edifice that has survived since Father Junipo Serra founded a Catholic mission here in the early 1800s. The future, meanwhile, is epitomized by the recent expansion of CA 52 along the park's northern border, a development that will allow developed San Diego, like its cousin Los Angeles, to continue spreading inland.

The ride starts from a little parking lot at the intersection of Jackson Drive and Mission Gorge Road. A descent and fording of the San Diego River lead to a fairly steep climb that provides great views of rugged terrain, and also the encroaching subdivisions. A single-track plunge gives the ride an alpine flavor before a wicked climb up to Fortuna Saddle intervenes. An abrupt descent toward Oak Canyon follows, until the trail meanders through enticing grasslands while swerving toward the Old Mission Dam.

In the fall, the brilliantly colored sycamores and willows surrounding the dam make it feel like a transplanted New England tableau. After a paved but carless descent alongside the lush San Diego River on the Father Junipo Serra Trail comes the return to the car and the awed realization that such an entertaining trail is so close to downtown San Diego.

General location: 10 miles east-northeast of downtown San Diego off Mission Gorge Road.

Elevation change: Climbs 740 feet (much of it over a short distance).

Season: Year-round, but crossing the San Diego River is not recommended after especially heavy winter rains. In addition, most of the trail is unshaded and hot on summer days.

Services: Water and rest room facilities can be found at the Visitor Center.

Hazards: Extremely steep and rocky hills on either side of Fortuna Mountain Saddle. Also watch out for a potentially deep river crossing in winter and spring. Rattlesnakes and poison oak exist throughout the park.

RIDE 1 • Mission Trails Regional Park

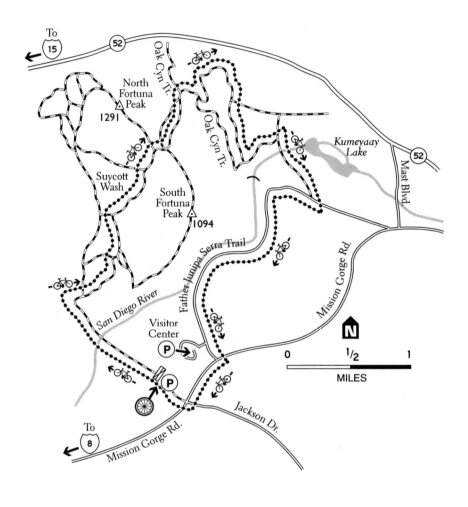

Rescue index: Though rugged, this is certainly a "town ride." Help is always nearby. Park rangers are stationed at the Mission Trails Visitor Center, which is reached at the end of ride.

Land status: Regional park.

Maps: A park trail map is available at the Visitor Center.

Finding the trail: Take Interstate 8 to Mission Gorge Road, about 6 miles east of downtown San Diego. Go northeast on Mission Gorge Road. When the businesses and residences give way to open land, get in the left lane. At 4.5 miles from I-8, turn left onto Jackson Drive, which immediately dead-ends in a dirt parking lot. A gate at the northwest end of the parking lot marks the beginning of the ride. Seriously heed any gate closure signs, as this park makes a practice of locking gates promptly at posted closing times.

Source of additional information:

Mission Trails Regional Park   www.mtrp.org
1 Father Junipero Serra Trail   (619) 668-3275
San Diego, CA 92119

Notes on the trail: Since the Visitor Center often can be swamped with traffic, this ride begins from the lesser-used Jackson Drive parking lot, which lacks facilities. If you require a park map, water, rest room, or more information, it's just a quick 0.4-mile jog to the Visitor Center along the well-marked Visitor Center Loop Trail. After your needs are met, return to the Jackson Drive parking area to start the ride. Begin by going around the gate at the northwest end of the parking lot and heading northwest on a fire road. The road almost immediately plummets into a canyon formed by the San Diego River. You'll reach a dirt road closely paralleling the river before hitting the water itself. Continue straight through the intersection and promptly cross the San Diego River. Be aware that this river can flow quickly after winter rains, so exercise caution.

After fording the river, there's a sharp climb to the ridgeline. Veer right at the ridge at 1 mile, and take a moment to reflect on the superlative views of wilderness. At 1.1 miles, turn right on the single-track marked "South Suycott/Mt. Fortuna." The trail is rutty at first and then studded with rideable waterbars. Veer slightly right at a junction at 1.4 miles, then take a quick left onto the main single-track path. You'll soon reach a shady picnic area. If it's hot and you need a break, stop here; there's no shade again for some time. Turn right at the junction with the main Mt. Fortuna road, at 1.9 miles. You can see the daunting climb to Fortuna Mountain Saddle that awaits you. At the intersection with the East Suycott Trail on your left at 2 miles, you'll have two options. You can continue straight and undertake the climb, or you can procrastinate and go left to make merry on the well-marked single-track trails of Suycott Wash in the shadow of CA 52 . If you choose this second option, just make sure to come back to the main Fortuna road eventually. (Mileage for this option is not included.)

The climb is gradual at first, but it soon becomes gnarly. At 2.4 miles, continue straight and upward, past a sign on your left leading to "North Suycott/West Fortuna/Shepherd Canyon." Even strong riders will probably have to walk portions of this climb. Reach Fortuna Mountain Saddle at 2.6 miles, between the peaks of North Fortuna and South Fortuna, and turn right. At 2.7 miles, turn left and plummet downhill at the ve-way junction, staying to the left of the green power pole. This section is also quite steep and rocky, so take care. Stay straight past the intersection with Oak Canyon Trail, on the left at 3.2 miles. Note how the scenery has become significantly more verdant and lush than on the west side of the saddle. At 3.3 miles, pass another Oak Canyon Trail sign, this one indicating that bikes are prohibited in that part of Oak Canyon. The occasionally rutty but mostly firm fire road you're traveling on begins to climb now. Stay on the main road and follow signs to "Old Mission Dam." Veer right at 3.7 miles, again following signs to the dam. At 3.9 miles, stay right again as the trail narrows at an unsigned intersection. Keep veering softly to the right until reaching a streambed. Cross the streambed at 4.5 miles and pick up the trail again (it will be located at approximately 1 o'clock). You're now bopping alongside a small creek. The trail splits, but from either fork you'll see a little wooden bridge crossing the creek. At 4.6 miles, go left and cross the bridge before climbing back to the main trail. Turn right on the main trail at 4.7 miles. Turn right again at 4.8 miles toward the Old Mission Dam Viewpoint. From the viewpoint take in the sight of the crumbling stone dam. When your eyes are sated, turn around and stay right as you cruise through the park's vast grasslands. Turn right at the trailhead kiosk at 5.2 miles. You'll soon cross two bridges before reaching paved Father Junipo Serra Trail (or FJST). At 5.4 miles, turn right again on FJST and glide down the pavement (which is closed to cars in this direction). The lush scenery surrounding the adjacent San Diego River is gorgeous. After passing the impressive Visitor Center, FJST ends at Mission Gorge Road. Turn right on Mission Gorge Road at 7.8 miles. At 8 miles, turn right on Jackson Drive. Reach the gate for the end of the ride at 8.1 miles.

RIDE 2 · San Clemente/Rose Canyons

AT A GLANCE

Length/configuration: 17.2-mile combination (in the form of two linked out-and-back rides: one 5.7 miles each way, the second, 2.8 miles each way)

Aerobic difficulty: Easy—all points on the ride are within 400 feet of each other in elevation

Technical difficulty: Moderate—lots of single-track, some of it narrow or off-camber

Scenery: Gorgeous willows, sycamores, and oaks; pretty stream; railroad and highways

Special comments: A town ride with miles of fun exploration possibilities, this is perfect for intermediates who want to stay close to home

The placement of Miramar Naval Air Station and its strict no-trespassing policies prevent this 17.2-mile out-and-back ride from coming together as a 9.5-mile loop. However, in this case, repeated terrain is not a bad thing. This city ride features so many exploration possibilities, it's fun to get one's bearings on the "out" portion and then explore on the "back" section.

The ride begins in Marian Bear Memorial Park, just south of CA 52. Riding west from the parking lot, riders begin curving alongside a small stream in wooded San Clemente Canyon. The trails are numerous here, but it's always

RIDE 2 • San Clemente/Rose Canyons

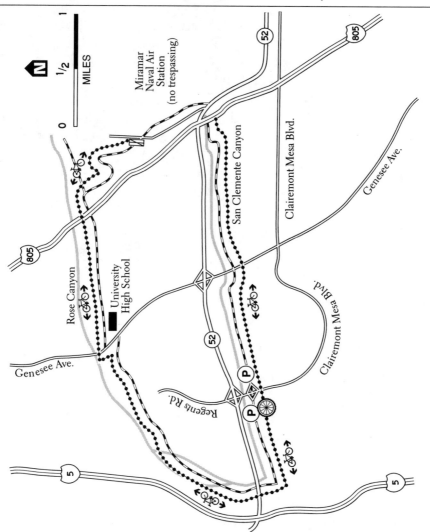

possible to orient yourself by using railroad tracks for bearings as you continue into Rose Canyon. The trail opens up there, and you can make some good time on the level dirt roads until you turn around at the gate to Miramar. On the way back, it's fun to explore places you missed on the way out. After re-entering San Clemente Canyon and returning to the parking lot, you are now ready to spin through the ride's most fun section. East of the parking lot, the number of side tracks explode. After just a little bit of tentative exploring, you'll reach your comfort zone and begin swooping from one side of San Clemente creek to the other. Though the intrusion of Miramar makes you turn around once more, you'll have too much fun to notice.

Don't spit while driving on San Diego's freeways; you might hit this bike.

Do be aware, however, that this route takes place in small urban parks where hikers, bikers, picnickers, and nature are all pushing for their space. It's likely that limits and regulations could change. Contact park officials for updated information before riding here.

General location: In San Diego, just south of CA 52 at Clairemont Mesa Road.

Elevation change: Approximately a 500-foot gain.

Season: Year-round.

Services: Rest rooms and water are available at Marian Bear Memorial Park.

Hazards: Narrow trails, rattlesnakes, and poison oak.

Rescue index: A ranger is sometimes on duty at Marian Bear Memorial Park. The route is always close to major roads and highways. Help is available in San Diego; call 911 in an emergency.

Land status: City parkland, municipal property.

Maps: USGS 7.5-minute quadrangle map: La Jolla.

Finding the trail: Take CA 52 to Clairemont Mesa Boulevard, and exit to the south. Turn right (west) into the Marian Bear Memorial Park parking lot and park. (Parking is divided into west and east lots that flank both sides of Clairemont Mesa Boulevard. However, you cannot make left turns from Clairemont Mesa Boulevard. Instead, use an underpass beneath Clairemont Mesa to go from one parking lot to the other.)

Sources of additional information:

City of San Diego
Parks and Recreation
    Department
Natural Open Space Parks
202 C Street
San Diego, CA 92101
(619) 685-1350

www.sannet.gov/park-and-
    recreation/parks/marbear2.shtml
www.sannet.gov/park-and-
    reacreation/parks/rosecan1.shtml

Cycle World
11675 Sorrento Valley Road
San Diego, CA 92121
(619) 792-2453

Notes on the trail: From the west parking lot, ride your bike west onto the main trail, which soon narrows and begins splitting off into fragments. Don't worry about staying on the "right" trail; there is none. Instead, just ride parallel to the stream and CA 52. No matter which trail you take, you'll probably cross the stream (which turns south) at 0.8 mile. If you keep your eyes open, you'll soon come to a T intersection with a set of railroad tracks. Go right, keeping a safe distance between you and the tracks. Do not cross the tracks or ride on them; this is considered trespassing. You'll soon pass under the intersection of CA 52 and I-5 while heading northeast. You're now in Rose Canyon, a flat but popular jogging and dog-walking spot. The trail isn't as scenic as San Clemente Canyon, but it's still a fun ride as you cruise up to Genesee Avenue, which you'll find at 3.8 miles. Cross Genesee at the traffic light at Centurion Road. Jog left (northeast) on Genesee below the campus of University High School. Then go right between the two yellow poles just to the northeast side of University High's driveway. Proceed east/northeast on the road through a rocky streambed. Head toward the tall I-805 bridge that spans Rose Canyon. You'll pass under the bridge at 5.2 miles. Now, turn right (southeast) up a steep utility road linking electrical towers. The road roller-coasters until 5.7 miles, where it reaches a gate on Miramar's property indicating that no trespassers are allowed at any time. This is the turn-around point. After returning the way you came, you'll emerge at the Marian Bear Memorial Park parking lot at 11.4 miles. The best is still to come. Just make sure you head mostly to the east as you meander along a main trail that forks off frequently. After a lot of fun exploring, you'll come to another intersection with I-805 at 14.3 miles. Turn around here and explore on the way back to your car, which you'll reach at 17.2 miles.

RIDE 3 · Los Penasquitos Canyon

AT A GLANCE

Length/configuration: 12-mile out-and-back (6 miles each way)

Aerobic difficulty: Easy; gentle terrain with some brief hills

Technical difficulty: Easy; occasional loose rocks and ruts

Scenery: Low, rocky bluffs line the brush-covered drainage

Special comments: Park features adobe structures built by Mexican settlers

This is an easy, out-and-back, 12-mile round-trip ride. The terrain is gentle over an unpaved two-wheel-drive road that is in good condition for most of its length. The road does have a few sandy spots, and some of the short hills contain loose rocks and ruts.

Los Penasquitos Canyon is six miles in length and lies in the midst of San Diego suburbia. Just a few minutes of pedaling will take you into the deep shade of sycamores, eucalyptus, live oak, pepper trees, and willows. The name, Los Penasquitos, means "the little cliffs," and alludes to the rocky bluffs that are visible from the road. Adobe structures built by Mexican settlers can be found at both ends of the park. The restored building at the eastern extreme, the Johnson Taylor Adobe, was once the center of activity in the canyon and now claims the honor of being San Diego's oldest rancho.

General location: Trail begins at the Los Penasquitos Canyon Preserve, 24 miles north of San Diego.

Elevation change: The ride starts at approximately 250 feet. You descend to 100 feet at the west end of the canyon—the turnaround point. Several small hills add an estimated 50 feet of climb to the ride. Total elevation gain is 200 feet.

Season: This trail can be ridden year-round. Wildflowers and light traffic in the early spring make this a good time to visit. Use is heavy on weekends and holidays, and the trail is popular in the late afternoon with people seeking exercise after work.

Services: You will find a water fountain and a chemical toilet at the trailhead. Bring your own water, because the water fountain is an unreliable source. All services are available in San Diego and surrounding communities.

Hazards: This route is heavily used. You are likely to encounter equestrians, hikers, picnickers, families, and children on school outings. Familiarize yourself with the guidelines of responsible trail cycling; be courteous and use common sense. Rattlesnakes inhabit the canyon and play an important role in the park's ecology.

Rescue index: Help can be found in the nearby community of Miramar.

Land status: This area is a preserve of the City and County of San Diego.

Maps: USGS 7.5-minute quadrangle maps: Del Mar and Poway Valley.

Finding the trail: The trail begins at the Los Penasquitos Canyon Preserve, 24 miles north of San Diego. From San Diego, take I-15 to the exit for Mira Mesa Boulevard. Follow Mira Mesa Boulevard west to Black Mountain Road. Go right (north) on Black Mountain Road for 2 miles to the Los Penasquitos Canyon Preserve entrance on the left (west) side of the road. Parking is available for day use only, and there is a $1 fee.

RIDE 3 • Los Penasquitos Canyon

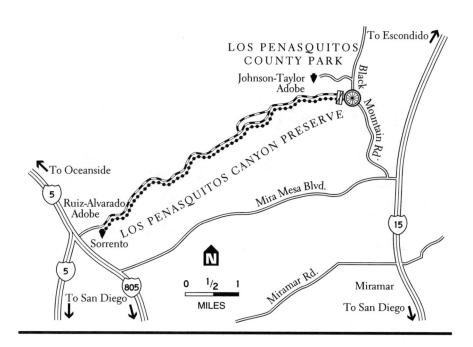

Sources of additional information:

County of San Diego Parks and
  Recreation
5201 Ruffin Road, Suite P
San Diego, CA 92123
(619) 694-3049

City of San Diego
  Parks and Recreation Department
Natural Open Space Parks
202 C Street
San Diego, CA 92101
(619) 685-1350
www.sannet.gov/park-and-
  recreation/parks/penasq.shtml

Notes on the trail: The trailhead is located at the northwest end of the Los Penasquitos Canyon Preserve parking lot. Lift your bike over the gate and follow the road to the turnaround point at the Ruiz-Alvarado Adobe. Return the way you came. Many of the preserve's trails are closed to bicycles; please obey all of the signs indicating closings.

The Johnson-Taylor Adobe House can be reached by entering the Penasquitos Community Park entrance, 0.3 mile north of the Los Penasquitos Canyon Preserve entrance on Black Mountain Road. Follow the Penasquitos Community Park entrance road west past the playing fields to the adobes. There is a 10 mph speed limit.

Los Penasquitos Canyon.

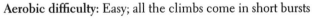

RIDE 4 · Lake Hodges

AT A GLANCE

CA

Length/configuration: 15.3-mile out-and-back ride (7.4 miles one way, slightly different 7.9 miles coming back)

Aerobic difficulty: Easy; all the climbs come in short bursts

Technical difficulty: Moderate; single-track options tend to drop quickly

Scenery: Alpine-looking Lake Hodges, rolling hills, lush creeksides

Special comments: A popular route during the day, this ride is fast becoming a nocturnal favorite for locals—but at any time of day, it's a scenic intermediate loop with single-track options for more advanced riders

This 15.3-mile route is scenic and easily accessible to most of San Diego, but it's also hot, full of other users, and a bit flat. Making lemonade out of lemons, advanced riders have turned this route into a nighttime bonanza, when the trails are uncrowded, the weather cool, and every little knoll becomes a challenge.

A group of cyclists from the local NiteRider Bicycle Lighting Systems Company go on their nocturnal Lake Hodges rides on Tuesday nights, and they were gracious enough to invite me along. Though it's always a bit unnerving riding with cyclists you've never met before, everyone was as helpful as could be. Still,

RIDE 4 • Lake Hodges

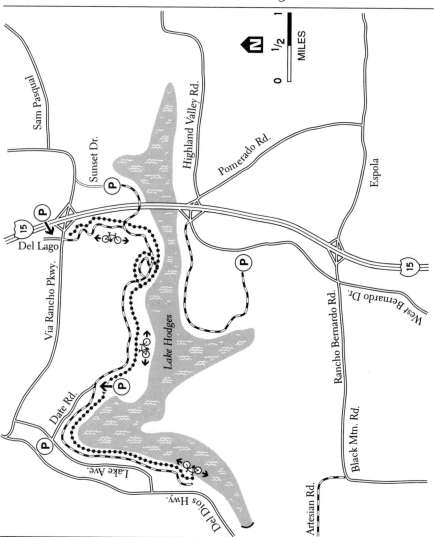

I was nervous. They had cycled here scores of times, and I had barely even gone night riding anywhere. But with the appropriate lighting system rigged to my bike, I got in line as we left a shopping center just off of I-15 in Escondido and pedaled up a narrow single-track.

It was daunting at first, but the great thing with night riding is that inhibition doesn't have time to strike—you don't have the chance to dwell on obstacles, and thus you're almost already past them before any hesitation kicks in. The fun terrain helped, too. We zigzagged from the crumbling asphalt frontage road onto single-track detours and back again. Even though it was night and a new area, the lake always provided a point of reference. I never once worried about getting lost. Riding on the west end of Lake Hodges was especially fun—the single-track curves every few feet, resulting in a sinuous and rhythmic ride. By the time we returned to our cars after more exploring, I was ready to ride Lake Hodges again the next week. But in case you don't have any experienced guides for the night ride, I've provided information below for a more established route in this area.

General location: 5 miles south of central Escondido, just off of I-15.

Elevation change: Approximate gain of 200 feet.

Season: Year-round, but avoid riding during the heat of the day in summer.

Services: A country store and cafe with phones, water, and rest rooms are available midway through the ride. All other services are available in Escondido.

Hazards: There are some tight single-track options; also, watch for automobile traffic in the parking lots traversed by the ride.

Rescue index: The route parallels city streets, where help is available.

Land status: County land, managed by San Dieguito Park Joint Powers Authority.

Maps: USGS 7.5-minute quadrangle map: Escondido. Lake Hodges online map available at www.sdrp.org/web/images/lakeweb.jpg.

Finding the trail: Take I-15 to the Via Rancho Parkway exit (5 miles south of Escondido) and go west. Turn right almost immediately on Del Lago and park on the street near the Texaco gas station or in the adjacent McDonald's parking lot (but if you park there, be sure to patronize McDonald's after the ride). To park at an established trailhead and ride the easily followed North Shore Lake Hodges Trail, go east instead of west on Via Rancho as it exits I-15. Drive 0.25 mile, then turn right on Sunset Drive. At the end of Sunset Drive is a parking area and trailhead for the North Shore Lake Hodges Trail.

Sources of additional information:

San Dieguito River Park
18372 Sycamore Creek Road
Escondido, CA 92025
(858) 674-2270
www.sdrp.org

Pacific Wind Design
(Mountain Bike Rentals)
(760) 735-8088

County of San Diego Parks
    and Recreation
5201 Ruffin Road, Suite P
San Diego, CA 92123
(619) 694-3049

NiteRider Technical Lighting
    Systems
(re: Tuesday night rides)
(858) 268-9316

Notes on the trail: The description that follows is an adventurous route that I rode for the first time for this book. If you don't have anyone guiding you as I did, you might be better off parking at the Sunset Drive trailhead (see "Finding the Trail" above) and simply riding east on the established, easy-to-follow North Shore Lake Hodges Trail, which winds to an end at the far southwest portion of the lake at 7.4 miles, for a 14.8-mile-long trip. For a little more challenge, however, do as I did and ride from the parking area near the McDonald's as follows: From the parking area, carefully cross to the southwest corner of Via Rancho Parkway and Del Lago (diagonally across from the Texaco station). Zero your odometer when you reach a small, anonymous single-track that drops away from Via Rancho. Go south on this unsigned trail. The trail almost immediately comes to a **T** intersection; go left. This single-track, traveling roughly parallel to I-15 on your left, climbs over a hillside. Pass over a cement culvert at 0.7 mile and pass through a chain-link fence to enter the Lake Hodges area. Your goal now is to reach the crumbling asphalt frontage road shadowing the lake. Take the single-track path at 0.8 mile (it's a hairpin left turn) to accomplish this. However, if you miss this turnoff and see another, then take it—it doesn't matter as long as you get to the frontage road. Take a right onto the crumbling asphalt for some mild spinning. Cross a creek at 1.9 miles and ride to a well-used single-track path climbing uphill on your right at 2.9 miles. Make sure to remember this intersection; you'll come back here eventually. But for now, turn right up the single-track. Almost immediately upon reaching a fence, make a left on an intersecting single-track. This path is level, firm, and narrow, with the occasional rock. At 3.9 miles, you'll reach a big boulder. Make a sharp left at the boulder and start down an inclined, rutted single-track. Just when it gets really steep, head right at an intersection at 4 miles. From here, it's a mostly gentle descent with a few sudden dips into creeks. At 4.4 miles, go right onto the asphalt frontage road once more. At 5.3 miles, go around a gate and into a parking lot at the intersection of Lake and Date Roads. There's a country store and a café on the right (north) side of the parking lot. (You will return here in a little bit, so decide whether to stop now or later.) Continue riding by turning south onto a single-track path (at 5.4 miles) that runs between Lake Hodges and Lake Avenue. There are numerous forks and splits here; feel free to ride any of them. The only rule is to not turn severely left (into the lake) or severely right (onto Lake Avenue). You'll ride into a mini parking lot after about a mile; just keep heading through it in the same direction and you'll find the trail once again. Finally, at 7.5 miles, you'll reach the end of the trail in the shadow of Lake Hodges Dam. Turn around here and ride back the way you came to the intersection you memorized earlier (it was at 2.9 miles on the way out; you'll reach it at 12 miles on the way back). From here, turn left on the frontage road. At 12.6 miles, veer left and head uphill on a rocky ascent. After cresting a small hill, go right at 13.2 miles and head downhill on a single-track. You're now in a beautifully wooded, lush landscape with vibrantly colored trees in autumn. Go right again along a cement wall, and you'll soon make a left turn at 13.5 miles onto the frontage road. After about a mile of riding, you'll turn left up the single-track you originally descended, which brings you back to the chain-link fence, the cement culvert, the anonymous single-track, and the intersection of Del Lago and Via Rancho Parkway at 15.3 miles.

RIDE 5 · Daley Ranch

AT A GLANCE

Length/configuration: 12-mile combination (0.7 mile each way, plus a 10.6-mile figure-eight loop) on fire road and single-track

Aerobic difficulty: Moderate; some short but steep climbs

Technical difficulty: Moderate; some rocky fire roads and a twisty single-track

Scenery: Ponds, grassy meadows, rock outcroppings, and views of Mt. Cuyamaca and Mt. Palomar

Special comments: Located in one of the newest mountain biking oases in San Diego, this intermediate ride spins past stark boulders, grassy meadows, and lush creeksides

As recently as 1996, the land that this 12-mile combination ride traverses was in danger of being bulldozed to make way for an enormous housing tract. Fortunately, conservancy groups and the city of Escondido rallied to save it. After pedaling through this diverse landscape, you'll understand why.

Beginning a few miles from the center of Escondido, the ride quickly climbs through rocky, boulder-strewn land. There are good views of adjacent Lake Dixon as the trail roller-coasters through the Diegan coastal sage/scrub ecosystem and into some grasslands. Ponds are sprinkled on both sides of the trail as you meander to the Ranch House, a 1928 redwood building that served as the headquarters for the Daley family dairy. This is a shady, cool place to stop for a break before climbing the steep Central Valley Loop Trail. As you approach the ranch's northern border, the route unveils a fun, quick single-track that leads to a steep downhill. Afterwards, a more mellow descent past ducks and ospreys returns you to the ranch entrance and the parking lot. It's now just a few minutes drive to a celebratory burrito in Escondido.

General location: Just a few miles northeast of central Escondido in San Diego's North County region.

Elevation change: Gain is approximately 800 feet.

Season: Year-round, but avoid riding during the heat of the day in summer.

Services: Pit toilets are available at Ranch House, but there are no other services on the trail. All services are available in Escondido.

Hazards: Trails are rocky, and rattlesnakes are present.

Rescue index: Park rangers regularly patrol this route, which is very close to the town of Escondido.

Land status: City parkland, private property, Bureau of Land Management (BLM) property.

RIDE 5 • Daley Ranch

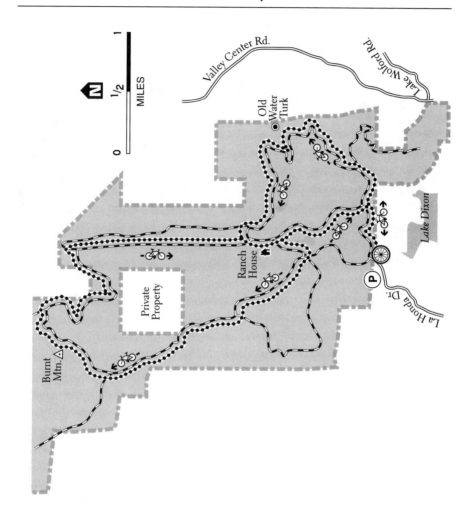

Maps: *Welcome to Daley Ranch* map and guide (free at the trailhead).

Finding the trail: Take I-15 to Escondido and exit at El Norte Parkway (it's one exit north of CA 78). Go east on El Norte approximately 3 miles. Following the signs to Lake Dixon, turn left on La Honda Drive. Drive uphill for 1.5 miles and turn left at the parking lot on your left just in front of well-signed Daley Ranch. The entrance to Lake Dixon is on your right. $2 fee.

The wide-open spaces of Daley Ranch.

Source of additional information:

City of Escondido
Daley Ranch
La Honda Drive
Escondido, CA 92027

(760) 839-4680
www.ci.escondido.ca.us/visitors/
uniquely/daley

Notes on the trail: From the parking area, turn left and enter Daley Ranch. Immediately after passing the trailhead sign, turn right onto the Ranch House Loop Trail. You will cross a bridge at 0.3 mile and ride up to an intersection with Chaparral Loop Trail at 0.7 mile. Go right, but remember the intersection; you'll be making a crucial turn here near the end of the ride. Keep straight past the intersection with Caballo Trail and stay on the main trail for some roller-coaster riding. Eventually you'll ride over a small hill and descend into what seems like a different climate—instead of stark and rocky, the landscape is now welcoming and grassy. At 3.3 miles, veer right and downhill as a pond appears on your left. Go left at 3.7 miles onto signed Jack Creek Meadow Loop. At 3.8 miles, head left at the turnoff to the Ranch House. This is a good place to take a quick break before tackling the meat of the ride. Go straight past the Ranch House (it's partially paved) and veer right at 4 miles onto Boulder Loop Trail/Central Valley Loop Trail. The climb is tough, probably the toughest you'll face on the whole ride. There are great views from the top of the hill, however, and after enjoying them, veer right onto Central Valley Loop. After a long stretch of ridge riding, Central Valley Loop merges with Engelmann Oak Loop at 6 miles. Go right. Then, after slogging through some sand and climbing a small hill, look to your left for a single-track. Turn left on the unnamed single-track, which twists and turns until intersecting with Engelmann Oak Loop at 6.9 miles. Go right so you can return to the Central Valley Loop, which you'll reach again at 7.4 miles. Turn left onto Central Valley Loop, which descends sharply into an intersection with Jack Creek Meadow Loop at 8.6 miles. Turn right and head slightly downhill all the way back to the Ranch House. Continue straight past the Ranch House once more, but this time veer left onto Ranch House Loop at 10.1 miles. You'll roller-coaster a little bit more until, during a big descent, you reach the easy-to-miss intersection with Chaparral Loop Trail at 11.3 miles (this is the intersection you were told to remember earlier in the ride). Make a sharp right onto Ranch House Loop instead of heading straight and left onto Chaparral Loop. After crossing the bridge once more, you'll return to the trailhead at mile 12.

RIDE 6 · Green Valley Loop

AT A GLANCE

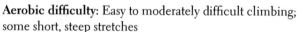

Length/configuration: 5-mile combination; a 4-mile loop and a 1-mile out-and-back (0.5 mile each way)

Aerobic difficulty: Easy to moderately difficult climbing; some short, steep stretches

Technical difficulty: Moderately difficult; hoof damage, ruts, and loose rocks

Scenery: Stands of live oak and ponderosa pine give way to chaparral as you climb away from the river

Special comments: Swimming in Sweetwater Creek is not recommended

This is a 5-mile trip consisting of a 4-mile loop and a 1-mile out-and-back spur. The riding is easy to moderately difficult with some short, steep sections of trail. The 40 miles of fire roads and trails here are in fair to good condition. Hoof prints, rutting, and loose rocks are found on the portion of the route that follows the California Riding and Hiking Trail.

This ride begins among mature stands of canyon live oak and ponderosa pine. You'll soon enter a chaparral plant community that allows unobstructed views from the trail into the park's interior valleys. Near the end of the ride you will reach the Sweetwater River and the Green Valley Falls. Several still pools dot the river, their reflective surface broken only by the occasional bather.

General location: The Green Valley Campground and Picnic Area in Cuyamaca Rancho State Park, approximately 50 miles east of San Diego.

Elevation change: The ride begins at 3,957 feet and climbs to 4,290 feet at the Arroyo Seco Primitive Campground. Undulations in the trail add an estimated 200 feet of climb to the ride. Total elevation gain: 533 feet.

Season: Seasonal color and comfortable temperatures make the spring and fall ideal times for riding in Cuyamaca Rancho State Park. This region sees heavy

RIDE 6 • Green Valley Loop

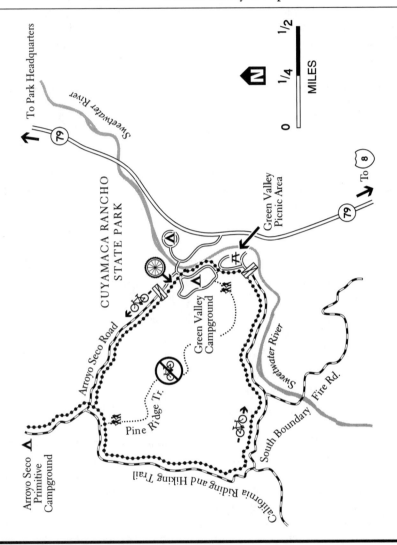

use during the summer months and also on weekends and holidays. Be prepared for cool evening temperatures if you are planning on camping here in the spring or fall.

Services: Water, rest rooms, phones, interpretive information, and camping facilities (including showers) are available at the Green Valley Campground. All services can be found at Lake Cuyamaca, just north, outside of the park, on CA 79.

Hazards: Part of this ride is on the California Riding and Hiking Trail. Keep an

Green Valley Trail.

eye out for equestrians. The route may be hoof-worn and rock-strewn in places. The park's bicycle speed limit is 15 mph.

Rescue index: Help is available at the Cuyamaca Rancho State Park Headquarters, 2 miles north of the Green Valley Campground and Picnic Area on CA 79.

Land status: State park.

Maps: A map of Cuyamaca Rancho State Park may be purchased at the park headquarters, and is also available at the entrance stations to the campgrounds. It is a good guide to this ride.

Finding the trail: Cuyamaca Rancho State Park is located on CA 79, about 12 miles south of Julian. From San Diego, take I-8 east to the exit for CA 79. Follow CA 79 north for approximately 9 miles to the Green Valley Campground and Picnic Area on the left (west) side of the highway. Turn left and follow the campground entrance road as it swings right (north). Stop and pay a $2 day-use biking fee at the fee station on the right. Continue in a northerly direction and go past the first campground. Cross the river and turn right into the second day-use parking area. Park your vehicle.

Source of additional information:

Cuyamaca Rancho State Park
12551 Highway 79
Descanso, CA 91916

(760) 765-0755
www.cuyamaca.statepark.org
cal-parks.ca.gov

Notes on the trail: From the day-use parking area, follow the signed Arroyo Seco Road for 1 mile to the sign for Green Valley. Continue straight for 0.5 mile to the Arroyo Seco Primitive Campground. Turn around and return to the intersection with the sign for Green Valley. Turn right here to follow the California Riding and Hiking Trail. In 0.3 mile, continue heading straight on the California Riding and Hiking Trail where Pine Ridge Hiking Trail goes left. Stay left at all the remaining intersections to reach the pavement at the Green Valley Picnic Area. Follow the exit signs north through the campground to your vehicle.

RIDE 7 · Cuyamaca Peak

AT A GLANCE

Length/configuration: 9.3-mile combination; a 6.3-mile loop and a 3-mile out-and-back (1.5 miles each way)

Aerobic difficulty: Difficult; demanding climb on paved Cuyamaca Peak Fire Road

Technical difficulty: Segments of the ride's dirt roads are rock-strewn and rough; a steep drop on pavement from the peak requires good bike-handling skills

Scenery: Awesome views from Cuyamaca Peak (into Mexico, on a clear day)

Special comments: Fun descent on Azalea Springs Road; ride passes through woods and meadows

This 9.3-mile loop (with a spur to Cuyamaca Peak) is a great ride if you love to climb. You'll start with 2.7 miles of strenuous uphill pedaling (very steep grade, not recommended for novices) on the one-lane, paved Cuyamaca Peak Fire Road. It is punctuated by a few very steep grades (up to 15%) and is closed to public motor traffic. Azalea Springs Fire Road and Milk Ranch Road are dirt, two-wheel-drive roads in mostly good condition (with some rough sections). The circuit is completed with 1.5 miles of paved cycling on CA 79.

On a clear day, the view from Cuyamaca Peak is incredible. You can see San Diego, the Pacific Ocean, the Salton Sea, and on into Mexico. Azalea Springs Fire Road is a beautiful trail that rolls downhill through deciduous forests, meadows, and past the bubbling Azalea Spring.

General location: Cuyamaca Rancho State Park is approximately 50 miles east of San Diego.

RIDE 7 · Cuyamaca Peak

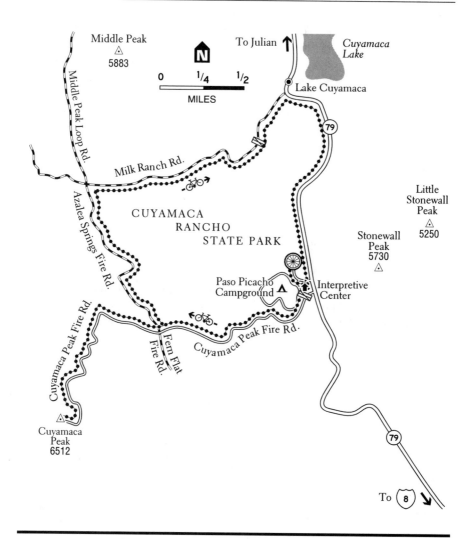

Elevation change: The ride starts at 4,870 feet and rises steadily to the 6,512-foot summit of Cuyamaca Peak. Cycling back down, you'll turn onto Azalea Springs Fire Road at 5,400 feet and drop to 4,800 feet at CA 79. Return along the highway to 4,870 feet. Total elevation gain: 1,712 feet.

Season: Spring through late fall. Dress in layers, for you will heat up while climbing to the peak, but it may be windy on top. Summer weekends and holidays can be extremely crowded.

Services: Water, rest rooms, phones, interpretive information, and camping facilities (including showers) are available at the Paso Picacho Campground. All services can be obtained at Lake Cuyamaca, just north outside the park on CA 79.

Hazards: The roads and trails in this park are popular with hikers and equestrians. Although rare, you may encounter service vehicles on Cuyamaca Peak Fire Road. Be mindful of your speed on the steep, paved descent from the peak; speed limit for bikers is 15 mph. The road is narrow and winding; your view of oncoming traffic is often obstructed. Milk Ranch Road is rock-strewn in places.

Rescue index: Help can be found at the Interpretive Center located near the entrance to the Paso Picacho Campground or at the park headquarters. The headquarters is off of CA 79 on the left (east) side of the highway, about 3 miles south of the Paso Picacho Campground.

Land status: State park.

Maps: The general map of Cuyamaca Rancho State Park, which can be purchased at the park headquarters and at the entrance stations to the campgrounds, is an excellent guide to this ride.

Finding the trail: Cuyamaca Rancho State Park is located on CA 79, about 12 miles south of Julian. From San Diego, follow I-8 east to the exit for CA 79. Follow CA 79 north for approximately 14 miles to the Paso Picacho Campground and Picnic Area on the left (west) side of the highway. If you enter the park via automobile, you will have to pay a small fee. Visitors entering by bike are admitted free, so some visitors park in turnouts on CA 79 (but a Forest Adventure Pass is required to park there).

Source of additional information:

Cuyamaca Rancho State Park
12551 Highway 79
Descanso, CA 91916

(760) 765-0755
www.cuyamaca.statepark.org
cal-parks.ca.gov

Notes on the trail: From the day-use parking area of the Paso Picacho Campground, exit the campground and turn right onto CA 79. Immediately turn right past the CDF Fire Station at the "Authorized Vehicles Only" sign. Walk your bike around the locked gate that closes Cuyamaca Peak Fire Road to most traffic. Follow Cuyamaca Peak Fire Road and reach the summit after 3 miles of riding. Return the way you came. After approximately 1.5 miles on the downhill return, turn left onto Azalea Springs Fire Road. It is an easy turn to miss, so watch closely for the signpost as you descend. In another 1.5 miles you come to a T intersection at Milk Ranch Road. Turn right onto Milk Ranch Road. This dirt road ends at CA 79. Turn right and follow the highway to the campground and your vehicle.

RIDE 8 · Noble Canyon

AT A GLANCE

CA

Length/configuration: 18-mile loop on pavement, single-track, and fire road

Aerobic difficulty: Very difficult; one long initial climb and several others

Technical difficulty: Very difficult; narrow trails, rocks, and tight switchbacks

Scenery: Gorgeous vistas from rocky ledges and the nearby Cuyamaca Mountains; spring wildflowers

Special comments: Nothing less than the quintessential downhill in San Diego County—absolutely not for beginners

This 18-mile downhill destroys the myth that Southern California doesn't have four distinct seasons. Summers are too hot to ride here, and winters can see a lot of snow. But in the fall and spring, the downhill in Noble Canyon is an advanced rider's delight, a must for both locals and tourists. In fact, they even call this the Noble Canyon National Recreation Trail. If the "National" designation means it's one of the country's best, no one would disagree.

Situated in the Laguna Range, which tends to be warmer and drier than the neighboring Cuyamacas, you'll climb an intermittent dirt and pavement road on this ride. It's easy to be lulled into thinking the climb will be moderate the whole way, only to encounter some truly sickening steeps. But it's a good way to earn vertical mileage, and that you will do as you turn onto Laguna Meadow Road. You'll cross Noble Canyon National Recreation Trail several times and be tempted to stop climbing and descend it. But be patient, you'll want to earn as much vertical on this trail as possible. After finally accessing the top of the trail from Sunrise Highway, you'll actually ascend some more. But after a half-mile, you'll begin to go down. And down. And down. And down some more. It's technically challenging but awesomely beautiful, with interspersing oak "tunnels" and rocky cliffside vistas. Even some uphill sections and a boulder field at the ride's end can't change the positive experience of this ride.

Just be aware that this is a multiple-use trail. Bikers share Noble Canyon with hikers and equestrians, so it is crucial that all bikers control their speed, especially on the trail's steep portions. Obey the triangular trail-user yield signs that you encounter along the way.

General location: The trail begins along Pine Creek Road north of the community of Pine Valley, about 45 miles east of San Diego.

Elevation change: About 2,700 feet. Ride starts at 3,740 feet and climbs to 5,400 feet, with some undulations in between.

Season: Fall and spring.

RIDE 8 • Noble Canyon

Services: Pit toilets are available at the trailhead. There's no water available on the ride. Water and limited services are available in Pine Valley and Guatay. All other services are available in Alpine, 15 miles west on I-8.

Hazards: Some very narrow single-track, rocky trails, crowds on weekends, and automobile traffic on roads.

Rescue index: Help is available in Pine Valley.

Land status: National forest.

Grinnin' and spinnin' in Noble Canyon.

Maps: *Noble Canyon National Recreation Trail Map* is available at Descanso District Office of the Cleveland National Forest. *Anza-Borrego Desert Region Recreation Map*, by Earthwalk Press, is available at sports outfitters.

Finding the trail: From San Diego, take I-8 east to the off ramp for Pine Valley. Exit the interstate and turn left. Travel north for 0.3 mile to Old Highway 80. Turn left onto Old Highway 80 and drive 1.2 miles to Pine Creek Road. Turn sharply right (just past the bridge) onto Pine Creek Road and drive 1.6 miles to the trailhead parking area on the right. Forest Adventure Pass required.

Source of additional information:

Cleveland National Forest
Descanso Ranger District
3348 Alpine Boulevard

Alpine, CA 92001-9630
(619) 445-6235
www.r5.fs.fed.us/cleveland

Notes on the trail: From the parking area, head north on Pine Creek Road. The pavement ends soon, but keep going uphill, choosing the obvious main road at a four-way intersection and veering right when Pine Creek Road gives way to Forest Service (FS) 14S04/Deer Park Road at 1.1 miles. The climb steepens considerably in parts for the next few miles, especially during a paved section of trail. After passing over a cattle guard, turn right onto Laguna Meadow Road at 3.3 miles. It's a pleasant ride for a while, and at 4.2 miles you'll cross Noble Canyon trail. If you need to bail out, do it here, or turn around and return the way you came. But try to stay with the trail, as there is some great riding here. You'll cross the Noble Canyon trail again, and at 6.2 miles, turn left toward Filaree Flat and

Sunrise Highway, County Road (CR) S1. The last stretch is asphalt, and at 7.3 miles turn right on the pavement of Sunrise Highway. Continue on CR S1 to the trailhead of Noble Canyon Trail at 7.9 miles. Turn right onto the single-track and enjoy the easy descent until the switchbacks and frequent crossings of Laguna Meadow Road begin slowing you down. At the last crossing of Laguna Meadow Road, go southwest on the single-track at 10.1 miles. There are some really rocky sections with ledge outcroppings here; so be careful. But also have fun on the smoother sections. You'll pass a small cave on your right at 13.9 miles and then veer slightly left at an intersection at 15.1 miles (sticking to the well-signed Noble Canyon Trail). You'll reach the end of Noble Canyon and return to the start at 18 miles.

RIDE 9 · Big Laguna Trail

AT A GLANCE

Length/configuration: 10.4-mile out-and-back ride on single-track, or shorter, easier 7.7-mile loop on single-track and pavement

Aerobic difficulty: Easy/moderate; some intermittent rises and a twisting trail at a mile-high altitude will keep you puffing

Technical difficulty: Moderate; stream crossings, narrow trail, and some rocky stretches demand your attention

Scenery: High mountain meadow, vibrant spring wildflowers, streams, stands of black oak, Jeffrey pines, Big Laguna Lake

Special comments: A much easier ride than its neighbor Noble Canyon, this route is a favorite during spring wildflower season

One of the most scenic rides in all of San Diego County, this is a fairly short but very worthwhile ride. The trail winds around Laguna Meadow, which explodes in color every spring during wildflower season. Even in other seasons, the views are exquisite: the meadow, the surrounding Laguna Mountains, the stands of sturdy oak trees, and the streams all vie for your attention.

As does the trail. You can ride it as part of a very fun out-and-back ride, or as a shorter loop. Either way, you won't forget its compelling twists, turns, ups, and downs for a long time.

General location: In the Laguna Mountains, fifty miles east of San Diego.

Elevation change: Approximately 600 feet.

Season: Fall and Spring are best, snowless winters are good also.

Services: No services on trail. Some services in the nearby communities of Mt. Laguna and Pine Valley. All services in Alpine.

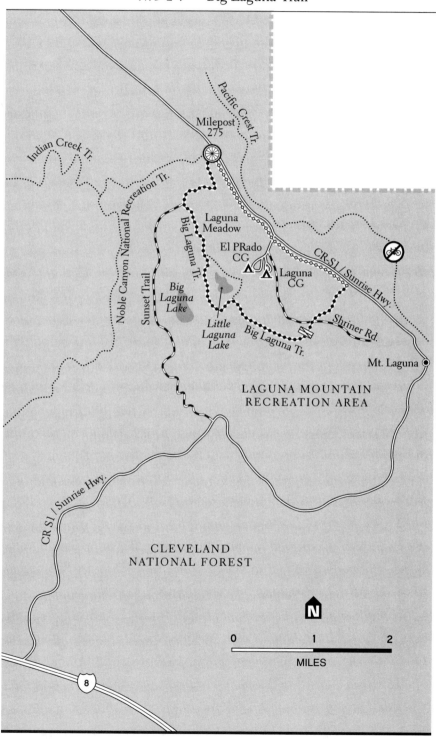

Hazards: Stream crossings, some rocky sections.

Rescue index: Help is available in Mt. Laguna and Pine Valley.

Land status: National forest.

Maps: *Anza-Borrego Desert Region Recreation Map* from Earthwalk Press, (800) 828-6277.

Finding the trail: From San Diego, take I-8 East past Alpine, Descanso Junction, and Pine Valley to County Road S1/Sunrise Highway. Exit here, and go left (north) on CR S1/Sunrise Highway for approximately 14 miles to milepost 27.5, which is where Noble Canyon National Recreation Trail intersects with Sunrise Highway. Park here. Forest Adventure Pass required.

Source of additional information:

Cleveland National Forest
Descanso Ranger District
3348 Alpine Boulevard

Alpine, CA 91901
(619) 445-6235
www.r5.fs.fed.us/cleveland

Notes on the trail: Begin by riding west on Noble Canyon National Recreation Trail (NCNRT). At 0.1 mile, while surrounded by a grove of California black oak, you reach the intersection with Big Laguna Trail. Go left on it. You roll on a nice section of trail about 5,600 feet in elevation to a Y intersection at 1.4 miles. To the right is Sunset Trail. Stay left on Big Laguna, and you soon enter Laguna Meadow, which bursts with color every spring. It's a very scenic place, but don't let it distract you too much. You want to go right at the next Y junction, so that you're continuing to ride southeast through the meadow instead of going left to El Prado campground.

You soon reach marshy Big Laguna Lake on the right. Keep on the trail, veering right at the next intersection to stay on Big Laguna Trail. You've now gained a taste of stream crossings, and the taste lingers with more splashing. After some more pleasant riding, you see signs pointing the way to the Pacific Crest Trail (PCT). Though you never ride the PCT itself (it's off-limits to bikes), you want to head in that direction on the main Big Laguna Trail.

After a rock-studded climb, you pass through a gate at 4.1 miles, and in a quarter mile or so, you come to a dirt road. Cross the dirt road, and resume riding on the trail, which is indicated by a brown trail sign. The trail widens into a dirt road, and then goes uphill to an intersection with a single-track trail on the left. (It's marked by another brown sign and a wooden post.) Take this single-track, which curves to an intersection with Sunrise Highway at 5.2 miles.

I normally prefer to ride loops, but when the single-track is this compelling, I change my mind. That's why I suggest turning around here and returning the way you came for a fun 10.4-mile ride. But if time, energy, or daylight are a factor, then simply go left on Sunrise Highway for an easy return back to the start (this option totals 7.7 miles).

RIDE 10 · Coyote Canyon

AT A GLANCE

Length/configuration: 30-mile point-to-point ride (requires car shuttle)

Aerobic difficulty: Moderate/difficult; short but steep climbing sections, some sand slogging

Technical difficulty: Difficult; rocky trails, stream riding, long rugged stretches, and sand

Scenery: The peaks of Cleveland National Forest, creekside willows, desert landscapes, canyons, and lush orange groves

Special comments: One of Southern California's epic descents, a must for all advanced riders with exploring in their blood

This 30-mile point-to-point ride was popularized by the now-defunct Coyote Canyon Clunker Classic festival, during which hundreds of riders would descend into the canyon on Super Bowl weekend. Unfortunately, the event was killed by its own success: When it got too big, the state of California put a severe limit on the number of participants, which defeated the whole purpose of an invite-all-comers group ride. The good news is, you can still have a tremendous amount of fun here.

Starting just over the San Diego/Riverside county line in Anza, say good-bye to the friends that drove you here and start rolling through a mostly level plain that soon ascends to the entrance of Anza-Borrego Desert State Park. A hairy, wild descent ensues as you careen down a branch of the San Jacinto Fault. But you can't worry about fault lines or tremors here. Besides, as fast as you're riding, you'll feel as if you could outrun an earthquake, right?

Bottoming out in Turkey Track (so named for the way the canyons are shaped here, like a turkey foot), you'll slog through some tough sand in a wash. You'll pedal (or struggle) through this wash for some time, and even ride through water for long periods near Middle Willows (crossing into San Diego County). Juking right to avoid riding through a wilderness area, you'll ride on an automobile road for a while before returning to the water below the Lower Willows. You'll bypass Vernon Whitaker Horse Camp, and then it's a flat ride into downtown Borrego Springs, where you can celebrate the end of an epic day with cold refreshments purchased from Borrego's fine merchants.

General location: Anza-Borrego Desert State Park, in southern Riverside County, northeast San Diego County.

Elevation change: Descend from 3,840 feet to 590 feet.

Season: October through May. (Coyote Canyon is closed between June 16 and September 15 to protect bighorn sheep water sources.)

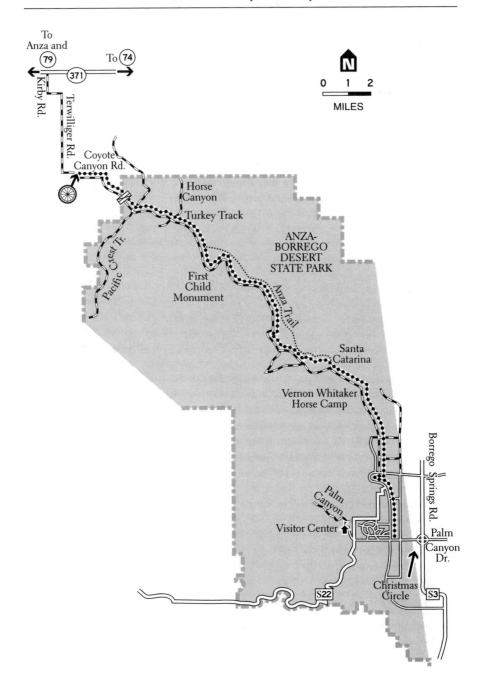

To
Anza and
79
To 74
371
Kirby Rd.
Terwilliger Rd.

N
0   1   2
MILES

Coyote
Canyon Rd.

Horse
Canyon

Turkey Track

Pacific Crest Tr.

ANZA-
BORREGO
DESERT
STATE PARK

First
Child
Monument

Anza Trail

Santa
Catarina

Vernon Whitaker
Horse Camp

Borrego Springs Rd.

Palm
Canyon

Visitor Center

Palm
Canyon
Dr.

Christmas
Circle

S22

S3

Exercise caution;
unmarked obstacles
do exist.

Services: No services are available on the trail. All services are available in Borrego Springs at the ride's end.

Hazards: Very rugged, remote country. Watch out for streams, rocky roads, and cacti.

Rescue index: Do not count on outside help. Be self-sufficient. Help is only available at the ride's end at State Park Headquarters.

Land status: Unincorporated county land, state park.

Maps: *Anza-Borrego Desert Region Recreation Map* from Earthwalk Press, (800) 828-6277. *San Diego Backcountry* from Tom Harrison Cartography, (800) 265-9090 or (415) 456-7940.

Finding the trail: This is a shuttle ride where the start and finish are 90 minutes apart. (For this reason, you're probably best off convincing a friend or loved one to go on a lovely desert drive—say from Anza to Borrego Springs—dropping you off at the first and picking you up at the latter.) But if you must shuttle, drive two cars southeast on CA 79 from the junction of CA 79 and I-15 in Temecula. You'll pass the intersection with CA 371, but keep going southeast. Turn east on CR S2, and then east on CR S22 into Borrego Springs. You'll soon reach a roundabout named Christmas Circle. Park the terminus car here, then retrace your route west/northwest on CR S22, CR S2, and CA 79. Only this time, you'll go north at the intersection with CA 371 at Aguanga. In 16 miles you'll reach the town of Anza and turn right (south) onto Kirby Road, which feeds you into Terwilliger Road. Continue south on Terwilliger to the intersection with Coyote Canyon Road. Park here, making sure you're neither blocking traffic nor obstructing a wash. Do not leave your car without first grabbing extra water, survival supplies, and bike tools.

Sources of additional information:

Anza-Borrego Desert State Park
Visitor Center (at CR S22 and
   Palm Canyon Drive)
P.O. Box 299
Borrego Springs, CA 92004
(760) 767-4684
cal-parks.ca.gov

Carrizo Bikes
P.O. Box 640
648 Palm Canyon Drive
Borrego Springs, CA 92004
(760) 767-3872

Notes on the trail: From the intersection with Terwilliger Road, ride east on Coyote Canyon Road 1.7 miles to a T intersection. Go right. At 3.5 miles, you'll arrive at the entrance to Anza-Borrego Desert State Park after a quick but lung-bursting climb. Staying on the main four-by-four road, drop down a rutted, rocky, but fast downhill. After almost 3 miles of speedy descent, you'll reach Turkey Track at 6.3 miles. Continue on the main trail as it gets sandy and turns into a wash. At 9 miles, pass the road leading to Alder Canyon on your right. Stay left and continue in the direction you've been riding. Just after crossing into San Diego County, you'll arrive at Middle Willows (at 12.5 miles) and begin riding through some water for a long period of time. At the junction with Monkey Hill Trail, follow the road to the right toward Salvador Canyon and enjoy the relief from the sandy wash terrain. Stay left at Salvador and again at Sheep Canyon. The road curves a bit until you reach Coyote Creek once more at Santa Catarina Springs at 18.6 miles. Keep riding south (down-canyon) on the automobile road. You'll pass a historical marker chronicling the achievements of Pioneer Juan Bautista de Anza. After leaving Santa Catarina Springs, you must leave the canyon via the bypass road. (That's so wildlife can safely water in the Lower Willows area.) After you climb up and over the bypass road, you embark on a rocky descent. You soon encounter three stream crossings. At the first, stay right on the main road. After a gate, you come to the second crossing. Cross it by following the auto road. You swing left (east) toward the upper part of Di Giorgio Road. There's a fork to the right which heads to Vernon Whitaker Horse Camp, but you want to stay left, heading toward the now-visible Borrego Valley floor. At the third stream crossing, just stay on the main trail, which soon brings you to Desert Gardens picnic area at 22 miles. Keep heading south, and at 26.5 miles you'll arrive at Borrego Springs Road. Turn right here. Borrego Springs Road winds around and almost doubles back on itself. Stay on it as it heads south to the center of town. It reaches Christmas Circle, where either a loved one or a loved car (or both!) are waiting to help you celebrate after 30 miles.

ORANGE COUNTY

Better known for its surfing, shopping, and suburbanizing than its cycling, Orange County is the dark horse of Southern California mountain biking. The image of Orange County as a flat plain where subdivisions and conservatives now grow in place of strawberries and oranges is not absolutely false, but it is severely limited. Let snobbish Los Angelenos to the north look down their noses at this region and part the "Orange Curtain" on a mountain bike yourself. I guarantee you'll be pleasantly surprised by the diversity and scope of riding here.

Most noticeably, you'll find an attitude and spirit about mountain biking that's refreshingly enthusiastic and unjaded. Maybe it's because cyclists here are a band apart from the Orange County stereotypes who would rather shop at Fashion Island or labor in Irvine's business parks. Whatever the cause, attitudes about outdoor recreation have changed a lot since President Nixon went for a stroll on the San Clemente beach in dress socks and wingtip shoes.

And although it's one of California's smallest, this county is home to some amazingly diverse terrain. From the rolling, wildlife-rich ranchland of Chino Hills State Park to the emerald green slopes of Crystal Cove State Park or the ruggedly gorgeous Santa Ana Mountains of Cleveland National Forest, Orange County has more satisfying rides than nearby Disneyland and Knott's Berry Farm combined. The "amenities" aren't bad either. Coastal winds keep the region mostly temperate (and rideable) when nearby Los Angeles is sweltering, and spring wildflowers and mustard grow so thick that they dye your riding shoes during excursions to Chino and Crystal Cove. Some of the best post-ride Mexican food anywhere is available here too, including Wahoo's Fish Tacos in Laguna and Las Golondrinas in San Juan Capistrano. In short, it's pretty easy to see why the swallows keep coming back to Orange County year after year. You will too.

RIDE 11 · Bell Canyon

AT A GLANCE

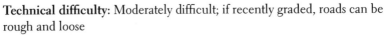

Length/configuration: 5.6-mile combination; a 3.6-mile loop and a 2-mile out-and-back (1 mile each way)

Aerobic difficulty: Moderately difficult; some short steep hills

Technical difficulty: Moderately difficult; if recently graded, roads can be rough and loose

Scenery: Rolling topography; woodlands, grasslands, and small creeks

Special comments: Bicycles are restricted to the park's dirt roads. Stay off the horse and hiking trails. Mountain lions reside in the park; they are unpredictable and dangerous

Bell Canyon loop is a 5.6-mile circuit in the Ronald W. Caspers Wilderness Park. The riding on Bell Canyon Trail is easy, with some short hills. Sun Rise and East Ridge Trails require additional effort, for they are steep in places. The route follows dirt fire roads in fair condition.

This large wilderness park, located in the western Santa Ana Mountains, has more than 25 miles of dirt roads suitable for mountain biking. Beginners can follow the scenic Bell Canyon Trail as it rambles past woodlands, grasslands, and streams.

General location: The Old Corral Picnic Area in Ronald W. Caspers Wilderness Park, 7.5 miles east of the city of San Juan Capistrano and approximately 60 miles southeast of downtown Los Angeles.

Elevation change: The trip starts at 470 feet on Bell Canyon Trail and ascends gradually to 530 feet at the intersection with Sun Rise Trail. The route then rises rapidly to 800 feet at the intersection with East Ridge Trail. Following East Ridge Trail, you drop to 760 feet, and then climb moderately to 900 feet at Pointed Hill. This is followed by a quick descent to the intersection with Cougar Pass Trail at 700 feet, and then rolling terrain to 720 feet at the intersection with Oso Trail. On Oso Trail you descend for 0.5 mile to Bell Canyon at 570 feet. From here it's a cruise down the canyon to the trailhead at 470 feet. Total elevation gain: 490 feet.

Season: Cyclists can enjoy this park at any time of the year. Trail use is light in the early spring, late fall, and winter.

Services: Water and rest rooms are available at the Old Corral Picnic Area. All services can be obtained in San Juan Capistrano.

Hazards: The rangers at the entrance station do a good job of informing you that you are entering a wilderness area characterized by certain dangers. Besides rattlesnakes, poison oak, and rugged terrain, they stress that mountain lions live within the park and are unpredictable and dangerous. Children have been

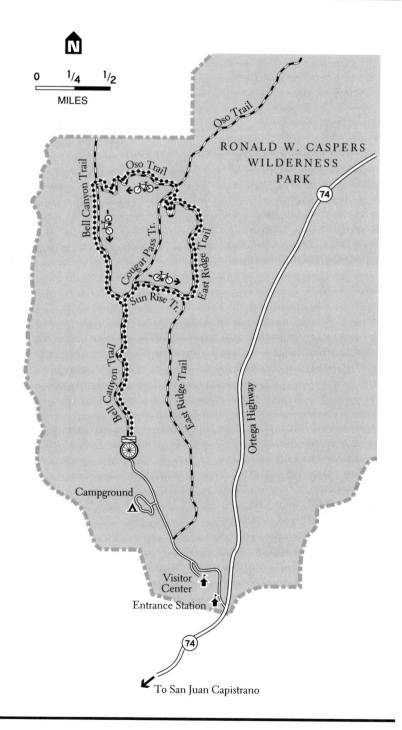

Ronald W. Caspers Wilderness Park.

attacked by lions, and as a result, kids are restricted to the Visitor Center and picnic areas. Minors should always be accompanied by an adult. This park is also popular with equestrians. Stay alert, especially when approaching blind corners. Loose rocks and sand make the steep descents on East Ridge and Oso Trails treacherous.

Rescue index: Help can be found at the entrance station during daylight hours. There is a pay phone at the Visitor Center. There are three emergency call boxes located along the Oso Trail.

Land status: Public park.

Maps: A *Caspers Wilderness Trail Guide* is available at the park entrance station and is a good guide to this trail.

Finding the trail: Follow I-5 to San Juan Capistrano and take the exit for Ortega Highway (CA 74). Travel east on CA 74 for 7.5 miles to the entrance of Ronald W. Caspers Wilderness Park on the left. Pay a day-use fee ($2 Monday-n-Friday, $4 weekends) at the entrance station and proceed to the extreme north end of the park's main road. Park your vehicle in the dirt parking area at the Old Corral Picnic Area.

Source of additional information:

Ronald W. Caspers Wilderness Park   San Juan Capistrano, CA 92675-0395
33401 Ortega Highway   (949) 728-0235 or (949) 831-2174
P.O. Box 395

Notes on the trail: All of the trails in this park are well marked, with named signposts. Begin this ride on Bell Canyon Trail, the dirt road that begins at a locked gate at the north end of the parking area. After 1 mile, turn right toward Cougar Pass Trail at signpost 14. Soon after, continue straight onto Sun Rise Trail at signpost 16 where Cougar Pass Trail goes left. Ride uphill to the top. Stay to the left here to follow East Ridge Trail north. Keep to the left at signpost 19 near Pointed Hill. Descend to Cougar Pass Trail and stay to the right heading north. Climb to Oso Trail at signpost 21 and turn left. Cycle to Bell Canyon Trail at signpost 20 and turn left. Follow Bell Canyon Trail downhill to the trailhead.

You may wish to walk the Caspers Nature Trail after your ride. It is located south of the Bell Canyon Trailhead near the old corral and windmill. The Visitor Center contains photographic displays and interpretive exhibits of the park's history and natural features.

RIDE 12 · San Juan/Old San Juan Trail

AT A GLANCE

Length/configuration: 19-mile single-track combination ride (6.8 miles each way, plus a 5.5-mile loop)

Aerobic difficulty: Moderate/difficult; a long climb on single-track—not horribly steep, but tough enough to get you breathing hard

Technical difficulty: Moderate/difficult; a narrow but fairly smooth trail

Scenery: Otherworldly rock outcroppings, outstanding views of Cleveland National Forest, and desert and alpine landscapes

Special comments: A single-track, lollipop-shaped ride with perhaps the best sustained downhill in Orange County

This 19-mile lollipop is a ride to make you feel smug and superior. Unlike a lot of riders in the region who sample the tasty downhill of San Juan Trail, you'll use your lungs and legs to get here, not your car. Sure, you could be a lemming and shuttle it too, but shuttling can be a hassle, it's good to scope out a downhill prior to cruising it, and besides, you could use the exercise.

Starting from Hot Springs Road in Cleveland National Forest, begin ascending the switchback-intense San Juan Trail, FS 6W05. If it's a weekend, you'll likely pass a lot of riders descending past you, some of whom might express admiration/amazement that you're riding up this instead of down. And granted, it's tricky climbing some of these switchbacks. But soon the trail levels out a bit as you continue coursing toward Sugarloaf Peak. Just as you start thinking that every mountain range in the United States has a Sugarloaf Peak and wondering what the hell a sugarloaf is anyway, you'll reach the intersection with Old San Juan Trail and Lunch Rocks, just below the summit of you-know-what. This is a sub-

RIDE 12 • San Juan/Old San Juan Trail

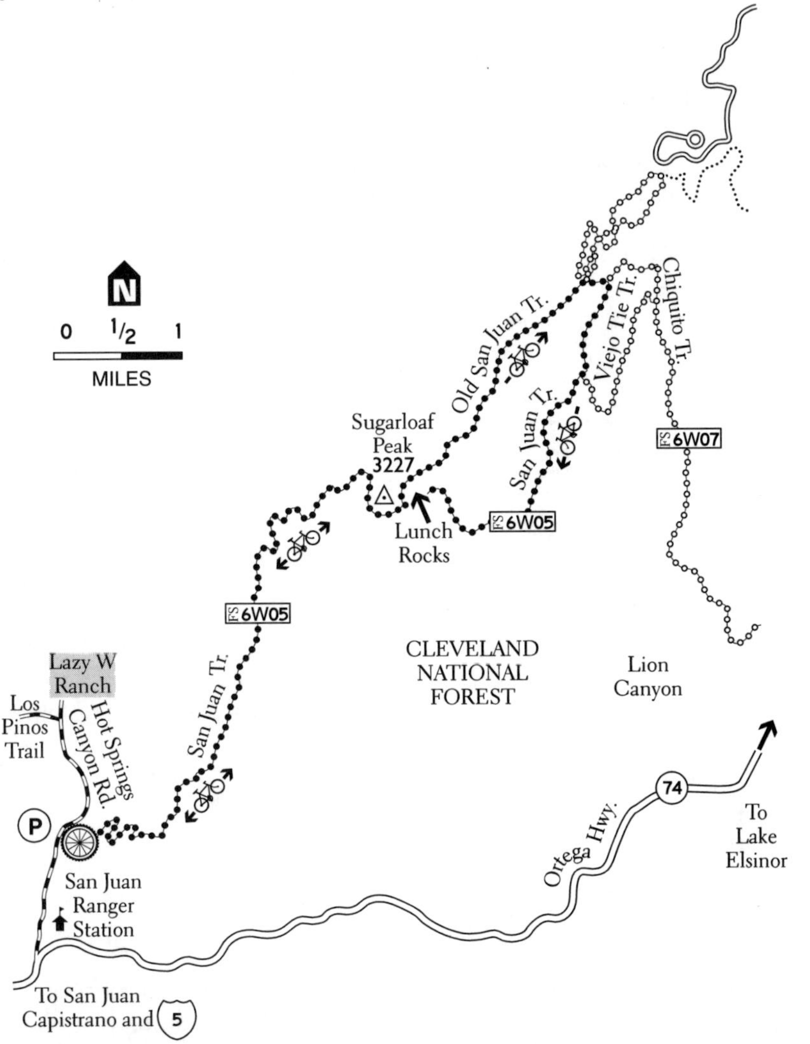

N

0   1/2   1
MILES

Old San Juan Tr.

Viejo Tie Tr.

Chiquito Tr.

6W07

Sugarloaf
Peak
3227

San Juan Tr.

6W05

Lunch
Rocks

6W05

CLEVELAND
NATIONAL
FOREST

Lion
Canyon

Lazy W
Ranch

Los
Pinos
Trail

San Juan Tr.

Hot Springs
Canyon Rd.

P

San Juan
Ranger
Station

Ortega Hwy.

74

To
Lake
Elsinor

To San Juan
Capistrano and 5

lime place to rest. The views are outstanding, the sandstone makes a great place to stretch out, and if you get bored, you can always sit back and watch bikers climbing and descending on both sides of you.

Veering up Old San Juan, you'll crest some knolls and then spin through a meadow before meeting up with the San Juan Trail again in the trip's only shady section. Some tight, cliffside single-track awaits as you return to Lunch Rocks and the beginning of the epic downhill back to Hot Springs Road. This part of the ride is always pretty, but it's downright gorgeous in the late afternoon, when soft orange light illuminates the entire Cleveland National Forest below you.

The sight is so magical, it made my otherwise speed-consumed riding buddy say, "Why am I trying to out-race this?" He then promptly stopped in his tracks, and we just looked at the scenery for ten minutes until we remembered the burritos at Las Golondrinas. You'll remember them too; after the end of this superlative ride, head down Ortega Highway. Just before you reach I-5, go left on Rancho Viejo Road, then right on Paseo Espada into a little shopping center. Las Golondrinas is on the right at 27124 Paseo Espada, (949) 240-3440. Bon appetit!

General location: In the Cleveland National Forest, approximately 13 miles from I-5 in San Juan Capistrano.

Elevation change: Approximately 2,400 feet, ranging from a low of 800 feet to a peak of 3,200 feet.

Season: Year-round. However, the route is mostly unshaded; avoid climbing the San Juan Trail in the heat of a summer day.

Services: Rest rooms are available at the trailhead. No other services are available on the trail. Bring plenty of water along. All other services are available in San Juan Capistrano.

Hazards: Narrow single-track with numerous switchbacks. The trail is heavily utilized by bikers, and collisions are not uncommon. Ride with extreme caution around blind corners.

Rescue index: This is a rugged trail not easily accessed by rescue personnel. Expensive helicopter rescues are necessary in case of bad accidents. In an emergency, help is available through San Juan Fire Station at the intersection of CA 74 and Hot Springs Canyon Road.

Land status: National forest.

Maps: USGS 7.5-minute quadrangle maps: Alberthill, Sitton Peak, and Cañada Gobernadora.

Finding the trail: Take I-5 to the Ortega Highway/CA 74 exit. Head east on CA 74 for 12.5 miles. Turn left on Hot Springs Canyon Road, which is marked by a sign reading "Lazy W Ranch" and is adjacent to the San Juan Fire Station. Proceed on Hot Springs Canyon Road about 0.5 mile to a large dirt parking area in a shady clearing. As you enter the parking area, San Juan Trail, FS 6W05, will be on your right, roughly across from the rest rooms. Park near here. Forest Adventure Pass required.

Sources of additional information:

Cleveland National Forest
Trabuco Ranger District
1147 East Sixth Street
Corona, CA 91719
(909) 736-1811
www.r5.fs.fed.us/cleveland

South County Cyclery
32302 Camino Capistrano
San Juan Capistrano, CA 92675
(949) 493-5611

Notes on the trail: From the parking area, head east on FS 6W05, the San Juan Trail. After a lot of switchbacks, the ascent becomes easier. Watch out for blind corners as you reach Lunch Rocks and the intersection with Old San Juan Trail on your left at 6.8 miles. Veer left on Old San Juan, which climbs over some knolls and through chaparral. There are game trails which intersect this trail; stick to the more established track. At the top of a knoll at 7.4 miles, veer left. At 8.1 miles you'll enter a grassy meadow. The trail heads to the right here, and so will you. The single-track goes under some low branches and is rutted. Just when it looks as if you're going to climb a steep hill, go right on the single-track path at 8.8 miles. By this point, you have moved from Old San Juan to the San Juan Trail. At 8.9 miles, you'll reach the intersection with the Chiquito Trail on your left. Head straight and slightly to the right here. You're now heading in a mostly southerly direction. This is a beautiful section which courses along a ridgeline and on a steep cliffside. Veer right at the intersection with Viejo Tie Trail and at any other questionable spots so that you remain on the San Juan Trail. At 12.3 miles you'll reach Lunch Rocks once more. Take a break here if you'd like to; the best is yet to come as you descend down the gorgeous San Juan Trail for more than 6 miles. Just make sure to ride carefully around blind corners. Return to the parking area at 19 miles.

RIDE 13 · Trabuco Canyon/West Horsethief

AT A GLANCE

CA

Length/configuration: 12.4-mile combination (2.7-mile out-and-back each way with 7-mile loop)

Aerobic difficulty: Moderate/difficult; a fairly grinding single-track ascent

Technical difficulty: Moderate/difficult; there are very tight switchbacks on Horsethief Trail

Scenery: Impressive canyon and lake views

Special comments: A profoundly fun lollipop-shaped ride whose out-of-the-way location prevents overcrowding

This is the epitome of a good loop ride: lots of single-track, a taxing but not frustrating climb, great views, diverse terrain, and a fun downhill. In 12.4 miles, this trail packs a lot of punch. A fairly long dirt road brings riders to the base of some of the highest mountains in the Santa Ana range. A shaded ascent up Trabuco Canyon on a single-track trail produces some gorgeous views. At times, the canyon seems utterly remote and unpopulated. (In fact, this ride was reviewed on a pleasant Saturday midmorning in July, yet no other riders, hikers, or equestrians were on the trail.)

The isolated feeling disappears once the trail reaches the Main Divide Road, which allows for grand views of Lake Elsinore and countless subdivisions, but it

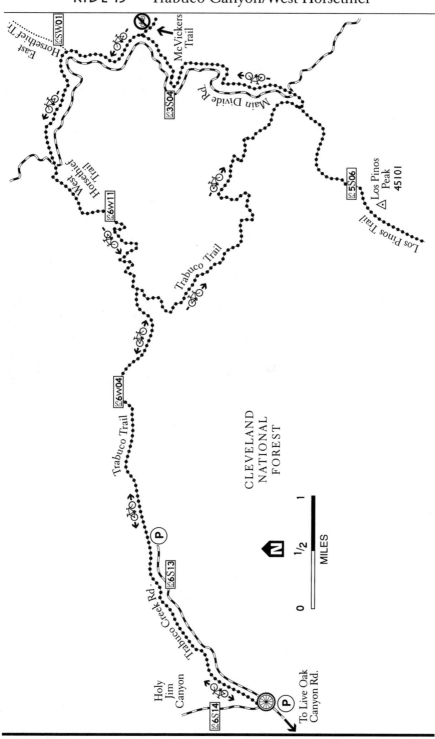

East Horsethief T.

3S01

McVickers Trail

3S04

Main Divide Rd.

West Horsethief Trail

6W11

Trabuco Trail

5S06

Los Pinos Peak 45101

Los Pinos Trail

Trabuco Trail

6W04

CLEVELAND NATIONAL FOREST

N

MILES
0   1/2   1

Trabuco Creek Rd.

P

6S13

Trabuco Trail

Holy Jim Canyon

6S14

P

To Live Oak Canyon Rd.

Riding up typically deserted Trabuco Canyon.

can still be eerily quiet. Descending the tight switchbacks of West Horsethief Trail demands good bike-handling skills and some dismounts for almost all riders. Once it returns to the valley floor, the ride turns into an easy, gradual descent back to the start point.

If you have the time or energy, scenic Holy Jim Falls are 1 mile up the Holy Jim Canyon trail. The trail demands a lot of portaging, so you might want to give your bike a rest and hike it instead.

General location: The Santa Ana Mountains in the Trabuco Ranger District of the Cleveland National Forest, roughly between Lake Elsinore and El Toro.

Elevation change: Starting at 1,740 feet and climbing to 4,194 feet. Total elevation change: 2,454 feet.

Season: Year-round.

Services: There's no potable water on the trail, but most services are available in El Toro and Lake Elsinore.

Hazards: There are steep drop-offs on West Horsethief Trail; watch out for prickly century plants and cacti.

Rescue index: This is a fairly remote ride on an underutilized trail. Be self-sufficient. Help is available in El Toro.

Land status: Part of the Trabuco Ranger District, Cleveland National Forest, U.S. Forest Service.

Maps: USGS 7.5-minute quadrangle maps: Alberthill and Santiago Peak. (A large map is posted at the trailhead, and the route is easy to follow.)

Finding the trail: From I-5, go east on El Toro Road 7.6 miles to Live Oak Canyon Road (also known as Cook's Corner). Turn right and proceed 4.4 miles. After crossing Rose Canyon Road and Trabuco Creek, turn left onto Trabuco Creek Road (it's a wide dirt road). Follow the dirt road for 4.7 miles (you'll pass a falconry range on the way). After passing a green shack on your left, you'll enter a parking lot next to the Holy Jim Canyon Trailhead. Park here. A Forest Adventure Pass is required.

Sources of additional information:

Cleveland National Forest
Trabuco Ranger District
1147 East Sixth Street
Corona, CA 91719
(909) 736-1811
www.r5.fs.fed.us/cleveland

Canyon Cyclery
26471 Portola Parkway, 1-B
Foothill Ranch, CA 92610
(949) 454-1221

Notes on the trail: From the Holy Jim Canyon Trailhead parking area, proceed east on Trabuco Creek Road, FS 6S13. (Do not go north onto Holy Jim Canyon, FS 6S14.) At 1 mile, after spinning through another parking lot, the trail becomes a single-track. After several stream crossings (many of them portages), you'll reach a junction with the Horsethief Trail at 2.7 miles. You'll come back here later, but for now head right. There are some gravelly sections as you pedal through exposed sage scrub. Eventually you'll find yourself clinging to a cliffside that offers abundant shade and some winding terrain. At 4.4 miles turn right at an intersection, and at 5.5 miles you'll reach Main Divide Fire Road, FS 3S04. Go left (north) for some fast roller-coaster ridge-top riding. There are great views of Lake Elsinore to the right and Trabuco Canyon to the left. After 2.5 miles, keep your eyes peeled to the left for the trailhead to West Horsethief Trail, FS 6W11. It's near some oak trees at 8 miles. Turn left here, stopping for lunch under the shady oaks if you're so inclined. While descending, first cling to a narrow ridge and then head right at a fork so that you drop below the ridge. The switchbacks are extremely sharp, as are the century plants you can fall into if you muff the switchbacks. (Believe me.) It's a fun descent once you get your rhythm, however, and the canyon floor arrives too soon. At 9.7 miles, veer right at the intersection with Trabuco Trail. Head back the way you came, reaching your car at 12.4 miles.

RIDE 14 · Whiting Ranch/The Luge

AT A GLANCE

CA

Length/configuration: 14.7-mile loop on single-track, pavement, and fire road

Aerobic difficulty: Moderate/difficult; occasional steep climbs

Technical difficulty: Moderate/difficult; single-track sections are sometimes rutted but rideable

Scenery: Riparian canyons, chaparral hillsides, the Pacific Ocean, and perhaps the most scenic oak woodlands in Southern California

Special comments: A squiggly loop with all sorts of variety. The terrain seems to change drastically every 20 minutes or so—a perfect ride for short attention spans

In Southern California, palm trees are the starlets, while the California live oaks are comparable to veteran character actresses. Sure, it's fun to look at the starlet palm trees and their beguiling, exotic shapes, but it's the character actress oaks who carry the day when the going gets tough. Whenever you desire some shade on a hot bike ride in these parts, it's the California live oaks that grant your wish.

There are a lot of trees on this 14.7-mile loop, and there's a lot of other diverse terrain as well. After spinning out of the parking area, you're immediately surrounded by sycamores and ferns adorning a creek. Go a little farther and climb a steep hill flanked by chest-high mustard in the spring. Bike down to a paved road and venture through rocky scrubland. Next it's up to clean-shaven Santiago Trail, victim of a massive brush fire in the fall of 1997. A little past the burn area, you'll descend past the picturesque Vulture Crags, where condors once gathered, and down the so-called "Luge," a rutted single-track that flies through a tunnel of vegetation. After some pavement and an optional stop at a biker bar (the other kind of biker, that is), it's up past a stable and down a stark ridge into the oak woodlands you've been craving. In other words, just a typical Orange County ride.

Note that the Whiting Ranch segments of this ride are very popular with families. The particular loop listed here is for more advanced riders, but families would do well here riding the level trails, especially Serrano Cow Trail and Live Oak Trail. Minors, however, should be under direct supervision at all times.

General location: In Whiting Ranch Wilderness Park and the Cleveland National Forest just north of Foothill Ranch.

Elevation change: Elevation ranges from a low of 800 feet to a high of 2,340 feet.

Season: Year-round, but avoid riding during the heat of the day in summer.

Services: All services are available in the shopping center directly adjacent to the trailhead (including Canyon Cyclery bike shop). Water is available at Four Corners.

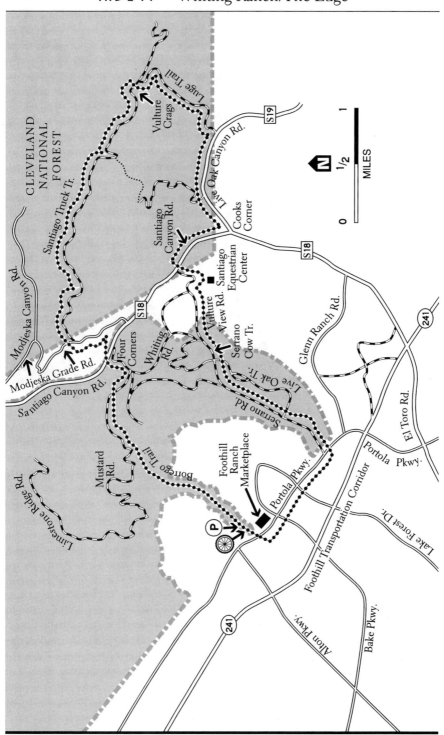

With the Vulture Crags
as a backdrop,
descending the rutted,
speedy Luge.

Rest rooms, food, beverages, and phones are available at Cook's Corner in the second half of the ride.

Hazards: Narrow rutted paths, and stream crossings; the trails are potentially crowded too.

Rescue index: The trail is always within easy riding distance of civilization.

Land status: County regional park and national forest.

Maps: A free Whiting Wilderness Park map is available from Canyon Cyclery just northeast of the trailhead in Foothill Ranch Marketplace. Also, refer to the USGS 7.5-minute quadrangle maps: El Toro and Santiago Peak.

Finding the trail: From I-5 in El Toro, take El Toro Road northeast 4.7 miles to Portola Parkway. Turn left (north) on Portola Parkway for 1.8 miles. Turn right on Market, then immediately go left into the well-signed parking lot. A small fee is charged. (You are immediately northeast of Foothill Ranch Marketplace, where Canyon Cyclery, a coffee house, and a grocery store are located.)

Sources of additional information:

Canyon Cyclery
26471 Portola Parkway 1-B
Foothill Ranch, CA 92610
(949) 454-1221

Whiting Ranch Wilderness Park
P.O. Box 156
Trabuco Canyon, CA 92678
(949) 589-4729
www.ocparks.com/whitingranch

Cleveland National Forest
Trabuco Ranger District
1147 East Sixth Street
Corona, CA 91719
(909) 736-1811
www.r5.fs.fed.us/cleveland

Notes on the trail: From the parking area, follow the signs pointing northeast to the trailhead of Borrego Trail. Go around the gate and ride north on the one-way Borrego Trail. (Invariably, however, you'll encounter cyclists going the wrong way, so ride cautiously.) The first part of this ride is fairly level, which attracts a plethora of novice riders. Watch out for them. Borrego narrows into a wide single-track and comes to a T intersection at 1.6 miles in front of a trail map display. Turn right here onto Mustard Road, a fire road that climbs abruptly to a saddle called Four Corners at 2.4 miles. Take a sip from the drinking fountain, then go left on a short climb toward a water tank. Descend past the water tank (on your right) by sticking to the primary road. It delivers you to a gate on paved Santiago Canyon Road at 2.8 miles. Head right, leaving Whiting Ranch Wilderness Park. Watch for speeding cars, and make your first left at 3 miles onto Modjeska Grade Road (which lacks a street sign, as of this writing). Ascend a fairly steep grade to a steel gate at the summit of a hill at 3.5 miles. Turn right here onto Santiago Trail (also known as Santiago Truck Trail). You're now in the Cleveland National Forest. Climb in an easterly direction through a burn area where all visible traces of vegetation were obliterated in the fall of 1997. Keep pedaling as you see evidence of the mountain healing itself. At 5.8 miles, stay left at an intersection. After a summit at 6.2 miles, you'll begin descending, but don't go too fast. Instead, keep your eyes peeled for a single-track intersection on your right. At 7 miles you'll reach a notch between two knolls and the intersection with the single-track Luge Trail (also known as Vulture Crags for the high cliffs to the west where condors once gathered). Turn right and head down this rutted but rideable single-track. At 8 miles, go right on a service road. After staying on the main trail, head left at a T-intersection with a dirt/paved road at 8.3 miles, and you almost immediately reach a gate at paved Live Oak Canyon Road. Go around the gate, and turn right on Live Oak Canyon Road. A mile-long paved descent takes you to Cook's Corner tavern at 9.5 miles. Turn right on Santiago Canyon Road and head up a gently climbing paved road. Turn left at 10.7 miles into Santiago Equestrian Center. Almost immediately you'll turn right onto a dirt road, just before the stables. Go around a gate and encounter a three-way junction at 10.8 miles. Turn left up Vulture View Road, which turns into a steep, sandstone single-track. You're now back in Whiting Ranch Wilderness Park. You'll come to an intersection at 11.7 miles. Turn right so that you pass directly underneath a large, jutting tree limb. Next, go left onto Serrano Cow Trail, a fire road that narrows considerably. Stay on Serrano Cow Trail through various intersections while winding through gorgeous live oak woodlands. At 12.8 miles, head left on Live Oak Trail, a twisty morsel that ends too quickly at 13.3 miles with a right turn onto Serrano Road. Follow Serrano as it hangs a left, goes around a gate, and finally ends at Portola Parkway at 13.7 miles. (Don't worry if you cannot follow these directions exactly. There is a large network of trails in this area; as long as you ride southwest on any of them, you'll eventually end up at Portola Parkway.) Turn right on Portola, returning to the parking lot at 14.7 miles.

RIDE 15 · Wood Canyon

AT A GLANCE

Length/configuration: 10.4-mile combination (4.6 miles out, 1.3-mile loop, and 4.5 miles back)

Aerobic difficulty: Moderate; some short, steep climbs with one longer climb on the Cholla Trail—otherwise mostly level

Technical difficulty: Moderate; a rocky, steep descent down Lynx Trail single-track, but otherwise easily navigable

Scenery: Pretty canyon environment, ranging from shady creekside trails to exposed desert terrain

Special comments: A popular, easily accessible ride tucked between encroaching subdivisions

This is a moderate 10.4-mile combination ride, essentially an out-and-back with a terminus loop. Taking place within the scenic Aliso and Wood Canyons Regional Park, the ride generally follows the wide, smooth Wood Canyon Fire Road, but most of the time it takes place on hard clay and dirt single-track. The most difficult ascent, on the Cholla Trail at the terminus loop, combines steep terrain with a loose surface. The Lynx Trail descent, on the other hand, is rocky and rutted; good bike-handling skills are essential here. The ride passes through riparian woodlands featuring California live oaks and California sycamores as well as desert scrub terrain. A fall on the Cholla Trail could land a rider on a prickly cactus. This is a year-round ride, but since much of the ride is unshaded, it's not recommended during extremely hot weather. To preserve the trails, the park is subject to closure for three days after heavy rains.

Aliso and Wood Canyons Regional Park is an extremely popular destination for mountain bikers of all abilities. On any given weekend, it's likely that riders ranging from racers-in-training to helmetless families carrying water jugs on their handlebars will be sharing the park. Curiously, when I rode here, it seemed as if the usual gender ratio of mountain bikers was reversed. This is about the only ride in Southern California where women riders appear to outnumber men.

Note that this is just one of many possible rides in the park. For more

RIDE 15 • Wood Canyon
RIDE 16 • Dripping Cave/Hollow Oak

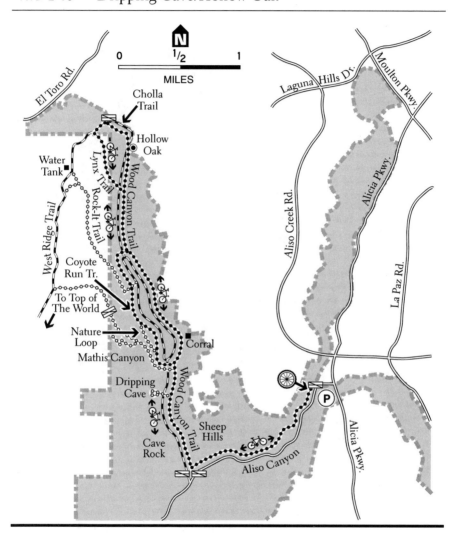

advanced riding, ride up Mathis Trail and veer left to Top of the World. It's a challenging uphill and a test of one's climbing skills.

General location: Within Aliso and Wood Canyons Regional Park in Laguna Niguel, approximately 4 miles south of I-5.

Elevation change: From just above sea level, the ride climbs gradually with a short, steep final push to an elevation of 700 feet. The descent mirrors the ascent.

Season: Year-round. The park is subject to closure three days after heavy rains.

Cacti, manzanita, and rocks: bring your tire liners to Wood Canyon.

Services: Water is available at the ranger station located at Gate 2, where Aliso Trail intersects with Wood Canyon Trail. All other services are easily found in Laguna Niguel.

Hazards: Steep drop-offs on Cholla and Lynx Trails, abundant cacti on Cholla Trail.

Rescue index: A park ranger is stationed at Gate 2, where Aliso Trail intersects with Wood Canyon Trail. Solar-powered emergency call boxes are located every mile along Wood Canyon Trail.

Land status: County regional park, open to mountain bikers except where indicated.

Maps: Free park maps are available at the trailhead at Gate 1 and at the ranger station at Gate 2.

Finding the trail: From I-5, exit on Alicia Parkway. Travel south approximately 4 miles. After the intersection with Aliso Creek Road, turn right onto the Aliso Water Management Agency (AWMA) Road. Cross over a bridge, veer to the left, and park in the lot. The ride starts at Gate 1 at the west end of the parking lot (next to the information kiosk where free maps can be obtained).

Sources of additional information:

South County Cyclery
32302 Camino Capistrano
San Juan Capistrano, CA 92675
(949) 493-5611

Aliso And Wood Canyon
  Wilderness Park
28373 Alicia Parkway
Laguna Niguel, CA 92677
(949) 831-2790
www.ocparks.com/alisoandwood
  canyons

Notes on the trail: From Gate 1, ride southwest on the paved Water Management Agency road. Signs will soon direct you to switch over to a dirt path that parallels the paved (but private) road. After 1.6 miles, turn right and pass through Gate 2 onto Wood Canyon Trail. Ride up this smooth fire road to the intersection with Mathis Road at 2.6 miles. Turn left and then almost immediately turn right onto the hard clay single-track of Coyote Run, also known as the Nature Loop. After a short, steep ascent and down again, bear right at all times, until you pass through a sycamore grove and reach Wood Canyon Creek. Intermediate riders will want to dismount before traversing this creek. At 3.7 miles, turn left on Wood Canyon Trail again. Gently rising and falling, the trail offers a lot of banked walls for riders who want to get a little horizontal. At 4.6 miles, Wood Canyon Trail comes to a stop in front of a large hill topped on the right side with homes. Turn left here onto the steep, loose Cholla Trail. Signs indicate that this trail is 1 mile in length, but it's doubtful that either your legs or odometer will register it being that long. At 5.2 miles, turn left on the vista-heavy West Ridge Trail and quickly left again at 5.3 miles on the Lynx Trail. This is a technical, rocky, and rutted descent that is dubiously marked as being 1.1 miles in length, but at just 5.9 miles you'll turn right back onto Wood Canyon Trail. Return the way you came, and at 10.4 miles you'll be back at Gate 1 and the parking lot.

RIDE 16 · Dripping Cave/Hollow Oak

AT A GLANCE

Length/configuration: 9-mile out-and-back (4.5 miles each way, with an optional, slightly different return route)

Aerobic difficulty: Easy; mostly level riding on fire roads

Technical difficulty: Easy; but easy/moderate if the optional return is selected

Scenery: Sandstone rock formations, caves, shady creekside trails, and desert scrub

Special comments: One of the more popular family rides in Orange County, and deservedly so

On the single-track near Hollow Oak; who said a family ride had to be dull?

This easy loop seems a lot shorter than its 9-mile length would indicate. Maybe that's because with its family-friendly diversions—including an elephant-shaped rock, a cave reputed to be an old-time bank robbers' hideout, and an optional nature loop—the ride seems to pass quickly.

Set in the immensely popular Aliso and Wood Canyons Regional Park, this ride is regarded as a perfect introduction to the sport of mountain biking. An easy, gentle downhill from the parking area leads to a ranger station where families can gear up for the scenic part of the route. Almost immediately, you'll pass Cave Rock, also known by its more fitting name, Elephant Rock, since it resembles a pachyderm in repose. You can't climb on this easily scarred sandstone, so let kids enjoy it from a distance. Then get pedaling again up to the signed turnoff to Dripping Cave. Rumor has it that bank robbers hid out here, using the holes carved in the rock to hold up tree branches from which they hung their supplies. It's fun to imagine holing up here long before the encroachment of subdivisions.

Now you'll encounter the meaty part of the ride: a gentle ascent through shade and a stream crossing to Hollow Oak at the end of Wood Canyon Trail. Rest a bit here while watching more advanced cyclists tackle the uphill of Cholla Trail, then turn around and descend. If you want a little variation, turn right across the creek and go left on Coyote Run Trail and its fun nature loop before rejoining Wood Canyon and returning home. Throughout the route, you'll find lots of nice places to pull over and picnic.

General location: Within Aliso and Wood Canyons Regional Park in Laguna Niguel, approximately 4 miles south of I-5.

Elevation change: Insignificant.

Season: Year-round. The park is subject to closure for three days after heavy rains.

Services: Water is available at the ranger station located at Gate 2, where Aliso Trail intersects with Wood Canyon Trail. All other services are easily found in Laguna Niguel.

Hazards: Trails can be crowded; take care when crossing the stream on the optional return route on Coyote Run Trail. Sound bell or shout when rounding "blind" corners.

Rescue index: A park ranger is stationed at Gate 2, where Aliso Trail intersects with Wood Canyon Trail. Solar powered emergency call boxes are located every mile along Wood Canyon Trail.

Land status: County regional park, open to mountain bikers except where posted.

Maps: Free park maps are available at the trailhead at Gate 1 and the ranger station at Gate 2.

Finding the trail: From I-5, exit on Alicia Parkway. Travel south approximately 4 miles. After the intersection with Aliso Creek Road, turn right onto the Aliso Water Management Agency (AWMA) Road. Cross over a bridge, veer to the left, and park in the lot. The ride starts at Gate 1 at the west end of the parking lot (next to the information kiosk where free maps can be obtained).

Sources of additional information:

Aliso and Wood Canyon
  Wilderness Park
28373 Alicia Parkway
Laguna Niguel, CA 92677
(949) 831-2790
www.ocparks.com/alisoandwood
  canyons

South County Cyclery
32302 Camino Capistrano
San Juan Capistrano, CA 92675
(949) 493-5611

Notes on the trail: From Gate 1, ride southwest on the paved water management agency road. Signs will soon direct you to switch over to a dirt path that parallels the paved (but private) road. After 1.6 miles, turn right (north), and pass through Gate 2 onto Wood Canyon Trail. Ride up this smooth fire road a few hundred yards until you see Cave (Elephant) Rock on your left. After taking a gander at the rock, keep going north up Wood Canyon Trail. At 2.3 miles, you'll reach a well-signed fork pointing the way to Dripping Cave on the left. Turn left, dismounting from your bike for the last bit of trail leading to Dripping Cave. Explore the cave, then turn around and return to Wood Canyon Trail and continue north. It's good gentle riding, first in an open meadow, then through a sycamore grove, and then out to open chaparral at Hollow Oak. When you come to the Cholla Trailhead on your left at 4.5 miles, turn around.

You're now heading south on Wood Canyon. At 5.4 miles into the ride, you'll reach the turnoff to Coyote Run Trail on your right and the optional return route. This option isn't recommended for young children, but if you don't mind crossing a creek and riding some narrow trails with one tricky but short climb, then it's a fun way to go back. The added distance is negligible. If you don't want to take the optional return, simply retrace your route on Wood Canyon Trail back to the start.

To take the optional return, turn right down the steep little decline to the creek, go up the other bank, and turn left on Coyote Run single-track. Head south, veering left at all forks. At a T-intersection with Mathis Canyon, turn left and then immediately right onto Wood Canyon Trail, where you'll soon pass Dripping Cave on your right. Retrace your route from here back to Gate 1 and the parking lot at 9 miles.

RIDE 17 · Moro Canyon

AT A GLANCE

CA

Length/configuration: 9.3-mile combination; a 6.1-mile loop and a 3.2-mile out-and-back (1.6 miles each way)

Aerobic difficulty: Moderately difficult; some steep climbing

Technical difficulty: Difficult; steeper roads and trails include rocks, ruts, and washboarding

Scenery: Grassy hills and oak-shaded draws; lovely ocean views

Special comments: You can find rides suited to all skill and fitness levels in Crystal Cove State Park

This is a moderately difficult 9.3-mile loop. Most of the climbing is gradual to moderately steep; there are some demanding uphills on West Loop Trail. Staying in control on the route's steeper downhills will require good bike-handling skills. You will encounter some rough terrain descents on Red-Tail Ridge, Rattlesnake, and West Cut-Across Trails; expect ruts, washboarding, and loose rocks. The ride follows hard-packed dirt fire roads and single-track trails in mostly good condition.

Although the Crystal Cove backcountry area is shared with equestrians and hikers (but no motorized vehicles), it has the reputation of being a "mountain bike park." Cyclists of all abilities will find agreeable trails to explore here. Moro Canyon Trail wanders through oak woodlands and is a pleasant path for beginners. The park's ridge trails, although steep in places, provide dramatic ocean views, challenging single-track riding, and great downhills. In the winter, coastal bluffs provide good vantage points for watching migrating gray whales.

RIDE 17 · Moro Canyon

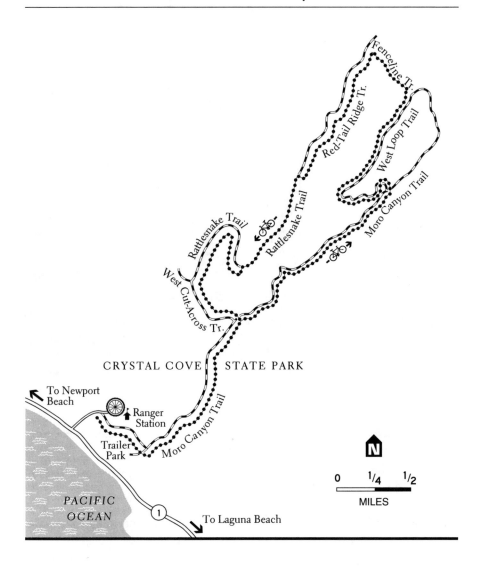

General location: Begins at the Moro Canyon parking lot in Crystal Cove State Park, 2.5 miles north of Laguna Beach and approximately 40 miles south of Los Angeles.

Elevation change: The loop starts at 110 feet above sea level, drops to 40 feet, and then gradually ascends Moro Canyon to 520 feet. West Loop Trail quickly climbs to 700 feet and then follows a ridgeline up to Fenceline Trail at 920 feet. Fenceline Trail rolls up and down and meets Red-Tail Ridge Trail at 920 feet. It is mostly downhill and rolling terrain from here. End with a 70-foot ascent back

The grassy hills of Moro Canyon.

to the trailhead. Tack on another 200 feet of climbing for undulations encountered over the course of the ride. Total elevation gain: 1,150 feet.

Season: Crystal Cove State Park is open year-round. Spring visits are pleasant; temperatures are mild, and the wildflowers are in bloom.

Services: Water, rest rooms, and a telephone can be found at the Crystal Cove State Park Ranger Station/Visitor Center. This facility is adjacent to the parking lot. All services are available in the community of Laguna Beach.

Hazards: Descend with care. Sections of Rattlesnake and West Cut-Across Trails are very steep and contain loose rocks and sand. Keep a keen eye out for other trail users; the park gets especially busy on weekends and holidays. Check your clothing and skin periodically for ticks after contact with brush and soil. Poison oak grows near the trail. Rattlesnakes reside in the park.

Rescue index: Help can be found at the Crystal Cove State Park Ranger Station/Visitor Center.

Land status: Public park.

Maps: A good topographic map of Crystal Cove State Park may be purchased at the Crystal Cove Visitor Center. A local cartographer has produced a mountain bike map of the park utilizing an aerial photograph. This map is also for sale at the Visitor Center.

Finding the trail: The ride begins from the Moro Canyon parking lot in Crystal Cove State Park. The park fronts the Pacific Coast Highway (CA 1) approximately 2.5 miles north of Laguna Beach and approximately 2 miles south of Newport Beach. From the highway, look for a small sign marking the entrance to Moro Canyon. Turn east into the park entrance and proceed to the entrance station. A day-use fee is required for parking.

Sources of additional information:

California Department of Parks
  and Recreation
Orange Coast District
18331 Enterprise Lane
Huntington Beach, CA 92648
(714) 848-1566

Crystal Cove State Park
8471 North Coast Highway
Laguna Beach, CA 92651
(949) 494-3539
cal-parks.ca.gov

Notes on the trail: Start the ride near the entrance station in the southeast corner of the parking area; you will find a trail here marked by an "Official Vehicles Only" sign. Follow this trail past a trailer park and down to the signed Moro Canyon Trail. Go uphill on Moro Canyon Trail. You'll arrive at a hub of trails after 3 miles of pedaling. Turn left here onto West Loop Trail where Moro Canyon Trail continues right. Climb for approximately 1.3 miles on West Loop Trail to a gate at single-track Fenceline Trail. Turn left onto Fenceline Trail and follow it for 0.5 mile to a **T** intersection. Turn left at this intersection onto Red-Tail Ridge Trail. After 0.8 mile, Red-Tail Ridge Trail narrows and becomes the single-track Rattlesnake Trail. Continue for 1 mile on Rattlesnake Trail to an electrical tower. Follow Rattlesnake Trail as it turns hard to the right here and widens to become a fire road. Follow the fire road for 0.8 mile to an intersection at West Cut-Across Trail. Turn left and follow West Cut-Across Trail down to Moro Canyon Trail. Turn right onto Moro Canyon Trail and return the way you came.

A portion of Crystal Cove State Park is designated as an underwater park. Scuba divers and snorkelers can explore reefs and kelp beds in a unique marine environment. There are 3.5 miles of beach and marine preserve with 32 walk-in environmental campsites. Contact the park for details.

RIDE 18 · Raptor Ridge Loop

AT A GLANCE

Length/configuration: 16-mile figure eight loop
Aerobic difficulty: Moderate overall, but demanding in spurts

Technical difficulty: Moderate; the tricky parts don't last long

Scenery: Rolling hills and abundant wildlife, especially birds of prey (they don't call it Raptor Ridge for nothing)

Special comments: One of many great rides in Chino Hills State Park, this is an especially fun loop

A t 16 miles, Raptor Ridge is a superb figure eight ride for intermediates as well as experts. If you ever find yourself looking for a route that will appeal to a large group of cyclists of varying abilities, this ride would make a great choice. The loop's mix of interspersed re-road climbs and single-track descents will keep the intermediates breathing easy and the experts whooping with joy. A hard-packed fire road up South Ridge delivers riders to a gentle winding single-track through Tarantula Canyon and the Four Corners picnic area. From there, a moderately ascending single-track carves up Raptor Ridge before delivering a rollicking descent into Upper Aliso Canyon Road and Chino Hills State Park headquarters. Another fire road climb is followed by a gentle decline back to Four Corners. From there, at the nexus of the figure eight, begins a long plunge into Telegraph Canyon and an earnest climb up Diemer Trail and South Ridge before the return to the start point. Now that you know the park, be sure to come back and ride some of the other trails here. And while in the area, make sure to visit the mind-stimulating and surprisingly non-sugarcoated interpretive displays at the Nixon Library. Afterwards, chow down at any of the restaurants along Yorba Linda Boulevard and reflect on how the area has changed since Tricky Dick lived here.

General location: In Chino Hills State Park, north of Yorba Linda.

Elevation change: This is a roller-coaster ride featuring several mini-ascents and descents, for a total gain of approximately 1,400 feet.

Season: A mostly unshaded route, it's best ridden between October and June or early in the morning on hot summer days.

Services: Potable water is available at the park headquarters, roughly halfway through the ride. All other services are available in nearby Yorba Linda, Placentia, and Brea.

Hazards: Some off-camber turns during the descent down Raptor Ridge.

Rescue index: This is a well-traveled route in a busy state park—help is always nearby. This route passes by the Visitor Center around mile 7; stop there if you need assistance. The Chino Hills State Park Rangers also maintain an emergency phone line at (909) 940-5661.

Land status: State park.

Maps: *Chino Hills State Park Trail Map* (available at the Visitor Center or by calling the park at the phone number listed later in this ride).

Finding the trail: From the Orange Freeway (57), exit at Yorba Linda Boulevard and go east for approximately 5 miles. (You'll pass the Nixon Library on the left.) Turn left onto curvy Fairmont Boulevard and travel north for 1.8 miles. Turn left onto Rimcrest (also heading north), traveling for 0.2 mile before parking on the

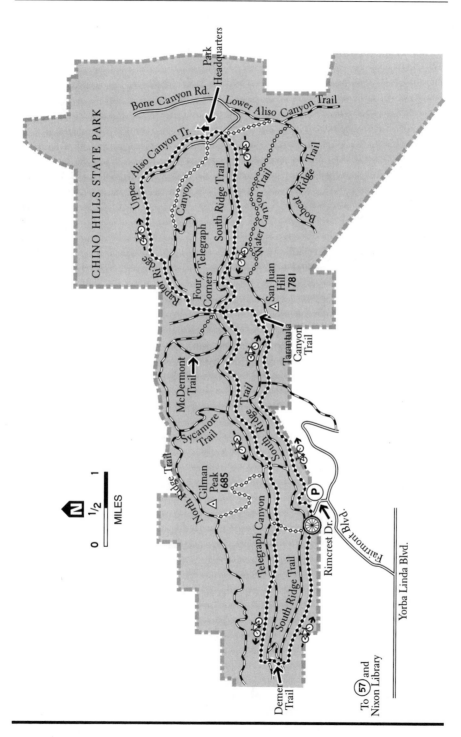

Entering raptor country in Chino Hills State Park.

right side of the street at the intersection of Blue Gum. (Note: This is a residential area that has experienced past conflicts with bikers urinating, undressing, and playing loud music in the area. Act responsibly or we could lose this parking area.)

Source of additional information:

Chino Hills State Park   (909) 780-6222
4195 Chino Hills Parkway, E165   cal-parks.ca.gov
Chino Hills, CA 91709

Notes on the trail: At 0.0 miles, the point where paved Rimcrest intersects with an unnamed dirt road, proceed northeast on the dirt road. After a few hundred feet, you'll come to a gate and a trailhead display. Go around the gate and begin riding South Ridge Fire Road to your right. After some quick climbs and small descents, the trail intersects with a utility road, but keep straight on South Ridge as it climbs toward San Juan Hill. At 2.7 miles, turn left on a descending single-track marked by a sign reading "Telegraph Canyon." (However, be aware that this is not in fact Telegraph Canyon but Tarantula Canyon. The misleading sign is actually indicating the destination of the single-track, which is Telegraph Canyon.) In any case, the single-track is narrow and sometimes rutty, but the pitch is gentle enough for almost any rider. Be on the lookout for tarantulas and lizards sunning themselves. At 3.2 miles, the path merges with a fire road but shortly resumes as a single-track. Bear left when the trail forks. At 3.8 miles, the single-track intersects with Telegraph Canyon Fire Road at the Four Corners picnic area. This is the nexus of the figure eight loop you're riding. Cross the fire road and head slightly to your right onto the Raptor Ridge single-track, snaking uphill. Have fun carving turns off the hillside as the path roller-coasters to an electrical tower at 4.5 miles. The trail passes right underneath the tower as it merges with a utility road. Keep your eyes and ears open here; you can frequently see hawks perched on the power lines and hear coyotes howling (even in the daytime) in the surrounding hills. Continue down the utility road. At 4.8 miles, make a sharp left back onto the single-track at a sign marked "Trail." This begins a grin-inducing, mile-long descent (though with some washed-out turns) down to Upper Aliso Canyon Fire Road at 5.8 miles. Turn right onto this fire road and descend to the paved Visitor Center road at 6.9 miles. Veer right past information boards, posted maps, a drinking fountain, and some picnic tables. The paved road comes to a T at 7.2 miles. Turn left and quickly make a sharp right back onto the South Ridge Fire Road at 7.2 miles.

The climbing is somewhat tough until you reach the unsigned connector road to Telegraph Canyon on your right at 8.7 miles. Head right on this road. At 9.1 miles, you'll intersect with Telegraph Canyon Fire Road (which roughly parallels South Ridge). Turn left here. The climbing soon ends, and you'll descend a gentle slope back to Four Corners at 9.6 miles. Continue straight (or west) down Telegraph Canyon. This is a 4-mile fire road descent that would be fun to bomb, but it's also one of the most well-traveled trails in the entire park—so resist the temptation, obey the posted speed limits, and ride responsibly.

At 11.9 miles, you'll pass Little Canyon Trail with access to South Ridge, but continue down and straight. At 12.6 miles, the trail intersects with a single-track trail known as Easy Street or Cheat Street. It's an appealing little climb, but unfortunately it's now closed to bikes. So keep plunging down Telegraph Canyon through several fun water crossings until you reach the Diemer Trail to South Ridge at 14.1 miles. Make a sharp left onto this double-track and begin climbing in earnest. At 14.6 miles you'll reach a saddle and the western end of South Ridge Fire Road. Turn left onto this road, which is aflame with wild mustard growing alongside it during spring. Though it's hard to imagine in fall or winter, the mustard is so thick here during the spring that it turns your sleeves and shoes yellow. There are some mini-descents here, but for the most part the road climbs until a south-facing vista at 15.6 miles. Take a gander at the encroaching housing subdivisions and see what this ride would look like if it weren't a state park. Then descend a steep face back to the gate where you started. Go around the gate and return to paved Rimcrest.

SAN JACINTO/
SANTA ROSA MOUNTAINS

On October 24, 2000, then-President Clinton signed legislation designating 272,000 acres of these mountains as the new Santa Rosa and San Jacinto Mountains National Monument. The new monument will be jointly administered by the BLM, U.S. Forest Service, California Department of Fish and Game, California Department of Parks and Recreation, the Agua Caliente Band of Cahuilla Indians, the Coachella Valley Conservancy, and a handful of county, city, and private land owners. Whew. At press time, it's difficult to predict how the new designation will affect mountain biking, but it's probable that visitors will look at these mountain ranges as more than mere backdrops for the golf courses of Palm Springs and Palm Desert—rather as destinations in their own right.

As biking attractions, these mountains are certainly worth some sort of honor as four-season attractions. After the heat of the summer and aridity of fall have passed, winter brings light amounts of refreshing rain and snow to this area. The moisture promotes the growth of spectacular spring wildflowers which seem to blossom in the most unlikely places—where rocks seem to be the only perennials.

Winter is especially fun. It's cooler here then, with comfortable temperatures among the barrel cacti of the valley floors of the low Colorado Desert. The only problem with visiting in winter is that this season is when the endangered Peninsular Ranges bighorn sheep enjoy their lambing season. As a result, the BLM might ask trail users to voluntarily refrain from hiking, biking, or riding horses on some of the trails listed. Check with the Monument before riding here in winter.

The good news is that summer, surprisingly, can be a good time to ride here. Even when it's blazing on the Coachella Valley floor, high-elevation rides on Thomas Mountain and Santa Rosa Mountain feature stretches of cool, comfortable riding through pine forests. What's more, lodging rates in the Coachella Valley drop by half at many hotels and resorts.

Regardless of what time of year you visit, you'll find fun riding in this sometimes stark, sometimes lush area. What's more, you can top off your experience with a soak in one of the area's abundant hot springs. Those golfers don't know what they're missing.

RIDE 19 · Thomas Mountain Road/Ramona Trail

AT A GLANCE

CA

Length/configuration: 17.4-mile loop on dirt road, single-track, and pavement.

Aerobic difficulty: Difficult; the climb up Thomas Mountain road is long and takes place at a fairly high altitude.

Technical difficulty: Difficult; some narrow single-track and very rocky sections

Scenery: Lake Hemet, mix of ecosystems: Jeffrey pines; sugar pines and alders; chaparral and scrub; and high desert landscapes all featured

Special comments: Lots of downhill after a long climb; a perfect ride for hot summer and fall day

This ride begins with a steady climb up Thomas Mountain before delivering a bounty of fun single-track descents. When the downhill is over, you can return to the start by riding the gentle grade on fast (but occasionally trafficky) CA 74, or ride a quieter dirt power line road. In either case, this route—like the nearby Palm Canyon Ride—allows you to ride through a variety of ecosystems. The difference is that here, the low point of the ride is still 4,400 feet above sea level. (The high point is around 6,700 feet.)

It's not uncommon for bikers to drive from the hot Coachella Valley dressed for warm weather, work up a sweat on the initial climb up Thomas Mountain, then freeze during the 10 miles of mostly downhill riding that follows. So do yourself a favor and bring extra layers, especially during spring and fall. Let your teeth chatter from the thrill of the descent, not the cold.

General location: About 30 miles southwest of Palm Desert via CA 74, and 11 miles southeast of Idyllwild.

Elevation change: Route gains 2,300 feet, climbing from start at 4,430 feet to high point of 6,700 feet.

Season: Spring to fall.

Services: Water, telephone, gas, and basic supplies may be available at Lake Hemet Market in the community of Lake Hemet. All services in Idyllwild, Hemet, and Palm Desert.

Hazards: Clawing manzanita bushes; some very rocky patches of trail.

Rescue index: Help can be found in Idyllwild, west of the route.

Land status: National forest.

Maps: "Trails Map of the Santa Rosa Mountains National Scenic Area," available at the San Jacinto Ranger District in Idyllwild, and at BLM Visitor Center south of Palm Desert on CA 74.

RIDE 19 · Thomas Mountain Road/Ramona Trail

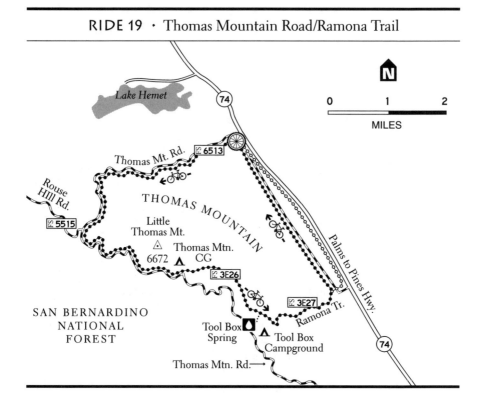

Finding the trail: From Palm Desert, go south, then west, then northwest on winding CA 74 for 32 miles to the intersection with Thomas Mountain Road (FS 6S13) on your left. (Note: You will first pass the southeastern terminus of Thomas Mountain Road at 27 miles; don't turn here, go another 5 miles until you reach the northwestern terminus at 32 miles. It's opposite milepost sign 64.25, and is marked by a brown road sign "6S13.") Go left on Thomas Mountain Road for 0.2 mile to a turnout on the right and park, making sure not to block the road. Forest Adventure Pass required.

Sources of additional information:

San Bernardino National Forest
San Jacinto Ranger District
54270 Pinecrest
P.O. Box 518
Idyllwild, CA 92549
(909) 659-2117
www.r5.fs.fed.us/sanbernardino

Palm Springs Cyclery
611 South Palm Canyon Drive
Palm Springs, CA 92262
(760) 325-9319

Santa Rosa and San Jacinto
    Mountains National Monument
Bureau of Land Management
Palm Springs South Coast Field
    Office
690 Garnet Avenue
P.O. Box 1260
North Palm Springs, CA 92258
(760) 251-4800
www.ca.blm.gov/palmsprings

Thomas Mountain Road.

Notes on the trail: Begin by riding in the same direction that you were driving, west, on Thomas Mountain Road/FS 6S13. The road starts climbing, and aside from a nice downhill just before mile 2, it's almost all uphill. Excellent views abound, however, and if you get in a steady groove, it goes pretty quickly. At 4.6 miles, cross over a cattle guard and stay left on Thomas Mountain Road past the intersection with FS 5S15, which goes right to Rouse Hill. You stay on the main road at all times and reach the beginning of some ridge-top riding around 6 miles into the excursion.

Shortly after passing FS 6N13D, leading up to a summit on your left, you arrive at a turnoff to a single-track trail at 7.6 miles. This is supposed to be FS3E27, but it's doubtful you'll see any signs as such. But the trail is marked with a sign that reads, "This Trail is Open To..." followed by icons for hikers, equestrians, and bikers, and a blue sticker reading "More Difficult."

Go left here and enjoy a rollicking single-track which seems to feature a little bit of everything. From carpets of pine needles to very bumpy rocks, you'll have several chances to test your technical ability. Though not actually named, the correct path is easy to follow, marked by signs exactly like the one where you first turned onto the single-track. After some fun rollercoastering through sugar pines and alders, you come to an intersection with a dirt road leading to Tool Box Springs Campground at 9.8 miles. Cross the dirt road and pick up the trail on the other side. Keep your speed in check, for at 10 miles on the left, you arrive at the junction with Ramona Trail (FS 3E26). There was no sign for Ramona Trail when I rode here, but it may be flagged with ribbon and will likely have bike tracks on it.

So turn left, point the Cannondale downhill and go: You'll have a blast. The trail throws a lot of variety at you: wonderful single-track, tight switchbacks, sand, rock waterbars, and red clay. And then, more rocks. You reach the trailhead at the bottom of Ramona Trail at 13.8 miles with a smile on your face. You now have two options for returning. You can either take the dirt road under the power lines back to Thomas Mountain Road and the start, or ride a little east to CA 74, and go left on the faster (but trafficky) CA 74. Either way, your final ride will total around 17.4 fun miles.

RIDE 20 · Santa Rosa Mountain/Sawmill Trail

AT A GLANCE

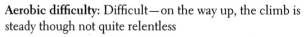

Length/configuration: 25.6-mile loop (on dirt road, single-track, and pavement)

Aerobic difficulty: Difficult—on the way up, the climb is steady though not quite relentless

Technical difficulty: Difficult; tight switchbacks and rocky fire roads demand good bike-handling skills

Scenery: Panoramic views of the Santa Rosa range; alpine ecosystems; huge expanse of Colorado desert

Special comments: A loop ride connecting a scenic hill climb and one of the newer trails in the region, this is fast becoming a local favorite

If you're ever in the Coachella Valley and think it's just too dang scorching to ride, think again. This 25.6-mile loop is a surefire beat-the-heat ride, rewarding cyclists with cool mountain breezes, a gurgling mountain spring, and an utterly refreshing single-track. Before the Sawmill Trail single-track was built in 1997 (to "mountain biker specifications," notes a local map), the Santa Rosa Mountain Truck Trail was worth riding simply for the scenery it offered. Now this route will thrill your adrenaline system as much as your optic nerves.

After a warm-up ride on pavement, you'll ascend Santa Rosa Mountain Truck Trail to a saddle where you can catch your breath in the high altitude. After a quick descent, the ascent takes over, switchbacking here, coursing along open hillsides there, all the way up to the inviting Santa Rosa Spring. After you refill water bottles and lungs, you come to the turnoff for Sawmill Trail. Hard-core riders might want to blast another 4 miles up to Toro Peak for a good climbing workout and 360° views of much of Southern California.

But the mortals among us will want to simply savor Sawmill's singular single-track, which switchbacks from one great panorama to another as it descends toward CA 74. Some demanding double-track and fast fire roads ensue as you make your way back to the start. Afterward, cap off the ride with a meal, fresh-

RIDE 20 · Santa Rosa Mountain/Sawmill Trail

baked cookie, or beverage at the Sugarloaf Cafe, less than a mile south of the start/finish on CA 74.

General location: 16 miles north of Palm Desert just off the Palms to Pines Highway (CA 74).

Elevation change: Climbs from a low of around 4,000 feet to 7,540 feet, with some ups and downs along the way, for a total gain of about 3,800 feet.

Services: Spring water available on trail, while food, water, phone and rest rooms can be found at the Sugarloaf Cafe on CA 74. All other services available in Palm Desert.

Hazards: Fast-changing weather, tight single-track, rutted roads.

Rescue index: Help can be found from the multitude of mountain bikers on the trail (and—on weekends at least—4x4 drivers).

Land status: National forest.

Maps: "Trails Map of the Santa Rosa Mountains National Scenic Area," available at San Jacinto Ranger District headquarters in Idyllwild, and at the BLM Visitors Center on CA 74.

Finding the trail: From the intersection of CA 111 and CA 74 in Palm Desert,

Truckin' through the Santa Rosa Mountains.

drive south on CA 74 for about 16 miles. When you see Pinyon Drive and Pinyon Flats Campground on the right, you want to go left on the paved road leading to the trailhead for Sawmill Trail. Go 0.4 mile to the paved parking loop on the left and park. Forest Adventure Pass required.

Sources of additional information:

San Bernardino National Forest
San Jacinto Ranger District
54270 Pinecrest Drive
P.O. Box 518
Idyllwild, CA 92549
(909) 659-2117
www.r5.fs.fed.us/sanbernardino

Santa Rosa and San Jacinto
Mountains National Monument
Bureau of Land Management
Palm Springs South Coast
    Field Office

690 Garnet Avenue
P.O. Box 1260
North Palm Springs, CA 92258
(760) 251-4800
www.ca.blm.gov/palmsprings/

Palm Springs Cyclery
611 S. Palm Canyon Drive
Palm Springs, CA 92262
(760) 325-9319

Notes on the trail: From the parking area, ride back to CA 74 (which you reach at 0.4 mile) and go left. Be careful; traffic can be fast on this stretch. If it hasn't been demolished, you'll pass an abandoned gas station on your left. Then, at 4.1 miles, you'll see FS 7S02, known both as Mt. Santa Rosa Road and Mt. Santa Rosa Truck Trail, on your left. Be extremely careful crossing CA 74, and make the sharp left on Mt. Santa Rosa Road. It won't be long before flatlanders begin noticing the altitude. At 5.8 miles, at the top of a small saddle, a welcome but brief 0.75-mile descent begins. As the road ascends once more, there are numerous intersections with other jeep trails, but the main road is always obvious. So don't worry about looking at the road, and instead feast your eyes on the views to the north of Mt. San Jacinto and Haystack Mountain.

Around 10 miles into the ride, the climb steepens, and it's pretty unrelenting until you reach Santa Rosa Campground. Keep going, and at 12.4 miles, feel free to take the short turnoff on the left to Santa Rosa Spring. Re-hydrate here (the locals do) and then resume climbing FS 7S02. In about a mile you pass a utility access road to a radio facility on the left. Go another 50 feet to the intersection with Sawmill Trail, FS 5E03, also on your left at 13.3 miles. If you really have a lot of energy, you can ride another 4 miles toward Toro Peak for great views, but that mileage isn't included here, because even great fire roads have trouble competing with the single-track you're about to enjoy.

So go left on Sawmill Trail and enjoy switchbacking through a beautiful alpine environment where the views are as big as the trees. The switchbacks demand a lot of you, but when you're in a groove, they are wondrous to ride. Or so I'm told.

After crossing a creek, you plunge through a chaparral zone and arrive at a double-track. Go right (east) with the double-track, enduring some brief, rocky climbs here and there. You then reach dirt Sawmill Road, which is a little easier to navigate but also pretty dang steep. It plunges most of 6 miles (with lots of switchbacks) back to Sawmill Trail Trailhead and the start of the ride, which you reach at 25.6 miles.

RIDE 21 · Palm Canyon

AT A GLANCE

Length/configuration: 28.4-mile point-to-point ride (requires car shuttle)

Aerobic difficulty: Moderate/difficult; a mostly downhill route, but with one extended climb and several short ascents

Technical difficulty: Difficult; though eminently rideable for the most part, this ride is too long to avoid traversing some rocky, loose, and off-camber terrain

Scenery: Alpine forests to low desert scrub, epitomized by views of massive Mt. San Jacinto in one direction and palm oases in the other

Special comments: Though not especially difficult to ride, this trip is hard-core in length, remoteness, and ruggedness — extra water and inner tubes are essential

It's hard to imagine a ride that gives a better introduction to its unique region than this 28.4-mile point-to-point trip. The ride embarks from the Santa Rosa Mountains, 18 miles north of Palm Desert off CA 74, known as the Palms to

Pines Highway. Consider this ride to be the Pines to Palms Descent, a trip that showcases the Santa Rosa Mountains' singular mix of alpine and desert ecosystems. Dropping gradually from Highway 74, a single-track clings precariously to mountainsides populated by abundant jackrabbits and deer before hitting the Palm Canyon floor. For a while it's hard to get into the flow of riding due to the frequent interruptions by sandy washes and some protruding thorn bushes. But eventually the trail settles into a groove above the canyon floor, increasing your speed and enjoyment. You might even find yourself racing down the single-track alongside a sprinting California Thrasher, which resembles a roadrunner. (Sad to report that they don't say "Beep Beep" when crossing your path.)

After joining a less scenic but very fast four-by-four road, the descent gives way to a gradual but sandy 3-mile climb up Dry Wash Road. After blinking several times to make sure the Mike Dunn Desert Riders Oasis isn't just a mirage, enjoy lunch at the Oasis' picnic tables and visit one of the port-a-potties before turning onto probably the most spectacular stretch of single-track in the Coachella Valley, known as the Hahn Buena Vista Trail. After a quick climb to Valentine Point, with its 360° panoramic view of the region, a sublime descent takes over. You cascade past picturesque desert gardens that look as if they were painted by Georgia O'Keeffe, around adrenaline-boosting but wholly rideable switchbacks, and down a grade that seems made for mountain bikers. Afterwards, a mildly ascending roller-coaster single-track takes you to Dunn Road for quick descending and bail-out opportunities if you need them. But if possible, stick to the hardcore route described below for a sampling of the area's well-known Goat Trails and an exit back into civilization near the town border between Palm Springs and Cathedral City.

Note: The BLM may ask trail users to voluntarily refrain from using this trail during the Peninsular Ranges Bighorn Sheep lambing season, which runs from January 1 to June 30. Check with the BLM's Palm Springs Field Office before riding here.

General location: Begins 18 miles north of Palm Desert, and ends in Palm Springs just north of the border with Cathedral City.

Elevation change: Drops approximately 4,000 feet, from 4,300 feet down to 280 feet, with a substantial 800-foot climb from 1,400 feet to 2,200 feet midway through the ride.

Season: October through May.

Services: Picnic tables and portable toilets are available midway through the ride, but there is no water on the trail. All services are available in Palm Springs, Cathedral City, and Palm Desert.

Hazards: Extremely narrow trail in places; occasional off-camber turns; abundant and diverse kinds of cactus, thorn bush, and manzanita can be a nightmare for tires. Bring extra tubes and a patch kit. Most importantly, be aware that the usually dry washes along the route are prone to flash floods. Avoid this route during high-intensity rain, and even on dry days be on the lookout for thunderstorm activity in the mountains above.

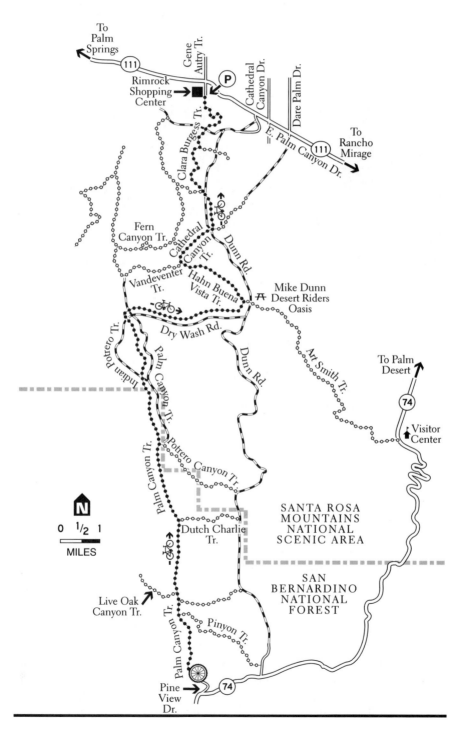

Taking in the buena vista on Hahn Buena Vista Trail.

Rescue index: Help is more readily available at the terminus of this ride than at the start. While the resort cities of the Coachella Valley are close in distance to this route, they are far in accessibility until the end. You must be self-sufficient. Be aware that most sections of this ride see little use — on a gorgeous, high-season weekend day when the valley was packed with people, this rider encountered only three other trail users over 28 miles of cycling.

Land status: San Bernardino National Forest, BLM land, some non-federal public lands.

Maps: "Trails Map of the Santa Rosa Mountains National Scenic Area," available at BLM's Santa Rosa Mountains National Scenic Area Visitor Center on Highway 74.

Finding the trail: Drive two cars slightly southeast of the intersection of Gene Autry Trail and Palm Canyon Drive/CA 111 in Palm Springs. (It's just northwest of the border with Cathedral City.) Turn south into the Rimrock Shopping Center (marked by a Von's supermarket) at 4733 East Palm Canyon Drive. Leave one car at the southeast end of the shopping center, either in the parking lot or on the unnamed road just to the southeast of the shopping center. In the second vehicle, turn right (south) onto Palm Canyon Drive/Highway 111. Proceed approximately 14 miles to the junction with Highway 74, the Palms to Pines Highway, in the town of Palm Desert. Turn right on Highway 74 and drive up a steep straight hill. (The helpful BLM/Santa Rosa Mountains National Scenic Area Visitor Center is 3.8 miles up Highway 74 on the left.) The road then switchbacks past Vista Point and a nature trail before climbing by the Sugarloaf Cafe. At 18.3 miles from the junction with Highway 111, turn right onto the broken pavement of Pine View Drive. (If you pass an abandoned gas station on your left, you've gone too far.) Drive 0.2 mile and park as far right as possible at the end of paved Pine View Drive, where the trail begins. Since you are in the San Bernardino National Forest at this point, you will need a Forest Adventure Pass to park here.

Sources of additional information:

San Bernardino National Forest
San Jacinto Ranger District
54270 Pinecrest Drive
P.O. Box 518
Idyllwild, CA 92349
(909) 659-2117
www.r5.fs.fed.us/sanbernardino

Santa Rosa and San Jacinto
    Mountains National Monument
Bureau of Land Management
Palm Springs South Coast
    Field Office

690 Garnet Ave.
P.O. Box 1260
North Palm Springs, CA 92258
(760) 251-4800
www.ca.blm.gov/palmsprings/santa_
    rosa_national_monument.html

Palm Springs Cyclery
611 South Palm Canyon Drive
Palm Springs, CA 92262
(760) 325-9319

Notes on the trail: From the end of paved Pine View Drive, proceed north on the rough trail, which is about halfway between a jeep road and a single-track 4x4 dirt road. Very soon, at 0.2 mile, turn right at an intersection marked by two unreadable rusted signs, one a yellow triangle, the other a gray rectangle. You're now on a narrow 4x4 road that drops gently for over a mile. At 1.5 miles, at a site marked by stone cairns, the trail takes a sharp left and plunges downhill. Stay on it. At 1.7 miles you will reach a trail sign that indicates you're now on Palm Canyon Trail 4E01, and you can either continue via the "Canyon Bottom" to the left or the "Ridge top" to the right. Stay right and climb up the ridge top. At 1.9 miles proceed through a cattle gate; if you can't step over it, make sure to close it behind you. The trail—whose width keeps changing—often clings precariously to the side of the ridge as it rises and falls. After about 3.5 miles, the trail descends in earnest down to Omstott Wash. At 4.2 miles, turn left on the path that parallels the wash (you'll see the back of a trail sign beckoning you). Almost immediately you'll pass the intersection with the popular Pinyon Trail. As a result, you will now see a lot more bike tracks. At 4.3 miles, after slogging through the sandy wash, veer left onto firmer ground and a path that's marked by thigh-high, notched wooden posts shaped like New York City's Citicorp Building. Continue straight past a trail sign that's facing away from you (don't bother reading this sign, it'll only confuse and mislead you). Near the 5-mile mark, the trail becomes a bit faint, and is further obscured by thick reeds partially blocking your way. Don't worry, however. Just veer right, follow the footprints, bike tracks, and even horse poop marking the way, and you'll be fine.

After meandering alongside a dry wash for a while, you'll climb a narrow, sandy chute past a beat-up sign at 6 miles reading "State Game Refuge." Soon, more notched wooden posts magically appear to guide you as you cross a plethora of washes. At 7.2 miles, at the signed intersection with Dutch Charlie

Trail on your right, continue straight. Likewise, stay straight past the signed intersection with Live Oak Spring Trail on your left at 7.6 miles. The trail really begins to rock now—the washes that have thus far interrupted your flow are no longer a problem.

After a couple of miles of fun cruising, you'll pass the signed Agua Bonita Spring (and a presumable source of emergency water) before merging with the signed Potrero Canyon 4x4 Road at 9.8 miles. Turn left here. Now you're on a rocky, rutted, steep jeep road, so watch your speed. At 11.2 miles, a sign informs you that you're leaving the San Bernardino National Forest and entering BLM land, but continue on the same road as it descends. If it's hot, do yourself a favor and stop at the unmissable palm oasis at 12.5 miles for a rare bit of shade. At 14 miles, at the T-intersection with unsigned Dry Wash Road, turn right. After 3 miles of sandy, occasionally frustrating climbing, turn left on Dunn Road (a smooth fire road) at 17.1 miles. Soon you'll reach the enticing Mike Dunn Desert Riders Oasis and the intersection with the Art Smith and Hahn Buena Vista Trails at 17.9 miles. After a picnic lunch and pit stop (rest rooms are available), find the Hahn Buena Vista trailhead directly across Dunn Road from the picnic tables and pedal up it. A very rideable single-track puts you at the summit of Valentine Point at 18.5 miles. Enjoy the 360° panoramic view, then start descending on the path just below and to the right of the big iron "Hahn Buena Vista" sign.

A wondrous, sublime descent takes you to the intersection with the Vandeventer and Cathedral Canyon Trails at 21.4 miles. From here, quickly veer right once (into a sandy wash) and then again (out of the wash) and onto the unsigned but obvious Cathedral Canyon Trail. Numerous bike tracks and stone cairns (stay to the right of them) point the way as the trail roller-coasters up to Dunn Road. At 22.9 miles, turn left on Dunn Road (still a dirt road), which cycles through a series of steep drops and rises. At 23.8 miles, shortly after topping out of one rise and beginning to descend again, keep your eyes peeled for a wide dirt road intersecting from the left. At first glance, the road seems to dead end almost immediately in a huge mound of dirt, but go left here anyway. Chances are, you'll see a bunch of bike tracks snaking around the mound to the left. Do the same thing, and you find a long double-track road unfurling to the north. Take it. (If you miss this turnoff or need to bail out of the ride, don't worry. By staying on Dunn Road, you'll eventually reach pavement. Once on pavement, just keep going downhill and northward, and you'll eventually reach Highway 111. Go left on Highway 111 through Cathedral City, and you'll reach your shuttle vehicle at the Rimrock Shopping Center.)

But let's assume you stayed on the double-track. The road is badly eroded in spots but always rideable. At 24.6 miles, near the beginning of a climb, you'll see a rock cairn and an attractive single-track with lots of wheel marks on your left. Take it and you're now in the "Goat Trails" area. (Again, if you miss this turnoff don't worry; by sticking on the double-track and heading north and downhill, you'll eventually come out on Highway 111, where you can turn left and ride to your car.) Back on the steep, loose terrain of the Goat Trails, look north to see Palm Springs Airport. If you always head toward the airport, you'll be fine. At 25 miles, another stone cairn appears on your left, but this time stay right. You're now on the Clara Burgess Trail. Head north on it until you reach the signed Clara Burgess trailhead at 25.2 miles. With your back to the trail sign, look northward for a dirt road climbing out of a wash. This is your trail. You'll have to carry your bike down the steep path into the wash (if the path looks impassably steep, go to your right where it's less daunting). Turn left on the road climbing out of the wash.

At 25.8 miles, upon reaching a summit marked by a cross, remind yourself to be careful. You can now see the airport again, and almost immediately you'll head right onto a trail leading downhill and toward the airport. From here, there's no single correct way to get down, so it's futile to confuse you with directions. Just go downhill or north at any one of the numerous intersections, heading toward the airport whenever possible. Eventually, you'll go down a markedly steeper and rockier slope and end up next to a massive boulder pile on your right at 27.9 miles. Turn left here and head downhill. At 28.4 miles, go around a gate and arrive at your car at the paved Rimrock Shopping Center.

RIDE 22 · Art Smith Trail

AT A GLANCE

Length/configuration: 16.7-mile out-and-back ride (8.35 miles each way)

Aerobic difficulty: Difficult; steep climbing and some hike-a-bike sections

Technical difficulty: Difficult; rideable if you're in a groove, frustrating if you're not

Scenery: Sheer canyons, a bounty of overlooks, desert oases, and, if you're lucky, bighorn sheep

Special comments: A very technical trail that's sublime on those days that you're feeling immortal—if you're feeling merely human, don't bother

From its origin in Dead Indian Canyon, this 16.7-mile out-and-back single-track route takes you through a diverse desert garden of cacti as you follow a couple of sandy washes into a canyon. The impeccably signed and maintained path then begins climbing sharply up switchbacks while passing signs erected in tribute to the trail's namesake, Art Smith. But just as you're musing what a guy Art Smith must have been to inspire such a beautiful trail, the switchbacks and rocks begin vying for your attention. You will likely dismount and carry your bike with frequency. This is annoying, because you know in your heart that if you had the gumption and derring-do you possess on your best riding days, the trail would be completely rideable. It's only then that a troubling but totally sensible realization arrives: of all the local riders who recommended this trail, none were older than 22! All of a sudden, everything makes sense. This is exclusively a ride for the young and young at heart. If you're riding like you're youthful, strong, and immortal, this is paradise. But if you feel old, blasé, or timid, it's an ordeal.

RIDE 22 · Art Smith Trail

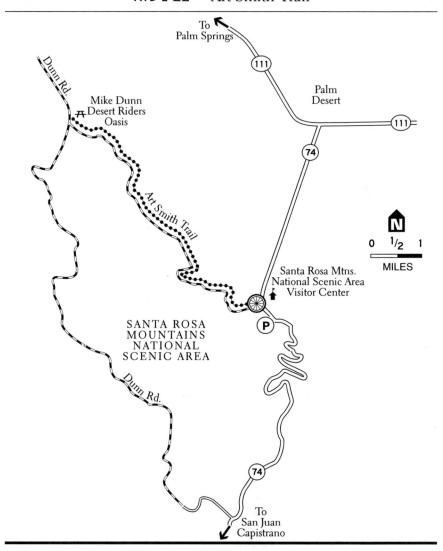

You thus steel yourself to be more like Art Smith, an ageless trail boss who spent his life exploring the Santa Rosa Mountains on foot and on horseback, and attack the route with more determination. The terrain assists you, as the trail reaches a shoulder to the east of Haystack Mountain and then becomes more navigable. Passing jaw-dropping scenic vistas, you feel like you're on top of the world when you reach a ridge top. You then meander past hundreds of century plants until you reach the Mike Dunn Desert Riders Oasis, an exemplary spot for a picnic before the thrilling descent back to the start.

Note: The BLM may ask trail users to voluntarily refrain from using this trail

The trailhead: one of the rare places where the Art Smith Trail is flat.

during the Peninsular Ranges Bighorn Sheep lambing season, which runs from January 1 to June 30. Check with the BLM's Palm Springs Field Office before riding here.

General location: 4 miles north of Palm Desert just off the Palms to Pines Highway (CA 74) in the Santa Rosa and San Jacinto Mountains National Monument.

Elevation change: Climbs 1,300 feet (from 1,000 to 2,300 feet), and then drops the same amount.

Season: October through May.

Services: Picnic tables and rest rooms are available at the trail's midpoint. Water, rest rooms, phones, maps, and area guides are available at the BLM's Santa Rosa and San Jacinto Mountains National Monument Visitor Center across the road from the trailhead. All other services are available in Palm Desert.

Hazards: Cacti; the trail is very narrow at times, with steep cliffsides.

Rescue index: Though this is rugged terrain, you're never more than 9 miles from CA 74 and the phones at the Santa Rosa and San Jacinto Mountains National Monument Visitor Center. Help is also available in Palm Desert.

Land status: BLM land.

Maps: "Trails Map of the Santa Rosa Mountains National Scenic Area," available at the BLM Visitor Center on CA 74.

Finding the trail: From the intersection of CA 111 and CA 74, drive south on CA 74. After 3.9 miles, turn right into a paved parking lot marked "Art Smith Trail." (You will have already passed the BLM Visitor Center.) The trailhead is at the north end of the parking lot.

Sources of additional information:

Santa Rosa and San Jacinto
Mountains National Monument
Bureau of Land Management
Palm Springs South Coast
Field Office
690 Garnet Avenue
P.O. Box 1260
North Palm Springs, CA 92258

(760) 251-4800
www.ca.blm.gov/palmsprings/ santa
_rosa_national_monument.html

Palm Springs Cyclery
611 South Palm Canyon Drive
Palm Springs, CA 92262
(760) 325-9319

Notes on the trail: Proceed from the trailhead on the well-signed single-track path. The trail almost immediately begins paralleling a dry wash by clinging to an adjacent cliffside. The desert landscape is incredibly picturesque, something you can really appreciate at 0.4 mile, when you have to ride through a sandy wash. Though the wash is wide and curvy enough to make you feel like you might be wandering off-route, if you look around you'll always see footprints, bike tracks, or, best of all, a trail sign. (Note: Here and whenever the trail signs disagree with established bike tracks or footprints, follow the trail signs.) Leaving the wash for terra firma, you soon pass by a big iron sign reading "Art Smith Trail—1977" and begin climbing in earnest. This section can either be pleasantly challenging or torturously frustrating depending on your daily aggressiveness quotient. In any case, you'll gain an appreciation for the trail's meticulous maintenance and informative signage. However, you might still feel as if the route is better suited to mountain goats than mountain bikes, and in a way you're right. You're in a State Game Refuge, home to shy bighorn sheep who thrive in the rocky, rugged terrain. Keep riding, and after 5 miles you'll bypass stoney, 3,808-foot Haystack Mountain on the left. The worst of the climb is now over, and for a long time you'll roller-coaster up to and alongside a ridgeline, avoiding prickly century plants while taking in splendiferous views. At 8.4 miles, you'll pour out of the trail and into the Mike Dunn Desert Riders Oasis picnic area. Take a well-deserved break and prepare for a challenging, technical descent back the way you came. (Be careful—those picturesque rocks are a lot more fun to experience with your eyes than your knees and elbows.)

RIDE 23 · The Goat Trails

AT A GLANCE

CA

Length/configuration: 7.7-mile combination (6.4-mile loop on dirt road, single-track, and pavement, plus a 0.6-mile single-track spur)

Aerobic difficulty: Difficult; climbs are short, can be steep

Technical difficulty: Difficult; narrow rocky trails, with a tricky hike-a-bike section

Scenery: Small canyons, palm trees, and urban landscapes

Special comments: A network of trails where getting lost is half the fun

Riding the Goat Trails always reminds me of the opening of Mark Twain's *Adventures of Huckleberry Finn*, where the author warns against the dangers of meticulously interpreting the book: "Persons attempting to find a motive in this narrative will be prosecuted; persons attempting to find a moral in it will be banished; persons attempting to find a plot in it will be shot." You deserve the same fate if you get meticulous and try to limit the Goat Trails to a single, definitive, carefully spelled-out route. That's because the Goat Trails are only as logical and rational as the goats—or bighorn sheep, or other local wildlife—that created this insane network of trails. So do as the goats or sheep do, and just meander here and there while seeking out nourishment in the form of sweeping turns, sudden descents, wash traverses, and exemplary views. Whichever way you ride, it's likely your total trip mileage will measure between 7 and 12 miles.

The biggest appeal of this particular 7.7-mile trip, and every other excursion in the Goat Trails, is its surprising proximity to Palm Springs. From fall to spring, this is where locals taking an after-work spin intersect with tourists getting a feel for desert riding on their first day of vacation. It's an unlikely mix, but it works, since in the Goat Trails you just follow your appetite. If you want to ride steep, rocky single-tracks, they're right there. If you'd rather pedal wide, smoother dirt roads, they're over this way. And chances are, both routes will intersect a dozen times. (However, all combinations are challenging to your lungs.)

The only thing you really have to remember here is the street address nearest to where you parked. From the Goat Trails you can always head downhill and north and wind up on East Palm Canyon Drive/CA 111, which brackets the trail. Once on East Palm Canyon Drive/CA 111, find the closest street address. Since address numbers increase the farther southeast you travel on East Palm Canyon Drive/CA 111, you'll only have to do a little math and then head right (southeast) or left (northwest) to find the street address where your car is parked. For post-ride vittles, be sure not to miss Las Casuelas Mexican restaurant on CA 111 in downtown Palm Springs.

Note: The BLM may ask trail users to voluntarily refrain from using this trail during the Peninsular Ranges Bighorn Sheep lambing season, which runs from

RIDE 25 · The Goat Trails

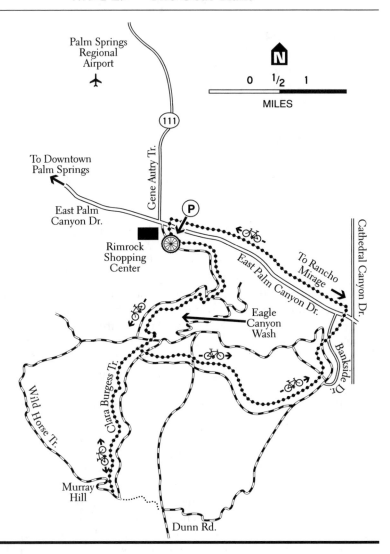

January 1 to June 30. Check with the BLM's Palm Springs Field Office before riding here.

General location: Roughly paralleling East Palm Canyon Drive/CA 111 in Palm Springs and Cathedral City.

Elevation change: Approximately 1,200 feet, depending on where you ride.

Season: October through May.

Services: None are available on the trail. All services are available in Palm Springs and Cathedral City.

Hazards: Cacti, a very narrow trail at times, and washes prone to flash flooding.

Rescue index: Though this is rugged terrain, you're never more than a couple of miles from the Coachella Valley's main artery, East Palm Canyon Drive/CA 111.

Land status: Municipal and non-federal public lands.

Maps: USGS 7.5-minute quadrangle maps: Palm Springs and Cathedral City (but be aware that neither these nor any other maps come close to depicting all the trails in the area), "Trail Map: Santa Rosa Mountains National Scenic Area," available in local sports stores and at the BLM Visitor Center outside of Palm Desert.

Finding the trail: Drive to the intersection of Gene Autry Trail and Palm Canyon Drive/CA 111 in Palm Springs. (It's just northwest of the border with Cathedral City.) Turn south into the Rimrock Shopping Center (marked by a Von's supermarket) at 4733 East Palm Canyon Drive. Park at the southeast end of the shopping center in the parking lot near the laundromat or on the unnamed road just to the southeast of the shopping center.

Sources of additional information:

Santa Rosa and San Jacinto
　　Mountains National Monument
Bureau of Land Management
Palm Springs South Coast
　　Field Office
690 Garnet Avenue
P.O. Box 1260
North Palm Springs, CA 92258

(760) 251-4800
www.ca.blm.gov/palmsprings/ santa_
　　rosa_national_monument.html

Palm Springs Cyclery
611 South Palm Canyon Drive
Palm Springs, CA 92262
(760) 325-9319

Notes on the trail: This is just one possible route in the Goat Trails. Because so many trails intersect up here, it's very difficult to follow any prescribed route. So don't worry about getting lost; it's much better to simply ride where you want to and just head downhill and northward when you get tired. From the southeast end of Rimrock Shopping Center, go around the gate a little ways up the dirt road leading uphill. At 0.5 mile, pass a boulder pile on your left and veer right up a steep hill. The road is rutted and loose, but not long. Just as the terrain is firming up and leveling off, turn right onto another dirt road at 1.1 miles. This road roller-coasters in a counterclockwise direction, and at times it's disorienting; you feel as if it might deliver you back to East Palm Canyon Drive before you're ready. But not to worry; at 2 miles turn right when your road intersects with a much more utilized road. Soon, this trail also embarks on a roughly counterclockwise semicircle through rocky terrain. The views improve as you begin climbing in earnest toward a rocky summit marked with a cross. At 2.6 miles, turn left on the road leading up to the summit and take in the view. (If it's late afternoon the hillsides around you will be positively orange and glowing.) Head downhill in the same direction toward Eagle Canyon Wash. Once in the wash, you'll have to dismount and portage your bike while clambering up a steep rock face. At 3.2 miles you've now climbed out of the wash, so get back on your bike and pedal south on a single-track toward the large iron "Clara Burgess Trail" sign in front of you. The single-track becomes increasingly technical as the trail enters a rugged, scenic canyon. There are a few intersections marked with cairns, but proceed mostly straight until the trail reaches the shoulder of a mountain and begins to descend at 3.8 miles. This is a good place to turn around, and doing so treats you to wide views of the Coachella Valley. Rumble back down back to the Clara Burgess Trail sign, and go right on a four-by-four road instead of entering Eagle Canyon Wash again. After a mile of roller-coaster riding, you'll reach a single-track at 5.4 miles. Veer left and clatter down toward a concrete water channel below. At 5.9 miles, you'll reach a crumbling pavement road paralleling the channel. Head downhill here toward civilization. At 6.2 miles, turn left on CA 111. At 7.7 miles you'll reach your car back at the Rimrock Shopping Center.

DESERT PARKS

The Desert Protection Act of 1994 changed the face of California's federal desert lands. Death Valley and Joshua Tree were upgraded from national monuments to national parks and gained significantly in total acreage. At the same time, Mojave National Preserve—formerly a BLM scenic area—was created under the auspices of the National Park Service. During winter, when snow, rain, or mud close down or impair many Southern California riding destinations, you'll be glad these strikingly scenic areas are protected. But while all three parks in this chapter benefited from the Desert Protection Act, the three have vastly different personalities.

Joshua Tree National Park is known as an outdoor enthusiast's paradise, but more for climbing and bouldering than biking. Interestingly, however, biking at Joshua Tree seems to take its cue from those old Avis rent-a-car ads: It may be #2, but it tries harder. The park actively encourages mountain biking, and—as of press time—had a general management plan that plotted out trails for bikes that would be off-limits to equestrians.

Farther north, Mojave National Preserve inhabits the "Lonely Triangle" between Interstates 15 and 40 and the California state line. Rough around the edges, Mojave is not as well-known among visitors, and its spectacular scenery is often bypassed. Ride here when you want to really get away from it all.

Death Valley is not only the largest of these three national park areas, it's the largest national park in the contiguous United States. And its size isn't the only imposing thing about Death Valley. Everywhere you look, attractions here use words such as "Bad," "Furnace," "Devil's," or "Funeral" to describe themselves. Don't be intimidated; like its counterpart desert parks, Death Valley in winter offers comfortable daytime temperatures, refreshingly clean air, and a surprising variety of flora and fauna.

When you ride here (and you absolutely should), make your experience enjoyable by taking some precautions. First, drink plenty of water even when it seems relatively cool. Second, watch out for thunderstorms anytime of year, and especially in summer and fall. The resulting flash floods can transform dry washes into roaring torrents in mere minutes. And finally, watch where you're going. First-hand author research proves beyond a doubt that those cactus needles are every bit as sharp as they look.

RIDE 24 · Pinkham Canyon

AT A GLANCE

Length/configuration: 23.8-mile out-and-back ride on dirt road and some pavement (11.9 miles to Snow Cloud Mine and return, with longer loop options available as well)

Aerobic difficulty: Moderate/difficult; climbs aren't horribly steep, but they are long

Technical difficulty: Moderate/difficult; the route has some sections which can be extremely loose and sandy

Scenery: Buttes, canyons, washes, cholla cactus, abundant wildlife

Special comments: A scenic, rugged ride through Joshua Tree National Park's two distinct desert ecosystems—fun as an out-and-back or a loop

This trip travels from the lower, dryer Colorado Desert to the higher-elevation, colder, and wetter Mojave, which results in a lot of changing topography. It can be ridden as an out-and-back as described here, or as one of two long dirt-and-pavement loops. Whatever your final choice may be, you'll first embark on a scenic, steady, sometimes fast uphill ride which delivers you to a road leading to Snow Cloud Mine. This is the route's turnaround point, but if you get this far, you have several options. You can return the way you came, enjoying a wonderful downhill back to the start. (I did it late in the day, and wound up finishing under a full moon with jackrabbits, kangaroo rats, and burrowing owls for company—a memorable way to cap off a ride.)

Or you can continue the way you've been heading, into the Cottonwood Mountains, circling downhill through Pinkham Canyon and returning on firmly packed dirt roads and pavement. Finally, you can fashion a slightly longer loop by riding Thermal Canyon, which cuts through the Cottonwood Mountains west of and roughly parallel to Pinkham Canyon. Thermal is shorter in length than Pinkham Canyon, but it's also less sandy—which is probably why the Park Service is promoting it as a trail which will connect to Berdoo Canyon, one that may be limited to bikers and hikers only—no motorists or equestrians. Whichever route you choose, this is a memorable way to explore some of Joshua Tree's most spectacular scenery.

General location: Southeast portion of Joshua Tree National Park.

Elevation change: Out-and-back route ascends from approximately 3,000 feet to 3,600 feet for a change of 600 feet. Loop route descends to 1,475 feet before climbing back to 3,000 feet, for an approximate elevation change of 2,125 feet.

Season: October through May.

Services: Rest rooms, water, vending machines, and maps are available at the Cottonwood Visitor Center at start of ride. All other services are available in surrounding communities.

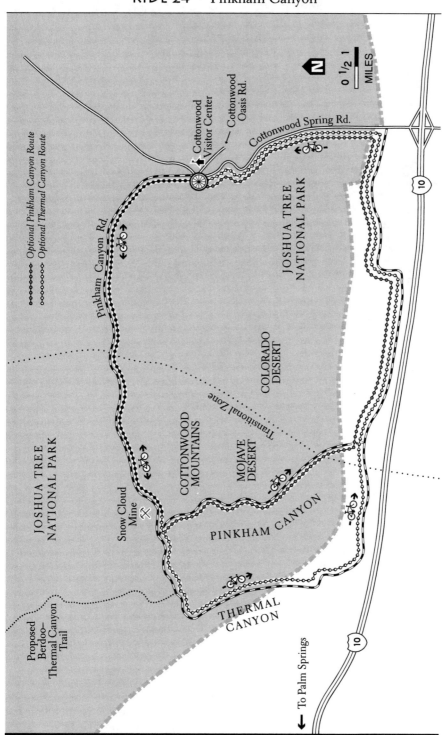

Rolling over sand in Pinkham Canyon.

Hazards: Flash flood danger, long exposed ride, cacti, and snakes.

Rescue index: Help is available at Cottonwood Visitor Center at start of ride.

Land status: National park.

Maps: The National Park Service's "Joshua Tree National Park" map comes with admission to the park. More detailed maps are available at Cottonwood Visitor Center.

Finding the trail: Enter Joshua Tree National Park from the Cottonwood Entrance near the city of Indio. Park in the Cottonwood Visitor Center parking area.

Sources of additional information:

Joshua Tree National Park
74485 National Park Drive
Twentynine Palms, CA 92277
(760) 367-5500
www.nps.gov/jotr

Camping Reservations
National Park Reservation System
P.O. Box 1600

Cumberland, MD 21502
U.S. and Canada: (800) 365-2267
International: (301) 722-1257
TDD (888) 530-9796

*Bicycling America's National Parks:
California*, David Story,
(Countryman Press, 2000)

Notes on the trail: From Cottonwood Visitor Center, go left on paved Pinto Basin Road, then immediately right onto dirt Pinkham Canyon Road. It's a bit sandy at first, but the road firms up very nicely by the time you reach a fork at 1 mile. Go left onto well-signed Pinkham Canyon Road, a dirt double-track. It's uphill through scenic Smoke Tree Wash, and compared to some other routes in the park, the ride is impeccably smooth. Washboards are remarkably absent as you spin past Mojave yucca and creosote bush. (If you're thinking this will make for an awesome downhill on the return trip, you're absolutely right.)

By this point in the climb, you will have noticed marker posts which register miles in increments of two (2, 4, 6, 8, etc.). Past Mile 8, the topography changes. As you leave Smoke Tree Wash, you enter the "transitional zone" where the lower elevation Colorado desert changes into the higher climes of the Mojave. After you pass a butte on your left, the road becomes much more sandy. Where you have been able to find terra firma before, now you begin fishtailing. The smooth, firm climb of the early miles is now but a memory. There are times where you'll likely have to walk your bike. Your goal is to make it to the Snow Cloud Mine turnoff on the right at 11.9 miles, but there's no shame in avoiding the sand and turning around earlier. If you make it to the Snow Cloud Mine turnoff, you can turn around there and zip down the wonderful downhill, ending your ride at 23.8 miles at Cottonwood Visitor Center.

Or, you can continue the way you've been heading, into the Cottonwood Mountains. As it enters Pinkham Canyon itself, Pinkham Canyon Road begins circling south (in a counterclockwise direction). Stay on it for some beautiful riding. At 20.1 miles, shortly after leaving the park boundary, you come to a T-intersection with the Colorado Aqueduct road. Go left on this dirt road, (paralleling Interstate 10) for more than 10 miles to its intersection with paved Cottonwood Spring Road at 30.8 miles. Go left, returning to the park, and ride over Cottonwood Pass and down to Cottonwood Visitor Center at 36.7 miles.

Finally, you can also fashion a slightly longer loop by riding Thermal Canyon, which cuts through the Cottonwood Mountains west of and roughly parallel to Pinkham Canyon. From the intersection with the road to Snow Cloud Mine, ride west for 0.7 mile, then veer right at the junction with Thermal Canyon. It's a shorter canyon than Pinkham, but it's also less sandy. After you emerge from Thermal Canyon, you reach the Aqueduct Road at 18.6 miles. Go left, reaching the junction with Pinkham Canyon Road at 22.8 miles. Proceed to Cottonwood Visitor Center by following the directions in the preceding paragraph, for a ride totaling 39.4 miles.

RIDE 25 · Geology Tour Road

AT A GLANCE

Length/configuration: 16.9-mile combination on dirt roads (5.4 miles each way to Squaw Tank, plus 6.1-mile loop through Pleasant Valley)

Aerobic difficulty: Moderate; some steady climbs made more difficult by road conditions

Technical difficulty: Moderate; expect some sandy sections and some rough road in the Pleasant Valley portion

Scenery: Black basalt of Malapai Hill, unusual rock formations, geological history, Joshua trees, Pushawalla plateau

Special comments: Make sure to pick up the nominally priced *Geology Tour Road Guide* from a visitor center or from the honor system box at the trailhead (but the box sometimes runs out of guides)

An out-and-back ride topped with a terminus loop, this tour provides an enlightening look at the unique geology of Joshua Tree National Park. Bring along the Park Service's *Geology Tour Road Guide* (available for a nominal fee at visitor centers and, on occasion, the trailhead), and both your quads and medulla oblongata will get a workout.

General location: Joshua Tree National Park.

Elevation change: From the start at 4,350 feet, the route descends to 3,200 feet. Factor in some other ups and downs for a total elevation gain of approximately 1,350 feet.

Season: October through May.

Services: Water and rest rooms are available at park campgrounds and visitor centers. All other services are available in surrounding communities.

Hazards: Be extremely aware of the weather; flash floods can turn dry washes into raging torrents in minutes. Dehydration occurs quickly here—drink lots of water.

Rescue index: Help is readily available from rangers who regularly patrol this area of the park.

Land status: National park.

Maps: The National Park Service's "Joshua Tree National Park" map comes with admission to the park.

Finding the trail: From either the West or North Entrance Stations in Joshua Tree National Park, take Park Boulevard into the interior of the park, heading toward Geology Tour Road. Turn south on Geology Tour Road and immediately park in the dirt day use area parking lot on the right, just south of the intersection with Park Boulevard.

Sources of additional information:

Joshua Tree National Park
74485 National Park Drive
Twentynine Palms, CA 92277
(760) 367-5500
www.nps.gov/jotr

Camping Reservations
National Park Reservation System
P.O. Box 1600

Cumberland, MD 21502
US and Canada: (800) 365-2267
International: (301) 722-1257
TDD (888) 530-9796

*Bicycling America's National Parks:
California*, David Story,
(Countryman Press, 2000)

RIDE 25 · Geology Tour Road
RIDE 26 · Queen Valley

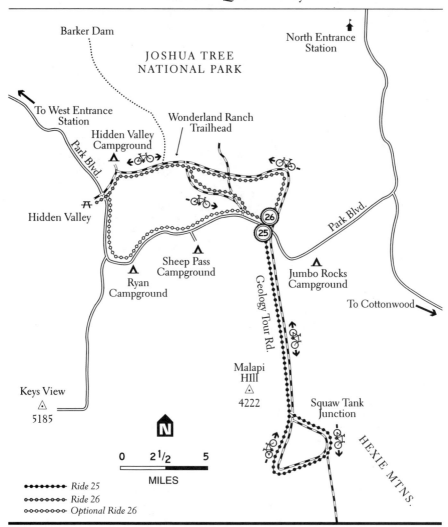

Barker Dam

JOSHUA TREE
NATIONAL PARK

North Entrance
Station

To West Entrance
Station

Wonderland Ranch
Trailhead

Hidden Valley
Campground

Park Blvd.

Hidden Valley

Park Blvd.

26
25

Sheep Pass
Campground

Ryan
Campground

Jumbo Rocks
Campground

To Cottonwood

Geology Tour Rd.

Malapi
HIll
4222

Squaw Tank
Junction

Keys View

5185

HEXIE MTNS.

N

0   2¹/₂   5

MILES

●●●●●●● Ride 25
○○○○○○○ Ride 26
○-○-○-○-○ Optional Ride 26

Notes on the trail: From the day-use area, head south (away from the paved road) on well-signed Geology Tour Road. The numbered markers that you see along the road correspond to the *Geology Tour Road Guide* you presumably picked up at the visitor center or trailhead. At first, the road is mostly flat and unchallenging, allowing you to easily check out the scenic stacked rock sculptures.

The road becomes a little steeper going downhill past the black basalt of Malapai Hill, and at 5.4 miles you reach the Squaw Tank junction. Refer to the interpretive guide for all the geological features in the area, then go left here,

Rocky scenery along Geology Tour Road.

onto the (clockwise) loop through Pleasant Valley. This road is classified as four-wheel-drive-only, and for good reason. The surface can be rough, even on a bike. Bumping along here, you pass mines, then cross a dry lakebed before reaching an intersection with Berdoo Canyon Road at 7.7 miles. Go right, staying on the loop. You're now heading toward Pushawalla Plateau, and you push a while to ascend the gentle hill to Pinyon Well Junction.

Some steady but mostly gentle climbing takes you back to Squaw Tank at 11.5 miles, at which point you retrace your way back to the start at 16.9 scenic miles.

RIDE 26 · Queen Valley

AT A GLANCE

Length/configuration: 12-mile loop or out-and-back on dirt roads and some pavement

Aerobic difficulty: Easy; dirt portion of route is fairly flat. There's some minor climbing on pavement, but you can skip that by making the route an out-and-back instead of a loop

Technical difficulty: Easy; a few soft, sandy sections pose the only impediment to riding

Scenery: Desert landscape, Joshua trees, rock formations, spring wildflowers, petroglyphs

Special comments: There are several bike racks along this route so you can secure your bike while taking short hiking detours; bring a lock

Queen Valley does a wonderful job of introducing visitors to the region. The easy, flat dirt roads of this route provide access to several short hiking trails that showcase Joshua Tree's rock formations and desert landscape. You can either ride this as an out-and-back on dirt or as a loop ride on paved Park Boulevard. Since the paved stretch is less scenic and longer, I recommend returning the way you came via dirt roads.

General location: Northern half of Joshua Tree National Park.

Elevation change: Insignificant.

Season: October through May. March and April tend to be the best for wild-flowers. Route is shadeless, so avoid riding during heat of the day.

Services: Rest rooms and water are available at ride midpoint at Hidden Valley Campground; all other services available in surrounding communities.

Hazards: Be extremely aware of the weather; flash floods can turn dry washes into raging torrents in minutes. Dehydration occurs quickly here—drink lots of water.

Rescue index: Help is readily available from rangers who regularly patrol this area of the park.

Land status: National park.

Maps: The National Park Service's "Joshua Tree National Park" map comes with admission to the park.

Finding the trail: From either the West or North Entrance Stations in Joshua Tree National Park, take Park Boulevard into the interior of the park, heading toward Geology Tour Road. Turn south on Geology Tour Road and immediately park in the dirt day-use area parking lot on the right, just south of the intersection with Park Boulevard.

Sources of additional information:

Joshua Tree National Park
74485 National Park Drive
Twentynine Palms, CA 92277
(760) 367-5500
www.nps.gov/jotr

Camping Reservations
National Park Reservation System
P.O. Box 1600

Cumberland, MD 21502
U.S. and Canada: (800) 365-2267
International: (301) 722-1257
TDD (888) 530-9796

Bicycling America's National Parks: California, David Story, (Countryman Press, 2000)

Notes on the trail: From the parking area, cross Park Boulevard and ride north (away from Geology Tour Road). You spin through a desert landscape about 1 mile to a hairpin intersection. Going straight leads you to the backcountry

Joshua trees loom over
the trail in Queen Valley.

"board" for hikers heading to Desert Queen Mine and Pine City. You want to go left on the hairpin turn, heading toward Hidden Valley. There are several Joshua trees along this section. Keep straight on the main road, bypassing several turnoffs as you ride parallel to Queen Mountain on your right. You also reach your first trailhead on the right, a short hiking trail which leads to Wonderland Ranch.

Park and lock your bike to take a quick hike through amazing monzogranite mounds and structures, then return to your bike, continue in the same direction, and you soon reach the turnoff for the Barker Dam parking area. Go right here, lock your bike up, and walk the 1.1-mile loop up to Barker Dam, a natural catch basin that has been augmented by human ranchers in an attempt to collect precious rainwater. If you're lucky enough to ride here shortly after a winter storm, the basin will look like a high alpine lake surrounded by granite outcroppings. Continuing to hike around the loop, you pass some Native American petroglyphs that were painted over by a clueless film crew trying to enhance the symbols' appearance. Fortunately, if you look hard enough, you can also find some untainted petroglyphs nearby, behind heavy brush.

Back on the bike, return to the main road, go right and you come to Hidden Valley Campground. To see rock climbers taking on sheer granite faces, take a spin through this campground loop. Then continue in the same direction until you reach Park Boulevard at approximately 5.5 miles into the ride. Go right, then immediately left to Hidden Valley nature trail. A 1-mile loop trail takes you into (as the name says) a concealed, picturesque valley surrounded by towering rock formations. Take a break at picnic area at the end of the loop, then return to your bike.

From here, turn right on paved Park Boulevard to loop back to the start on pavement, or better yet, backtrack the way you came on dirt. But this time, veer right on the unsigned turnoff just past the Wonderland Ranch hiking trail. This track eventually leads you back to paved Park Boulevard. Go left on Park Boulevard, which returns you to the start at around 12 miles, depending on how many trails you explored.

RIDE 27 · Cinder Cones Loop

AT A GLANCE

Length/configuration: 28.9-mile combination (3.4 miles out and back (1.7 miles each way) plus 25.5-mile loop) on rugged jeep roads

Aerobic difficulty: Moderate/difficult; route is long, which makes the climbs seem tougher

Technical difficulty: Moderate; rugged roads will demand all your bike-handling skills

Scenery: Volcanic cinder cones (a National Natural Landmark), lava tube, Cima Dome, mines, and mountain vistas

Special comments: Bring a flashlight to explore the lava tube. Keep your bike on the road during this trip; wilderness areas often start right at roadside

Twisting past a lava tube, alongside cinder cones, and through the striking desert scenery of Mojave National Preserve, this ride is dry, dusty, and a whole lot of fun. You'll pass many attractions on this ride, the first being a group of 32 cinder cones. Left over from ancient lava flows, the cones give an eerie feel that permeates the entire ride.

Spinning through intriguing desert topography, you next reach the Lava Tube, a volcanic cave created when flowing lava cooled and hardened on the outside, but hot lava in the inside kept moving, leaving empty air in its wake. If you have a flashlight, explore this cool, dark cave. (Ask a ranger for precise directions on getting there.)

Surprisingly, for a period in the late 1990s, this part of the preserve drew visitors not for its volcanic legacy, but for a phone booth! To be sure, it was quite a sight to come across a phone booth in such a desolate area, and somehow the booth started getting more and more attention, until its international renown

RIDE 27 · Cinder Cones Loop

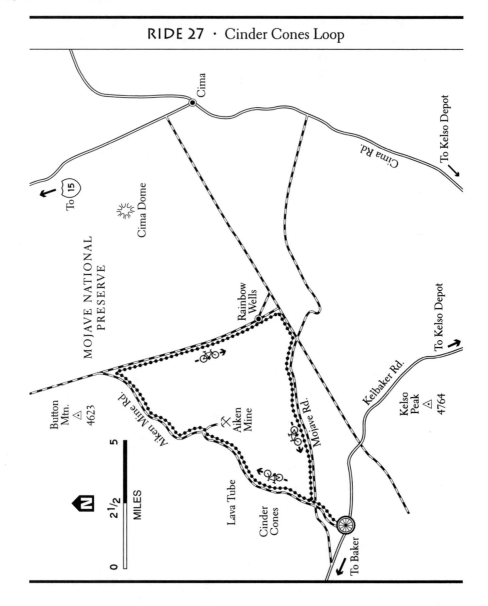

reportedly drew more visitors than the fragile desert landscape could sustain, leading to the booth's removal in 2000.

Though the phone was a nice safety valve in this remote section of the preserve, embrace the primitive and you'll have a fun time roller-coastering back to the start.

General location: Mojave National Preserve, approximately 15 miles northwest of Kelso Depot.

Elevation change: Ride starts at 3,200 feet, ascends to 4,700 feet, and returns, for an elevation gain of 1,500 feet.

Kicking up a little Mojave dust on the Cinder Cones Loop.

Season: October to May.

Services: None on trail. Basic supplies available at Cima General Store a few miles north of route.

Hazards: Long ride in exposed area; cacti; snakes. Exercise caution if exploring lava tube caves.

Rescue index: Help is available through Mojave National Preserve rangers, but be aware that this route experiences light traffic.

Land status: National preserve.

Maps: "Recreation Map of the Mojave National Preserve" from Tom Harrison Cartography, (800) 265-9090 or (415) 456-7940.

Finding the trail: From the town of Baker, go approximately 19 miles southeast on Kelbaker Road to the junction with Aiken Mine Road on the left. Park in such a way that you do not block any roadways.

Sources of additional information:

Mojave National Preserve
222 E. Main Street, Suite 202
Barstow, CA 92311
(760) 255-8801
www.nps.gov/moja

Baker Information Center
72157 Baker Boulevard
P.O. Box 241
Baker, CA 92309
(760) 733-4040

*Bicycling America's National Parks:
California*, David Story,
(Countryman Press, 2000)

Notes on the trail: From the junction of Aiken Mine Road and Kelbaker Road, ride northeast on the dirt Aiken Mine Road. You soon pedal by the Cinder Cone National Natural Landmark on your left. Around the 4.5-mile mark, you approach the Lava Tube, a cool, dark cave which you can explore if you've brought a flashlight.

Afterward, keep riding north on Aiken Mine Road to the Aiken Mine itself at 7.7 miles. Leaving the mine site, the road curves and rollercoasters a bit in the shadow of Button Mountain on the left. At 12.6 miles, you reach an intersection with a long straight road heading to Rainbow Wells, where the incongruous phone booth used to stand. Turn right, heading south. You're now riding at the edge of the massive, granite Cima Dome on your left. You climb gently for a bit, then descend more steeply to Rainbow Wells. Staying right at a Y-junction at 18.3 miles, you reach a power line road at 19.2 miles. Go right here and right again at 20.7 miles. This second right puts you on historic Mojave Road, one of the first routes through the imposing Mojave Desert. It can be rough and sandy in places, but it's downhill most of the way to Aiken Mine Road at 27.2 miles. Go left on Aiken Mine Road back to the start at 28.9 miles.

RIDE 28 · Hole-in-the-Wall to Mid Hills Loop

AT A GLANCE

Length/configuration: 19.3 miles (18.5-mile loop from Hole-in-the-Wall to Mid Hills and return, with 0.4-mile spur out-and-back to the Mid Hills campground) on pavement and dirt

Aerobic difficulty: Moderate; one steady climb interrupted by a few steep faces and sometimes sandy road

Technical difficulty: Easy/moderate; wide gentle roads prevail; sandy, soft portions may cause some problems

Scenery: Volcanic formations, mesas, changing ecosystems, brilliant wildflowers in spring

Special comments: This loop between Mojave National Preserve's two park campgrounds is renowned for its scenery and has been designated an official "Back Country Byway" of the U.S.

There's something about the designation "Back Country Byway" which connotes easygoing wandering, and that's the right way to think about this ride.

RIDE 28 · Hole–in–the–Wall to Mid Hills Loop

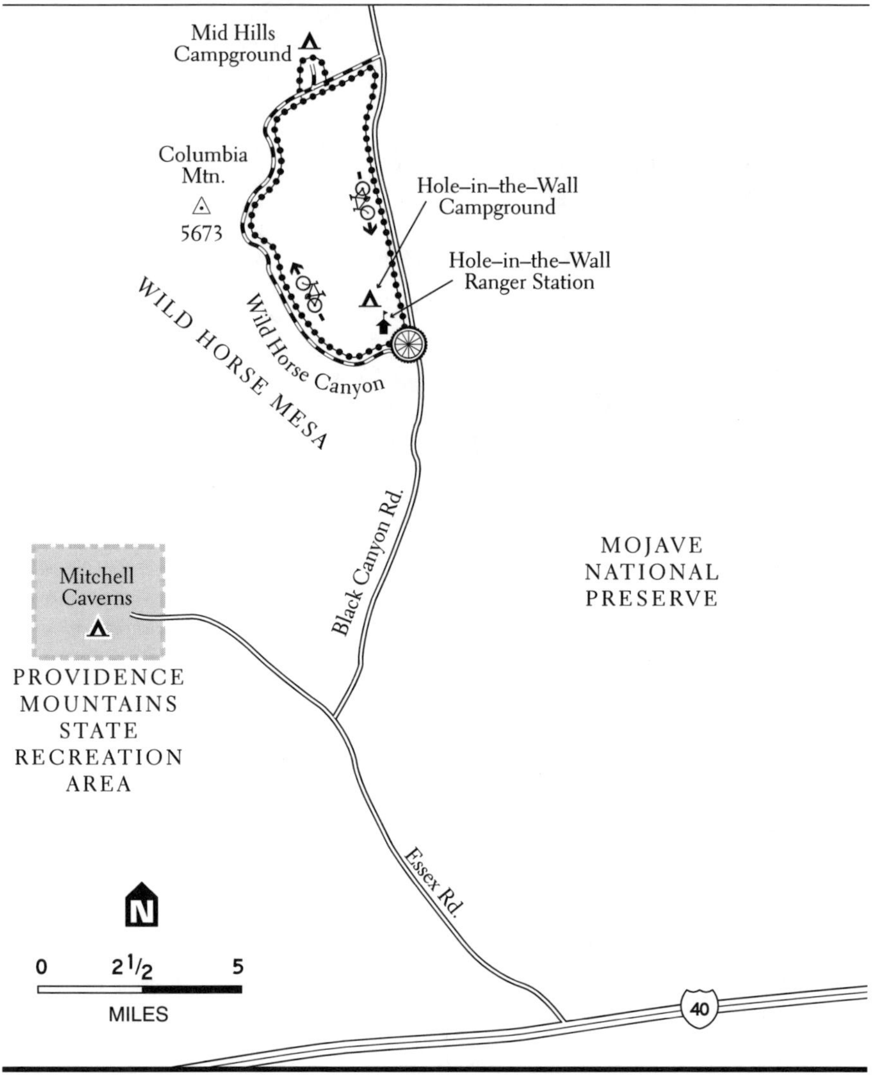

Mid Hills
Campground

Columbia
Mtn.

△
5673

Hole–in–the–Wall
Campground

Hole–in–the–Wall
Ranger Station

WILD HORSE MESA

Wild Horse Canyon

Black Canyon Rd.

MOJAVE
NATIONAL
PRESERVE

Mitchell
Caverns

PROVIDENCE
MOUNTAINS
STATE
RECREATION
AREA

Essex Rd.

N

0   2¹/₂   5
MILES

40

The route's rush of scenery is much more compelling than its adrenaline rush, so stop and smell the flowers along the way. There are a lot of 'em, as you gradually spin through one ecosystem after another, from cholla cactusland to sagebrush landscapes, and into a quasi-alpine piñon pine/juniper forest.

This is probably the only route where you'd ever take a detour just to see a campground, but the views from the tent sites of Mid Hills are exemplary; the New York and Providence mountain ranges are right there, and you've got a nice perspective on the massive granite Cima Dome on the northwest side of the

Who needs a mule? Loaded for bear at Hole-in-the-Wall.

campground. Afterwards, a mostly downhill cruise on dirt and pavement returns you to the start.

General location: Mojave National Preserve, near Hole-in-the-Wall Ranger Station.

Elevation change: Ride begins at 4,400 feet, and tops out at 5,600 feet, for a gain of 1,200 feet.

Season: October to May.

Services: Rest rooms and limited water available at start of ride at Hole-in-the-Wall Ranger Station. Basic supplies available at Cima General Store a few miles northwest of route.

Hazards: Exposure to sun and wind; snakes.

Rescue index: Help is available through Mojave National Preserve rangers, but be aware that Hole-in-the-Wall Ranger Station is only open seasonally. You may want to call the park for a schedule to find when the station will be staffed during your visit.

Land status: National preserve.

Maps: "Recreation Map of the Mojave National Preserve" from Tom Harrison Cartography, (800) 265-9090 or (415) 456-7940.

Finding the trail: Take I-40 to Essex Road on the southern boundary of the park. Go north on Essex Road approximately 10 miles to the junction with Black

Canyon. Veer right on Black Canyon and go approximately 9 more miles to the Hole-in-the-Wall Ranger Station on the left. Park here. (Before driving away after the ride, check under your car to make sure no desert tortoises are there.)

Sources of additional information:

Mojave National Preserve
222 E. Main Street, Suite 202
Barstow, CA 92311
(760) 255-8801
www.nps.gov/moja

Baker Information Center
72157 Baker Boulevard

P.O. Box 241
Baker, CA 92309
(760) 733-4040

Bicycling America's National Parks: California, David Story, (Countryman Press, 2000)

Notes on the trail: Starting at the Hole-in-the-Wall Ranger Station, ride east back to Black Canyon Road. Turn right on Black Canyon, and briefly descend for 0.2 mile to Wildhorse Canyon Road on your right. It's marked, but you might see a "No shooting" sign before the road sign. Turn right here and rollercoaster a bit before embarking on a gradual climb. Passing the trailhead for the hiking path to Mid Hills, you stay on Wildhorse Canyon Road and enter the canyon itself, which is flanked by Flat-Topped Wildhorse Mesa.

At 9.8 miles, after riding through stands of piñon pine, you reach the turnoff to Mid Hills Campground. Go left here for 0.4 mile, and check out the views. After exploring, get back on your bike, backtrack to Wildhorse Canyon Road, and go left (east) for two miles to Black Canyon Road. Go right, descending the somewhat dusty part of Black Canyon Road as you spin by massive Table Mountain. Continue to the turnoff to Hole-in-the-Wall and the start of the ride at 19.3 miles.

RIDE 29 · Greenwater Valley

AT A GLANCE

Length/configuration: 17.2-mile combination ride (5.6-mile out-and-back (2.8 miles each way) plus 11.6-mile loop) on dirt roads

Aerobic difficulty: Moderate; climb is fairly gentle up to the loop portion of ride, steeper on the loop traveling to the old mining community

Technical difficulty: Moderate; road can be soft in some stretches

Scenery: Old mining community ruins, desert flora, Black Mountains, Greenwater Range

Special comments: Exploring a short-lived mining community, this ride offers a glimpse into Death Valley's past

RIDE 29 · Greenwater Valley

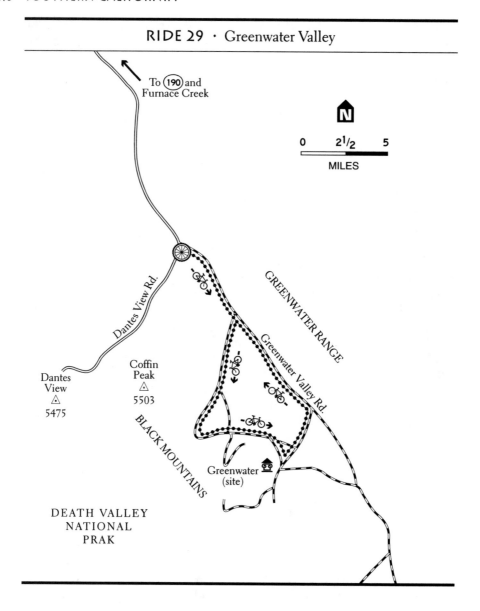

This excursion rambles through a pavement-free section of Death Valley National Park. The ride heads south on a dirt road that is occasionally washboarded and loose, but it's almost always possible to pick out a line over terra firma. After settling into a steady cadence on the gradual uphill between the Black Mountains on your right and the Greenwater Range on your left, you notice that something's different about this ride, but you can't initially put your finger on it. Then it comes to you: Looking straight ahead, there are no mountains fencing you off—a unique perspective for Death Valley. In fact, it sort of

Long, long views of Death Valley await you here.

feels like an ocean is waiting for you on the other side of the valley, or that you're biking toward the edge of the world.

Before you get there, however, you begin climbing to loop through the old mining community of Greenwater. Though only ruins exist here now, the area was once a booming city. After a copper strike in 1905, wildly exaggerated promotions of the land's wealth lured speculators here by the hundreds. Eventually swelling to over 1,000 people, the town boasted a post office, stores, two newspapers, and even a men's magazine. All pretty impressive considering there wasn't even a water source—water had to be hauled in by mule. When the mining proved to be a bust, everyone left, creating a ghost town by 1909. Your own stay here will also soon come to an end, as you descend back to Greenwater Valley Road and an easy coast back to the start.

General location: Death Valley National Park, 17 miles southeast of Furnace Creek Visitor Center.

Elevation change: From the start near 3,200 feet, the ride ascends to 4,750 feet and returns, for an approximate change of 1,550 feet.

Season: October to May.

Services: None available on-trail; all services available at Furnace Creek.

Hazards: Total exposure to sun and wind; exercise caution if exploring near old mines.

Rescue index: Area is lightly trafficked; nearest help is available 12 miles away at Furnace Creek.

Land status: National park.

Maps: The National Park Service's "Death Valley National Park" map comes with admission to the park.

Finding the trail: From Furnace Creek Visitor Center, go 12 miles south on CA 190, then turn right on Dante's View Road. Go 7.3 miles to the junction on your left with dirt Greenwater Valley Road. Park in the small gravel lot on your right (across Dante's View Road from Greenwater Valley Road).

Sources of additional information:

Death Valley National Park
P.O. Box 579
Death Valley, CA 92328-0579
(760) 786-2331
www.nps.gov/deva

Camping reservations:
(800) 365-2267 (CAMP)
reservations.nps.gov/index.cfm

Furnace Creek Inn and
   Ranch Resort
P.O. Box 1
Death Valley, CA 92328
(760) 786-2345
www.furnacecreekresort.com

Bicycling America's National Parks:
   California, David Story,
   (Countryman Press, 2000)

Notes on the trail: From the gravel parking area just across Dante's View Road, ride south toward the Greenwater Valley sign. The road is occasionally soft, but you can usually find firm ground at the right or left edge of the road.

At 2.8 miles, turn right on the dirt road leading up to the Furnace mining site. This section is much steeper, and you'll sweat as you climb up to the Furnace site at 6.3 miles. Explore the rubble, then get back on your bike and veer right toward the site of Greenwater mining town, which you reach at 9.6 miles. After some more exploring off the bike, remount and head downhill on an obvious dirt road back to Greenwater Valley Road, which you reach at 11.4 miles. Go left and return to the start at 17.2 miles.

RIDE 30 · Twenty Mule Team Canyon

AT A GLANCE

Length/configuration: 4.5-mile loop on dirt road and pavement

Aerobic difficulty: Easy; gradual climbs

Technical difficulty: Easy; graded, firm dirt road

Scenery: Sandstone rock outcroppings, Panamint Mountains, and (nearby) Golden Canyon at Zabriskie Point

Special comments: A family-friendly ride that's scenic, short, and surprisingly quiet

If you ever thought the hills were talking to you, urging you to come mountain biking, this ride proves you're not crazy. That's because the hills on this trip are eroding remnants of an ancient lake bed which are constantly shifting. When the temperature changes dramatically (at sunrise and sunset), their contractions/ expansions are actually audible. If it sounds too bizarre to believe, remember that this is Death Valley, a unique place. And when it comes to introductory rides in this amazing national park, this 4.5-mile loop starting at the intersection of Twenty Mule Team Canyon and CA 190 is hard to beat.

Unlike several of the other back roads here, the surface of one-way Twenty Mule Team Canyon is beautiful packed dirt, not loose gravel. If you've been riding elsewhere in the park, the sudden deliverance from spin-outs is liberating. When my wife and I rode here, she was so grateful for terra firma that she shot past the starkly beautiful creosote bushes and clusters of desert holly like a mule cut loose from pulling a wagon full of borax. (That's a regional simile. Sorry.) As I caught up with her, the canyon closed around us and the road roller-coastered through gorgeous terrain. It was everything a mountain biker looks for: no traffic, plenty of winding hills, and great views. We enjoyed it so much we intended to linger there, but our bikes gobbled up the terrain too quickly and in no time we were back at CA 190 and the gentle descent to our car.

The experience of this ride is enhanced if you combine it with a visit to nearby Zabriskie Point (just 1.2 miles north) right at sunrise. Watching Golden Canyon light up under the snowy peaks of the Panamint Range is a wonderful experience. Then, before it gets too hot, hurry over to Twenty Mule Team Canyon for the possibility of hearing the hills "speak" during your ride. Afterward, head to Furnace Creek Ranch's coffee shop to cap off the morning right.

General location: In Death Valley National Park, approximately 5 miles south of Furnace Creek.

Elevation change: Approximately 300 feet of elevation gain.

Season: October through May. Early mornings are best, but they can be chilly.

Services: No services are available on the trail. All services (except bike repair) are available in Furnace Creek.

Hazards: Automobile traffic on CA 190.

Rescue index: Trail is within 3 miles of CA 190 at all times. Help is available 5 miles away at the Furnace Creek Ranger Station.

Land status: National park.

Maps: The National Park Service's "Death Valley National Park" map comes with admission to the park., The Automobile Club of Southern California's "Guide to Death Valley National Park" is available at all AAA offices. Also, "Death Valley National Park" is available from Tom Harrison Cartography, (800) 265-9090 or (415) 456-7940, www.tomharrisonmaps.com.

Finding the trail: From Furnace Creek Visitor Center, go right on CA 190 5 miles to the intersection with Twenty Mule Team Canyon Road. Park in the turnout well off CA 190 so that you are not blocking traffic.

RIDE 30 · Twenty Mule Team Canyon

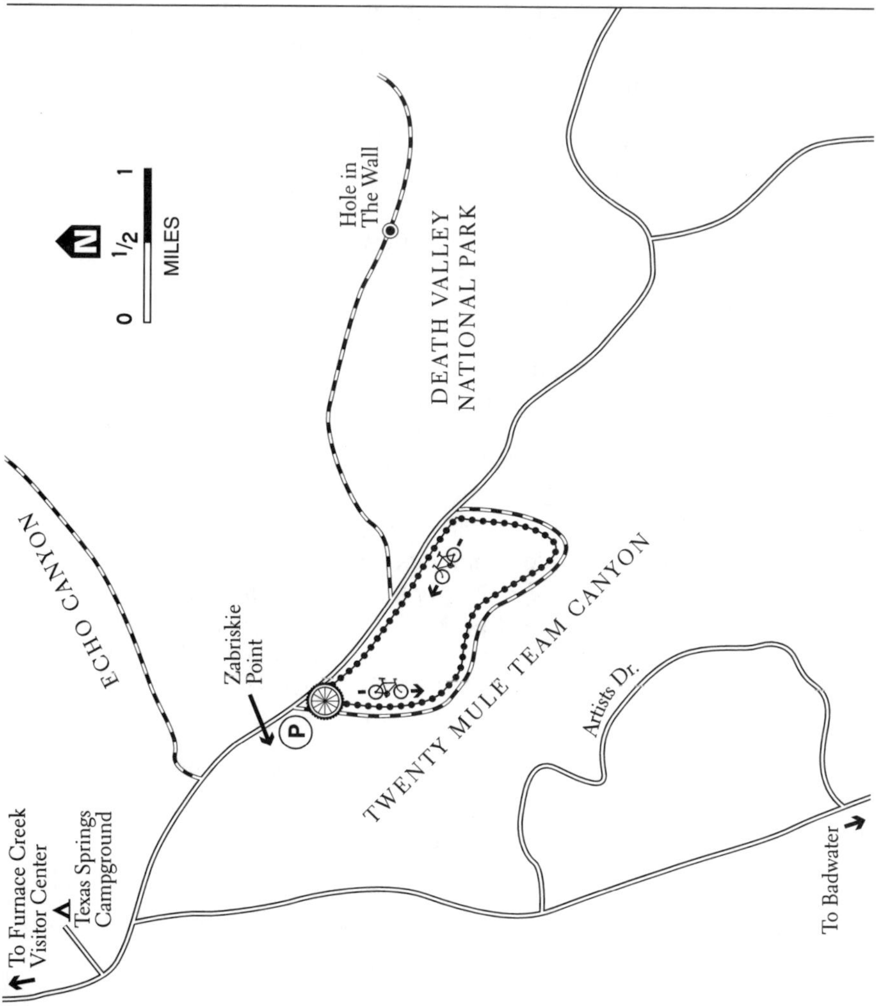

Sources of additional information:

Death Valley National Park
P.O. Box 579
Death Valley, CA 92328-0579
(760) 786-2331
www.nps.gov/deva

Camping reservations:
(800) 365-2267 (CAMP)
reservations.nps.gov/index.cfm

Bicycling America's National Parks:
  California, David Story,
  (Countryman Press, 2000)

A three-biker team entering Twenty Mule Team Canyon.

Notes on the trail: From the intersection of CA 190 and Twenty Mule Team Canyon, head south on Twenty Mule Team Canyon on the one-way dirt road. The road roller-coasters through open land and into a canyon, passing wild rock formations. Stick to the primary road at all times until it curves around and intersects with CA 190 at 2.8 miles. Turn left on CA 190, being careful to watch out for automobile traffic. There are a lot of gawking motorists here; assume that they cannot see you and ride alertly. At 3.8 miles, you'll reach the intersection with Hole in the Wall Road, one of Death Valley's notorious gravel roads. Keep riding straight on CA 190, reaching your car at 4.5 miles.

RIDE 31 · Aguereberry Point

AT A GLANCE

Length/configuration: 13-mile out-and-back (6.5 miles each way)

Aerobic difficulty: Difficult; begins with a good warm-up; climb becomes steep after first 3 miles

Technical difficulty: Difficult; rugged road poses little difficulty as you climb; good bike-handling skills are required for the steep, rough return

Scenery: Beautiful view of Death Valley from Aguereberry Point

Special comments: Road handwrought by Pete Aguereberry in the early 1900s

This out-and-back, 13-mile round-trip ride takes you into the high desert of Death Valley. The first mile is level, and then you'll begin climbing—gradually for two miles and then steeply to the top. The return requires good bike-handling ability due to the fast and sometimes rough nature of the descent. Except for some washboarding, this hard-packed two-wheel-drive dirt road is in good condition.

At Aguereberry Point you will be rewarded with a panoramic view of Death Valley. Furnace Creek, Devil's Golfcourse, and the snowcapped peaks of the Sierra Nevadas can be seen from this high place in the Panamint Mountains. On the way back, a short side trip will take you to the Eureka Mine and remnants of a once-thriving mining town. Pete "Pierre" Aguereberry and Shorty Harris discovered gold here in 1905. Pete worked the mine until his death in 1945. He took pleasure in taking tourists up to see the fine view of Death Valley. Aguereberry built the road himself—hence, Aguereberry Point Road.

General location: Begins 20 miles south of Stovepipe Wells, in Death Valley.

Elevation change: This trip begins at 4,885 feet and climbs to a high point of 6,435 feet at Aguereberry Point. Total elevation gain: 1,550 feet.

Season: The late fall through spring is the best time to ride in Death Valley. The high elevation of this route makes for comfortable temperatures, especially when compared to conditions found on the valley floor. Traffic is usually light because of the road's distance from the main Visitor Center at Furnace Creek.

Services: There is no water available on this ride. All services are available in the town of Stove Pipe Wells.

Hazards: Special care should be taken when approaching bends in the road. Motorists will not be looking for cyclists and may be driving fast. Be prepared for sudden changes in the weather. Wear sunscreen and carry lots of water.

Rescue index: Help can be obtained in Stovepipe Wells.

Land status: National park.

Maps: A map of Death Valley National Park is available at the Visitor Center in Furnace Creek. It is a good guide to this ride.

Finding the trail: From Stovepipe Wells Village in Death Valley National Park, go southwest on CA 190 for 9 miles, then go left on CA 178 (Emigrant Canyon Road) for 12 miles to Aguereberry Point Road. Go left and park 100 yards up Aguereberry Point Road from CA 178.

Sources of additional information:

Death Valley National Park
P.O. Box 579
Death Valley, CA 92328-0579
(760) 786-2331
www.nps.gov/deva

RIDE 31 · Aguereberry Point

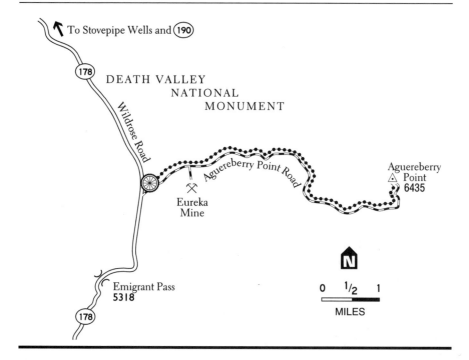

Camping reservations:
(800) 365-2267 (CAMP)
reservations.nps.gov/index.cfm

Bicycling America's National Parks:
California, David Story,
(Countryman Press, 2000)

Notes on the trail: Follow Aguereberry Point Road to the turnaround spot at Aguereberry Point. On the return, about 1 mile from the parking area, Eureka Mine can be seen on the hillside to your left. Turn left to check out the mine. It is well worth a visit.

RIDE 32 · Titus Canyon

AT A GLANCE

Length/configuration: 27-mile dirt road point-to-point ride (involving car shuttle) from NV 374 to the floor of Death Valley

Aerobic difficulty: Moderate/difficult; two climbs, one long and gradual, the other short and steep, with a very long downhill

Technical difficulty: Moderate; dirt roads are occasionally soft or gravelly

Scenery: Colorful mountains, spectacular rock formations, ghost town, petroglyphs, deep narrows

Special comments: The jewel of all Death Valley routes, this excursion on a one-way dirt road demands logistical planning but delivers stunning sights

Cyclists pedal over mountain passes, past rock formations, through old mining towns, alongside petroglyphs, and into an extremely narrow canyon on this memorable ride. The only hitch is that it demands some logistics, requiring either a car shuttle, hitchhiking, or a very tough return trip by bicycle. Even with a shuttle, there is a fair amount of climbing at the start of this ride. But the climb allows you to feel as if you have earned the wonderful downhill portion, which drops a vertical mile in 14 miles of fun riding. The most memorable part of this trip is the scenery, which grabs your attention even more than the compelling downhill.

General location: Death Valley National Park, roughly halfway between Furnace Creek and Scotty's Castle.

Elevation change: Ride starts at an elevation of 3,600 feet, rises to a summit at 5,250 feet, then descends all the way to 165 feet.

Season: October to May.

Services: None available on trail; all services available at Furnace Creek and Stovepipe Wells.

Hazards: Long ride in lightly trafficked area; temperatures can vary greatly between Death Valley Floor and Red Pass, nearly a mile higher in elevation.

Rescue index: Nearest help is available in communities of Stovepipe Wells and Furnace Creek.

Land status: National park.

Maps: The National Park Service's Death Valley National Park map comes with admission to the park. The AAA map, "Guide to Death Valley National Park," depicts the entire ride.

Finding the trail: Driving two cars, go northwest on CA 190 from the Furnace Creek Visitor Center. After 12 miles, stay right toward "Scotty's Castle" when CA 190 turns left toward Stovepipe Wells. You shortly pass Daylight Pass Road on your right, to which you'll soon be returning. Go 14 more miles to the intersection with Titus Canyon Road on your right. Park as close as you can to this intersection, making sure to not block any roadway and avoiding washes that could be prone to flash flooding. Leave terminus car here. In the origin car, return to Daylight Pass Road, and turn left following signs to Beatty, NV. The road climbs very steeply to Daylight Pass (elevation: 4,317 feet) at which point it enters Nevada and becomes NV 374. Continue another 7 miles, then turn left onto Titus Canyon Road. (You're now outside the park boundary). One hundred yards from NV 374 is a parking area on the left. Leave your origin car here.

RIDE 32 · Titus Canyon

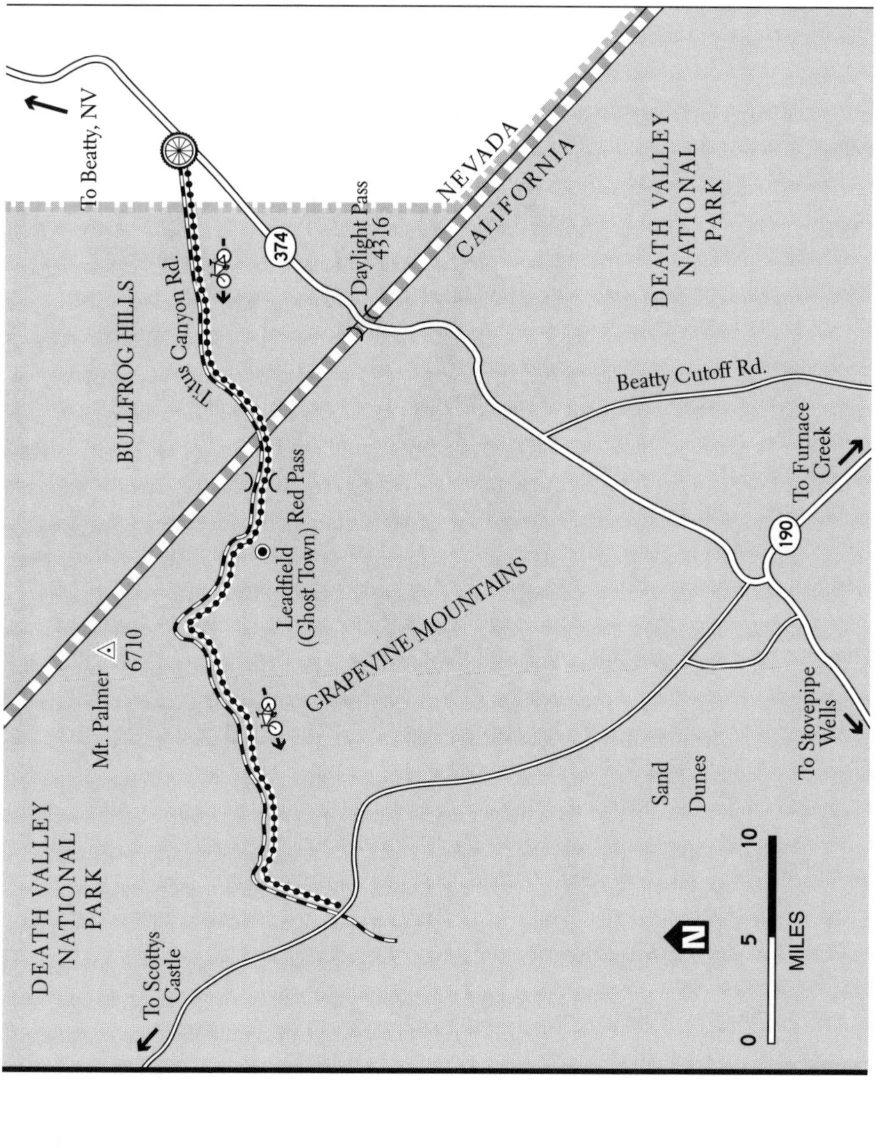

Sources of additional information:

Death Valley National Park
P.O. Box 579
Death Valley, CA 92328-0579
(760) 786-2331
www.nps.gov/deva

Camping reservations:
(800) 365-2267 (CAMP),
reservations.nps.gov/index.cfm

Entering the Narrows at
Titus Canyon.

Furnace Creek Inn and
  Ranch Resort
P.O. Box 1
Death Valley, CA 92328
(760) 786-2345
www.furnacecreekresort.com

*Bicycling America's National Parks:
California*, David Story,
(Countryman Press, 2000)

Notes on the trail: Begin riding away from NV 374 and up gently rising Titus Canyon Road. (You are outside the park boundary here.) At 1.9 miles, you pass a cattle guard and enter the park, at which point the road becomes one-way (east to west). Though the road is washboarded, loose, and steep in sections, it's usually possible to find a firm riding surface.

After 9.8 miles, you come to the summit of White Pass, and it looks like it might be all downhill from here. It's not. You descend for a while, then climb fairly steeply again to 5,250 feet, at appropriately named Red Pass (there's iron in them thar hills) at 12.7 miles. Now it's downhill to the 1920s boom/bust town of Leadfield at 15.9 miles. Soon after, you'll encounter a wall where the geologic pressure was so great it bent layers of rock into wavy ribbons.

Just when you think the scenery can't get any more striking, you coast into the main fork of Titus Canyon, where sheer limestone walls rise high above you. Near Klare Spring, where you have a decent chance of seeing bighorn sheep, there are Native American petroglyphs (marked by a NPS sign). Around the 23-mile mark, you reach "The Narrows," where the canyon walls are only 18 feet apart. Go slowly here—it's a magical place. Reaching the end of the canyon at 24.3 miles, you emerge into a dirt parking area and back into Death Valley itself. If you turn back and look where you came from, you only see an almost imperceptible slot in the impenetrable Grapevine Mountains. It's hard to believe there's a canyon in there. Now turn back to the road, and coast a fast 2.7 miles back to your terminus car, arriving there after 27 miles of spectacular riding.

SAN BERNARDINO MOUNTAINS

Though a lot of mountain ranges in California seem to rise out of deserts, the San Bernardinos represent some of the most dramatic geological contrasts in the state. Stretching nearly 50 miles, the San Bernardinos (or San Berdoos as they're sometimes called), form a lush, thickly wooded border between the higher elevation Mojave Desert to the north and the lower Colorado Desert to the southeast. With these deserts as neighbors, it's hard to understand how the San Berdoos could serve as Southern California's primary winter resort center. But believe it: The area supports several ski areas, and in 1993, it even experienced a white-out snowstorm in June.

But for three seasons every year, this is prime mountain-biking country. The same wooded slopes, pristine mountain ponds, clear air, and gurgling streams that once provided grizzly bears with comfortable habitat are now yours to experience. Don't be misled by the name Big Bear Lake, however. Though grizzlies were once so abundant that trappers caught 22 of them in a couple of days near Baldwin Lake in 1845, they're extinct from this region now. (Of course, at that rate, how could they not be?)

While you might not see grizzlies in this region, you will see great panoramic views from the Keller Peak lookout tower, endless mountain ridges along Skyline Drive, excellent lake vistas on the loop near Delamar Mountain, and best of all, some of the most buffed single-track paths in California unfurling beneath your tires on the Santa Ana River Trail. So leave the bear repellent at home, and enjoy. You can't go wrong spending a summer weekend riding, relaxing, and resorting here.

RIDE 33 · Santa Ana River Trail

AT A GLANCE

Length/configuration: 28.1-mile out-and-back (14 miles each way)

Aerobic difficulty: Moderate/difficult; all climbs are long and gradual except for the one at the ride's end

Technical difficulty: Moderate/difficult; the single-track is fairly narrow for most of the ride, but it's rarely treacherous

Scenery: Santa Ana River Valley, alpine forests

Special comments: Simply put, one of the longest, best single-tracks in this or any other region

On the slopes of nearby Snow Summit, skiers have a name for moguls that turn from hard and unforgiving to soft and pliant: "ego bumps." That's because any skier can look good skiing them. Consider this ride, then, to be an "ego single-track." This 28.1-mile out-and-back ride's terrain is so conducive to ostensibly technical but actually easy riding that everybody looks good here.

Starting just east of the quaint hamlet of Angelus Oaks, the ride drops quickly to the trailhead of the Santa Ana River Trail. From there, you're initially so busy crossing creeks, curving through lodgepole pine groves, and roller-coasting over knolls that you'll hardly have time to notice that you're gradually going uphill. It's not until a third of the way through your route that you notice you've been ascending most of the way. This is also the point where you'll start noticing that this area is home to what must be the largest squirrels ever known. You could swear that they're jackrabbits or even foxes when they sprint across the trail in front of you.

Anyway, after crossing Glass Road, you'll gently climb some more, and as a result, excellent views of surrounding mountain ranges and the Santa Ana River Valley appear to your left. But the views here aren't important, the terrain is. Simply put, it's more of a thrill to glide along this single-track than to look away from it.

Reaching the turnaround spot at South Fork Parking/Picnic Area, eat and prepare for a mellow ride back the way you came. But the return trip turns out to be better than you'd anticipated. The trail rocks and rolls on the loamy dirt while you duck and dodge trees, stones, and manzanita. In fact, by the time you reach Middle Control Road and the start of the climb back to your car, you're thinking, "It'll take a costly plastic surgeon to get this grin off my face." Lucky for your pocketbook, the nearly 3-mile climb back to your car will save you the expense. So turn right promptly on CA 38 to Angelus Oaks and the Oaks Restaurant, where you can spend the money you just saved on a delicious burger and a beer. Amazingly, premium beer brands are only a quarter more than common domestics. So splurge—this trail deserves a celebration.

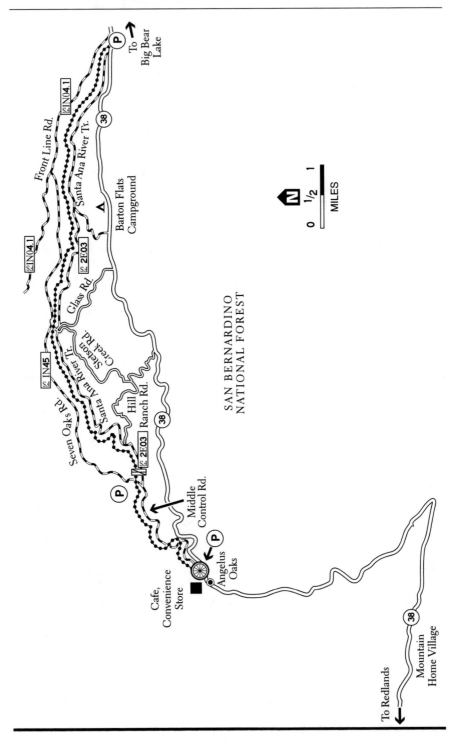

Jason is happy: 22 more miles of this single-track to go.

General location: Just east of the hamlet of Angelus Oaks off of CA 38 in the San Bernardino National Forest. 19 miles from I-10 in Redlands; 31 miles from Big Bear Lake.

Elevation change: Not significant.

Season: May through October.

Services: No services are available on the trail. Food, phones, rest rooms, and water are available in Angelus Oaks. All services are available in Big Bear Lake and Redlands.

Hazards: Narrow trails with some steep drop-offs; ice patches are possible during fall and spring.

Rescue index: The trail runs parallel to CA 38, which can usually be reached without too much effort. Help is available at the U.S. Forest Service's Mill Creek Ranger Station.

Land status: National forest.

Maps: The "San Bernardino Mountains Recreation Topo Map" is available in local sports stores and at Mill Creek Ranger Station.

Finding the trail: From I-10 in Redlands, go north on Orange Avenue/CA 38. CA 38 passes through the communities of Redlands and Mentone before reaching Mill Creek Ranger Station (on the right) at 9 miles. Keep going uphill on CA 38 to Angelus Oaks, a small enclave containing a gas station, cafe, and general store. Stay on CA 38 and go 0.3 mile east of Angelus Oaks. Turn left into a gravel parking lot just east of a dirt road named Middle Control Road. (But if the sign is still turned halfway around as it was during this writing, the dirt road seems to be named Mill Creek Road.) In any case, park in the gravel lot, making sure to stay well off to the side of CA 38. A Forest Adventure Pass is required.

Sources of additional information:

San Bernardino National Forest
San Gorgonio Ranger District
34701 Mill Creek Road
Mentone, CA 92359
(909) 794-1123
www.r5.fs.fed.us/sanbernardino

Team Big Bear Mountain Bike
  Center (open May to October)
880 Summit Boulevard
P.O. Box 2932
Big Bear Lake, CA 92315
(909) 866-4565

Notes on the trail: Leave the gravel parking lot and ride downhill on the dirt Middle Control Road (regardless of how it is signed). You'll plunge into a shady forest on a road that's sometimes eroded and sandy. At 2.9 miles, turn right at the intersection with FS 2E03, Santa Ana River Trail. After some modest climbing, stay right at an intersection with an unnamed road at 4.1 miles. This route is well signed, and if you always follow signs for FS 2E03, you'll be fine. At 4.5 miles cross Forsee Creek, which can flow fast during early summer. The trail crosses another creek and begins roller-coastering. The climb intensifies just before reaching paved Glass Road at 7.7 miles. Turn left on Glass Road for 60 feet, then right onto FS 2E03 once more (it's unmarked at this point). There are no long uphills, but you'll gradually ascend to 11.3 miles, where you'll intersect with a trail leading up to Barton Flats Campground and FS 1N45 leading down to the Santa Ana River. Ignore both of these routes and continue straight on FS 2E03. At 13.5 miles, pass the intersection with a trail on the right, which offers a short-cut to CA 38. Keep heading straight and you'll reach pavement and the beginning of the South Fork Parking/Picnic Area at 14 miles. It's a good place to sit in the sun or shade (depending on the season) and fuel up for the rollicking single-track descent to come. When you're done eating, turn around and return the way you came. The going is much faster as you cruise on the buffed, beautiful path all the way back to Middle Control Road at 25.1 miles. Turn left for a very taxing climb back to your car at 28.1 miles.

RIDE 34 · Skyline Drive

AT A GLANCE

Length/configuration: 18.3-mile loop

Aerobic difficulty: Difficult; initial 3-mile climb begins steeply then becomes moderate; lots of ups and downs (and easy riding too)

Technical difficulty: Moderately difficult; most of the ride is on good gravel roads; some washboarding

Scenery: Grandview Point affords a truly grand view of San Gorgonio Mountain and Ten Thousand Foot Ridge

Special comments: Route briefly joins CA 18; exercise caution on this busy highway

Here is a hard, 18.3-mile loop that is well worth the effort involved. The trail begins with a 3-mile climb that is steep for the first mile and then becomes less difficult. Once the Skyline is reached, the riding becomes easier. As you cycle along the ridge, you'll traverse a series of hills, losing elevation overall. After passing the trail to Grandview Point, there are several short climbs and two moderately steep ascents that are both over a mile long. There is plenty of descending. Two-thirds of the ride is on two-wheel-drive dirt roads. These are in good condition with some washboarding on some of the steeper sections. There is 1 mile of good single-track trail. The remainder of the trip is on paved roads in good condition.

An abundance of top-notch fire roads have helped make the Big Bear Lake area a mecca for mountain bikers. Skyline Drive is a favorite of locals and visitors alike. In addition to a great road surface, it offers spectacular scenery. Grandview Point is the best place to take in the view of 11,510-foot San Gorgonio Mountain and Ten Thousand Foot Ridge.

General location: The Snow Summit Ski Area, in the town of Big Bear Lake.

Elevation change: The ride starts at 7,040 feet and climbs to a high point of 8,100 feet. The trail undulates after reaching the ridge, adding an estimated 1,000 feet of climbing to the ride. Total elevation gain: 2,060 feet.

Season: Late spring through fall. Mornings and evenings can be brisk, but day-time temperatures are perfect for riding. Avoid the crowds by planning to visit Big Bear Lake before Memorial Day or after Labor Day.

Services: There is no water available on this ride. All services are available in the town of Big Bear Lake.

Hazards: Ride defensively and predictably, especially near the end of the loop where you will be traveling through Big Bear Lake on CA 18. Watch for traffic at all times. The last mile of the trip is on a twisty, downhill single-track trail.

Rescue index: Help can be found in the town of Big Bear Lake.

Land status: National forest.

Maps: USGS 7.5-minute quadrangle maps: Big Bear Lake and Moonridge.

Finding the trail: From I-10 in Redlands, take the Orange Street exit. Follow Orange Street north for 0.5 mile and turn right (east) onto Lugonia Avenue (CA 38). Follow CA 38 for approximately 60 miles to Big Bear Lake and CA 18. Follow CA 18 around the south side of the lake to reach the community of Big Bear Lake. Go left (south) on Summit Boulevard for about 1 mile to the Snow Summit Ski Area parking lot.

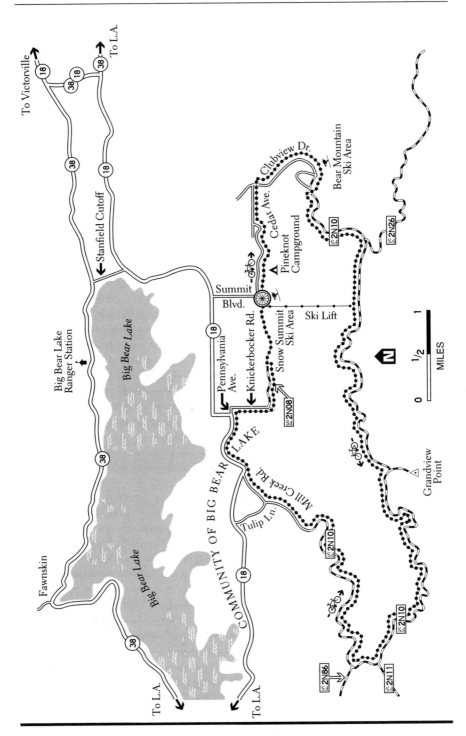

To Victorville

To L.A.

18

38 18

38

To L.A.

38

18

Stanfield Cutoff

Clubview Dr.

Bear Mountain
Ski Area

Cedar Ave.

Pineknot
Campground

2N10

2N26

Big Bear Lake
Ranger Station

Big Bear Lake

Summit
Blvd.

Ski Lift

Snow Summit
Ski Area

N

Knickerbocker Rd.

Pennsylvania
Ave.

18

2N08

1/2

1

0

MILES

Big Bear Lake

COMMUNITY OF BIG BEAR LAKE

Mill Creek Rd.

Grandview
Point

Tulip Ln.

2N10

Fawnskin

Big Bear Lake

18

38

2N10

2N86

2N11

38

To L.A.

To L.A.

View from the Skyline.

Sources of additional information:

San Bernardino National Forest
Big Bear Ranger District
41397 North Shore Drive,
    Highway 38
P.O. Box 290
Fawnskin, California 92333
(909) 866-3437
www.r5.fs.fed.us/sanbernardino

Big Bear Discovery Center
North Shore Drive, Highway 38
P.O. Box 66
Fawnskin, CA 92333
(909) 866-3437
www.bigbeardiscoverycenter.org

Big Bear Chamber of Commerce
www.bigbearchamber.com

Big Bear Lake Resort Association
630 Bartlett Road
Big Bear Lake, CA 92315
(800) 424-2327
www.bigbearinfo.com

Team Big Bear Mountain Bike
    Center (open May to October)
880 Summit Boulevard
P.O. Box 2932
Big Bear Lake, CA 92315
(909) 866-4565

Notes on the trail: The ride begins in the southeast corner of the Snow Summit
Ski Area parking lot. Follow the sign toward the Pine Knot Campground on

paved Cedar Avenue. Ride past the campground. The road changes to dirt and turns to the left before coming to the T-intersection of Cedar Avenue and Switzerland Drive. Turn right to continue on Cedar Avenue. After 0.5 mile you will reach another T-intersection at Clubview Drive. Turn right and climb on Clubview Drive past the Bear Mountain Ski Area. A short distance beyond the ski area, the road changes to a dirt surface. Soon after leaving the pavement you'll arrive at the signed FS 2N10. Turn left onto FS 2N10. You will stay on FS 2N10 for nearly 13 miles. Fourteen miles from the start of the ride you'll enter a residential area where the road surface turns to pavement. The road name changes at this point from FS 2N10 to Mill Creek Road. After 1.3 miles on pavement you'll arrive at the intersection of Mill Creek Road and Tulip Lane. Turn right to stay on Mill Creek Road. Continue on Mill Creek Road for another 0.5 mile to Big Bear Boulevard (CA 18). Turn right onto Big Bear Boulevard (CA 18). Follow it through town for 0.8 mile to Pine Knot Drive. Continue straight onto Pennsylvania Avenue where CA 18 goes left and follows Pine Knot Drive. After 0.2 mile on Pennsylvania Avenue, turn right onto Knickerbocker Road. Climb on this paved road for 0.5 mile where you will see FS 2N08, a dirt road, to your left. Turn left onto FS 2N08 and follow it a short distance to where the road becomes a single-track trail. Go around some boulders that partially block the trail. Stay on this single-track for 1 mile, passing behind residential developments to the parking lot of the Snow Summit Ski Area and your parked vehicle.

The Skyline is also accessible to less energetic cyclists. For a fee, you and your bike can ride a Snow Summit chairlift to the ridge. Make inquiries at the Team Big Bear Mountain Bike Center at the Snow Summit Ski Area.

RIDE 35 · Delamar Mountain

AT A GLANCE

Length/configuration: 10.5-mile loop

Aerobic difficulty: Moderately difficult; a steady climb; the first half-mile is steep

Technical difficulty: Moderately difficult; descent requires good bike-handling skills, but the rest of the ride is less demanding

Scenery: Nice views of Big Bear Lake and the surrounding mountains

Special comments: This road ride can handle traffic earlier in the spring than some other area routes

This 10.5-mile loop requires a moderate amount of strength. The ascent, though only steep for the first 0.5 mile, is steady and 4.5 miles long. The downhill is fast and potholed, requiring good riding technique. Most of the trip is on unpaved, two-wheel-drive roads in good condition. The first 0.5 mile and the last 2 miles are on pavement.

RIDE 35 · Delamar Mountain

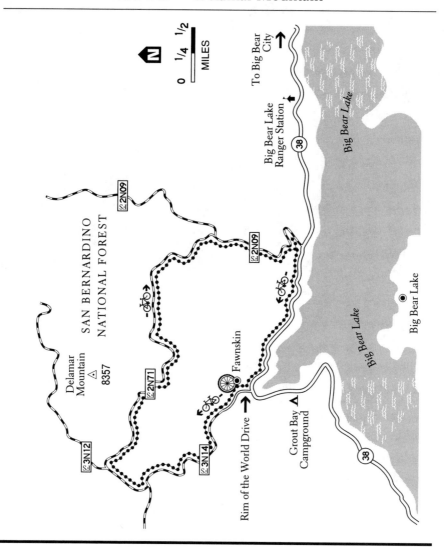

This route is an excellent introduction to mountain biking in the Big Bear Lake region. It is quite easy and takes in some great scenery. As the road winds up and around Delamar Mountain, views open up to include Big Bear Lake, the San Gorgonio Wilderness, and the San Gabriel Mountains. The roads receive good sun exposure and are often free of snow in the early spring.

General location: Begins in the town of Fawnskin, adjacent to Big Bear Lake.

Elevation change: Starts at 7,000 feet and reaches a high point of 7,500 feet on FS 2N71. The route descends on dirt to CA 38 at 6,775 feet and ends back at

Big Bear Lake from Delmar Mountain.

7,000 feet in Fawnskin. Ups and downs along the way add an estimated 100 feet of climbing to the ride. Total elevation gain: 825 feet.

Season: Spring and fall afford the best temperatures for riding. Nights can be cold, so be prepared if you plan to camp. The region becomes busy with vacationers in the summer.

Services: There is no water available on this ride. All services are available in Fawnskin and nearby communities.

Hazards: "Street-legal" vehicles are permitted on the fire roads in the forest. Campgrounds are located off these roads and there is bound to be some traffic. If at all possible, avoid weekends and holidays from Memorial Day until Labor Day. Care should be taken on CA 38; this stretch of highway contains some blind corners.

Rescue index: Assistance can be found in the town of Fawnskin or at the Big Bear Ranger Station. The ranger station is located on the north side of Big Bear Lake on CA 38, 3 miles east of Fawnskin.

Land status: National forest.

Maps: USGS 7.5-minute quadrangle map: Fawnskin. You can obtain an information sheet on mountain biking and a general map of the area at the Big Bear Ranger Station.

Finding the trail: From San Bernardino, take CA 330 to the town of Running Springs. Head east on CA 18 for 14 miles, then go left on CA 38 for 3 miles, following signs to Fawnskin. Turn north on Rim of the World Drive and almost immediately you'll come to a fire station. Park here, obeying all posted regulations. Forest Adventure Pass required while parking in San Bernardino National Forest.

Pass the Big Bear Ranger Station after 1 mile. Three miles beyond the ranger station you will enter the town of Fawnskin. Automobiles may be parked in legal zones on the streets of Fawnskin.

Sources of additional information:

San Bernardino National Forest
Big Bear Ranger District
41397 North Shore Drive,
　Highway 38
P.O. Box 290
Fawnskin, California 92333
(909) 866-3437
www.r5.fs.fed.us/sanbernardino

Big Bear Discovery Center
North Shore Drive, Highway 38
P.O. Box 66
Fawnksin, CA 92333
(909) 866-3437
www.bigbeardiscoverycenter.org

Big Bear Chamber of Commerce
www.bigbearchamber.com

Big Bear Lake Resort Association
630 Bartlett Road
Big Bear Lake, CA 92315
(800) 424-2327
www.bigbearinfo.com

Team Big Bear Mountain Bike
　Center (open May to October)
880 Summit Boulevard
P.O. Box 2932
Big Bear Lake, CA 92315
(909) 866-4565

Big Bear Visitor Center
North Shore Drive, Highway 38
　(3 miles east of Fawnskin)
(909) 878-3333

Notes on the trail: In Fawnskin, follow Rim of the World Drive north. Soon the pavement ends, and the road becomes FS 3N14. After approximately 2 miles of riding you will intersect with FS 3N12. Turn right onto FS 3N12. Ride about 0.5 mile to an intersection with FS 2N71 and turn right. Stay on FS 2N71 as it traverses the south side of Delamar Mountain. Turn right at the intersection with FS 2N09. Follow FS 2N09 downhill to CA 38. Turn right onto CA 38 and follow the highway for 2 miles back to Fawnskin.

RIDE 36 · Artic Canyon Overlook

AT A GLANCE

Length/configuration: 19.5-mile combination; a 12.5-mile loop and a 7-mile out-and-back (3.5 miles each way)

Aerobic difficulty: Difficult; tough climbing

Technical difficulty: Difficult; route includes a technical motorcycle trail; demanding descents on rough roads

Scenery: Lovely views into desert from the Arctic Canyon Overlook

Special comments: Most of the roads on this route are unmarked; the ride requires good route-finding skills

Here is a challenging ride for experienced cyclists. This 19.5-mile loop includes demanding climbs and steep, technical descents. Approximately 15 miles of the trip is on unpaved, two-wheel-drive roads in good condition. After 5 miles of pedaling, the route becomes a bouldered, sometimes sandy four-wheel-drive road. Later it turns into a rough motorcycle trail. There are uphill sections where the trail is rocky, rutted, and soft. This extremely rough portion is 5 miles long. The last 10 miles of the loop are on good dirt roads.

Upon reaching Arctic Canyon Overlook you will catch a glimpse of the desert off to the east. Take some time to scramble up the rocks and take in the marvelous view of Arctic Canyon, the Lucerne Valley, and the East Mojave Desert.

Local cyclists speak of a ghost that haunts the forest and decides who will stay in the saddle and "clean" this ride. May the ghost be with you.

General location: Begins in the town of Big Bear City, adjacent to Big Bear Lake.

Elevation change: The ride starts at 6,830 feet and climbs for 3.5 miles to 7,390 feet. From here it levels off for a mile and then ascends again for nearly 4 miles to a high point of 8,000 feet. Next, the trail drops to 7,500 feet before rising again, this time to 7,750 feet. The route continues by going downhill to 7,300 feet, rolling down and up to 7,400 feet, and finally descending back to the start at 6,830 feet. Rolling topography adds an estimated 200 feet of climbing to the ride. Total elevation gain: 1,720 feet.

Season: Late spring through fall. The Big Bear Lake region can get very busy in the summer.

Services: There is no water available on this ride. All services are available in Big Bear City.

Hazards: FS 3N32 can be treacherous; the utmost care should be taken on the downhill sections of this road. Due to the popularity of Holcomb Valley Campground in the summer, FS 3N16 can become busy with motor vehicles; avoid weekends and holidays between Memorial Day and Labor Day.

Rescue index: Help may be obtained in Big Bear City or at the Big Bear Ranger Station on CA 38.

Land status: National forest.

Maps: USGS 7.5-minute quadrangle maps: Fawnskin and Big Bear City. Also carry the San Bernardino National Forest map.

Finding the trail: From I-10 in Redlands, take the Orange Street exit. Head north on Orange Street for 0.5 mile and turn right (east) onto Lugonia Avenue (CA 38). Follow CA 38 for approximately 60 miles to Big Bear Lake. Follow the highway across the Stanfield Cutoff (a road over an earthen dam) to the north side of the lake. Turn right (east) onto CA 18 toward Big Bear City. After about 2 miles you will see a sign for Van Dusen Canyon and Holcomb Valley. Turn left (north) here onto Van Dusen Canyon Road and follow it to the end of the pavement. Park in the large dirt pullout on the right. Forest Adventure Pass required.

RIDE 36 · Arctic Canyon Overlook

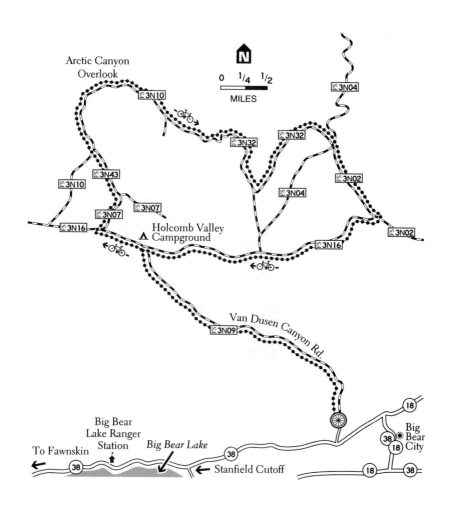

Sources of additional information:

San Bernardino National Forest
Big Bear Ranger District
41397 North Shore Drive,
 Highway 38
P.O. Box 290
Fawnskin, California 92333
(909) 866-3437
www.r5.fs.fed.us/sanbernardino

Big Bear Discovery Center
North Shore Drive, Highway 38
P.O. Box 66
Fawnksin, CA 92333
(909) 866-3437
www.bigbeardiscoverycenter.org

Big Bear Chamber of Commerce
www.bigbearchamber.com

The Lucerne Valley from
Arctic Canyon Overlook.

Big Bear Lake Resort Association
630 Bartlett Road
Big Bear Lake, CA 92315
(800) 424-2327
www.bigbearinfo.com

Team Big Bear Mountain Bike
 Center (open May to October)
880 Summit Boulevard

P.O. Box 2932
Big Bear Lake, CA 92315
(909) 866-4565

Big Bear Visitor Center
North Shore Drive, Highway 38
 (3 miles east of Fawnskin)
(909) 878-3333

Notes on the trail: Many of the FS roads described in this ride are unmarked. We
suggest that you use the recommended maps and a compass as directional aids.

Follow the signed FS 3N09 north for 3.6 miles to FS 3N16 at a sign for Holcomb Valley Campground. Turn left onto FS 3N16. Ride for about 1 mile on FS
3N16 to FS 3N07 on the right at a sign for Wilbur's Grave and Arctic Canyon.
Turn right and follow FS 3N07 for 0.5 mile to FS 3N43 on the left. Turn left
onto FS 3N43 and follow it for 1.8 miles to the unsigned Arctic Canyon Overlook. Although no signs indicate a change, you are now on FS 3N10. Continue
past the overlook for about a mile to an unmarked fork in the road. Stay left.
There is an obscure landmark just after you veer left at the fork—a sign on the

left that reads "Greenhorn Claim" (partially hidden by trees). It is 1.1 miles from this landmark to a T-intersection at FS 3N32. Turn right onto FS 3N32. A short distance down the road brings you to another poorly marked intersection. A sign reads "No Green Sticker Vehicles." Turn left here to continue on FS 3N32. From this turn it is 1.5 miles to FS 3N02. Turn right onto FS 3N02 and follow it for 1.3 miles to FS 3N16. Turn right onto FS 3N16. Follow this road for approximately 3 miles to FS 3N09, which will be on the left. Turn left onto FS 3N09 and descend back to your vehicle.

RIDE 37 · Keller Peak/National Children's Forest

AT A GLANCE

Length/configuration: 12.5-mile combination ride (a 12.1-mile out-and-back ride, with legs of 6 miles, plus a 0.2-mile spur)

Aerobic difficulty: Easy/moderate; the climb is long but not particularly steep

Technical difficulty: Easy; smooth fire roads and even smoother pavement

Scenery: Snow Valley Ski Area, Lucerne Valley, numerous peaks, and the nature displays at National Children's Forest

Special comments: A choice ride for all beginners and intermediates, but it's especially good if you're towing kids either in a bike trailer or in a rear rack seat; you won't mind the climb, and they'll love the National Children's Forest

With its views from a fire lookout tower and its spur to the National Children's Forest, this 12.4-mile combination would make a great family ride. The only problem is that most kids lack the endurance for a 6-mile climb, no matter how gentle it is. But if you have a Burley trailer, this is the place to take it. Granted, most manufacturers don't recommend taking either type of child-carrying conveyance off-pavement, but the dirt portion here is uncommonly smooth.

Starting just west of Running Springs near Deer Lick Children's Forest Visitor Information Center and Fire Station, the ride climbs paved Keller Peak Road (FS 1N96) toward the National Children's Forest. It's a steady climb at a 3.7% grade. But the paved surface and the few minor descents combine to make it easy going. The altitude might affect some people, however. After turning right past the turnoff to National Children's Forest, forge ahead on dirt up to the summit of Keller Peak, where a fire lookout is open to visitors, 9 a.m. to 5 p.m., seven days a week, from Memorial Day to Labor Day. Enjoy a tour of the tower, soak in some views, and have fun gliding down to the National Children's Forest for some exploring and touring on foot.

RIDE 37 · Keller Peak/National Children's Forest

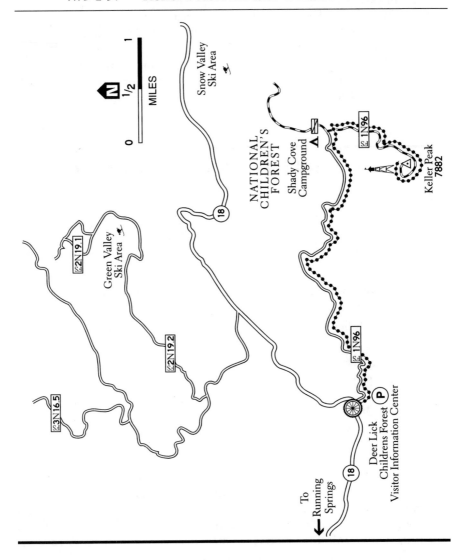

This area was badly burned in 1970, and because children helped replant trees here the Forest Service honored their aid by dedicating the site to children. A self-guided nature trail is informative and entertaining for young and old alike. Just note that you cannot ride your bike on the nature trail. You might want to bring a bike lock along for peace of mind, but there's probably nothing to worry about. After you exhaust the tour, wake up with a rapid (but not scary) descent back to Deer Lick.

General location: In the San Bernardino National Forest, about 7 miles east of Lake Arrowhead and just east of Running Springs.

Like the sign says, the San Bernardino Mountains is one place you don't want to pass on Forest Adventure.

Elevation change: 1,882 feet, from 6,000 feet to 7,882 feet.

Season: Late spring, summer, and fall. The lookout tower is only open from Memorial Day through Labor Day. FS 1N96 is closed in winter.

Services: In addition to the Visitor Information Center in Deer Lick Fire Station, there's a campground at the Children's Forest Interpretive Trail, tours of Keller Peak Lookout Tower, and water and rest rooms at the Children's Forest Interpretive Trail. All other services are available in Running Springs.

Hazards: Automobile traffic on paved sections, high altitude, and lightning on summer afternoons. If dark storm clouds appear threatening, turn around and head for lower elevations.

Rescue index: Help can be found at Keller Peak Lookout or at Deer Lick Fire Station along the ride's route.

Land status: National forest.

Maps: The San Bernardino National Forest map. Also, "Franko's Map of Big Bear!" and the "San Bernardino Mountains Recreation Topo Map" are available at sports stores.

Finding the trail: From Lake Arrowhead, take CA 18 east through Running Springs. Less than a mile east of Running Springs, turn right onto FS 1N96 and park. (Note: there is a limited amount of parking available here.) Forest Adventure Pass required.

Sources of additional information:

Children's Forest Association
San Bernardino National Forest
28104 Highway 18
P.O. Box 350
Sky Forest, CA 92385
(909) 337-5156
www.r5.fs.fed.us/sanbernardino

Team Big Bear Mountain Bike
   Center (open May to October)
880 Summit Boulevard
P.O. Box 2932
Big Bear Lake, CA 92315
(909) 866-4565

Notes on the trail: From the parking area, go east and uphill on paved FS 1N96. The road climbs steadily on pavement to the turnoff with National Children's Forest at 4.2 miles. Turn right on FS 1N96, which turns into dirt here. Keep climbing, and at 7,100 feet the road levels out some more. On your right, you'll have beautiful views of the Santa Ana River drainage and the cities of Redlands and San Bernardino. You'll reach the Keller Peak Lookout at 6 miles. Have fun on a tour of the tower, then turn around and descend back to the National Children's Forest turnoff at 7.9 miles. Veer right up to the Phoenix Trail at 8.1 miles. Dismount and walk along the Phoenix Trail. After exploring, remount your bike and retrace your way back to FS 1N96, then retrace your route back to FS 1N96. Take a right down the pavement and return to your vehicle at 12.5 miles.

RIDE 38 · Mr. Toad's Wild Ride

AT A GLANCE

Length/configuration: 30.4-mile combination (2.6-mile out-and-back [1.3 miles each way] plus 27.8-mile loop) on dirt road, jeep trail, and pavement

Aerobic difficulty: Difficult; climbs are not dastardly, but this is a long ride in high-altitude country

Technical difficulty: Moderate/difficult; most of ride takes place on fun fire roads, but some rough jeep trails and stream crossings make it a little tough

Scenery: Alpine lakes, forests, streams in big dose

Special comments: A big ride which gives an expansive tour of the Big Bear area and its communities; allow most of the day for it

It seems every mountain bike community has some trail named "Mr. Toad's Wild Ride," but few are probably this long or scenic. The name is said to originally come from cross-country skiers, not bikers, and it makes sense. Some of this terrain would be a lot hairier on skis than on bikes. It's not a technical single-track paradise, but with big climbs, big descents, and big rollercoaster sections, it's an epic all of its own.

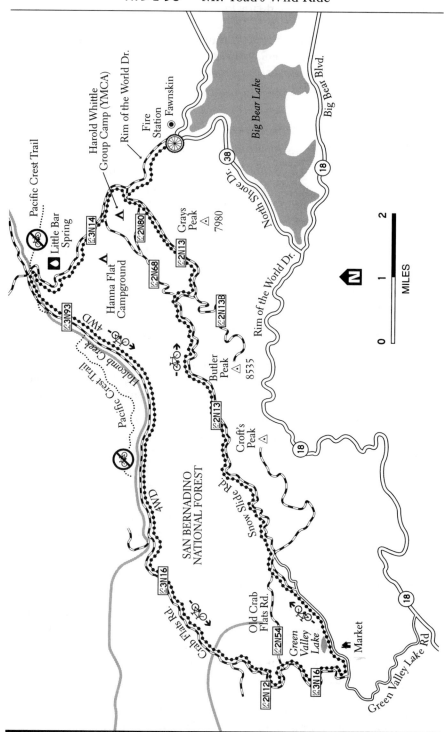

The ride takes place in the picturesque Fawnskin area on the north shore of Big Bear Lake, and climbs gradually to the Whittle Camp before a wonderful descent toward Little Bear Springs. You'll then head left along Holcomb Creek for a long, bouncy downhill. You pay for the vertical with a long, nearly 8-mile climb which brings you the scenic community of Green Valley Lake and a market serving wonderfully cold drinks. A rollercoaster section on beautiful Snow Slide Road brings you back to Fawnskin, where you'll find eateries to cap your ride off in style.

General location: On the north shore of Big Bear Lake, in the town of Fawnskin.

Elevation change: Approximately 2,400 feet.

Season: May to November; summer can be hot and crowded.

Services: Riders will find services in the communities of Fawnskin (at start/finish of ride) and in Green Valley Lake (near the ride's midpoint).

Hazards: Vehicular traffic on Forest Service roads, streams, rocky terrain in spots.

Rescue index: Help is available through Big Bear Ranger Station, 3 miles east of ride's start.

Land status: National forest.

Maps: USGS 7.5-minute maps: Fawnskin, Butler Peak, and Keller Peak.

Finding the trail: From San Bernardino, take CA 330 to the town of Running Springs. Head east on CA 18 for 14 miles, then go left on CA 38 for 3 miles, following signs to Fawnskin. Turn north on Rim of the World Drive and almost immediately you'll come to a fire station. Park here, obeying all posted regulations. Forest Adventure Pass required while parking in San Bernardino National Forest.

Sources of additional information:

San Bernardino National Forest
Big Bear Ranger District
41397 North Shore Drive,
    Highway 38
P.O. Box 290
Fawnskin, California 92333
(909) 866-3437
www.r5.fs.fed.us/sanbernardino

Big Bear Chamber of Commerce
www.bigbearchamber.com

Big Bear Lake Resort Association
630 Bartlett Road
Big Bear Lake, CA 92315
(800) 424-2327
www.bigbearinfo.com

Notes on the trail: Leave the fire station and pedal north (and up) Rim of the World Drive, which turns to dirt FS 3N14 at 0.5 mile. Keep climbing gradually to the intersection with 2N13 on left at 1.3 miles. Don't go left here; instead loop around counterclockwise until you reach Whittle Camp at 2 miles. Veer right, staying on 3N14, enjoying a fun descent to Little Bear Spring and Holcomb Creek at 4.4 miles. Go left on FS 3N93, a rough jeep road, which gets even rougher pretty quickly.

You'll enjoy bouncing alongside Holcomb Creek to an intersection at 10.4 miles. Veer left on Crab Flats Road, FS 3N16. Climb to 13.2 miles, and go left at a T-intersection with FS 2N12. Climb to 15.3 miles, where the road changes back to 3N16, and veer right. (Do not go left onto FS 2N54.) You reach paved Green Valley Lake Road at 17.1 miles. Go left (northeast), stopping to refresh yourself at the market on the right.

After a break, keep riding in the same northeast direction on Green Valley Lake Road, and at 18.5 miles, go left onto dirt Snow Slide Road, FS 2N13. You quickly reach the intersection with another section of Crab Flats Road (FS 2N54) on the left at 19.3 miles. Veer right, staying on Snow Slide Road, FS 2N13. You embark on a long rollercoaster ride through beautiful alpine country. At a junction at 26.8 miles, go right on FS 2N13 (which provides access to the road up to Butler Peak), and veer left at 27 miles (heading away from Butler Peak). Stay on FS 2N13 until you reach FS 3N14 at 29.1 miles, which you rode up earlier. Go right on FS 3N14, which descends into Rim of the World Drive and brings you back to the start at a long (but fun) 30.4-mile ride.

SAN GABRIEL MOUNTAINS

Nineteenth-century explorer and naturalist John Muir made it his business to explore uncharted mountain ranges. Yet when Muir first encountered the San Gabriel Range, even he was a bit intimidated: "I have never," Muir wrote, "made the acquaintance of mountains more rigidly inaccessible." Though the San Gabriels remain steep and rugged to this day, they are no longer inaccessible. Though startlingly close to downtown Los Angeles, these mountains offer an easy chance to get away—far, far away—from it all.

The history of the San Gabriels is a checkered one. The same qualities that made these mountains so daunting back in John Muir's day appealed to banditos and rustlers who would hide out here after raids on ranches in the fledgling communities outside Los Angeles. (The hideout aspect continues; even today, the remote canyons of Angeles National Forest are home to secret marijuana stashes and shallow graves.) Yet the mountains also attracted the righteous, and in the 1890s, the San Gabriels boomed in popularity during the 30-year Great Hiking Era. It was during this time that entrepreneurs built hotels, restaurants, and even railroads in the San Gabriels to serve hikers trying to beat the heat of Los Angeles. Perhaps due to its usage, the Angeles was the first National Forest in California, and only the second in the United States.

Since these mountains soar to a height of over 10,000 feet, it's still a nice place to beat the heat. Indeed, there's nothing quite like biking through cool mountain breezes on a ridge top in the San Gabriels. You inhale Jeffrey pine-scented air while the desert heats up on one side of you and the Los Angeles Basin spreads out on the other. It won't be long before you start figuring out ways to access all 14 rides in this region.

RIDE 39 · Blue Ridge "d"

AT A GLANCE

CA

Length/configuration: 18.6-mile combination (a 6.9-mile loop with a spur that's 5.9 miles each way)

Aerobic difficulty: Moderate; intermittent, untaxing climbs on the fire road, with a quick but tough pavement climb at ride's end

Technical difficulty: Moderate; there are a few tricky switchbacks on one of the smoothest, most scenic single-tracks in all of the San Gabriels

Scenery: The highest mountains in the San Gabriels, including Mt. Baden Powell and Mt. San Antonio; the desert floor of the Antelope Valley, and a gorgeous oak and sycamore forest

Special comments: Combining a fine high-altitude training ride and one of the area's most captivating single-tracks, this trip is a must for all riders looking to increase their endurance while having fun at the same time — it's also probably the best-smelling ride in this book

This 18.6-mile combination ride is in the shape of a lowercase "d," which can only stand for "delightful." Partly circumnavigating the Mountain High Ski Area near Wrightwood, this exquisitely pine- and vanilla-scented route is fun in late spring and summer, and jaw-droppingly stunning in the fall.

From its start next to the appropriately named Inspiration Point (not the same as the Inspiration Point in Ride 48) on Angeles Crest Highway (CA 2), the ride ascends an old paved road through a high alpine meadow that burned in a big fire in 1997. As the road steepens, you might be surprised by the sudden sight of a ski chairlift hanging above you, courtesy of Mountain High Ski Area. The pavement ends as you pass through Blue Ridge Campground and leave the ski area and civilization behind. Though firewood dealers and their trucks are no strangers here, the smooth road and panoramic ridge views of the high Mojave Desert to the north and alpine forests to the south more than make up for any man-made distractions.

The road becomes progressively more rugged before dead-ending on the side of Wright Mountain, where you can experience even more wide-scale views. A roller-coaster descent past sweet-smelling Jeffrey pines returns riders to the Blue Ridge Campground. From there, a buffed, stunning, unforgettable single-track snakes down a ravine between Mountain High West and Mountain High East. You'll think you're in New Hampshire while cruising down a perfect grade, coursing by deciduous trees, and even rattling over handmade bridges. You'll pay for such a descent with a rigorous climb up CA 2 to return to your vehicle, but it's well worth the price. Afterward, drive to Wrightwood for a selection of rustic, homey cafés and bakeries.

General location: A few miles west of Wrightwood in the Angeles National Forest.

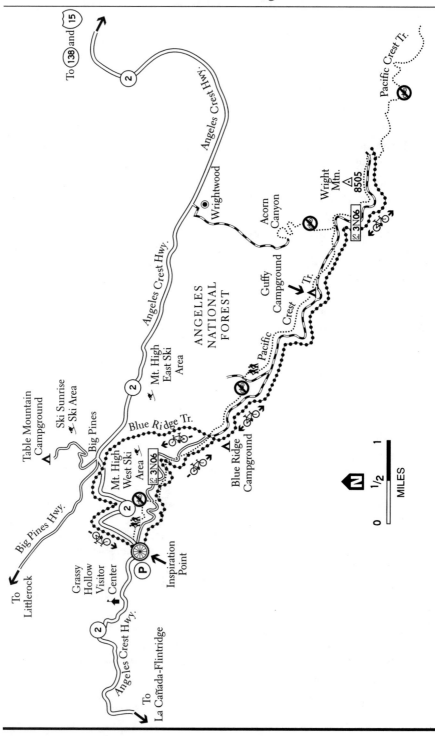

When it comes to single-track, the "d" in this ride's name stands for delicious.

Elevation change: The ride gains 1,950 feet in elevation. Moreover, the entire ride takes place above 7,000 feet, which makes the ride a substantial workout.

Season: May to October (with wildflowers in the spring and summer and brilliantly colored trees in the fall).

Services: Rest rooms are available in the Blue Ridge Campground, with all other services available in Wrightwood.

Hazards: Speeding firewood trucks on Blue Ridge Road, automobile traffic on CA 2, and tight switchbacks on the single-track descent.

Rescue index: The trail sees a lot of usage near the Blue Ridge Campground, but much less at the end of the spur to Wright Mountain. The town of Wrightwood is within easy biking distance, as is the Grassy Hollow Visitor Center, located less than a half-mile from the trailhead.

Land status: National forest.

Maps: *The Trail Map of the Angeles High Country* is available from Tom Harrison Cartography, (800) 265-9090 or (415) 456-7940. Also refer to the USFS Big Pines Recreation Area map, and USGS 7.5-minute quadrangle maps: Mt. San Antonio and Mescal Creek.

Finding the trail: From Wrightwood, go west on CA 2 approximately 6 miles to Inspiration Point, a large parking lot with benches and map displays on the south side of CA 2. (If you reach Grassy Hollow Visitor Center, you've gone too far.) From the San Gabriel Valley, head east on CA 2 approximately 50 miles from La

Cañada-Flintridge. After passing Grassy Hollow Visitor Center on the north, look for Inspiration Point on the south side of CA 2. From the Antelope Valley, take CA 138 to CA N4, the Big Pines Highway. Head north on CA N4 to the junction with CA 2, and turn right. Inspiration Point is approximately 2 miles from the junction on your left. Regardless of your point of departure, park in the large parking lot at Inspiration Point. Forest Adventure Pass required.

Sources of additional information:

Angeles National Forest
Santa Clara/Mojave Rivers
  Ranger District
Mojave Work Center
29835 Valyermo Road
P.O. Box 15
Valyermo, CA 93563
(661) 944-2187
TDD (661) 944-2189

Grassy Hollow Visitor Center
(on CA 2, 6 miles west of
  Wrightwood)
Usually open holidays and weekends
  10 a.m.–4 p.m.; open
  intermittently on weekdays
(626) 821-6737

Notes on the trail: First, stretch out your stiffened driving muscles while taking in the stunning views from Inspiration Point. Warm now? Then head east out of the parking lot and onto FS 3N06, also known as Blue Ridge Road. FS 3N06 is a sometimes steep, crumbling pavement road. At 0.9 mile, you'll come to the first of many intersections with Pacific Crest Trail, which is off-limits to bikes. At 1.2 miles, pass under your first Mt. High ski lift. The road levels out slightly as you ease into Blue Ridge Campground and pass Blue Ridge Trail at 2.4 miles. Stay straight as the road turns to dirt. A mile or so after climbing past Mt. High's snowmaking reservoir pond, the road descends on a silky-smooth stretch of fire road. You'll pass the entrance to Guffy Campground at 5.3 miles and the intersection with FS 3N39 at 5.7 miles. In both cases, stay straight on FS 3N06, which resumes climbing. As the ride passes through groves of Jeffrey and Ponderosa pine, the sweet smell of vanilla beckons you to take in even more oxygen. You might need it at 8.3 miles, where the road deadends on Wright Mountain, home to breathtaking views. Return the way you came back to Blue Ridge Campground and turn right on the trailhead for Blue Ridge Trail at 14.1 miles, just past a Mt. High ski lift. You descend a spectacular but short single-track. Flattering superlatives will clutter your mind as you cross a bridge at 16.3 miles and then bid a sad farewell to the single-track as you reach CA 2 at 16.4 miles. Turn left on this highway, which forks at the shuttered Big Pines Visitor Center (destroyed in a 1987 arson fire). CA N4 heads off to the right, while CA 2 climbs to the left. Stay on CA 2 for nearly 2 miles of sweaty ascending. Return to your car at Inspiration Point at 18.6 miles.

RIDE 40 · Manzanita Trail

AT A GLANCE

CA

Length/configuration: 12.5-mile loop on pavement, fire road, and single-track

Aerobic difficulty: Moderate; one bumpy, somewhat steep fire road ascent

Technical difficulty: Difficult; tight, twisting single-track with big drop-offs

Scenery: Thick forests, with maples, oaks, and sycamores blazing with color during November

Special comments: The epitome of what you want in a mountain bike ride: a gradual warm-up ascent, a challenging climb when you're ready to hammer, and a rollicking single-track downhill that's longer than the uphill

If other trail users knew mountain biking could be as fun as it is on this gorgeous 12.5-mile loop, they'd sell their horses and kick away their walking sticks. Were this trail a little closer to the major population centers in Los Angeles County, it would be justly famous. As it is, it's a nearly secret treasure that's worth repeated plundering.

Taking place in the underused Valyermo District of the Angeles National Forest, the ride begins with a gentle climb on pavement up FS 4N11, also known as Big Rock Creek Road. The grade is perfect for warming up the muscles that stiffened during the long drive to get here, and you'll be ready to hammer up steeper stuff when the pavement turns to dirt just after passing Camp Fenner, a conservation camp run by the California Department of Corrections. (Even if you're riding solo on a tandem, don't pick up hitchhikers here.)

The dirt fire road is bumpy, steep, and—when completely engulfed in a winter storm cloud—quite wet. It even has a few wet spots on dry days. This road is open to motorized vehicles, but it would be a surprise to see any. Instead, look to your right, across a small canyon, to see a thin trail clinging to the side of the mountain. That's the Manzanita Trail, and it's absolutely worth your climb. FS 4N11 saves its best for last, challenging you with a final steep face until you reach Angeles Crest Highway, CA 2. From here you can cross busy CA 2 to picnic at the Vincent Gulch rest stop and use the facilities (a rest room is available here), or hop on the Manzanita Trail immediately. Coursing and switchbacking through gorgeous, wooded terrain, the trail is always a hoot, even during sporadic climbs. You'll likely feel such a connection to the trail that even the occasional spring remnants of crusty snow won't deter you. This is simply a classic single-track, the kind that leaves you smiling and begging for more.

Note: At press time, this trail was not open to mountain bikes due to necessary trail work. It will probably be open by the time you read this, but call the Mojave Work Center just to be sure before riding here.

RIDE 40 · Manzanita Trail

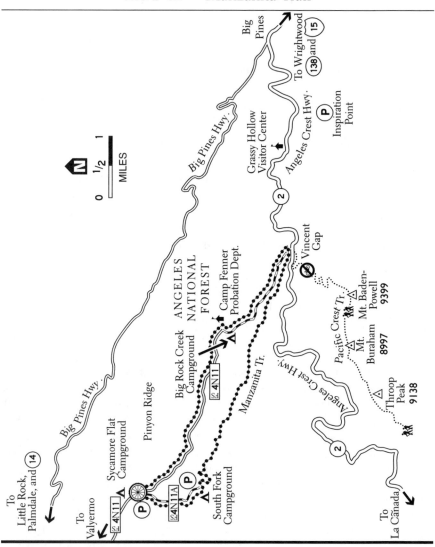

General location: 9 miles southeast of the town of Pearblossom and CA 138 in the Valyermo District of the Angeles National Forest.

Elevation change: 2,100 feet over a gentle uphill pavement section, a fairly rigorous fire road ascent, and intermittent single-track climbing.

Season: April through November (with wildflowers in the spring and summer and brilliantly colored trees in the fall).

Services: Rest rooms are available at Vincent Gulch Rest Area midway through the ride; other services are available in Pearblossom and Valyermo.

Heading into the elements on the Manzanita Trail.

Hazards: Extremely narrow, loose trail in places. Definitely not a ride for the squeamish or timid.

Rescue index: Help can be found from the Mojave work station near the beginning of ride.

Land status: National forest.

Maps: *The Trail Map of the Angeles High Country* is available from Tom Harrison Cartography, (800) 265-9090 or (415) 456-7940. Also refer to the USFS Big Pines Recreation Area map and USGS 7.5-minute quadrangle maps: Valyermo and Crystal Lake.

Finding the trail: Access CA 138, the Pearblossom Highway, from either CA 14 to the west or I-15 to the east. Take CA 138 to the town of Pearblossom. Go south on Longview Road for 0.4 mile. Go left (east) on Avenue W, which soon turns into Valyermo Road. Winding southeast, Valyermo Road passes through the picturesque hamlet of Valyermo and a ranger district office 5.6 miles from CA 138. Soon, turn right on Big Rock Creek Road. After passing through Sycamore Flat Campground, park at the turnout adjoining the road leading to South Fork Campground (9 miles from CA 138).

Sources of additional information:

Angeles National Forest
Santa Clara/Mojave Rivers
  Ranger District
Mojave Work Center
29835 Valyermo Road

P.O. Box 15
Valyermo, CA 93563
(661) 944-2187
TDD (661) 944-2189

| Grassy Hollow Visitor Center (on CA 2, 6 miles west of Wrightwood) | Usually open holidays and weekends 10 a.m.–4 p.m.; open intermittently on weekdays; (626) 821-6737 |

Notes on the trail: Ride north on Big Rock Creek Road (FS 4N11). At 3.4 miles, pass Camp Fenner and start riding up the dirt section of FS 4N11. The ride is fairly steep to the intersection with CA 2 at 5.6 miles. Head across CA 2 for a rest at Vincent Gulch Rest Area if you'd like. But if you're eager to get on the single-track, just head immediately to your right. A few dozen yards to the west of where you emerged from FS 4N11 is the Manzanita Trailhead, accessible through a gap in the wooden rail fence. A map display allows you to get your bearings—the dotted blue line is your route, the Manzanita Trail. The trail swoops, zings, and dives for almost 3 delicious miles. At 8.4 miles, you'll come to a boulder field that can be disorienting. If you can't pick up the trail, head toward 10 o'clock and you'll hook up with it again. After some intermittent climbing, you will reach the intersection with the Big Rock Creek Campground Trail at 9.7 miles. Stay on the Manzanita Trail by going straight. Around the 10-mile mark, the trail becomes very rocky as it traverses a steep talus slope. The hillside is very loose here, and it's a good idea to dismount. After some switchbacks, at 10.7 miles you'll reach a very plausible-looking trail which intersects with the elbow of a switchback. Though it looks as if it might lead in the correct direction, ignore this trail and go left. The switchbacks soon give way to a very fast but sandy descent. At 11.4 miles, you'll reach South Fork Campground. Turn right on the main access road, which descends for nearly a mile back to Big Rock Creek Road. At 12.5 miles, you'll reach your car and the end of the trip.

RIDE 41 · Marshall Canyon

AT A GLANCE

Length/configuration: 3.1-mile loop on pavement, fire road, and single-track

Aerobic difficulty: Moderate; climbs can be kind of tough

Technical difficulty: Moderate; a lot of single-track and stream crossings, but it's never excessively steep or technical

Scenery: Views of San Gabriel Valley; Mt. San Antonio; chaparral landscape; lush forests of alders, willows and sycamores; abundant wildlife

Special comments: A fun, easily accessible ride where bikers can get back to nature very quickly in terrain that's quite diverse

This route is just one of several rides you can sample in the Marshall Canyon/Claremont Hills region, and I'm not even sure it's the best. There's something about this area that's kind of magical—you can be having the time of your life riding through the gorgeous streamside single-tracks here, but you also get the feeling there's something you're missing. As if gnomes and elves are making even more merry a few leafy glades over.

That may be because the network of trails and fire roads here seems to offer so many different possibilities around every bend. I got lost the first time I rode here, and ended up talking to a number of bikers, equestrians, and hikers. They all had a different trail to suggest, another view to recommend, a separate story to tell. Directions and nomenclature of trails seemed totally contradictory from person to person. But everybody was exceedingly friendly. In fact, I would say without a doubt that the relationship between bikers and equestrians here was the most cordial and helpful I've ever seen.

Keep it that way by riding responsibly. Take the following route description as a suggestion, or go out and explore on your own. For instance, if you're more in the mood for cool, glade-type riding than fire roads, you can start by riding the described route in reverse, and cycling uphill from the finish alongside the concrete wash. You'll be in lush single-track in a quarter of an hour. But wherever you go, you're sure to experience the Marshall Canyon magic yourself.

General location: In the foothills of the San Gabriel Mountains, just north of the towns of Claremont and La Verne.

Elevation change: The route climbs from 1,180 feet to 2,450 feet, with some ups and downs for an elevation gain of 1,350 feet.

Season: Year-round, but the route can be very wet and muddy after rains. To prevent trail damage, do not ride immediately after rainstorms.

Services: No water on the trail; all services available in towns of La Verne and Claremont.

Hazards: Vehicular traffic on paved portions; stream crossings; snakes and poison oak can be found along the route.

Rescue index: You are never far from civilization on this ride; call 911 for help.

Land status: City land, city park, private land, county land, county park.

Maps: *Thomas Guide: Los Angeles County* (pages 570-571), is probably the easiest map of the area to decipher and is widely available. Also, USGS 7.5-minute maps: Glendora and Mt. Baldy, but they don't show all the trails in the area.

Finding the trail: Take I-210 East to its terminus at Foothill Boulevard in La Verne. Keep going east for about a mile on Foothill Boulevard to Wheeler Avenue . Go left on Wheeler, then right at the next major block on Base Line Road for a little more than a block. Park on city streets near La Verne Heights Elementary School on Base Line Road, obeying all posted regulations.

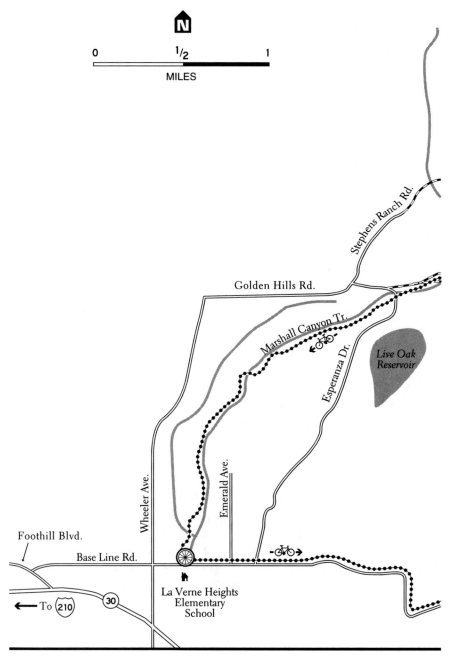

ANGELES NATIONAL FOREST

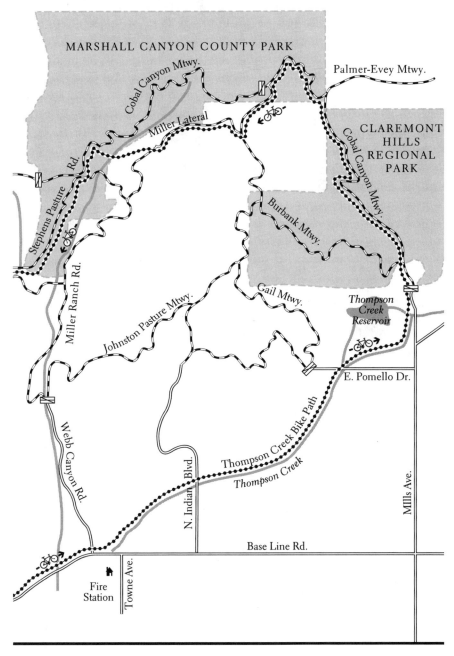

MARSHALL CANYON COUNTY PARK

Cobal Canyon Mtwy.

Palmer-Evey Mtwy.

Miller Lateral

CLAREMONT HILLS REGIONAL PARK

Cobal Canyon Mtwy.

Stephens Pasture Rd.

Burbank Mtwy.

Miller Ranch Rd.

Johnston Pasture Mtwy.

Gail Mtwy.

Thompson Creek Reservoir

E. Pomello Dr.

Webb Canyon Rd.

Thompson Creek Bike Path

N. Indian Blvd.

Thompson Creek

Mills Ave.

Base Line Rd.

Towne Ave.

Fire Station

Getting lost is its own reward in Marshall Canyon and the Claremont Hills.

Sources of additional information:

Foothill Cyclery
1147 Foothill Boulevard
La Verne, CA 91750-3328
(909) 593-1111

Claremont Hills Wilderness Park
(909) 399-5431

www.ci.claremont.ca.us

Incycle Bicycles
561 W Arrow Highway
San Dimas, CA 91773-2912
(909) 592-2181

Notes on the trail: Again, this is just one possible route through the area; take it as an introduction to the region, but feel free to explore on your own. Begin by riding east on Base Line Road for 2.2 miles. You'll come to a fire station just before Towne Avenue. Opposite the fire station, on the left side of the road, is a gate for Thompson Creek Trail (a paved bike path). Turn left (being very careful while crossing Base Line Road) and begin riding up Thompson Creek Trail. The trail takes you to Mills Avenue, which you reach at 4.6 miles. Go briefly uphill to the gate for Claremont Hills Wilderness Park. Enter the park at the gate, and begin riding up what soon becomes Cobal Canyon Motorway (don't be dissuaded by the name; cars and motorcycles are prohibited, though you may see some of the latter).

Climb to a T-intersection with Palmer-Evey Motorway on the right at 6.4 miles. Go left, staying on Cobal Canyon, and after a bit more of climbing, you level out and reach an intersection with Johnson Pasture Motorway at 7.2 miles. Stop and take in the views. Wherever you go from here, it's pretty much downhill. There is a gate on your right, marking the beginning of Marshall Canyon County Park and the continuation of Cobal Canyon. On your left is a sign for Claremont Hills Wilderness Park. There are a number of places you can explore, but I recommend pointing your Cannondale straight and riding onto Johnson Pasture Motorway. You'll climb a short incline to a nice ridge with good views of Mount San Antonio (Baldy) behind you. Ride off the ridge and keep your eyes peeled for a yellow sign (at 7.6 miles) marked "Johnson Past." and "Miller." Take a right here onto Miller Lateral, which connects to Miller Ranch Road. (Don't worry about the sign which says "Private Property"—as long as you stay on the road itself, you are not trespassing.)

You are soon riding on county land anyway, as you quickly climb and descend a knoll. At the bottom of the descent (just before another climb), again keep your eyes peeled, this time for a brown three-way trail user yield sign. Veer right here onto some very nice but all too short single-track, which, at 8.7 miles, drops you out onto a fire road (it's the bottom portion of Cobal Canyon Road). Go left here for some easy cruising on the fire road.

Go left at the first T-intersection you come to with a fire road, and then veer left immediately onto the single-track, at around 9.5 miles. (There is a whole network of trails in this area, and it's easy to wonder if you're on the right trail. Don't worry; if you miss the single-track, you can pick it up again by riding south on the fire roads and looking for signs reading "Marshall Canyon Trail.")

But let's say you're where you're supposed to be, riding the single-track. You'll come to a couple of intersections. Go right at the first, softly left at the second (going softly right at the second puts you onto the dirt Stephens Pasture Road). You'll quickly spin along some very fun single-track with a number of stream crossings. At 10.6 miles, after some great riding, you make a sharp turn to the right and go up a short but steep hill. It seems totally counterintuitive; like you're riding the wrong way. But keep going as you pass a white water tank on the right and emerge in a clearing with some stables.

It initially looks as if the trail disappears here. Don't worry, just go left, keeping the corral on your left, and you'll pick up the trail again at the far side of the clearing. You're soon riding alongside a golf course, and you'll even enjoy a stretch where you actually ride on the course's paved cart path. You leave the cart path on the obvious trail, and splash across more streams and spin through cool, leafy groves. You'll enjoy some ups and downs until you come to a wash and a debris basin where the trail seems to peter out. Head to the right of the debris basin, and begin riding alongside the paved wash. You are now riding between residential streets, but it's all downhill, and kind of fun. Keep right where the wash forks, and you emerge onto Base Line Road across from La Verne Heights Elementary School (between Wheeler Avenue and Valencia Drive) at 13.1 miles.

RIDE 42 · Mount Baldy

AT A GLANCE

Length/configuration: 9.6-mile out-and-back (4.8 miles each way)

Aerobic difficulty: Difficult; most of the climbing is moderately difficult; steeper grades lead to the top of Thunder Mountain

Technical difficulty: Moderately difficult; a four-wheel-drive road in good condition with some loose rock; the return descent is more demanding than the climb

Scenery: Good view of the surrounding mountains and valleys from the summit of Thunder Mountain

Special comments: A brief side trip (at the start of the ride) takes you to the base of 100-foot San Antonio Falls

This is an out-and-back, 9.6-mile round-trip ride up and down Mount Baldy. The first 3.6 miles occur over a moderately steep ascent of 1,600 feet to the Baldy Notch. A steeper climb of 685 feet over 1.2 miles takes you close to the top of Thunder Mountain. The first 0.5 mile is on a one-lane paved (but degraded) road. This changes to a hard-packed four-wheel-drive road in good condition with some sections of loose rock. The ride requires a moderate amount of technical skills and a good amount of strength.

The roar of rushing water can be heard soon after starting the ride. At the end of the pavement, San Antonio Falls comes into view. A side trail brings you to the base of the 100-foot falls. The dirt road continues up the mountain to the Mount Baldy Ski Lift's Notch Lodge and Baldy Notch. Continuing past the lodge, you'll arrive at a scree slope that leads to the top of Thunder Mountain. A short hike to the summit affords a terrific view of the surrounding area.

General location: Begins near the end of Mount Baldy Road, approximately 14 miles north of Upland.

Elevation change: The trip gets under way at 6,200 feet, climbs to 7,800 feet at Baldy Notch, and continues on to 8,485 feet near the summit of Thunder Mountain. Another 100 feet is gained with an optional hike to the top of Thunder Mountain. Total elevation gain: 2,285 feet (hike not included).

Season: Late spring through fall. The climb will warm you up, but once at the top you may cool off quickly. Be prepared with extra clothing, especially a windbreaker. Weekends and holidays can be busy.

Services: Water and rest rooms are available seasonally at several picnic areas en route to the ride. All services can be found in the town of Mount Baldy, 5 miles south of the trailhead on Mount Baldy Road. The Mount Baldy Ski Lift's Lodge at Baldy Notch includes a cafeteria-style restaurant. It may be open on summer weekends; call the resort for more information.

RIDE 42 · Mount Baldy

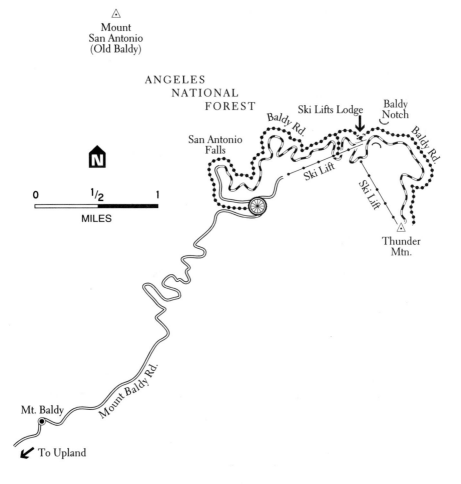

Hazards: The paved section to San Antonio Falls sees a fair amount of foot traffic; slow down and warn unsuspecting hikers of your approach. Vehicular traffic is restricted, but the road is used by the Forest Service and Mount Baldy maintenance workers.

Rescue index: Help is available in the town of Mount Baldy.

Land status: National forest.

Maps: USGS 7.5-minute quadrangle maps: Mount San Antonio and Telegraph Peak.

Finding the trail: Follow I-10 east from Los Angeles and take the exit for Mountain Avenue/Mount Baldy. Stay on Mountain Avenue for 6 miles to reach Mount Baldy Road. Turn right onto Mount Baldy Road and drive north for about 8 miles to the closed Movie Slope Restaurant on the right. The trail begins approximately 0.3 mile north of the Movie Slope Restaurant; look for a dirt road on the left (west) side of Mount Baldy Road. Park at the start of the dirt road or on the side of Mount Baldy Road.

Sources of additional information:

Angeles National Forest
San Gabriel River Ranger District
110 North Wabash Avenue
Glendora, CA 91741
(626) 335-1251

Mt. Baldy Ski Lifts
(909) 982-0800
www.mtbaldy.com

Mt. Baldy Schoolhouse
  Visitor Center
Mt. Baldy Road
Mt. Baldy, CA 91759
(909) 982-2829

Notes on the trail: Walk your bike around the gate and begin riding. Follow the road for 3.5 miles to the Mount Baldy Ski Lift's Notch Lodge. Pass the back of the lodge and turn right to follow the road uphill to Baldy Notch and views of the Mojave desert. Stay to the right and climb on the road to its end near the base of Thunder Mountain. Park your bicycle and hike up the scree slope to reach the top of Thunder Mountain. Return the way you came.

RIDE 43 · West Fork Road/Red Box-Rincon Road with Beginner Option

AT A GLANCE

Length/configuration: 30.3-mile loop or beginner option 13.6-mile out-and-back (6.8 miles each way)

Aerobic difficulty: Difficult; long ride; over 3,800 feet of climbing; beginner out-and-back option is easy

Technical difficulty: Moderately difficult/difficult; most of the ride is on dirt and gravel roads; steeper segments are rough; beginner out-and-back option is easy, taking place on a paved road

Scenery: Lush canyon and exposed riding through live oak and shrub-covered hillsides; nice views of San Gabriel Canyon Recreation Area

Special comments: A compellingly scenic ride regardless of what option you choose

RIDE 43 · West Fork Road/Red Box–Rincon Road

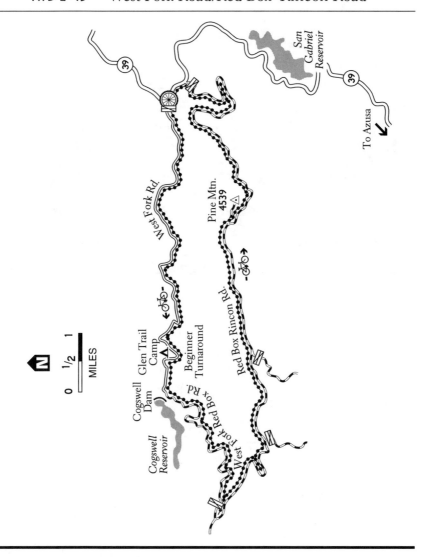

This 30.3-mile loop requires a moderate amount of technical skill. You must be a strong cyclist to manage the ride's length and nearly 4,000 feet of climbing. The first 6.8 miles wind gradually up a paved road to the Glenn Trail Camp. From there, beginners can return for an easy cruise through nice scenery. All others will continue on the road, which rises sharply and continues past the Glenn Trail Camp for 0.75 mile to the end of the pavement. The climbing becomes moderately difficult as you move onto dirt. The ascent continues for 6.4 miles and contains occasional steep sections. Then the road rolls up and down steeply as it follows a ridge. After a few more miles, the descents become longer and begin to outnumber the

San Gabriel Canyon Recreation Area from Red Box Rincon Road.

climbs. The trip ends with a welcome 8.4-mile downhill. Over 70% of this ride follows unpaved, four-wheel-drive roads in fair to good condition. Some of the steeper ascents and descents are rocky and worn.

General location: Begins at the intersection of CA 39 and West Fork Road in the San Gabriel Canyon Recreation Area, 11 miles north of Azusa. Azusa is about 20 miles east of downtown Los Angeles.

Elevation change: The long ride has a total elevation gain of 3,865 feet. The beginner option gains 425 feet.

Season: Early spring through late fall. There are times when it is sunny in the canyons and cloudy on the mountain ridges; be prepared with an extra layer of warm clothing.

Services: There is no water available on this ride. All services are available in Azusa.

Hazards: The first 2 miles of this route can be busy with hikers and fishermen in the summer and on holiday weekends. There may be Forest Service vehicles on the fire roads. Padded cycling gloves are a must for the rapid, bumpy descent to CA 39.

Rescue index: Help can be found in Azusa.

Land status: National forest.

Maps: USGS 7.5-minute quadrangle maps: Azusa, Glendora, and Mount Wilson.

Finding the trail: The trail begins at West Fork Road and San Gabriel Canyon Road (CA 39), 11 miles north of Azusa. From Los Angeles, drive east on I-10 to the exit for Azusa Avenue/CA 39. Follow Azusa Avenue/CA 39 north through the town of Azusa. Entering the San Gabriel Canyon Recreation Area, the road name changes to San Gabriel Canyon Road/CA 39. Keep an eye on the mileposts. West Fork Road begins near milepost 27. There's a parking area on the left near the trailhead. There is more parking and a rest room just a little farther north, across the bridge. A permit must be purchased to park anywhere in the San Gabriel Canyon Recreation Area on weekends and holidays.

Source of additional information:

Angeles National Forest
San Gabriel River Ranger District
110 North Wabash Avenue

Glendora, CA 91741
(626) 335-1251
www.r5.fs.fed.us/angeles

Notes on the trail: Due to the number of unsigned roads found on this loop, a bicycle odometer is recommended for this ride. All mileage notes in the description below are cumulative. Cyclists proficient at route-finding may decide that the suggested topographic maps and a compass are sufficient directional aids.

Follow West Fork Road as it climbs past the residences at Cogswell Dam. At 6.8 miles, beginners will want to turn around at Glenn Trail Camp, returning the way they came for a ride totaling 13.6 miles. All others continue on the road, which turns into the dirt West Fork–Red Box Road at mile 7.6. Turn left at the gate at 13.2 miles onto Red Box Rincon Road. You will follow Red Box Rincon Road for more than 16 miles to CA 39. Stay left (uphill) at the intersection at 15.7 miles. Turn left at the intersection at 16.3 miles. Continue straight at 16.7 miles. Turn left at 18.8 miles. At 21.5 miles, stay right and downhill. At 29.9 miles you will arrive at CA 39; turn left and return to your vehicle.

RIDE 44 · Chilao Flat Figure 8 ½

AT A GLANCE

\ **CA** \

Length/configuration: 21.3-mile combination ride on fire road, single-track, and pavement (in the form of an 18.9-mile loop shaped like one-and-a-half figure eights, plus a 1.2-mile spur to the top of Mt. Hillyer); shorter options are possible

Aerobic difficulty: Difficult; several steep hills, but none are especially long

Technical difficulty: Difficult; very tight single-track with numerous switchbacks, sandy surfaces

Scenery: Stunning rock formations, gorgeous high alpine forests, expansive views of San Gabriel backcountry

Special comments: A beautiful ride where the scenery seems to change every hundred yards, it offers numerous opportunities to bail out if you need to

I call this 21.3-mile ride a figure 8 ½ since it's in the shape of one full figure 8, plus half of one. In other words, three loops. The scenery is just stylized enough to remind you of Fellini, but the country is better known as the wild landscape once employed by notorious 1870s bandito Tiburcio Vasquez as a hideout. After soaking in the area's views, grunting up to an overlook over Mt. Hillyer, and bouncing down the fun but supremely technical Silver Moccasin Trail, you might want to hide out here just to ride some more.

The ride begins at the Chilao Flat, named for one of Vasquez' men, Jose Gonzalez. Regarded to be "hot" with a knife, Gonzalez was nicknamed "chilia pepper" and eventually, Chilao. In summer, the area gets hot despite its mile-high elevation, so begin climbing up Forest Service 3N14 early. This fire road offers scenic views of the Angeles high country to the northwest as it gently climbs up the north side of Mt. Hillyer. The route then drops on pavement to Horse Flats Campground, where you take a tough spur to the summit of Mt. Hillyer. If you can ride the whole thing without dabbing, you richly deserve the sublime views from the massive stone outcroppings atop Mt. Hillyer. Vasquez hid out right here, but you'll likely be content to merely eat lunch.

A tight, sometimes sandy, always fun single-track descent ensues on the Silver Moccasin Trail, requiring all your technical riding skills. Also, make sure not to let your eyes drift to the fantastic collection of rock formations adorning the trail. Just when you think this trail has got to end, it explores more terrain, eventually winding up in Charlton Flats Picnic Area. If you're beat, you can return to the start, but it's very worthwhile to go visit Vetter Mountain Fire Lookout via a climb (which is paid off with yet another looping single-track descent). After the Vetter Mountain detour, you take a quick spin up the dirt Mt. Mooney road, and finish off three loops of very fun biking.

General location: 28 miles northeast of La Canada (along CA 2).

Elevation change: Several climbs result in a 2,200-foot approximate gain.

Season: April to December; but winter months are okay if it hasn't recently snowed. Carry insect repellent at all times.

Services: Phone, water, rest rooms at Chilao Visitor Center. On weekends, you can buy food 0.25 mile north of Chilao Visitor Center on CA 2 at Newcomb's Ranch bar and cafe. All other services available in La Canada.

Hazards: Steep, sandy single-track, lots of waterbars, rocks alongside trail. Insects can be a problem; bring repellent.

Rescue index: This ride is always within riding distance of busy CA 2, and its triple-loop-figure-eight shape brings you close to both a visitor center and a ranger station at the beginning, middle, and end of the ride.

Land status: National forest.

Maps: *Trail Map of the Angeles Front Country,* from Tom Harrison Cartography,

5N04

Alder Saddle

Rosenita Saddle

N

0   ½   1
MILES

3N14

Mt.
Hillyer
6162

Santa Clara Divide Rd.

Mt. Hillyer Trail

Horse Flats
Campground

3N17

3N18

Loomis Ranch Rd.
(Private)

3N14

11W06

Silver
Moccasin
Trail

Three Points

2

Angeles Crest Hwy.

Ranger
Station

Chilao
Fire
Station

Chilao
Visitor
Center

Silver
Moccasin
Trail

Chilao
Campground

Coulter
Campground

P

CalTrans Facility

(Tough
Climb)

Mt.
Mooney

Vetter
Mountain
Trail

Lookout
Tower

Vetter
Mountain
5908

2

Charlton
Flats

3N16B

Angeles Crest Hwy.

(800) 265-9090 or (415) 456-7940, www.tomharrisonmaps.com. Available at sports stores in La Canada.

Finding the trail: From Interstate 210 in La Canada, drive uphill (northeast) CA 2 for 28 miles to the second turnoff to Chilao Flat (not the one diagonally across from a CalTrans equipment yard). Go left for just a few hundred feet, and park on the left, across the road from the Chilao Visitor Center. Forest Adventure Pass required.

Sources of additional information:

Chilao Visitor Center
Star Route 2
La Cañada, CA 91011
(626) 796-5541

Angeles National Forest
Los Angeles River Ranger District
4600 Oak Grove Drive
Flintridge, CA 91011

(818) 790-1151,
    TTD: (818) 790-9523
www.r5.fs.fed.us/angeles

Sport Chalet
920 Foothill Boulevard
La Cañada-Flintridge, CA 91011-0339
(818) 790-9800

Notes on the trail: Ride left (away from CA 2) on the road you came in on. You're heading toward the Chilao Campground, following signs pointing the way toward the Ranger Station. At 0.9 mile, turn right on Forest Service 3N21, following the sign pointing to the Ranger Station. In front of the Ranger Station, veer right onto well-signed FS 3N14. The pavement gives way to dirt at 2.1 miles, and a sandy, gradual climb ensues up a jeep road. If you ride in the morning, you'll have some welcome shade here. At 4.5 miles, turn right and ascend the paved Santa Clara Divide Road (FS 3N17) for 0.25 mile.

You're now at Rosenita Saddle. Head downhill on the pavement of FS 3N17, past a trail leading to the summit of Mount Hillyer (it's off-limits to wheeled travel, however). Instead, point your wheels downhill and descend to the turnoff for Horse Flats Campground. Go right on the paved road to Horse Flats, and reach a cul-de-sac and the end of the pavement at 5.5 miles. You're now right at the nexus of the Silver Moccasin Trail and the Mt. Hillyer Trail.

I strongly recommend climbing the Mt. Hillyer Trail for everyone who loves challenges that pay off with great views. So go sharply right onto the Mt. Hillyer Trail, which climbs steeply on tough, technical, and sandy single-track. Don't get frustrated if you have to dismount from time to time; the views from the top of Mt. Hillyer (which you reach at 6.7 miles) are extraordinary and make all your effort worthwhile.

At the top, take a well-deserved break on the abundant rocks crowning the summit. These rocks provide for some excellent nature viewing, so take a load off and relax—you'll need it for the challenging single-track to come. Heading back down the single-track Mt. Hillyer Trail, you bounce around rocks and through switchbacks, gaining rhythm as you go. At 7.7 miles, the trail deposits you back near Horse Flats Campground. Veer softly to the right whenever you can, trying to stay southwest of the paved campground road. At 7.9 miles, you're back near the intersection with well-marked Silver Moccasin Trail, FS 11W06. Head right on it, staying with the trail as it heads down toward Chilao Campground. You ride over a plethora of waterbars and intersect with Chilao Road once more at 9.7 miles. Jog left. (If you need to bail out for any reason, just follow the paved road back to nearby Chilao Visitor Center.) Otherwise, go immediately right on the well-marked Silver Moccasin Trail again. This is an especially buffed single-track which rolls over pine needles and fallen leaves. Stay on the path as it crosses a paved road once more at 10.2 miles.

An especially rollicking descent takes you to a canyon floor at 11.1 miles. Turn left and begin climbing once more, this time with feeling. At 12.3 miles, you reach a gate at the fork of two paved roads. If you're so tired that you want to miss one of the best vistas in the San Gabriels at Vetter Mountain Fire Lookout, go left on paved Charlton Flats Campground road and skip ahead to the paragraph beginning, "Take this paved road..." (Your mileage won't match, but you'll be able to follow the route without any problem.)

Otherwise, to see the great panorama at Vetter Mountain, go around the gate and right at the paved road that forks to the right. It's a fairly gentle climb to another gate at 13.8 miles. Go right here (a left takes you to CA 2), and climb to where the pavement ends at 14.6 miles. You'll find two dirt roads. Take the farthest one, FS 3N16B, which leads to Vetter Mountain. The climb becomes steeper as you grind up to the top at 15.3 miles. Gratefully dismount your bike, and scramble up to the Vetter Mountain Fire Lookout for its staggering views.

After you get your breath back, return to your bike for some fun single-track riding. Start riding back the way you came for a few hundred feet, then turn onto the well-signed Vetter Mountain Trail. It's a fun, switchbacky descent that's easier than the more technical stuff you've tackled earlier. You'll cross the paved road (which you just climbed to ascend Vetter Mountain) a couple of times, and glide by a picnic table before you plunge into a little ravine surrounding a creek. Climb out of it, keep going, and you'll soon find yourself at a paved road at 16.9 miles. Turn right. You've now completed the half figure 8 at the southern end of this ride. Congratulations.

Take this paved road, and you wind through the Charlton Flats area, passing picnic sites as you go. At 17.5 miles, go left on Angeles Crest Highway (CA 2) for 100 feet, then turn right on a paved road which quickly turns to dirt. You're now climbing Mt. Mooney, a healthy ascent. At the saddle at 18.3 miles, go left, avoiding all gates and fences.

A good descent returns you to CA 2 at 19.8 miles. Go right on it. There are some great views off to the right of the San Gabriel Wilderness Area. Spin up this stretch of CA 2 to the second Chilao turnoff at 21.2 miles. Turn left and return to the start at 21.3 miles.

RIDE 45 · Red Box-Rincon Road/Shortcut Canyon

AT A GLANCE

Length/configuration: 23.5-mile loop

Aerobic difficulty: Demanding; long ride with lots of climbing

Technical difficulty: Difficult; some good sections of dirt fire road; some rocky and sandy stretches; scree slope crossings

Scenery: Ride hugs exposed, brush-covered hillsides; notable exception— sycamore-shaded West Fork River

Special comments: Challenging route for fit and experienced cyclists

This loop covers 23.5 miles. It requires much strength and endurance, as well as good bike-handling skills. You will lose elevation for the first 5.6 miles to the West Fork Campground (with one short, hard uphill). From the campground, ride for 3.2 miles over moderately difficult to strenuous terrain. This is followed by a fast drop on Shortcut Fire Road to the West Fork of the San Gabriel River (with one brief, steep ascent). The 6.3-mile climb from the river up Shortcut Canyon to the Angeles Crest Highway is unrelenting. The cycling along the highway is half "fun descent" and half "this would be easy climbing if I weren't so tired."

The first 9.3 miles are on a dirt, four-wheel-drive road in good condition (with one short paved section). Shortcut Fire Road is rocky, loose, and sandy. Walking your bike over scree slides may be necessary. The Angeles Crest Highway is a paved two-lane highway.

Experienced cyclists will enjoy the challenging nature of this excursion. About 12 miles into the trip you'll come to the West Fork. The river is a welcome sight. Sycamores provide shade and a perfect spot to refresh yourself before beginning the long grind up Shortcut Canyon.

General location: Begins at the Red Box Station parking lot, 14 miles northeast of La Cañada-Flintridge on the Angeles Crest Highway (CA 2).

Elevation change: The ride commences at Red Box Station at 4,666 feet and then drops to 3,100 feet at the West Fork Campground. From here, you ascend to 4,040 feet at a water tank (near a trail that leads to Newcomb Saddle). From this crest you descend to the West Fork of the San Gabriel River at 3,200 feet and then pedal up to the Angeles Crest Highway at 4,800 feet. On the highway you drop to 4,400 feet, climb to 4,800 feet, and end at 4,666 feet. Add 300 feet for additional hills encountered en route. Total elevation gain: 3,240 feet.

Season: Spring and late fall. The uphill on Shortcut Fire Road is too exposed to recommend this loop as a summer ride.

Services: Water, a telephone, and pit toilets are available outside the closed ranger station at Red Box Station. All services can be found in La Cañada-Flintridge.

Hazards: Vehicular traffic may be encountered on the dirt fire roads described in this ride. Just after the Valley Forge Campground you will negotiate a creek crossing (3.4 miles from the start). It is paved and can be very slick. The descent on Shortcut Fire Road is rocky and steep; lower your saddle and stay in control. The Angeles Crest Highway has little or no shoulder, and traffic rushes along. The left turn from the highway into Red Box Station at the end of the loop is particularly dangerous. It is on a blind corner; cyclists may wish to pull onto the right shoulder, dismount, and walk their bikes across.

RIDE 45 · Red Box-Rincon Road/Shortcut Canyon

Rescue index: Help can be obtained in La Cañada-Flintridge.

Land status: National forest.

Maps: USGS 7.5-minute quadrangle maps: Chilao Flat and Mount Wilson.

Finding the trail: From I-210 (east of Los Angeles) take the exit for the Angeles Crest Highway (CA 2) in La Cañada-Flintridge. Drive northeast on the Angeles Crest Highway for approximately 14 miles to the Red Box Station parking lot on the right (south) side of the highway. Park in the parking lot; Forest Adventure Pass required.

Sources of additional information:

Angeles National Forest
Los Angeles River Ranger District
4600 Oak Grove Drive
Flintridge, CA 91011

(818) 790-1151,
   TTD: (818) 790-9523
www.r5.fs.fed.us/angeles

Notes on the trail: From the parking lot, turn left onto Red Box Rincon Road. After 1 mile of riding you will come to an intersection with signs pointing left toward the Valley Forge and West Fork Campgrounds. Turn left, stay on the main road, and continue past both campgrounds. Three miles beyond the West Fork Campground the road levels out and you'll pass a water tank and a trail to

Newcomb Saddle on the right; continue straight on the main road. Pass the Tumbler Shooting Area on the left. Watch for the signed Shortcut Fire Road on the left as you begin to descend. Turn left (one-half mile beyond the water tank) and pass your bike over the gate to follow Shortcut Fire Road downhill. Ride on Shortcut Fire Road for 9 miles to the Angeles Crest Highway. Turn left and follow the highway back to Red Box Station.

RIDE 46 · Mt. Wilson/Big Santa Anita Canyon

AT A GLANCE

CA

Length/configuration: 18.6-mile point-to-point ride (requires car shuttle); or a 29-mile loop ride

Aerobic difficulty: Strenuous; ascending to Mt. Wilson is certainly one of the steepest sustained climbs in all of Southern California

Technical difficulty: Very tough; narrow trails, tight switchbacks, rocks, and roots

Scenery: Mind-boggling Front Range views of the Los Angeles Basin, forests, and streams

Special comments: One of the most challenging rides in this book; definitely not for beginners

This 18.6-mile adventure is surely one of Southern California's most demanding rides—but it's equally rewarding. Though commonly undertaken as a point-to-point trip, the loop option is quite palatable given that the majority of its extra 11 miles are downhill. The only downside to this trip is that in order to ride the whole trail as listed here, you have to go on a weekend, since the access gate to Skyline Park is only open from 10 a.m. to 4 p.m. on Saturday and Sunday.

But there's little else wrong with this ride. Climbing from Pinecrest Drive in Altadena, you'll huff and puff up the dastardly steep Mt. Wilson Toll Road to Henninger Flats, a shady oasis with rest rooms and water. Stop here for a much needed break before climbing once again on a more gradual but still taxing incline.

After a lot more climbing, the Mt. Wilson Toll Road reaches an intersection with Mount Wilson Trail which can be used to reach Chantry Flat in case you've come up here on a weekday. Otherwise, you'll keep ascending to Mount Wilson and a well-deserved lunch in the pavilion in Skyline Park. After a look at the Mt. Wilson Observatory, you'll start a technical but fun descent down Sturtevant Trail. A quick climb to Mt. Zion brings more views, and then an amazing descent follows through Hoegee's Camp and along lower Winter Creek Trail. One final bit of climbing delivers you to Chantry Flats, your car, and the regret that you didn't pack a cooler with cold drinks to celebrate your epic ride.

RIDE 46 · Mt. Wilson/Big Santa Anita Canyon

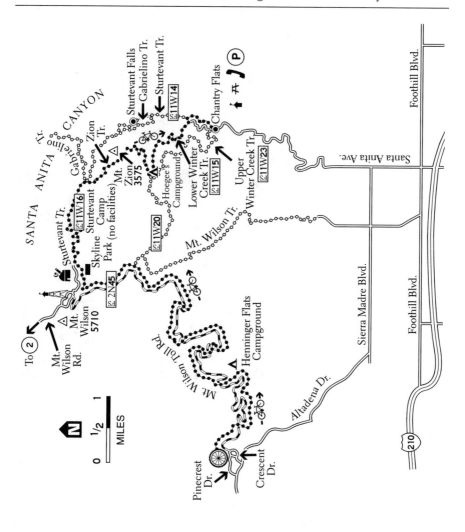

General location: About 4 miles north of I-210 in Altadena and Sierra Madre.

Elevation change: Massive: The start point is at 1,400 feet, and the summit is at 5,710 feet. That's 4,300 feet in one 9-mile climb. Add approximately 600 feet during the ride's ups and downs, and the total is about 4,900 feet.

Season: Year-round but with conditions: ride on a weekend; time your ride to avoid the Toll Road in the heat of the day in July; don't attempt climbing Mt. Wilson when the snow level is below 6,000 feet; and watch out for insects in June.

Threading the needle in
Big Santa Anita Canyon.

Services: Water is usually—but not always—available at Henninger Flats and
Skyline Park. Rest rooms are available at both of the above. All services are available in Sierra Madre and Altadena.

Hazards: Crowded trails below Henninger Flats are likely on weekends;
demanding climb; steep drop-offs, tough switchbacks on Sturtevant Trail;
numerous stream crossings.

Rescue index: Mt. Wilson Toll Road is accessible to Forest Rangers (call 911),
but single-track trails are rugged and remote. Be prepared for all sorts of conditions and weather, and be self-sufficient.

Land status: Angeles National Forest.

Maps: *Trail Map of the Angeles Front Country* available from Tom Harrison
Cartography, (800) 265-9090 or (415) 456-7940, www.tomharrisonmaps.com.
(However, the very beginning of Mt. Wilson Toll Road is off the map; otherwise
this map is excellent.) The "Big Santa Anita Canyon—Mt. Wilson Area" map is
available from Angeles National Forest. The "San Gabriel Mountains Recreation Topo Map—Western Section" is available at local bike stores.

Finding the trail: If shuttling, take I-210 to Santa Anita Avenue and travel north nearly 6 miles to the Chantry Flats parking area. Drop off the terminus car (a Forest Adventure Pass is required). In the second car, turn around and descend the way you came. After 5 miles, turn right on Sierra Madre Boulevard for 3 miles, then right on New York Drive for a mile, then right on Altadena Drive for a mile, right on Crescent Drive, and right on Pinecrest Drive. The trailhead is marked by a massive fence and gate, (open from sunrise to 6:30 p.m. PST and 8:30 p.m. PDT) which is impossible to miss. But you must park at least 300 yards away from it and then come back. If not shuttling, head to the trail directly by taking I-210 to Altadena Drive. (If coming from the east, exit at San Gabriel Boulevard and head straight at the bottom of the off-ramp until you intersect with Altadena Drive.) Head north on Altadena Drive approximately 3.5 miles, turn right on Crescent Drive, and then right onto Pinecrest to the trailhead mentioned above.

Sources of additional information:

Angeles National Forest
Los Angeles River Ranger District
4600 Oak Grove Drive
Flintridge, CA 91011
(818) 790-1151
TTD: (818) 790-9523
www.r5.fs.fed.us/angeles

Pasadena Cyclery
1670 East Walnut Street
Pasadena, CA 91106
(626) 795-2866

Pro Bikes of Arcadia
142 East Huntington Drive
Arcadia, CA 91006
(626) 447-3181

Notes on the trail: Ride through the gate at Pinecrest Drive and briefly downhill into Eaton Canyon. Enjoy this descent; it's your last for quite some time. At the end of a bridge, climb up and to the left. After 2.7 miles of steep, unshaded ascending, you'll reach Henninger Flats. Veer slightly left and head toward some white buildings. At a T intersection, stop and use the most welcome drinking fountain on the face of this Earth (it's on your left). Then get pedaling again, climbing to the right and uphill on Mt. Wilson Toll Road. There's a lot more shade now as you gradually switchback up to a nice vista spot with views of San Gorgonio and Mt. Baldy at 4.8 miles. Keep climbing, and at 5.3 miles you'll get your first glimpse of the radio towers atop Mt. Wilson. The road gets looser and rockier as you arrive at the intersection with a trailhead on your right at 7.6 miles. This is the Mt. Wilson Trail, which descends through Little Santa Anita Canyon and also connects to Hoegee Trail. If pressed for time, you could ride Mt. Wilson to Hoegee Trail to Hoegee's Camp, pass Upper Winter Creek Trail, and finally go right at Lower Winter Creek Trail, picking up the directions below at 16.2 miles. But you're smart and allotted a whole day to this ride, so keep climbing Mt. Wilson, which you'll finally summit at 9.2 miles. Congratulations! Now ride to your right and enter Skyline Park, which is open on weekends only. At 9.4 miles you'll reach a trail sign pointing to the left. You'll come back here in a bit, but for now veer right and up the dirt path next to the red rail fence. You'll ascend counterclockwise to the pavilion, where more spectacular views and picnic tables await. Have lunch, then circle back down to that trail sign and follow it. Sticking to the main road, you'll see signs pointing to "Trail" and "Echo

Point." Follow them. After passing to the left of a chain-link fence on a narrow dirt path, you'll reach the trailhead of Sturtevant Trail on your right at 10.4 miles. (The left option takes you to dead-end Echo Point.) If you like to lower your seat on technical descents, do so now. This is a fun but tricky single-track downhill on narrow, switchback trails. It eventually levels out at Sturtevant Camp at 3,200 feet, which you reach at 13.3 miles. Now go right on Upper Zion Trail, which is initially too steep to ride. It becomes gentler, however, as you spin up to the Mount Zion saddle at 14.4 miles. Take the short 0.1-mile spur on the left to the summit of Mount Zion at 3,575 feet. There are great views here if the chaparral is not too high. Returning to the Zion Trail at 14.6 miles, go left. Fast but tight, this is perhaps the best downhill section of the entire trip, a bonanza for experts. At Hoegee's Camp at 16.2 miles, go downhill on Lower Winter Creek Trail. This is a beautiful area, thick with sycamores, ferns, waterfalls, and stream crossings. After traversing Winter Creek numerous times, you'll intersect with the Gabrielino Trail at 17.9 miles. Turn right over the bridge for a short but steep pavement climb to Chantry Flats. (Don't be alarmed by a sign reading "Chantry Flats 5.5 miles"—that's only if you backtrack and take Upper Winter Creek from Hoegee's.) Going the correct way, you'll reach Chantry Flats parking area at 18.6 miles. If you didn't shuttle, ride back to your car at Pinecrest in Altadena by following the directions that start "In the second car . . ." in the "Finding the Trail" section earlier.

RIDE 47 · Mt. Wilson/Gabrielino Trail

AT A GLANCE

CA

Length/configuration: 29.2-mile point-to-point ride

Aerobic difficulty: Strenuous; ascending to Mt. Wilson is certainly one of the steepest sustained climbs in all of Southern California

Technical difficulty: Very tough; extremely narrow trails, steep drop-offs, and countless water crossings

Scenery: Stunning views of the Los Angeles Basin; even better high alpine vistas of San Gabriel Front Range, riparian habitats, waterfalls, and wildlife

Special comments: An extremely challenging but rewarding all-day ride; definitely not for beginners

Like its sister ride, the Mount Wilson/Big Santa Anita Canyon trip, this excursion tackles the climb up grueling Mt. Wilson Toll Road. But where its sibling only descends 9 miles, this trail goes downhill for a whopping 20! (Albeit with quite a few more portages.) Allot an entire day to this trip—you'll likely need it.

Climbing from Pinecrest Drive in Altadena, you'll huff and puff up the dastardly steep Mt. Wilson Toll Road to Henninger Flats, a shady oasis with rest

RIDE 47 · Mt. Wilson/Gabrielino Trail

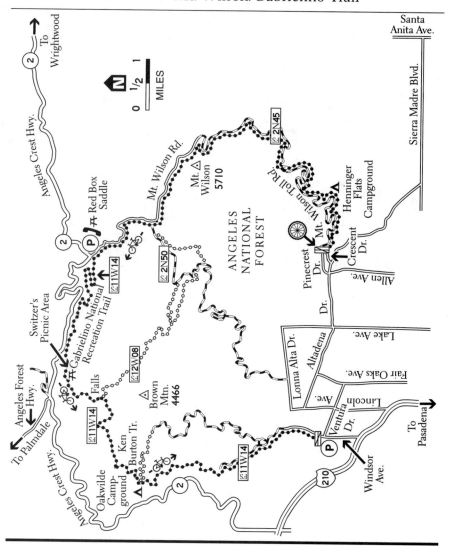

rooms and water. Stop here for a much needed break before climbing again on a more gradual but still taxing incline.

I guarantee that you can amaze your riding pals if, instead of gasping for every little breath, you calmly recount the history of Mount Wilson. It goes something like this: In the 1890s, Benjamin Wilson first looked at the unnamed peak you're ascending as a source of timber for his vineyard. Later, like a good Californian, he turned entrepreneur and charged hikers and equestrians a toll to ascend the road he built to the cool and bracing 5,710-foot summit of Mt. Wilson. He even built a hotel up there for weary travelers, which was heavily utilized during the

Rolling through the oasis at Henninger Flats.

San Gabriels' "Great Hiking Era" from the 1890s to the 1930s. The arrival of Angeles Crest Highway obviated the need for a toll road, and Wilson's road was deeded to the Forest Service.

After more ascending, you'll reach the summit of Mount Wilson. This is normally a gorgeous rest spot, but if the flies are out, keep going. You'll descend the paved road to Red Box Saddle and the crossing of the Gabrielino Trail. This is such a primo single-track that the Forest Service has even labeled it a national recreation trail.

Spin through Switzer's picnic area and turn left for some very advanced riding. The trail is narrow and impossibly scenic. You simply cannot believe trails, mountains, and vistas like this exist so close to downtown Los Angeles. After miles of great descending, you'll begin the first of many stream crossings, which could get monotonous if it weren't for the scenery and complimentary, summer-fruiting blackberries awaiting you at trailside between June and August. Finally, finish up with a spin through the Arroyo Seco and arrive at your shuttle car muddy, tired, and sweaty—but most of all, exultant.

General location: In the Los Angeles River Ranger District of the Angeles National Forest, north of Altadena and Pasadena.

Elevation change: Massive! The start point is at 1,400 feet, the summit is at 5,710 feet, and the finish is at 1,200 feet. Tack on some climbing during the "downhill portion" and overall that's 4,700 feet of climbing, 4,900 feet of descent.

Season: Year-round but with some conditions: Time your ride to avoid the Toll

Road in the heat of the day in July; don't attempt climbing Mt. Wilson when snow level is below 6,000 feet; and watch out for insects in June.

Services: Water is usually, but not always, available at Henninger Flats, Skyline Park at the summit of Mt. Wilson, and at Red Box Station. Bring your own to be safe. Rest rooms are available at Henninger Flats and Red Box Station. All services are available in Pasadena and Altadena.

Hazards: Crowded trails on weekends below Henninger Flats; demanding climb; exceedingly steep drop-offs; tough switchbacks; countless stream crossings. It's essential that you telephone the Los Angeles River Ranger District (see Sources) to check on the condition of the Gabrielino Trail between Switzer's Picnic Area and Oakwilde Campground before embarking on this ride. The Gabrielino Trail is an extremely advanced trail in good condition; if damaged, it would be impassable and dangerous.

Rescue index: Help is usually available at Henninger Flats, the summit of Mt. Wilson, and Red Box Station along the ride's route. However, single-track portions are extremely rugged. Be prepared for all sorts of conditions and weather, and be self-sufficient.

Land status: Angeles National Forest.

Maps: The "Trail Map of the Angeles Front Country" is available from Tom Harrison Cartography, (800) 265-9090 or (415) 456-7940, www.tomharrison maps.com. (However, note that the very beginning of Mt. Wilson Toll Road is off the map; otherwise this map is excellent.) The San Gabriel Mountains Recreation Topo Map—Western Section is available from Fine Edge Productions, (760) 387-2412.

Finding the trail: This is a shuttle ride. Drive two cars on I-210 to the Arroyo/Windsor Exit in Pasadena. Go north from the off ramp on Windsor Avenue for 1 mile. Turn left into the unsigned parking lot before Windsor intersects with Ventura Street in a sharp turn to the right. Park the terminus car here. In the second car, go east at the intersection of Windsor and Ventura. Turn left at Fair Oaks Avenue, then right onto Altadena Drive. Continue to Allen Avenue. Take a left on Allen, then an immediate right onto Pinecrest Drive. Continue on Pinecrest to the trailhead. It is marked by a massive fence and gate, and is open from sunrise to 6:30 p.m. PST and 8:30 p.m. PDT—it's impossible to miss. But you must park at least 300 yards away from it and then come back.

Sources of additional information:

Pasadena Cyclery
1670 East Walnut Street
Pasadena, CA 91106
(626) 795-2866

Sport Chalet
920 Foothill Boulevard
La Cañada, CA 91011
(818) 790-9800

Angeles National Forest
Los Angeles River Ranger District
4600 Oak Grove Drive
Flintridge, CA 91011
(818) 790-1151
TTD: (818) 790-9523
www.r5.fs.fed.us/angeles

Notes on the trail: Ride through the gate at Pinecrest Drive and briefly downhill into Eaton Canyon. Enjoy this descent; it's your last for quite some time. At the end of a bridge, climb to the left. After 2.7 miles of steep, unshaded ascent, you'll reach Henninger Flats. Veer slightly left and head toward some white buildings. At a T intersection, stop and use the greatest drinking fountain on the face of this Earth on your left. Then get pedaling again, climbing to the right and heading uphill on Mt. Wilson Toll Road. There's a lot more shade now as you gradually switchback up to a nice vista spot with views of San Gorgonio and Mt. Baldy at 4.8 miles. Keep climbing and at 5.3 miles you'll get your first glimpse of the radio towers atop Mt. Wilson. As the crow flies, it seems quite close. But you're not a crow, so shut up and keep climbing. The road gets looser and rockier as you arrive at the intersection with the Mt. Wilson Trailhead on your right at 7.6 miles. Keep climbing on the toll road, and you'll finally reach the summit of Mt. Wilson at 9.2 miles. Congratulations!

After catching your breath, veer softly to the right of the knoll with all the radio antennae and begin descending the paved road to Red Box. Be extremely careful here; you're likely to encounter a lot of motorists who have little mountain-driving experience. Reaching Red Box at 13.9 miles, turn left into the parking lot and head for the northwest corner, site of the trailhead to the Red Box Gabrielino NRT Trail. Start riding down it. The Gabrielino Trail between Red Box and Switzer's Camp is a jewel with firm single-track and a rush of forest scenery. Watch out for hikers, especially on blind turns. At 16.2 miles stay left on the main trail, which descends in a westerly direction. Soon you'll be riding parallel to a stream that always seems to draw unwary riders into falling into it. Nature-trail signs soon begin cropping up as you approach Switzer's Camp. At 18.3 miles, cross a bridge and briefly hit pavement. Turn left, heading downhill until the pavement ends at the well-marked Gabrielino Trail. Ride onto the Gabrielino.

After some portaging and stream crossings, the trail climbs sharply up from a creek. The hillside is so steep and the trail so narrow in this section that a tall chain-link fence has been erected to protect users from falling. At 19.8 miles, you'll reach the turnoff to Bear Canyon. There's a great waterfall down there, but it's not worth the climb back up, so veer right and slightly uphill. The views are astounding here, and so is the descent. If you're not squeamish about the narrow trail or steep cliffsides, you will be mightily impressed.

After riding on some extremely narrow paths for a long time through some heavily wooded sections, your forearms start screaming. Thankfully, the trail levels out by the time you reach Oakwilde Camp at 23.5 miles. Riding through the camp, you'll soon arrive at a set of concrete stairs. Go left and bounce right down those stairs, following the obvious trail. Crossing and recrossing a streambed innumerable times makes for slow going for a while. The trail also may seem to vanish at times, but by keeping your eyes peeled, you'll always find it again. Around the 24-mile mark, look for some 6-foot-tall blackberry bushes on the right. From mid-June to early August, they make a perfect snack. At 24.4 miles, a sign points the way to Pasadena. Follow it, and start climbing a quarter-mile incline. Take in the great views alongside a fence guarding the narrow trail and then plunge downhill over rideable rubber waterbars. At 25 miles, you'll spill out onto the Arroyo Seco floor and the Paul Little Picnic Area. Now follow the main

Arroyo Seco trail left and downhill toward Pasadena. If you somehow managed to stay dry up to this point, get over it—over the next mile, you will surely get wet. Eventually, the endless stream crossings give way to scenic bridges. There are more users on this section of the Arroyo Seco, so stay in control as you roll through Gould Mesa Campground and return to pavement at 28 miles. Stay straight, and ride back up the gently sloping pavement to the parking lot and your terminus car at 29.2 miles.

RIDE 48 · Inspiration Point

AT A GLANCE

Length/configuration: 13.7-mile combination; a 6.1-mile loop and several out-and-back segments, totaling 7.6 miles of riding

Aerobic difficulty: Difficult; steepest climbing is encountered in the first 2.5 miles

Technical difficulty: Demanding; dirt roads include loose rocks, sand, and ruts; trails are narrow, exposed, and filled with obstacles

Scenery: Views of San Gabriel Mountains and sprawling megalopolis

Special comments: Mt. Lowe was once a thriving tourist attraction; interpretive displays describe aspects of the mountain's history

This is a moderately difficult, sometimes strenuous loop with some one-way spurs. The ride is 13.7 miles long. The first 2.5 miles are a tough ascent on paved FS 2N50. From here the climbing becomes more moderate and the route changes to a two-wheel-drive dirt road. The road was originally built for electric streetcars, but they could not surmount a grade steeper than 7%. This dirt portion of FS 2N50 allows for good traction with only short stretches of sand, loose rocks, and rutting. The descent on the single-track Sam Merrill Trail to Echo Mountain requires a high degree of technical skill, as does the return to FS 2N50 on Echo Mountain Trail. These trails hug canyon walls, are extremely narrow, and contain steep switchbacks. Sheer drop-offs are common. Sections of these single-tracks are rutted and sandy, and they present obstacles like old railroad ties, exposed tree roots, and rocks. Some segments of the trails have been "knocked down" into the canyon. Carrying your bike over these degraded areas will minimize further damage and help assure you safe passage.

After 1.8 miles of riding, you'll come across the first of several interpretive displays depicting aspects of a once-popular tourist attraction located here. In 1893, entrepreneur Thaddeus Lowe opened his Mount Lowe Railway. It employed a steep incline railroad and trolleys to bring sightseers into the San Gabriel Mountains. Also of interest are sighting tubes at Inspiration Point that aid in identifying distant landmarks.

RIDE 48 · Inspiration Point

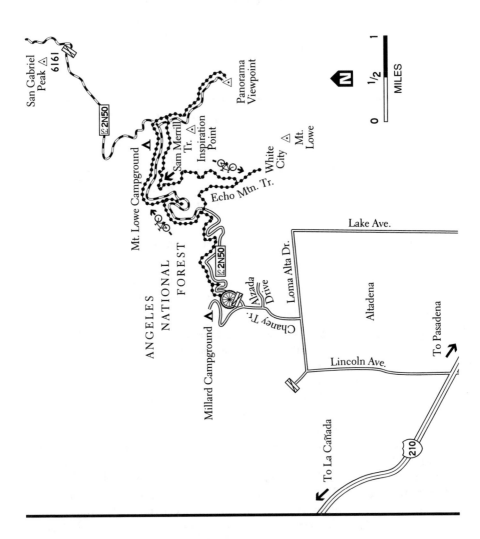

General location: The route starts at the end of Chaney Trail above Altadena, approximately 15 miles north of downtown Los Angeles.

Elevation change: The paved road begins at 2,080 feet, turns to dirt at 3,480 feet, and then climbs to a high point of 4,500 feet at Inspiration Point. The route drops to 4,400 feet at Panorama Point before returning to 4,500 feet and descending on the Sam Merrill Trail to Echo Mountain at 3,207 feet. This is followed by a climb to 3,480 feet along Echo Mountain Trail, and then a quick downhill on pavement to 2,080 feet. Total elevation gain: 2,793 feet.

Horseshoe Curve and
Millard Canyon.

Season: This circuit is suited to year-round travel. Winter rains and hot temper-atures in the summer are limiting factors. Sweet-smelling Spanish broom is in bloom throughout the spring.

Services: There is a water spigot just past the start of the ride and one at the inter-section of Sam Merrill and Echo Mountain Trails. But these sources cannot be guaranteed, so bring all of the water you will require with you. All services are available in Altadena and neighboring communities of the Los Angeles area.

Hazards: You are likely to see other mountain bikers and hikers using these roads and trails; control your speed while descending. Sam Merrill and Echo Mountain Trails are narrow and contain many obstacles. Walk your bike where necessary. You may encounter Forest Service and utility-company vehicles on FS 2N50.

Rescue index: Help can be found in Altadena.

Land status: National forest.

Maps: USGS 7.5-minute quadrangle maps: Mount Wilson and Pasadena.

Finding the trail: From I-210 (east of Los Angeles) take the exit for Lincoln Avenue and follow Lincoln Avenue north through Altadena. After 1.8 miles on

Lincoln Avenue, turn right (east) on Loma Alta Drive. Follow Loma Alta Drive for 0.6 mile to Chaney Trail. Turn left (north) on Chaney Trail. Stay left on Chaney Trail at the Y intersection with Alzada Drive. Climb on Chaney Trail approximately 1 mile beyond Alzada Drive to another intersection at a sign for Brown Mountain Road and Millard Canyon. Stay to the right at this intersection and park in the pullout on the right near the locked gate. Do not block the gate. Forest Adventure Pass required.

Source of additional information:

Angeles National Forest
Los Angeles River Ranger District
4600 Oak Grove Drive
Flintridge, CA 91011

(818) 790-1151
TTD: (818) 790-9523
www.r5.fs.fed.us/angeles

Notes on the trail: Pass around the side of the gate and climb on the paved, unsigned FS 2N50. Go past Echo Mountain Trail on the right and continue on FS 2N50 as it turns to dirt. Pass the Mount Lowe Campground on the left after approximately 5 miles of riding on FS 2N50. At 0.25 mile beyond the Mount Lowe Campground, turn right at the sign for Inspiration Point. Notice the small sign for Sam Merrill Trail on the far right, partially hidden by vegetation, as this ride follows Sam Merrill Trail on the return. Continue to Inspiration Point (0.25 mile from the turnoff of FS 2N50), and on to Panorama Viewpoint, 1 mile past Inspiration Point at a water tank. Return the way you came, turning left down Sam Merrill Trail (Trail 12W14). Sam Merrill Trail is rough and fragile; to avoid it you can turn left at this point onto FS 2N50 and retrace your path to your car. Sam Merrill Trail will take you to Echo Mountain Trail. Turn left onto Echo Mountain Trail and pass a water spigot and a trail to Castle Canyon on your left. Continue straight on Echo Mountain Trail to the trail's end at the concrete foundations of White City. Turn around and return on Echo Mountain Trail, continuing on the main trail as side trails branch off. Turn left onto FS 2N50 and descend to your vehicle.

RIDE 49 · Josephine Saddle/Strawberry Peak

AT A GLANCE

Length/configuration: 16.6-mile loop on fire road, single-track, and pavement

Aerobic difficulty: Difficult; a strenuous climb up to Josephine Saddle with intermittent, steep single-track climbs

Technical difficulty: Very difficult; an exceedingly narrow trail with steep drop-offs

Scenery: Huge expanses of the front and backcountry of the western San Gabriels, including Mt. Gleason, Pacifico Mountain, and dramatic, varying views of Strawberry Peak

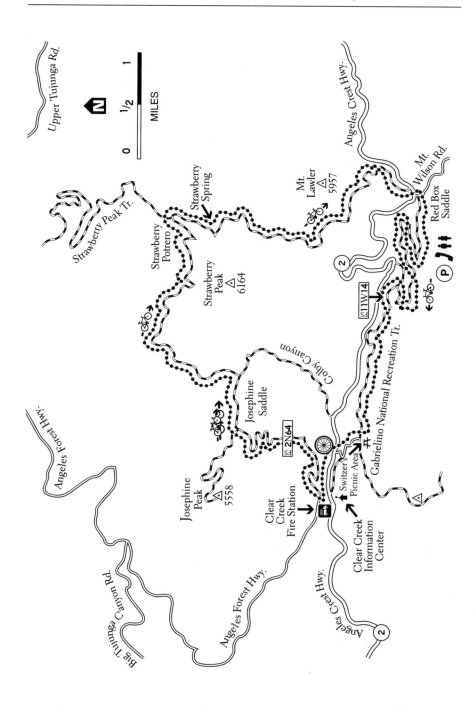

Special comments: A single-track feast on some of the most challenging but fun paths in the area—definitely not for beginners or the squeamish

Some days everything comes together. Some days you get to experience, all at once, the joy of crisp fall weather, the buzz of riding in a way that transcends your usual capacities, and even the confidence of a bike performing just the way its supposed to. Maybe it's luck, but more likely there's a mystical appeal to some trails that bestows good fortune. This is one of those trails.

This 16.6-mile loop begins inauspiciously as it ascends a steep but unremarkable fire road toward Josephine Peak. But if you can wipe the sweat out of your eyes, you'll notice how the desert-like scrubland becomes more striking as it merges with the alpine ecosystem above it. The scenery and riding are not bad, you'll think, as you reach a saddle between Josephine and Strawberry Peaks. From here, however, the terrain becomes spectacularly striking, and the single-track becomes increasingly challenging.

Circling around dramatic Strawberry Peak on a narrow, clinging mountain trail, the views are never less than jaw-dropping; the single-track is never less than thrilling. Surrounded by stately Jeffrey pines, you'll drop into the lush oasis of Strawberry Potrero for a bit before ascending toward a shoulder between Strawberry Peak and Mt. Lawler. From here, the ride speeds up to the Red Box parking area, then shifts into high speed down the Gabrielino Trail into Switzer's Camp. It's only when you get to your car that you'll realize you've just ridden more than 14 miles of pure single-track.

General location: 10 miles north of La Cañada in the Angeles National Forest.

Elevation change: 1,400 feet, much of it in the initial fire road climb to Josephine Saddle.

Season: Year-round, as long as you don't ride up to Josephine Saddle during the heat of a summer day. Don't ride within a few days of winter storms either; snow often falls at the upper altitudes of this ride, but usually melts soon.

Services: Water and rest rooms are usually available at Red Box, two-thirds of the way through the ride. All other services are available in La Cañada.

Hazards: Exceedingly narrow single-track with steep drop-offs; watch out for poison oak.

Rescue index: This area is deserted on weekdays, and curiously not that busy on weekends, so don't count on passersby. Help is available in La Cañada and at Clear Creek Ranger Station at the beginning of the ride.

Land status: National forest.

Maps: The "Trail Map of the Angeles Front Country" is available from Tom Harrison Cartography, (800) 265-9090 or (415) 456-7940; www.tomharrison maps.com.

Finding the trail: From the intersection of I-210 and CA 2 in La CaÒada, take CA 2 (Angeles Crest Highway) north into Angeles National Forest. After 9 miles of twisting roads, you'll reach the intersection with Angeles Forest Highway. The parking lot to Switzer Picnic Area is on the right, 0.45 mile past the Angeles Forest Highway. Park here. A Forest Adventure Pass is required.

Sources of additional information:

Clear Creek Information Station
Junction of CA 2 and Angeles Forest Highway
(818) 355-0712 (Friday and Sunday only; hours vary)

Angeles National Forest
Los Angeles River Ranger District
4600 Oak Grove Drive

Flintridge, CA 91011
(818) 790-1151
TTD: (818) 790-9523
www.r5.fs.fed.us/angeles

Sport Chalet
920 Foothill Boulevard
La Cañada, CA 91011
(818) 790-9800

Notes on the trail: From the parking lot, turn left (downhill) on CA 2/Angeles Crest Highway. At 0.6 mile, turn right onto the Angeles Forest Highway. In less than 100 yards, turn right on the gated dirt road marked "Josephine Road" (FS 2N64). The road climbs sharply, which allows you to get your bearings fairly quickly. You're heading toward the saddle between the strawberry-shaped peak on the right and the steep summit on the right. The terrain seems unable to make up its mind here—it's both alpine and high desert. The smells of eucalyptus and creosote are intoxicating, and you'll forget how hard the climb is as you reach the saddle at 3.1 miles. Go right. At 3.6 miles, keep left past the intersection with Colby Canyon Trail. You're now on a narrow single-track that starts to circle Strawberry Peak in a clockwise direction. Tight, narrow, but stupendously scenic, this part of the ride is utterly compelling. At 5.5 miles, a rocky vista provides amazing north-facing views. A big descent leads to the sandy but lush valley floor known as Strawberry Potrero. The trail is harder to follow here, but if you stay to the right of the lone picnic table, you'll be fine. At 7 miles, you'll reach a **Y** junction. Head right and start climbing a sporadically tough trail, one that will likely result in some dismounts. At 7.6 miles you'll reach Strawberry Spring, which is often dry during and just following drought years. The climb eases as you reach a saddle between the east side of Strawberry Peak and Mt. Lawler at 8.9 miles. Now, cling to Mt. Lawler for a little more than a mile. Far below you is CA 2; at times it seems that one careless turn could send you tumbling all the way down to the roadway. At a fork in the trail at 10.3 miles, head left (downhill). The descent really opens up, and it's fun, fast flying all the way down to CA 2. Turn right on CA 2 and then take an immediate left into the Red Box Saddle area. At the northwest corner of the parking lot, at 11.4 miles, is the trailhead to the Red Box Gabrielino NRT Trail. Start riding down it. (However, if you're pressed for time, you can follow CA 2 from Red Box all the way back to your car.) The Gabrielino Trail between Red Box and Switzer's Camp is a jewel with fast, firm single-track and a rush of forest scenery. At 13.7 miles, keep left on the main trail, which descends in a westerly direction. Soon you'll be riding parallel to a stream—be aware that this stream always seems to catch unwary riders. Around the 15-mile mark, nature trail signs begin cropping up as you enter Switzer's Camp. At 15.8 miles, you'll cross a bridge and hit pavement. Veer right and follow the pavement uphill for a taxing climb back to your car and the end of a stupendous ride at 16.6 miles.

RIDE 50 • Brown Mountain/Ken Burton and El Prieto Options

AT A GLANCE

CA

Length/configuration: Ken Burton Option: 15.1-mile combination (2.6 miles out-and-back (1.3 miles each way), plus a 12.5 mile loop) on pavement, fire road, and single-track; El Prieto Option: 8.8-mile combination (2.6 miles out-and-back (1.3 miles each way), plus a 6.2-mile loop) also on pavement, fire road, and single-track

Aerobic difficulty: Difficult—the climb up Brown Mountain for both options is relentless

Technical difficulty: Difficult—the switchbacks on the Ken Burton Trail are some of the tightest in the area; the El Prieto Trail is nearly as demanding

Scenery: Sun-baked south-facing slopes, verdant north-facing mountains, and riparian ecosystems along the Arroyo Seco; on the Ken Burton Option, there's an optional spur to an impressively large (but man-made) waterfall

Special comments: Less than 20 minutes from downtown Los Angeles, the two options for this route function as both hammerhead training rides and meccas for those who love tight single-tracks

The harder ride choice on this route is the Ken Burton Option, and it delivers an unsparing body blow. It leaves you with a sweaty back, waterlogged feet, and an inspired noggin. But you won't mind a bit. Because long after you forget the hot, grueling climb and endless stream crossings, you'll still be impressed by how much of a positive impact mountain bikers can have on a trail system if they work together.

Starting from a point overlooking the famous Jet Propulsion Laboratory in Pasadena, the route climbs up Brown Mountain Road, a steep and unforgiving taskmaster. (The El Prieto Option begins two thirds of the way through the grueling climb and offers an amazing, but somewhat brief, single-track descent—a near-perfect after-work ride.) The road climbs again past the turnoff for El Prieto, and you'll be sweating for certain before it levels out a bit. Eventually, your destination, a saddle below Brown Mountain peak, becomes visible and you ride a little faster. Through salt-stinging eyes, you see a sign marking the beginning of the Ken Burton Trail, the first new path built in the San Gabriels in over 40 years. Working with the Forest Service, the laudable Mt. Wilson Bicycling Association built the trail to serve as a link between Brown Mountain and the Arroyo Seco, thereby paying tribute to the memory of the late Ken Burton.

Impeccably maintained and consistently challenging, the trail is a memorable tribute. Scores of tight switchbacks on this incomparably scenic hillside

RIDE 50 · Brown Mountain/Ken Burton & El Prieto Options

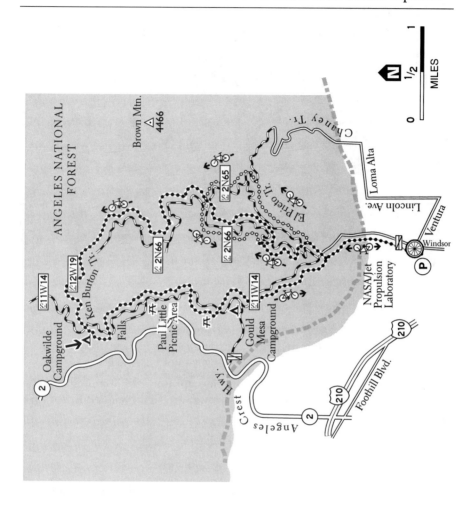

deliver cyclists into the lower Arroyo Seco trail just above Oakwilde Camp. Dozens of stream crossings, many of them unrideable, slow your progress, but the lush riparian landscape is so cool and inviting, you won't really mind that much. As if that weren't enough, there are even deliciously juicy (and fully edible) blackberries growing alongside the trail in spots from mid-June to late August. After the water crossings cease, the trail becomes more populated, so slow down and enjoy the mostly gentle descent back to your car.

General location: Just northeast of Pasadena.

Taking the road less traveled at Brown Mountain Saddle.

Elevation change: Ken Burton Option features a climb of 1,600 feet, from 1,200 feet to 2,800 feet. The El Prieto Option has a gain of 1,160 feet.

Season: Year-round as long as you don't ride up Brown Mountain during the heat of a summer day. Avoid this route during heavy rains—a mountain biker died here during a flood in early 1998.

Services: Water is available in spots along the Arroyo Seco portion of the ride. The ride passes through several campgrounds, many of which are booked in the summer.

Hazards: Very tight single-track with steep drop-offs, challenging stream crossings, and poison oak.

Rescue index: There is a ranger station at the end of the Arroyo Seco trail where help can be obtained.

Land status: National forest.

Maps: *Trail Map of the Angeles Front Country*, from Tom Harrison Cartography, (800) 265-9090 or (415) 456-7940, www.tomharrisonmaps.com.

Finding the trail: Take Interstate 210 to the Arroyo/Windsor Exit in Pasadena. Go north from the off ramp on Windsor Avenue for 1 mile. Turn left into the unsigned parking lot before the road takes a sharp bend to the right. Park here; the ride begins from the north end of the parking lot.

Sources of additional information:

Angeles National Forest
Los Angeles River Ranger District
4600 Oak Grove Drive
Flintridge, CA 91011
(818) 790-1151
TTD (818) 790-9523
www.r5.fs.fed.us/angeles

Pasadena Cyclery
1670 E. Walnut Street
Pasadena, CA 91107
(626) 795-2866

Notes on the trail: From the parking lot, head north where three paved roads immediately come together. Take the middle road and go around the gate. You're now in the often crowded lower Arroyo Seco (literally "Dry Ditch"—a glaring misnomer). At 1.3 miles turn right at the sign which points the way to "Lower Brown Mountain Road." You're now on Forest Service 2N66, which soon turns to dirt. Stay on the main road past Forest Service employee residences and the junction with El Prieto Canyon Trail. The road doesn't waste any time as it climbs sharply out of the wooded Arroyo Seco and onto the exposed south-facing slope of Brown Mountain. You gain a great deal of elevation up to a saddle and the intersection with FS 2N65 at 4.2 miles. Here is where you must make the choice between the longer Ken Burton or shorter El Prieto Options. If you want to ride the longer route, skip ahead to the paragraph "Otherwise, to keep going...".

El Prieto Option riders should go right at this point to descend a fun fire road known for its banked turns. Don't go too fast, however, for at 5.5 miles, you'll reach the somewhat easy-to-miss turnoff for the single-track El Prieto Trail. And, believe me, you don't want to miss it. The trail descends lush El Prieto Canyon, where it crosses a stream, flows off natural jumps, and ends too quickly. Try to ride slowly here—there are other users, and you don't want to rush through this amazing single-track, anyway. At 7.3 miles you reach Brown Mountain Road again and turn left, soon reaching pavement and the fork you passed earlier. Make your way back to the start on the paved road overlooking the Jet Propulsion Laboratory, for a total ride of 8.8 miles.

Otherwise, to keep going on the Ken Burton Trail, turn left at the saddle/intersection of FS 2N65 and FS 2N66. You have another 0.25 mile of tough ascent, and then it becomes much easier. The trail sometimes descends in spots. At 5.6 miles, you reach an intersection with a spur leading to a shady overlook. Stay right and continue uphill. The views of the L.A. Basin increase as you reach a saddle below the summit of Brown Mountain at 7 miles.

Here, signs mark the beginning of the Ken Burton Trail, also known as FS 12W19. If you're the type that prefers to lower your seat before tricky descents, by all means start lowering. The next 2 miles are staggeringly beautiful but somewhat perilous—your technical riding skills will be in full demand. At 9.4 miles you cross a stream feeding into the Arroyo Seco drainage and immediately intersect with the Gabrielino Trail. Go left and ride through Oakwilde Campground. You'll soon arrive at a set of concrete stairs. Go left and bounce right down those stairs, following the obvious trail. You cross and recross a streambed innumerable times, and as a result it's slow going for a while.

The trail also may seem to vanish at times, but by keeping your eyes peeled, you'll always find it again. Around the 10-mile mark, look for some six-foot-tall blackberry bushes on the right. From mid-June to early August, they make a perfect snack. At 10.3 miles, a sign points the way to Pasadena. Go the way it indicates, and start climbing a 0.25-mile incline. Take in the great views alongside a fence guarding the narrow trail and then plunge downhill over rideable rubber waterbars. At 10.8 miles, you emerge onto the Arroyo Seco floor at the Paul Little Picnic Area. (If you have time, instead of going left on the Gabrielino Trail, go straight out on a quarter-mile spur to a picturesque waterfall cascading down from the Brown Canyon debris dam. Just note that any mileage incurred on such a spur is not included here.)

Back at Paul Little, follow the main Gabrielino trail downhill toward Pasadena. If you somehow managed to stay dry up to this point, get over it. Over the next mile, you will surely get wet. Eventually, the endless stream crossings give way to scenic bridges. There are more users on this section of the Arroyo Seco, so stay in control as you roll through Gould Mesa Campground and return to pavement and the Brown Mountain Road turnoff at 13.8 miles. Stay straight, and ride back up the gentle sloping pavement to the parking lot at 15.1 miles.

RIDE 51 · Mendenhall Ridge/Pacoima Canyon

AT A GLANCE

Length/configuration: 28-mile combination (2.9 miles each way, with a 22.2-mile terminus loop)

Aerobic difficulty: Moderate; there are only two significant climbs, one long and gentle, the other short and fairly steep

Technical difficulty: Tough; the primary descent is rocky, narrow, manzanita-strewn, and full of water crossings

Scenery: Grand views of the San Gabriels high country, plus a shady, oak- and sycamore-lined canyon

Special comments: A paradox of a ride: easy to climb but difficult to descend, this is also one of the San Gabriels' most accessible yet least utilized trails—a wise fall or winter selection for intermediates to experts

This 28-mile lollipop-shaped combination ride allows cyclists to easily access the backcountry of the Angeles National Forest's Pacoima Canyon. Barely exceeding 5,000 feet in elevation, this route makes a good choice for those late fall, winter, and early spring days when your other favorite, long San Gabriel rides are covered in snow. But since few others go back here, don't ride alone, and be self-sufficient.

Starting a mere 7 miles from I-210, a fire road gradually climbs to Mendenhall Ridge. It then graciously traverses from one side of the ridge to the other in

RIDE 51 · Mendenhall Ridge/Pacoima Canyon

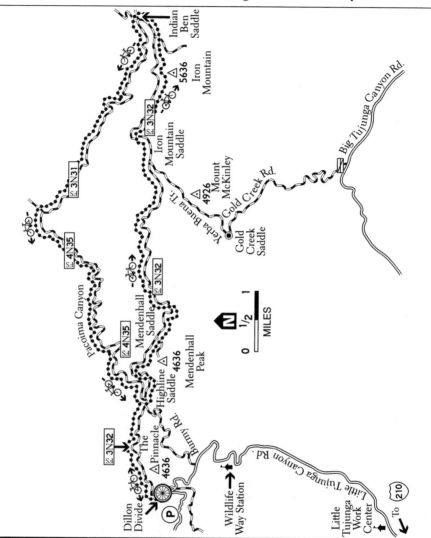

order to treat riders to compelling views of both Pacoima Canyon and the front range of the San Gabriels. You keep waiting for the climb to get nasty, but it never does, even as the surroundings become more and more alpine. From the choice lunch spot at Indian Ben Saddle, embark on a rocky, mostly single-track descent into Pacoima Canyon that encompasses all the challenges you missed during the climb. Technical riding skills are required here as you dodge rocks, flee grasping manzanita, and cross one picturesque stream after another. It's not a bad idea to ride here in the fall, when football is on your mind. That's because you'll often face the kind of dilemmas running backs encounter, like: "If I lower my shoulder and do a Bronko Nagurski on that manzanita, can I still pull a Barry Sanders juke around that boulder?"

Better to give your brakes a rest once in a while and let the beautiful sycamores and oaks soothe you until you reach the canyon floor and a welcome fire road. After a steep climb back to the Mendenhall Ridge road, it's all downhill back to the start.

General location: 7 miles north of San Fernando in the Tujunga District of the Angeles National Forest.

Elevation change: From 2,700 feet to 5,300 feet in initial ascent, with a steep 400-foot climb near the ride's end.

Season: October through June, with prime foliage in late October through November.

Services: No services are available on or near the trail. All services are available in San Fernando.

Hazards: Very rugged terrain, rocks, clawing manzanita, and stream crossings. In addition, keep your ears and eyes open for target shooters—though shooting is now illegal in this area, it's occasionally still practiced.

Rescue index: Though physically close to civilization, this is rugged, remote country that sees little use. Don't ride alone here.

Land status: National forest.

Maps: USGS 7.5-minute quadrangle maps: Condor Peak and Sunland. Also, the *Trail Map of the Angeles Front Country* is available from Tom Harrison Cartography, (800) 265-9090 or (415) 456-7940, www.tomharrisonmaps.com.

Finding the trail: From I-210 in San Fernando exit at Osborne Street and go north from the off ramp. Get in the left lane immediately and turn left onto Osborne Street. Osborne Street turns into Little Tujunga Canyon Road. (Visit the Los Angeles River Ranger District Office at 12371 North Little Tujunga Canyon Road for more information.) The road becomes progressively steeper and more twisty. Just when the road begins to descend, 7.6 miles from I-210, you'll find Dillon Divide and the intersection on the east (or right-hand) side of the road with FS 3N32. Park in the small parking area here (being careful not to block the gate) or at any one of the dirt turnouts a few hundred yards away. A Forest Adventure Pass is required.

Sources of additional information:

Los Angeles River Ranger District
Little Tujunga Work Center
12371 Little Tujunga Cyn.
San Fernando, CA 91342
(818) 899-1900
TTD (818) 899-1620
www.r5.fs.fed.us/angeles

Vicious Cycles
7965 Foothill Boulevard
Sunland, CA 91040
(818) 352-2454

Notes on the trail: From the intersection of FS 3N32 and Little Tujunga Canyon Road at Dillon Divide, go east on FS 3N32. The first few hundred yards may be the steepest on the entire trail, but don't despair. The fire road is mostly smooth and gentle, and in no time you'll reach the junction with FS 3N37 on your right at 2.8 miles. Stay left on FS 3N32 and keep spinning uphill, past the junction with FS 4N35 at 2.9 miles. This is where you'll be climbing out of Pacoima Canyon later, but for now, you're riding on the massive loop section of this combination ride. Just before the 5-mile mark, the road crosses from the north to the south side of Mendenhall Ridge, giving beautiful views of the San Gabriel Front Range. A small descent here and there interrupts the climb as the road traverses between the two sides of the ridge. At 9.2 miles, pass the shot-up trailhead sign marking the Yerba Buena Trail on your right. Soon afterwards, the surrounding terrain becomes markedly more alpine, with shady pine trees and cool air pockets keeping you refreshed.

After about 12 miles of climbing, you'll glide down to Indian Ben Saddle and the intersection with FS 3N31 hard on your left at 12.9 miles. Be sure to clamber up to the circular helipad/watertank at Indian Ben Saddle for lunch and some mesmerizing views of Strawberry Mountain, Josephine Peak, and Mt. Wilson. Now head west on FS 3N31 down into Pacoima Canyon. The single-track is rough, rocky, and technical but dry. At 16.4 miles you'll reach the canyon floor. Depending on the upkeep of the trail, you may or may not notice that FS 3N31 has changed into FS 4N35. Don't worry about it in any case; by continuing downhill and westerly in the direction you've been traveling, you'll be fine. Presently you'll encounter numerous creek crossings. If the trail ever seems to vanish, just continue downstream and keep your eyes peeled, and eventually you'll find the path. After miles of boulder bashing and stream thrashing, the single-track transforms into a fire road at 18.3 miles. It's a welcome change of pace, and the next 4 miles pass quickly until the road veers left and begins climbing sharply at 22.2 miles. There's a puny downhill or two, but it's mostly steep ascents here. Turn right at the intersection with an unmarked fire road at 24.2 miles, and right again back onto the "stick" part of the lollipop at the intersection with FS 3N32 at 25.1 miles. It's all downhill from here, and you'll return to your car at 28 miles.

RIDE 52 · La Tuna Canyon

AT A GLANCE

Length/configuration: 9.7-mile loop on fire road, single-track, and pavement

Aerobic difficulty: Moderate/difficult; steady, occasionally tough fire road climb

Technical difficulty: Difficult; the single-track is steep and narrow

Scenery: Outstanding city views of the San Gabriel Valley, Burbank, and Glendale, and vistas overlooking the Front Range of the San Gabriels

Special comments: An unexpectedly excellent single-track makes this the crown jewel of rides in the Verdugo Hills.

Starting near the towns of La Crescenta and Montrose, the route climbs a short but sometimes tough fire road. Do it on a clear day, and you'll be amazed how each switchback delivers yet another unanticipated view of the San Gabriels. Just when you think the scenery can't get any more spectacular, you reach a saddle boasting a nearly 360-degree view of greater Los Angeles. All mountain bikers who have recently moved to L.A. should ride up here. On a clear day, you can easily make out the Santa Susana, Santa Monica, Santa Ana, and sometimes even the San Bernardino mountain ranges you grow to love as a Southern Californian mountain biker.

After a fun descent down a ridge-top fire road, you'll turn onto an unobtrusive, unmarked single-track. It's like another world here, with tunnel-like lush vegetation, picturesque little streams, and even an abandoned truck or two. The single-track rises and falls and eventually pops out on La Tuna Canyon Road, where a pavement climb brings you back to your car. From there, take I-210 to Pennsylvania Avenue and go south. Keep going on Honolulu Avenue and follow signs to charming downtown Montrose (just east of La Crescenta) where numerous cafés wait for you to celebrate this little gem of a ride.

General location: On the north edge of the Verdugo Hills, just west of La Crescenta and Montrose.

Elevation change: 1,600-foot gain, 1,300 feet of it in one fire road climb, with the rest on pavement at the ride's end.

Season: Year-round, but avoid climbing the fire road in the heat of a summer day.

Services: None are available on the trail. All services are available in La Crescenta and Montrose.

Hazards: Poison oak appears on the single-track portion of the ride.

Rescue index: There are no phones on the trail, but the trail is never far from La Tuna Canyon Road and civilization.

Land status: Santa Monica Mountains Conservancy Parkland (even though it's not in the Santa Monica Mountains).

Maps: The *Trail Map of the Angeles Front Country* is available from Tom Harrison Cartography, (800) 265-9090 or (415) 456-7940, www.tomharrisonmaps.com. Online map available at ceres.ca.gov/smmc/latunamap.htm.

Finding the trail: Take I-210 to La Tuna Canyon Road in La Crescenta. Directly across La Tuna Canyon Road from the eastbound I-210 off-ramp is a gated road with a moderate-size parking area in front of the gate. Park here, being careful not to block any traffic going through the gate.

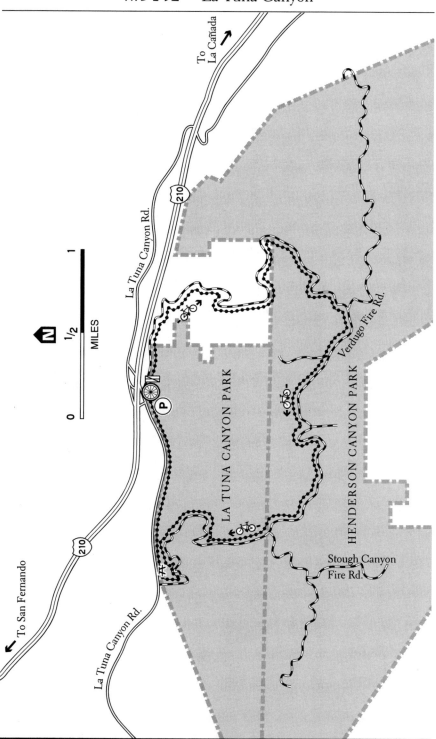

To La Cañada

210

La Tuna Canyon Rd.

N

MILES

0   ½   1

To San Fernando

La Tuna Canyon Rd.

210

P

LA TUNA CANYON PARK

HENDERSON CANYON PARK

Verdugo Fire Rd.

Stough Canyon
Fire Rd.

Sources of additional information:

Santa Monica Mountains
   Conservancy
5750 Ramirez Canyon Road
Malibu, CA 90265-4474
(310) 589-3200
ceres.ca.gov/smmc

Montrose Bike Shop
2501 Honolulu Avenue
Montrose, CA 91020
(818) 249-3993

Notes on the trail: From the parking area, go around the gate and start pedaling up a paved road. At 0.4 mile, turn right onto a steep (but still paved) road. After a quarter mile or so of very tough climbing, the pavement gives way to dirt. You're now on Hostetter Fire Road, and right away there are great views of the San Gabriels and its eponymous valley. The climb eases a bit, and at 3.6 miles, you'll reach a T-intersection with Verdugo Fire Road. Outstanding views of Burbank, Glendale, Universal City, Griffith Park, and even the Pacific Ocean accompany you as you go right and downhill. At 4.4 miles stay right at a Y-junction. The downhill increases in steepness, and you can really fly along this ridge. Keep your eyes peeled for a trail descending into a narrow canyon on your right, which you'll encounter at 6 miles. (If you reach Stough Canyon Fire Road, you've gone too far.) Turn right onto the trail, a single-track that plunges down to the stream-lined bottom of rugged La Tuna Canyon. Stay on the obvious trail at all times, even when you leave the canyon floor and it feels as if you're climbing way too high above the visible La Tuna Canyon Road. After a lot of zigzags and switchbacks, the trail descends again to a streambed. Stay right on the trail through here and you'll reach La Tuna Canyon Road and a small picnic area at 8.4 miles. Turn right on this road, which features fast traffic and narrow lanes, and ride until you reach the parking area at 9.7 miles.

SAUGUS DISTRICT
AND MT. PINOS

The two areas grouped together in this region at first seem to have little in common. Mt. Pinos, at 8,832 feet, is the tallest mountain in the White Mountains range. On the other hand, the ridges and hills of the Angeles National Forest's former Saugus District (recently renamed the Santa Clara/ Mojave Rivers Ranger District), are runts compared to their siblings in the San Gabriel Mountains high country. Here, most peaks are less than 5,000 feet. Moreover, when bikers in the Saugus District are suffering in sweltering heat, riders on Mt. Pinos may be cycling through snow.

And yet the two areas have a kinship. Standing between California's immense Central Valley to the north and the mountains which define the Los Angeles Basin to the south, these areas are linked by a single roadway, Interstate 5, which provides easy access to the region's farthest reaches. Both areas are uncrowded, undiscovered, and under an hour's drive from the San Fernando Valley.

At one time, grizzly bears foraged for food in these mountains, and antelope played in the plains below. They may be gone now, but another endangered Californian is just starting to make a comeback in the area. The California condor, which was facing near-certain extinction, is now being slowly reintroduced into the area. Keep your eye out for this magnificent bird as you cruise over the round, chaparral-covered knolls of the Saugus District or circle Mt. Pinos on a pine-scented single-track.

It's also interesting to note that the area is home of one of the few roadways listed on the National Register of Historic Places. The Old Ridge Route was originally built in 1915 to provide early motorists a way to travel through the rugged area where the San Gabriels, Tehachapis, and coastal ranges come together. Indeed, the Ridge Route is sometimes credited for keeping California together when some politicians wanted to divide the north from the inaccessible south. Soak in the local lore while you make some rugged history yourself.

RIDE 53 · Sierra Pelona/Five Deer Trail

AT A GLANCE

Length/configuration: 11.3-mile combination (2.1 miles each way, plus a 7.1-mile loop) on single-track and fire road

Aerobic difficulty: Moderate; a steady climb, steep in a few sections

Technical difficulty: Moderate/difficult; a technical single-track made easier by a mostly gentle grade

Scenery: Spring poppies, thirst-quenching views of Bouquet Reservoir, and unimpeded sights of the Tehachapis and San Gabriels

Special comments: A moderate ride in terms of challenges and views, but off the charts when it comes to fun single-tracks

For some reason, this area is more popular with anglers, dirt bikers, and even hunters than cyclists. In fact, accidentally riding this 11.3-mile combination on the first day of deer hunting season can be downright terrifying. But then, if any single-track in the region is worth taking a bullet for, it's the Five Deer Trail.

Starting 17 miles north of Saugus, the ride climbs FS 6N08, an exposed fire road with only a taste of shade near the woodsy Artesian Spring. You then push past an assortment of Off Highway Vehicle (OHV) trails until you reach a ridge with all sorts of unimpeded views. There's nothing majestic here, mostly just chaparral and sage, but you can sure see for a long way. Given the ordinary terrain, it comes as a surprise when you discover how magical Five Deer Trail is. The route is a sinuous delight, seeming to travel through every bit of moisture and shade this area has to offer. This is one of those trails that somehow seems to offer significantly more downhill than uphill. Don't ask why, just accept it as you fly back down to FS 6N08, then descend some more back to your car.

General location: 17 miles north of Saugus in the Santa Clara/Mojave Rivers Ranger District of the Angeles National Forest.

Elevation change: Approximately 1,400 feet in one steady climb.

Season: March through November. Spring brings blossoming matilja poppies, which are especially prevalent after wetter-than-normal winters.

Services: No services are available on the trail. All services are available in Saugus.

Hazards: Dirt bikers and all-terrain vehicles; hunters (especially around the start of deer season in early November); and loose, rocky trails in sections.

Rescue index: Help is available at Santa Clara/Mojave Rivers Ranger District office, approximately 9 miles south of the start of the ride on Bouquet Canyon Road.

Land status: National forest.

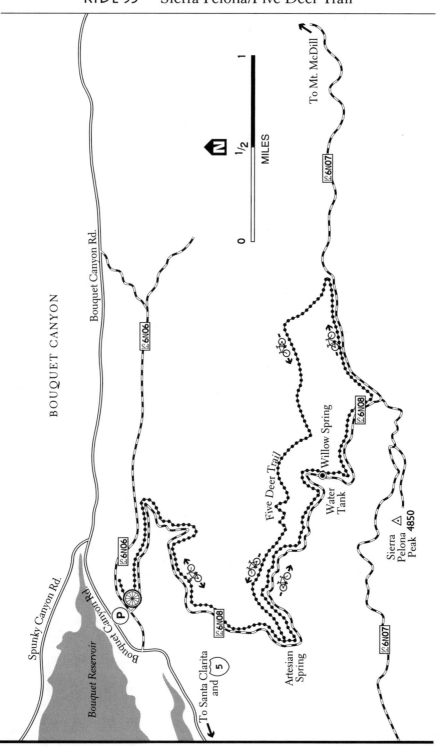

Maps: USGS 7.5-minute quadrangle map: Sleepy Valley.

Finding the trail: Take I-5 into the Santa Clarita Valley, exit at Valencia Boulevard, and go east approximately 4 miles. Turn left (north) on Bouquet Canyon Road. Eight miles from Valencia Boulevard, you'll pass the Santa Clara/Mojave Rivers Ranger District office, a good place to bone up on the area. After another 8 miles, approach Bouquet Reservoir. When the reservoir's banks begin to retreat away from the road on your left side, start looking on your right for FS 6N08. Turn right onto this dirt road. (Though it's marked with signs warning it's not suitable for two-wheel-drive vehicles, the road is in fact quite smooth; you could drive a long way up it if you had to.) But you don't have to; just go about 200 yards to where FS 6N08 intersects with FS 6N06. Park well to the side to avoid blocking traffic on the road. A Forest Adventure Pass is required.

Sources of additional information:

Angeles National Forest
Santa Clara/Mojave Rivers
   Ranger District
30800 Bouquet Canyon Road
Saugus, CA 91350
(661) 296-9710

TTD (661) 296-9710
www.r5.fs.fed.us/angeles

Cycle 2000
26867 Bouquet Canyon Road
Santa Clarita, CA 91355
(661) 296-5538

Notes on the trail: Start climbing up FS 6N08, which travels east before some hairpin turns and switchbacks redirect it in a southerly direction. At 2.1 miles, you'll reach shady Artesia Spring camp, an unofficial parking lot/base camp for hunters, dirt bikers, and even cyclists. This is also where you'll be returning on FS 14W14 (Five Deer Trail). But for now, keep climbing out of the shade of Artesia Spring. Though numerous OHV tracks intersect with this road, stay on the main trail (which is a lot less rocky than the OHV paths). At 4.5 miles, you'll reach the Sierra Pelona summit. Take in the expansive views, then head left on the ridge trail FS 6N07. It feels as if you're on the ridge for much more than 0.8 mile, but you're really not. It just seems longer for the same reason Christmas Eve lasts forever when you're a kid: anticipation. In any case, keep your eyes peeled to the left of the ridge for Five Deer Trail, which may or may not be signed (any signs would say "FS 14W14"). You're in the right area after descending a steep little ridge face to the left of a big oak tree. At 5.4 miles, you can see a number of bike and motorcycle tracks turning sharply left and downhill. Follow them, for this is indeed FS 14W14/Five Deer Trail. Though paths intersect it from time to time, the main trail is obvious except at a fork at 5.8 miles. Turn left here. There are a couple of steep sections and even some tiny uphills, but it's all quite rideable and fun for more than 3 miles. At 9.1 miles cross over an OHV road and continue heading straight, reaching FS 6N08 once more at 9.2 miles. Turn right and fly down this now-familiar road to your vehicle at 11.3 miles.

RIDE 54 · Elderberry Forebay/Cienaga Loop

AT A GLANCE

Length/configuration: 27.1-mile combination (2.7 miles each way, plus 21.7-mile loop) on fire road, macadam, OHV routes, and some single-track

Aerobic difficulty: Difficult; there are several climbs, some of them quite strenuous

Technical difficulty: Moderate/difficult; some very steep, rocky descents

Scenery: Spring wildflowers, bird's-eye views of Lake Castaic, plus views of mountains stretching to the farthest reaches of the Tehachapis and San Gabriels

Special comments: A long ride in rugged terrain that boasts spectacular views of Lake Castaic; though not for beginners or squeamish intermediates, this half-day ride is a choice excursion for those times when you want a trail all to yourself

There's a lot to look at on this 27.1-mile combination ride, but one thing you probably won't see is other trail users. Given the route's scenery, diverse terrain, and challenges, this condition might change one day. But until then, this area is ripe for the taking.

Located 11 miles from I-5 in Castaic, the ride begins on FS 6N32 in a shady canyon next to the Warm Springs Rehabilitation Center, which treats drug and alcohol addiction. The shade soon gives way to a treeless fire road. There's virtually no shade for another 20 miles, so don't be shy with the sunscreen. A modestly graded but consistent uphill takes you up to a saddle where the loop part of the ride begins on FS 7N13. More moderate climbing delivers you near the summit of Warm Springs, from which point you descend into the lovely Necktie Basin. In spring, this area is aflame with poppies and other wildflowers and makes for a good picnic spot if the ground isn't too wet. After some short uphills and downhills, Lake Castaic comes into view. It's odd when you compare the heavily utilized lake to the sparsely employed trails surrounding you. Boaters don't lack for company, that's for sure.

You're now so high above the lake that it seems as if there's no way you could descend directly down to it, but you do. The plunge is rocky, vertical, and, curiously, lined with wonderfully scented rosemary bushes. According to firsthand author research, it's easy to lose control on the loose, steep trail and perform a face-plant into a surprisingly prickly rosemary bush. If such an event happens to you, the rest of the ride may just make you think that someone has clamped your nose inside a wonderfully fragrant piece of Italian focaccia bread—a bizarre though not entirely unpleasant sensation.

In any case, one way or another you'll eventually reach man-made Lake Castaic's adjoining Elderberry Forebay. As you wind around Elderberry Forebay on

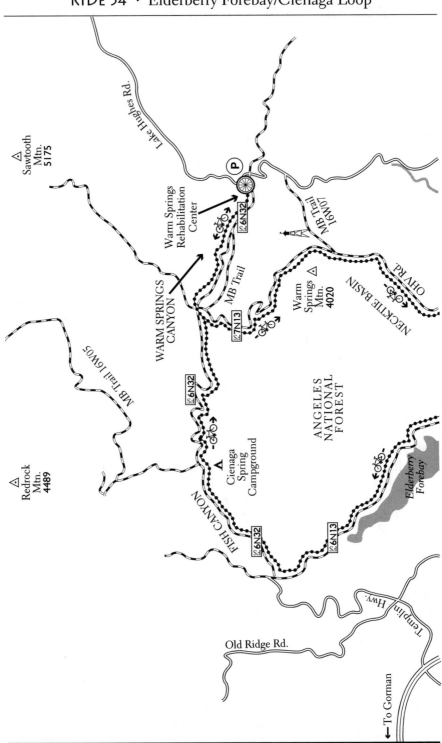

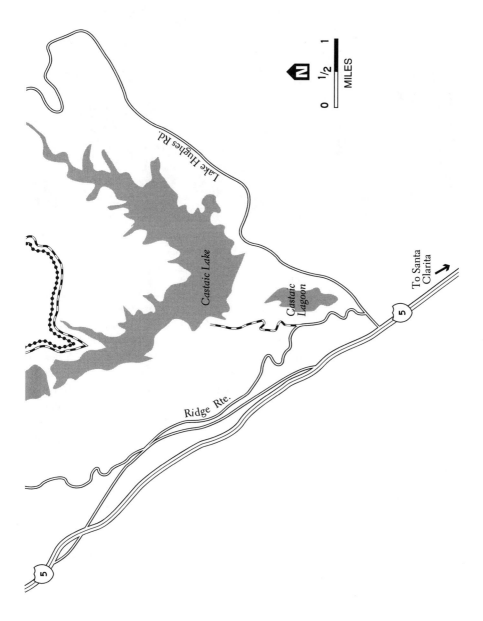

It's no mistake; that's indeed Lake Castaic.

level terrain, it's hard to keep yourself from musing what a great sound "Elderberry Forebay" makes. It could be the name of a character from a Victorian romance novel, or even the moniker of a psychedelic hippie band from the 1960s. The name stays on your lips long after you leave the water's edge and turn right to climb up shady, narrow Fish Canyon to Cienaga Camp. A good portion of your riding in this section takes place on a concrete-lined creekbed—so it's not the place to be during wet weather. After quaint, woodsy Cienaga Camp, the ascent intensifies, and it's a grind to finish the loop and return to the saddle where FS 6N32 and FS 7N13 intersect. Go down the way you came and you'll reach the end of the ride.

General location: 11 miles northeast of I-5 at Castaic in the Saugus District of Angeles National Forest.

Elevation change: An initial climb of approximately 1,500 feet (from 2,400 feet to 3,900 feet) followed by several smaller climbs and descents.

Season: Year-round, but avoid this trail for several days after major rainstorms and during especially hot days.

Services: There's a campground with pit toilets at Cienaga Camp. All other services are available in Castaic. (Bike shops can be found in Santa Clarita.)

Hazards: Very steep, rocky descents; prevalent, sharp rosemary bushes; and significant stream riding.

Rescue index: Remote and rugged despite its proximity to Lake Castaic. There are phones at Warm Springs Rehabilitation Center at the end of the ride, but this area is off-limits to visitors. Do not enter unless it's an emergency.

Land status: National forest.

Maps: USGS 7.5-minute quadrangle maps: Whitaker Peak and Warm Springs Mountain.

Finding the trail: Take I-5 into the Santa Clarita Valley and exit at Lake Hughes Road in Castaic. Proceed northeast on Lake Hughes Road for 11 miles to the junction with Warm Springs Road. Park on the small gravel parking turnout immediately north of Warm Springs Road. A Forest Adventure Pass is required.

Sources of additional information:

Angeles National Forest
Santa Clara/Mojave Rivers
   Ranger District
30800 Bouquet Canyon Road
Saugus, CA 91350
(661) 296-9710

TTD (661) 296-9710
www.r5.fs.fed.us/angeles

Cycle 2000
26867 Bouquet Canyon Road
Santa Clarita, CA 91355
(661) 296-5538

Notes on the trail: From the gravel parking lot, go around the gate on the west side of Lake Hughes Road and proceed westbound on FS 6N32/Warm Springs Road. After some sandy climbing, reach a saddle and a four-way intersection at 2.7 miles. Stay to the far left, go around a gate, and begin climbing FS 7N13. At 6.1 miles, just before the gated road on the left leading to Warm Springs Lookout Tower (destroyed in a fire), turn right and head downhill through pretty Necktie Basin. The trail roller-coasters to 8.3 miles, at which time the descent down a narrow OHV road to Elderberry Forebay takes over. Watch out for loose, rocky, and rutty terrain as well as the occasional dirt biker. At 10.6 miles go around a gate, and a third of a mile later, the OHV road ends at the junction with a crumbling macadam road. Turn right onto the road and stay right when it forks at 11.4 miles. After some roller-coastering, the road begins a grind of a climb at 12.4 miles. The climb soon levels off as you begin riding on unsigned FS 6N13 while shadowing the banks of Elderberry Forebay for 5 miles. You'll gain views of the massive pipes extending down from Templin Highway to a power plant at the north end of Elderberry Forebay and eventually pass the plant as you come to a gate at 17.4 miles. Go around the gate and stay right. The road itself is Forest Service property, and the surrounding terrain is state-owned land off-limits to exploration, so stay on the road. Also remain vigilant, for just when you begin noticing yellow posts marked "CA State Property" you'll want to be ready to turn right at 18.1 miles on FS 6N32, which really should be signed but (as of this writing) is not. (If you intersect with a single-lane bridge on your left, then you've gone too far by about a third of a mile.) Heading northeast on FS 6N32, enter Fish Canyon, which narrows and becomes shadier. At times, it's so tight that you end up riding on the concrete creekbed, which can be slippery with algae. At 20.2 miles, cycle through Cienaga Camp and some more stream crossings. Stay on FS 6N32 by veering right at the northeast end of Cienaga Camp. (Make sure you're not riding directly north on FS 6N32C.) An initially tough but mostly moderate climb brings you back to your first saddle and the intersection with FS 7N13 at 24.4 miles. From here, you have two options to return to the start. You can veer left and descend FS 6N32 (which you climbed at the beginning of the ride), which brings you back to the parking area at 27.1

miles. Or, for a single-track challenge, go right on FS 7N13 for a few hundred feet and turn left on the unsigned trail which drops into Warm Springs Canyon. When I rode here, the Forest Service hadn't signed this path, but it's called the Allegheny Trail. The Forest Service labels it as a "mountain bike trail," and at press time it was in good shape and fun to ride as it descends on some tight single-track. But it features countless stream crossings and is very prone to flood damage. It's a good idea to call the Santa Clara/Mojave Rivers Ranger District office at the number above to check on trail conditions. If it's rideable, you'll have a good time descending through the canyon, then rejoining FS 6N32. Go right on FS 6N32 for 0.9 mile back to the start. Veer left and descend FS 6N32 the way you came until you reach the parking area at 27.1 miles.

RIDE 55 · Burnt Peak/Upper Shake

AT A GLANCE

Length/configuration: 14-mile combination; 12-mile out-and-back (6 miles each way) and a 2-mile out-and-back (1 mile each way)

Aerobic difficulty: Difficult; plenty of steep grades

Technical difficulty: Moderately difficult dirt and gravel road ride; sections of washboarding, loose rocks, and ruts

Scenery: Views of Tehachapi Mountains and Antelope Valley

Special comments: Pretty picnic spot at Upper Shake Campground; large pines shade site

This out-and-back, 14-mile round-trip is recommended for strong cyclists and determined intermediates. The entire circuit is on unpaved four-wheel-drive roads in fair to good condition. The first two miles climb moderately on FS 7N23. This is followed by a relentlessly steep and fairly technical one-mile ascent on FS 7N23A. The next mile brings some relief as the road descends and then rolls up and down moderately. From here, the route climbs sharply for two miles to the summit of Burnt Peak. The steep sections of FS 7N23A contain some washboarding, loose rocks, and ruts.

The predominant vistas on the way to Burnt Peak are of the Antelope Valley and the Tehachapi Mountains. Once on top, you'll obtain a panoramic view of the surrounding countryside. On the return from the peak, take a side trip to the Upper Shake Campground. This is a cool, quiet spot with large shade trees and picnic tables.

General location: Begins at the intersection of FS 7N23 and Pine Canyon Road, 4.3 miles west of Lake Hughes in the Santa Clara/Mojave Rivers Ranger District of the Angeles National Forest, approximately 80 miles north of downtown Los Angeles.

RIDE 55 · Burnt Peak/Upper Shake

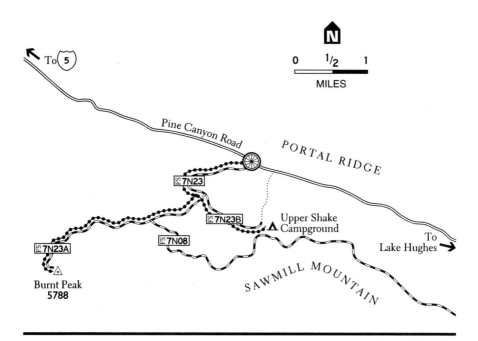

Elevation change: The ride starts at 4,265 feet and climbs to a high point of 5,790 feet atop Burnt Peak. On the return you drop to 4,465 feet at the Upper Shake Campground. From the campground you climb to 4,665 feet and then descend to 4,265 feet at Pine Canyon Road. Total elevation gain: 1,725 feet.

Season: Early spring through late fall. It may be cooler and windy at the crest of Burnt Peak; be prepared with warm clothing. Weekend and holiday traffic can be heavy.

Services: There is no water available on this ride. All services can be found in the town of Lake Hughes.

Hazards: The roads described in this ride access public campgrounds and see a fair amount of vehicular traffic. Be careful when approaching blind corners.

Rescue index: Help is available in the town of Lake Hughes.

Land status: National forest.

Maps: USGS 7.5-minute quadrangle map: Burnt Peak.

Finding the trail: The route begins at FS 7N23 and Pine Canyon Road. From downtown Los Angeles, follow I-5 north for approximately 60 miles to the exit for CA 138/Quail Lake/Lancaster. From points north, take I-5 south 6 miles beyond Tejon Pass to the exit for CA 138/Quail Lake/Lancaster. Proceed east on CA

138/Lancaster Road for 4.2 miles, to an intersection where CA 138/Lancaster Road goes left and Pine Canyon Road/N2 goes straight. Continue straight on Pine Canyon Road/N2 toward Lake Hughes and Elizabeth Lake. After approximately 15 miles you'll come to a sign on the right that reads "Upper Shake 3 miles, Sawmill Campground 5 miles, Burnt Peak 7 miles." This is the start of FS 7N23. Park in the pullout at the beginning of the road; cars may be left overnight.

Source of additional information:

Angeles National Forest
Santa Clara/Mojave Rivers
   Ranger District
30800 Bouquet Canyon Road

Saugus, CA 91350
(661) 296-9710;
TTD (661) 296-9710
www.r5.fs.fed.us/angeles

Notes on the trail: Follow FS 7N23 for 2 miles to the intersection with FS 7N23B and FS 7N23A; turn right onto FS 7N23A toward Burnt Peak. Continue straight at the sign reading "Burnt Peak 3 miles." Reach the ride's first turn-around point at the Burnt Peak microwave towers. Return the way you came. At the intersection with FS 7N23 and FS 7N23B, turn right onto FS 7N23B and follow it to the Upper Shake Campground. The Upper Shake Campground is the ride's second turnaround point. Return the way you came.

RIDE 56 · Liebre Mountain/Golden Eagle Trail

AT A GLANCE

CA

Length/configuration: 16.4-mile loop on broken pavement, fire road, and single-track

Aerobic difficulty: Difficult; initial mile of climb up Liebre Mountain is quite tough, but most grades are fairly gentle

Technical difficulty: Moderate/difficult; single-track portions are sometimes quite technical

Scenery: Confluence of several mountain ranges, Pyramid Lake, open grasslands, oak woodlands, golden eagles, Antelope Valley, and (in spring) abundant poppies

Special comments: A ride that dabbles in history as well as scenery, it's well worth the trip from Los Angeles

The ride begins on the Old Ridge Route, one of only three roadways in California to be listed on the National Register of Historic Places. After the turn of the 20th Century, there was actually talk that Southern and Northern California should be divided into two states because the mountain ranges south of Bakersfield were nearly impenetrable. The Old Ridge Route, originally built in 1915, changed all that. The Old Ridge Route carved through this confluence of the San Gabriel and Tehachapi mountain ranges, making it possible to drive from Castaic to Gorman in a day or two. It was an especially curvy drive. The road wound around mountains instead of blasting through them because there was simply no room in the budget for dynamite. But every spring, the area erupts with vivid explosions—of color. The late March–early April blooming season of brilliant orange poppies is something to see.

Oh, and the ride's pretty good too. After a spin on the broken pavement of the Old Ridge Route, an initially tough climb up Liebre Mountain's fire road brings you to the beginning of the mountaintop Golden Eagle single-track. Its a wonderful, sinuous trail, but can be so overgrown in spots that it may not be worth riding its lower section. Whether you ride the entire loop as prescribed here or modify it in your own way, you'll have a good time making your own history here.

General location: In the northwest section of the Saugus District of the Angeles National Forest, about 10 miles southeast of Gorman.

Elevation change: Ride begins at about 3,800 feet, and climbs to 5,700 feet, with some undulations, for a total gain of approximately 2000 feet.

Season: April to December; snow can close roads in winter.

Services: No water on trail. Most services available in Gorman.

Hazards: Be extremely mindful of autos on the fire road; it's easy to forget they're allowed on it. In November, deer hunters are common here.

Rescue index: Help is available in Gorman, about 10 miles from the trailhead.

Land status: National forest.

Maps: Angeles National Forest map, available from the Forest Service and local bookstores, or USGS 7.5-minute quadrangle map: Liebre Mountain (Golden Eagle portion is not depicted)

Finding the trail: From Los Angeles, take I-5 north to CA 138. Go east 4.2 miles and turn right on Pine Canyon Road/County Road N2. After 2.6 miles, veer right onto Old Ridge Route/FS 8N04. Continue 0.5 mile, and park on the right near the ruins of Sandberg's Summit Hotel. Forest Adventure Pass required.

Sources of additional information:

Angeles National Forest	Saugus, CA 91350
Santa Clara/Mojave Rivers	(661) 296-9710
Ranger District	TTD (661) 296-9710
30800 Bouquet Canyon Road	www.r5.fs.fed.us/angeles

Notes on the trail: From the ruins of Sandberg's Summit Hotel, turn right (south) on FS 8N04/The Old Ridge Route (sometimes called "Ridge Road"). The broken-pavement road curves and gently rises for 2.6 miles to the intersection on the left with dirt FS 7N23. Go left here, and begin climbing in earnest. The first 0.75 mile of the climb is by far the toughest of the entire route, so don't despair. You'll do fine.

Stay on the main road, which is officially designated as a "Back Country Discovery Trail," bypassing all intersections with other dirt roads. You climb through scenic grasslands until about 6.5 miles, when the road begins to level off. The

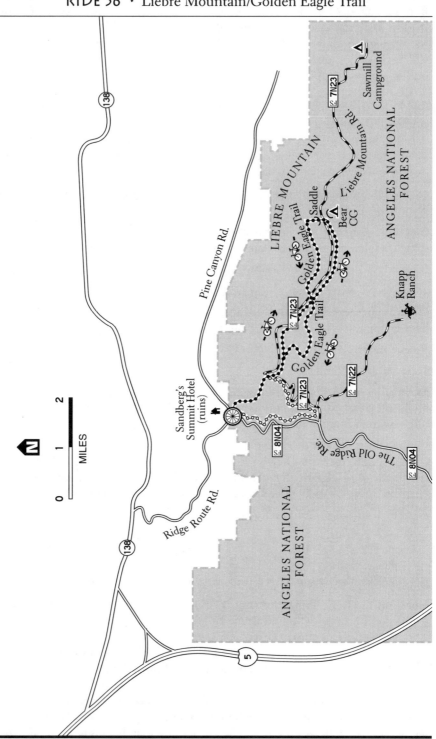

From the Golden Eagle Trail, you can see the mountains that almost split California in half.

panoramic views you've enjoyed now tend to close up as you enter California black oak country. The oak trees are full of mistletoe, creating a scenic backdrop for some roller-coaster, ridge-top riding. On one side of the ridge you'll see the brown Antelope Valley and the Tehachapis, on the other, you can see the craggy high peaks of the San Gabriels, which appear over the nearby, rounded ridges of the Sierra Pelona area.

The scenery is compelling, but the single-track you're about to ride is even more captivating. At 9.8 miles, keep your eye out for an intersection on the left with a double-track road that is perpendicular to the road you're on. You'll pass one double-track that heads left shortly before FS 7N23 crests a small rise. This isn't the right route, so don't take it. Instead, keep on the main road and look for the double-track that intersects FS 7N23 directly at the top of a little crest. Go left here, then left again at 10 miles when you reach a fence. You're now on the single-track Golden Eagle Trail, which clings to the fence for a while, then begins curving around oaks. At 11.3 miles you come to a big ravine. Drop into it, then curve right to climb out. As splendid views of the Antelope Valley open up in front of you, take the first sharp left (on an unmarked trail).

At 10.6 miles, you reach 7N23 again. Go left for about 0.25 mile, so that you're riding up and over a small rise. At the bottom of the small descent, go right at the intersection with a single-track trail, which is the continuation of the Golden Eagle Trail. The single-track rolls along, roughly paralleling 7N23. It's pretty easy to follow, except for a stretch at 11.9 miles, where you cross a dirt road, and the single-track disappears, replaced by double-track. Ride the double-track for about 300 feet, and keep your eyes peeled for a single-track trail on the right. Take it to resume riding on Golden Eagle, which grants some great views of Pyramid Lake.

At 13.8 miles, you reach 7N23 again. Jog briefly left on 7N23 to pick up the Golden Eagle again on the other side. But it can be a gamble to bike this section: if it's overgrown, it's simply not much fun to ride. So here's what you should do: If time, daylight, or fatigue are a factor, simply ride down 7N23 (watch out for cars), and go right on FS 8N04 returning the way you came for a longer, but quite possibly faster, ride of about 20 miles. Otherwise, give the Golden Eagle a chance, following it until it pours out onto FS 8N04 at 16.3 miles. Go right on FS 8N04 for just a few pedal strokes back to the start at 16.4 miles.

RIDE 57 · South Ridge/North Ridge

AT A GLANCE

Length/configuration: 6.4-mile loop on single-track and pavement

Aerobic difficulty: Moderate; one deadly hill, otherwise it's gentle and rolling

Technical difficulty: Moderate; some loose surfaces, and a few cross-country ski jumps that can take you by surprise

Scenery: Sequoias, Jeffrey Pines, and snow (even when it's scorching down in Los Angeles)

Special comments: A moderately challenging, fun loop in a beautiful setting—a superb summer getaway ride

This 6.4-mile loop offers a way to experience Mt. Pinos' sublime mountain biking terrain without suffering the pain of climbing or the stigma of relying on a car shuttle. If you're going to spend more than a day in the Mt. Pinos area (and you should), ride this trip first. It makes a superb introduction to the region.

The best time to ride here is when the rest of the Southland is scorching. On a day when Santa Ana winds are blowing 110° temperatures into Los Angeles, bikers up here can often be up to their shaved shins in snow.

After inhaling mightily to draw the pure Mt. Pinos air into your lungs, start by climbing up and over a hill and down to paved Mt. Pinos Road for a quick jog before rejoining a fire road meandering through a forest. This road becomes nastily steep, but it's over quickly, and the rest of the ride is a mostly downhill romp through woodsy, high-alpine terrain. At the end of the ride, the South Ridge Trail section is especially fun, combining a beautiful single-track and compelling views with regularly placed cross-country ski jumps which are perfectly shaped for airborne mountain bikers.

General location: 17 miles west of I-5 in the Mount Pinos District of the Los Padres National Forest.

RIDE 57 · South Ridge/North Ridge

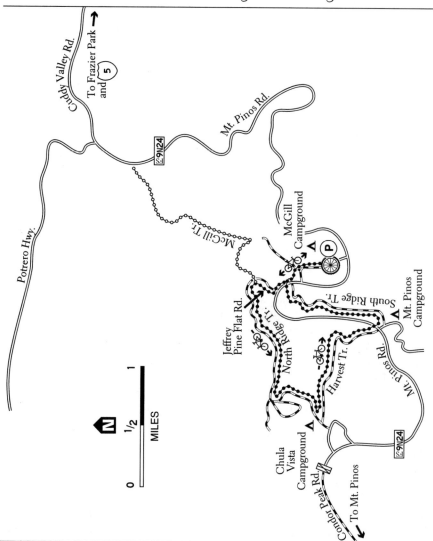

Elevation change: Approximate gain of 550 feet.

Season: June to October.

Services: Pit toilets and water (sometimes) are available on the trail; food is available in Frazier Park. Bike shops are a rarity in these parts—bring your own tools.

Hazards: Unexpected snow or ice on the trail.

Rescue index: The trail is always close to Mt. Pinos Road and to civilization.

Land status: National forest.

Maps: USGS 7.5-minute quadrangle map: Cuddy Valley.

Finding the trail: From Los Angeles, follow I-5 approximately 85 miles north to the exit for Frazier Park and Frazier Mountain Road. This exit is 3 miles north of Gorman and 1.5 miles south of Lebec (near Tejon Pass). Follow Frazier Mountain Road west through the community of Frazier Park. Approximately 7 miles from I-5, in the small community of Lake of the Woods, Frazier Mountain Road becomes Cuddy Valley Road (at the intersection with Lockwood Valley Road). Continue straight (northwest) for another 5 miles where you'll come to a poorly marked intersection. A sign here points right to Pine Mountain Club. Stay left on Cuddy Valley Road as it veers south toward Mt. Pinos; do not go toward Pine Mountain Club. From this intersection you will drive approximately 5 miles of twisting mountain road to the entrance for the McGill Campground on the right. Enter the campground and stay to the right at the camping pay station. Veer hard to the right and park in the small parking lot. A Forest Adventure Pass is required.

Sources of additional information:

Los Padres National Forest
Mount Pinos Ranger District
34580 Lockwood Valley Road

Frazier Park, CA 93225
(661) 245-3731; TTY (661) 245-0521
www.r5.fs.fed.us/lospadres

Notes on the trail: From the parking lot, veer left onto McGill Trail (it's at the left-hand side of the campground in front of you). After a quick little climb you'll reach a three-way junction at 0.25 mile. Turn left on the single-track and descend to Mt. Pinos Road. Go right here, past the South Ridge trailhead on the opposite side of the road, and then turn right on unsigned but obvious Jeffrey Pine Flat Road at 0.7 mile. Veer left at an unsigned intersection a little further on. At 1.1 miles you'll reach an intersection with a trail climbing a hillside. Stay straight, however, until the fire road seems to come to an end at 1.8 miles. Where the fire road ends, a double-track takes over, rising with daunting steepness. Climb this double-track even if it means walking your bike. The grade eases off, and soon you'll be riding in primo cross-country skiing terrain. At 2.9 miles, pass the intersection with Meadow Trail and go straight. At 3.1 miles, arrive at a rock barrier and an intersection where several different trails meet. Turn left down the single-track and pass the outskirts of Chula Vista Parking Lot. In short succession you'll pass the Chula Vista Campground and the Knoll Ridge Trail. At 4.4 miles, turn left on Mt. Pinos paved road, and then quickly right into Mt. Pinos Campground. Stay left through the campground, and find the trailhead for South Ridge at 4.7 miles. Turn left here for one of the most satisfying single-tracks in the book. A gentle grade allows for speed, while cross-country ski jumps encourage jumping, or at the very least, floating over the jumps. Reaching Mt. Pinos Road again at 6 miles, turn right, jog left and uphill on the McGill Trail to the small summit, and then ride back down to your car at 6.4 miles.

RIDE 58 · Mt. Pinos Loop

AT A GLANCE

Length/configuration: 21-mile combination: two loops — 8.4 miles and 3.6 miles long; 3 out-and-back legs comprising a total of 9 miles of pedaling

Aerobic difficulty: Moderately difficult to demanding; relatively high elevation makes the ride more strenuous

Technical difficulty: Moderate; conditions vary greatly over the course of the outing; pavement, good single-track, and degraded dirt roads

Scenery: Nicely forested trails; good views from Mt. Pinos summit

Special comments: Sweet single-track descents

This 21-mile loop (with out-and-back sections) is moderately difficult to strenuous, depending on your level of conditioning and acclimatization to the altitude. The trail conditions vary. One minute you're cycling along an excellent hardpacked dirt single-track trail; the next finds you dodging rocks on a degraded four-wheel-drive fire road. Some of the riding requires good bike-handling skills. There are 10 miles of cycling on good pavement.

A long paved climb allows you to enjoy some great descents on trails; climbing on the pavement is the easier way up. Terrific single-track riding and the views from the summit of Mt. Pinos highlight this ride.

General location: The ride begins at the McGill Campground on Mt. Pinos in the Los Padres National Forest (approximately 20 miles west of I-5, midway between Los Angeles and Bakersfield).

Elevation change: Total elevation gain: 2,880 feet.

Season: Late spring through early fall. Snow can be expected from December through April. Avoid busy weekends and holidays.

Services: Piped water can be obtained seasonally at McGill and Mt. Pinos Campgrounds. Services available in Frazier Park include gas, groceries, a restaurant, drug store, and telephones. There are also limited services available in Lake of the Woods. The nearest lodging is in Gorman.

Hazards: Trails on Mt. Pinos are heavily used by hikers and other recreationists; remember to yield right-of-way. Trails may narrow unexpectedly and contain hidden obstacles such as tree roots, rocks, sand, and ruts. Expect traffic on the paved Cuddy Valley Road. Mountain weather is unpredictable; carry raingear.

Rescue index: Help can be found in Lake of the Woods, Frazier Park, and the Chuchupate Ranger Station (about 1 mile south of Cuddy Valley Road on Lockwood Valley Road in Lake of the Woods). The closest hospital is in Bakersfield.

Land status: National forest.

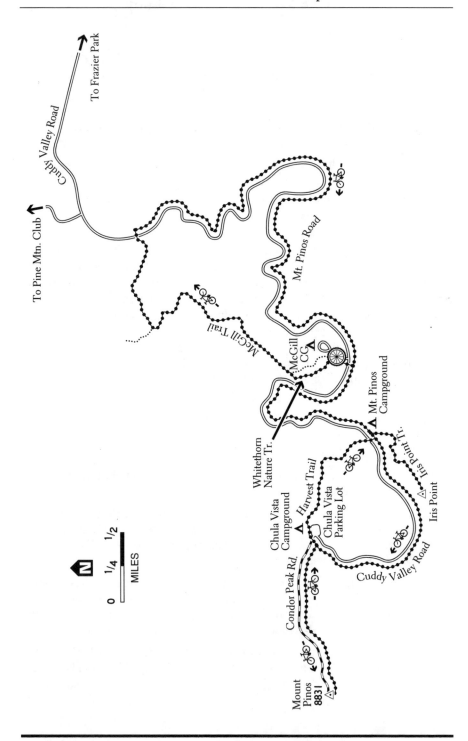

To Frazier Park

Cuddy Valley Road

To Pine Mtn. Club

N

0   1/4   1/2
MILES

Mt. Pinos Road

McGill Trail

McGill CG

Whitethorn Nature Tr.

Chula Vista Campground

Harvest Trail

Chula Vista Parking Lot

Mt. Pinos Campground

Iris Point Tr.

Iris Point

Cuddy Valley Road

Condor Peak Rd.

Mount Pinos 8831

Maps: USGS 7.5-minute quadrangle maps: Sawmill Mountain and Cuddy Valley.

Finding the trail: From Los Angeles, follow I-5 approximately 85 miles north to the exit for Frazier Park and Frazier Mountain Road. This exit is 3 miles north of Gorman and 1.5 miles south of Lebec (near Tejon Pass). Follow Frazier Mountain Road west through the community of Frazier Park. Approximately 7 miles from I-5, in the small community of Lake of the Woods, Frazier Mountain Road becomes Cuddy Valley Road (at the intersection with Lockwood Valley Road). Continue straight (northwest) for another 5 miles where you'll come to a poorly marked intersection. A sign here points right to Pine Mountain Club. Stay left on Cuddy Valley Road as it veers south toward Mt. Pinos; do not go toward Pine Mountain Club. From this intersection you will drive approximately 5 miles of twisting mountain road to the entrance for the McGill Campground on the right. Enter the campground and stay to the right at the camping pay station. Here you will find a hiker's parking lot available for day use; no overnight parking is allowed. Forest Adventure Pass required.

Sources of additional information:

Los Padres National Forest
Mount Pinos Ranger District
34580 Lockwood Valley Road

Frazier Park, CA 93225
(661) 245-3731; TTY (661) 245-0521
www.r5.fs.fed.us/lospadres

Notes on the trail: The ride starts directly across from the fee pay station for campers using the McGill Campground. Here you will find the trailhead for Whitethorn Nature Trail/McGill Trail. Bikes are permitted on the nature trail, but you may find it more enjoyable to walk and read the posted information. After 0.5 mile you'll come to a junction of trails at a bench. In front of you, three trails branch off. Take the trail to the right. You will pass a sign immediately on the right describing manzanita and then reach another intersection where you pick up McGill Trail; stay straight as Whitethorn Nature Trail goes hard to the right. Travel 2 miles on McGill Trail to an unmarked intersection; stay right. Ride 1 more mile and arrive at Cuddy Valley Road. Turn right and climb on pavement for 8 miles to Chula Vista Parking Lot. At the parking lot, turn left onto Condor Peak Road. Stay left at intersections on Condor Peak Road to reach the summit of Mt. Pinos. On the way back from the summit you can go left to another viewpoint at some microwave towers, but be aware that the Chumash Wilderness lies just West of the summit, and bikes are prohibited there.

Return down Condor Peak Road to Chula Vista Parking Lot. At the east end of the parking lot you will find a trail that takes you to the Chula Vista Campground. You will reach an intersection of trails on the outskirts of the campground. Continue straight (the trail to the left takes you to some pit toilets). A short distance beyond the campground you'll come to a couple of signs; one points right to Knoll Loop. The other directs you left onto Harvest Trail, but Harvest Trail is actually straight ahead. The trail is obvious as it goes downhill and is heavily gullied. Follow Harvest Trail for a little more than 0.5 mile to an intersection with a ski trail that goes right (west); continue straight to stay on Harvest Trail. Just beyond the intersection with the ski trail, you come to a T-intersection. Turn right and ride about 100 yards to paved Cuddy Valley Road. Turn left and follow Cuddy Valley Road downhill to nearby Mt. Pinos Campground. Here you will find Iris Point Trail (a dirt fire road) on the right. The trail is partially blocked by piles of earth and is signed "Iris Point—1 mile." Follow Iris Point Trail. Nearing Iris Point, you will come to an intersection; veer left to reach the viewpoint. Return the way you came from Iris Point to Cuddy Valley Road and turn right. It is about 2 miles down to the McGill Campground. Turn left into the campground to reach your parked vehicle.

Although the described ride is more than 20 miles long, it could easily be broken into smaller loops or one-way rides. Families might enjoy a ride from their campsite at Mt. Pinos Campground to Iris Point and back. The outstanding views from the summit of Mt. Pinos can be experienced by making a 4-mile round-trip on Condor Peak Road from the Chula Vista Parking Lot. If you can arrange it, get dropped off at the Chula Vista Parking Lot, ride Harvest Trail, Cuddy Valley Road, and McGill Trail, and get picked up at the bottom. This eliminates the paved climb altogether!

SANTA MONICA MOUNTAINS

The Santa Monica Mountains have one of the most important jobs in California: they make Los Angeles livable. Sure, the Pacific Ocean is nice, but the beaches, bike paths, and volleyball courts near the water can never provide the solace and quiet of these incredibly accessible mountains. Stretching 46 miles from Point Mugu in Ventura County to Griffith Park in the heart of the city, these mountains define the Los Angeles megalopolis geographically as well as culturally. They give the San Fernando Valley a separate attitude from the city, insulate the hippie-style community of Topanga, and isolate the wealthy enclaves of Malibu. But more importantly, they make for a year-round mountain biking paradise in a Mediterranean climate that only exists in five regions throughout the world.

One of the few east-west mountain ranges in the United States, the Santa Monicas are dwarfed by their other east-west neighbors, the San Gabriels and the San Bernardinos. The tallest peak, Sandstone, is only 3,111 feet above sea level. Yet there's something special about mountain biking here. Maybe it's the wooded canyons, the rugged backcountry, the surprisingly prevalent wildlife, or the gorgeous streams heading inexorably toward the ocean. One thing's for sure—this area would be a destination for mountain bikers no matter where it existed. It's just kind of nice that it's within incredibly close range of the second-largest city in America.

In short, whether you're pedaling on a family tour through Paramount Ranch or hammering along the rugged Paseo Miramar/Topanga Loop, this is an endlessly amusing place to ride. It's no exaggeration: This truly is the Entertainment Capital of the World.

RIDE 59 · Betty B. Dearing Trail

AT A GLANCE

Length/configuration: 3.3-mile loop on single-track, fire road, and pavement

Aerobic difficulty: Easy; a short climb on pavement

Technical difficulty: Easy; smooth riding throughout, with one narrow section of single-track

Scenery: City views, chaparral-covered hillsides, and panoramic vistas of the San Fernando Valley

Special comments: A wilderness area in the middle of a major metropolis, this ride is both a great family excursion and an after-work refresher

This 3.3-mile loop offers vivid proof to Los Angeles' claim that it contains more wilderness area within its city limits than any other metropolis. Poised between the Hollywood Hills, Beverly Hills, and the San Fernando Valley, this trail is close to everything, but more importantly it's a lot of fun.

The ride starts in Coldwater Canyon Park, home to the mountain patrol headquarters for the Los Angeles Fire Department beginning in the 1920s. Rangers would canvass the hilltops on horseback watching for fires; now it's your turn to cruise the same ridges on your steed, the trusty mountain bike. Coldwater Canyon Park is now home to TreePeople, an advocacy group for the planting and nurturing of trees in Los Angeles. After touring TreePeople's family-friendly displays, you'll spin past shady Depression-era Works Progress Administration (WPA) stone walls and staircases and out to the first of many panoramic vistas. Keeping an eye out for hikers and dogs, you'll ride into neighboring Wilacre Park. Next, embark on a pleasant downhill to the streets connecting Hollywood to the Valley. A pavement climb brings you back to the park, and a nifty little single-track tunnel brings you to the TreePeople headquarters and the realization that you're pretty lucky to be a mountain biker in this town.

General location: In Los Angeles' Coldwater Canyon Park and Wilacre State Park at the intersection of Mulholland Drive and Coldwater Canyon Avenue, between Beverly Hills, the Hollywood Hills, and the San Fernando Valley.

Elevation change: Insignificant.

Season: Year-round.

Services: Drinking fountains, rest rooms, phones, and information displays are available at the trailhead. All other services are available in the San Fernando Valley or Beverly Hills.

Hazards: Automobile traffic on paved sections, crowded trails.

Rescue index: The trail is never more than a mile from Coldwater Canyon Park trailhead, where phones and staff are present.

RIDE 59 · Betty B. Dearing Trail

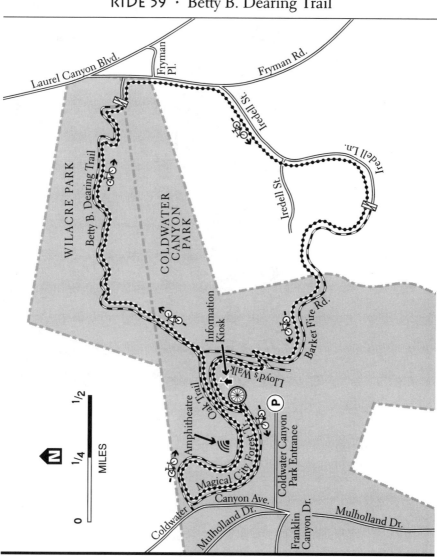

Land status: City park, Santa Monica Mountains Conservancy Parkland, city streets.

Maps: The "Guide to Coldwater Canyon Park" is available for a nominal donation at the park. Also refer to *The Thomas Guide: Los Angeles County*, (available at bookstores and drugstores throughout Los Angeles).

Finding the trail: Take Coldwater Canyon Avenue north from Beverly Hills or south from US 101 in the San Fernando Valley to the intersection with Mulholland Drive, and turn east into the single-lane driveway marked "Coldwater Canyon Park: Home of TreePeople." From I-405, exit at Mulholland and go east

Fighting weekend traffic on the Betty B. Dearing Trail.

4.5 miles to the intersection with Coldwater Canyon Avenue, then follow the directions listed previously. Park in the northeast end of the lot; the ride starts next to a brown sign above a drinking fountain that reads, "Welcome to Coldwater Canyon Park."

Sources of additional information:

Coldwater Canyon Park/TreePeople
12601 Mulholland Drive
Beverly Hills, CA 90210
(818) 753-4600

Santa Monica Mountains
    Conservancy
5750 Ramirez Canyon Road
Malibu, CA 90265-4474
(310) 589-3200
ceres.ca.gov/smmc/

Bicycle Shack
12059 Ventura Place

Studio City, CA 91604
(818) 763-8915

Beverly Hills Bike Shop
854 S. Robertson Boulevard
Beverly Hills, CA 90210-0000
(310) 275-2453

I. Martin Imports
8330 Beverly Boulevard
Los Angeles, CA 90048-2632
(323) 653-6900

Notes on the trail: From the drinking fountain and welcome sign in the northeast end of the parking lot, go downhill on a dirt path marked by a small sign, "Magic Forest Nature Trail Begins Here." Continue straight past the immediate intersection with Lloyd's Walk. Ride very slowly in this area; there are usually children present. At 0.1 mile you'll approach a gate; veer to the right side of it so that you parallel Coldwater Canyon Avenue for 100 feet or so. Then turn right onto a fire road that soon connects you to Oak Trail. Passing the amphitheater on your left, you'll emerge into a suddenly treeless Y junction at .4 miles. Go left onto the Betty B. Dearing Trail. The trail curves over some small hillsides and into a scenic meadow with great views as you begin descending. At 1.4 miles, the dirt fire road gives way to a crumbling macadam road. Keep an eye out for unleashed dogs and novice bikers as you descend to a gate at 1.8 miles. Go around the gate and turn right on Fryman Road. Go right on Iredell Street at 2 miles, then left on twisty Iredell Lane at 2.4 miles. At the end of Iredell Lane, ride onto the dirt road at 11 o'clock. A half-mile climb ensues back toward the Y junction you encountered earlier. Shortly before you arrive at the Y, make a sharp hairpin left onto a path at the end of a red rail fence. Make another sharp right at the other end of the red fence. You're now on the tunnel-like single-track of Lloyd's Walk, which kids seem to love. Lloyd's Walk soon returns you to the trailhead at 3.3 miles.

RIDE 60 · Kenter Fire Road/Whoop-De-Doos

AT A GLANCE

Length/configuration: 3.7-mile out-and-back ride (1.7 miles on the way out, 2 miles on the way back)

Aerobic difficulty: Moderate; some fairly steep fire-road climbs

Technical difficulty: Moderate/difficult; single-track humps that are easy when you're comfortable with the technique but daunting if you're not

Scenery: Pacific Ocean, million-dollar homes, city views

Special comments: A fire road with a special detour on a long stretch of constant whoop-de-doos; a must for fun-seekers

An ideal ride for Los Angelenos who don't have much time to have a lot of fun. This 3.7-mile ride is easy to reach, short, and full of amusement park thrills. Bring your kids (at least the nonskittish ones) here and the days of forking out big bucks at Disneyland, Universal Studios, and Magic Mountain may be over.

This year-round ride delivers expansive views right from the start, thanks to its location on a ridge high above Mandeville Canyon. The fire road is steep in spots, but it's also interspersed with little descents that relieve the climb up to a water tank. If it's clear, you can enjoy the views for a while, but remember it's

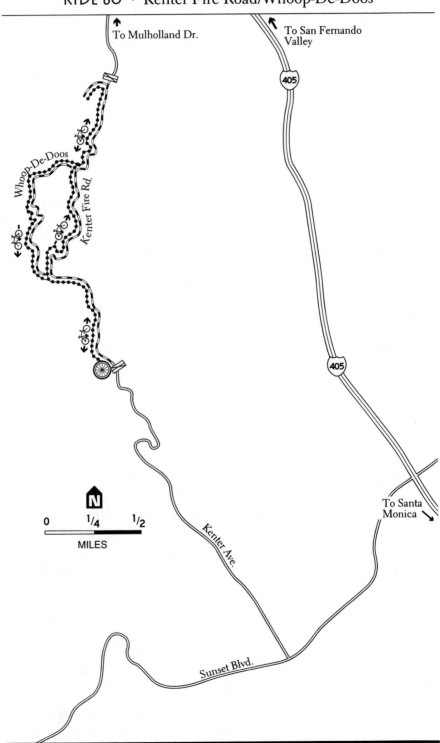

To Mulholland Dr.

To San Fernando Valley

405

Whoop-De-Doos

Kenter Fire Rd.

405

N

0   1/4   1/2

MILES

Kenter Ave.

To Santa Monica

Sunset Blvd.

Whooping it up on the
whoop-de-doos.

your somatosensory system that gets the most out of this ride, not your eyes.
That's because on the way back down, you'll turn off the fire road to engage the
famous Kenter whoop-de-doos.

Rumor has it that dirt bikers originally constructed this mile-long stretch of
jumps and bumps, but it's almost totally a mountain bikers' province now. And
the secret to mountain biking here is to have a relaxed technique. I've seen newcomers adapt to it perfectly in just one go but also rigid intermediate couples
nearly divorcing each other because they persistently seized up on the bumps by
remaining too tense.

The key is to let the bumps slow you down, not your brakes. Positioning your
feet at 3 and 9 o'clock on the pedals, lightly straddling the saddle, and keeping
your elbows bent is the way to go — every bump is thus shock-absorbed by your
arms and body. As you crest a bump, the handlebar comes up harmlessly toward
your face, then falls away as you start down again. It's a lot of fun. What's more,
if there are no other trail users in your path, you can jump the bumps — but that's
a whole other technique.

General location: In the Santa Monica Mountains, approximately 2 miles north
of Sunset Boulevard in the community of Brentwood.

Elevation change: Total gain is approximately 550 feet.

Season: Year-round.

Services: No services are available on the trail or at the trailhead. All services are available in Brentwood.

Hazards: Whoop-de-doos, which aren't for everybody.

Rescue index: Trail is within 2 miles of civilization at all times.

Land status: City, state park land.

Maps: USGS 7.5-minute quadrangle map: Beverly Hills. (Though the whoop-de-doos section is not mapped.)

Finding the trail: Take I-405 into the Los Angeles basin. Exit at Sunset Boulevard in Brentwood and go west approximately 1.5 miles to Kenter Avenue. Turn right on Kenter, which climbs steeply on pavement through posh neighborhoods. Kenter Avenue ends at a gate 2.1 miles from Sunset Boulevard; park on the side of the road here. Make sure to curb your wheels; the street is quite steep.

Sources of additional information:

Helen's Cycles
2501 Broadway
Santa Monica, CA 90404
(310) 829-1836

Supergo Bike Shops
501 Broadway
Santa Monica, CA 90401
(310) 451-9977

Notes on the trail: Go north around the gate and begin climbing Kenter Fire Road. Almost immediately you'll reach a vista point on your left. Kick aside the abundant broken glass and take in the view if it's a clear day; otherwise take a right on the narrow dirt path at 0.1 mile that comes immediately before the paved road descends into Mandeville Canyon. This path climbs north toward electrical towers and soon descends. At 0.2 mile veer right, staying on the main utility road linking the electrical towers. At 1 mile, the main road is just starting to drop when you notice a very steep electrical tower access road on your right. No, you don't have to climb it. Instead, keep the steep access road on your right at 3 o'clock and look to your left at the trail snaking along the side of a mountain at 7 o'clock. This is the start of the Whoop-De-Doos Trail, to which you will shortly return. But for now, stick to the main fire road, which eventually climbs toward a large white water tank. At 1.6 miles, pull even with the water tank and head left on an electric tower access road, which reveals great vistas of the entire Los Angeles Basin at 1.7 miles. Turn around and return the way you came to 2.4 miles, where you memorized the start of the whoop-de-doos. Pedal to the right and onto the trail. Using a good, relaxed technique, you'll come out on the main fire road at 3.3 miles. Turn right and ride back to your car at 3.7 miles.

RIDE 61 · Westridge/Sullivan Canyon

AT A GLANCE

Length/configuration: 11.1-mile loop on pavement, fire road, and single-track

Aerobic difficulty: Moderate; after a very steep but short pavement climb, it's all fairly gradual

Technical difficulty: Moderate; there are some rocky sections and stream crossings

Scenery: Pacific Ocean, gorgeous sycamore-lined canyon, and riparian habitats

Special comments: Perhaps the most popular ride anywhere in Los Angeles, this is a classic loop: a fire road ascent followed by a single-track downhill through a canyon where it always feels like autumn

This 11.1-mile loop was the first place I ever rode upon moving to Los Angeles from a ski town in Colorado. Going in, I didn't expect much; after all, how could the second-largest city in the country compare to the Rockies? But this ride changed my whole perspective. If you have any doubts about the area's wealth of biking opportunities, pedal this route, and you'll be a convert too.

Starting from an affluent hilly neighborhood above Brentwood, this tour climbs a dauntingly steep paved road in its first mile. If it's too much, please don't give up. Instead, walk your bike to the gate and the beginning of the dirt fire road—I promise you, you'll be glad you did. The gently climbing fire road keeps you spinning in a comfortable gear as you gain ridge-top views of the Pacific and Sullivan Canyon to your left. Stop at an overlook (there are several on this road) and check out the sycamore trees lining the canyon bottom alongside a creek. Soon enough, you'll be riding through those.

But for now, keep climbing to San Vicente Mountain Park located at the site of an ABAR radar tower. This tower was linked with Nike missiles stationed in the Sepulveda Wash in the San Fernando Valley from the mid-1950s to 1960s. Taking advantage of San Vicente Peak's prime location between the Los Angeles Basin and the Valley, the ABAR tower could detect enemy bombers from 100 miles away.

After some exploring, cruise down Mulholland and along Sullivan Ridge before dropping into Sullivan Canyon. This route often changes shape due to flooding and Southern California Gas Company maintenance (the company has a substantial but subterranean pipeline in the canyon). When the gas company regraded, widened, and poured gravel over the trail in 1995, I thought the canyon would never be fun again. But the canyon is unarguably a living organism, and it seems to favor bikers. Though the canyon will surely flood again, somehow the gravel will be pulverized, single-track routes will blossom, and it will become gorgeous once more. Enjoy it any time, but go in the fall when the sycamores change color for a little bit of New England right here in Southern California.

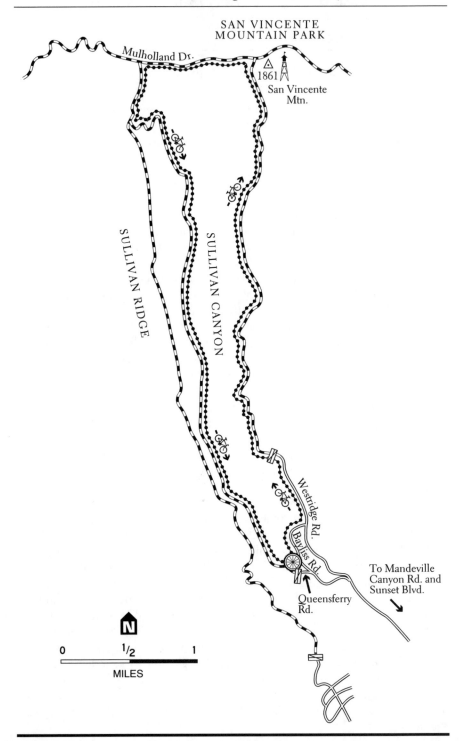

SAN VINCENTE
MOUNTAIN PARK

Mulholland Dr.

1861
San Vincente
Mtn.

SULLIVAN RIDGE

SULLIVAN CANYON

Westridge Rd.

Bayliss Rd.

To Mandeville
Canyon Rd. and
Sunset Blvd.

Queensferry
Rd.

N

0   1/2   1

MILES

Shade happens.

General location: Just north of Brentwood, approximately 2.5 miles west of I-405.

Elevation change: 1,200 feet (from 700 feet to 1,900 feet).

Season: Year-round.

Services: There's a water fountain, vending machine, rest rooms, and displays at San Vicente Mountain Park. All other services are available in Brentwood.

Hazards: Automobile traffic on paved sections, rocky trail sections, and stream crossings.

Rescue index: You'll never be alone on this ride; the route begins and ends in residential neighborhoods. Help is available in Brentwood.

Land status: City streets, state-owned lands, Santa Monica Mountains Conservancy Parkland, and (briefly) Topanga State Park.

Maps: *Trail Map of the Santa Monica Mountains East* is available from Tom Harrison Cartography, (800) 265-9090 or (415) 456-7940, www.tomharrison-maps.com. Also refer to the *Thomas Brothers' Guide to Los Angeles,* (available in bookstores and drugstores throughout Los Angeles).

Finding the trail: From I-405, go west on Sunset Boulevard approximately 2.3 miles. Turn right on Mandeville Canyon Road, go 0.2 mile, then turn left on Westridge Road. Ascend twisty Westridge for 2 miles, then turn left onto Bayliss. Go about a third of a mile to the intersection with Queensferry. Park in this vicinity, making sure to obey posted parking signs. (Note: This is a residential area that has experienced past conflicts with trail users urinating, undressing, and playing loud music in public. Act responsibly or we could all lose this parking area.)

Sources of additional information:

San Vicente Mountain Park
(310) 858-7272

Santa Monica Mountains
Conservancy
5750 Ramirez Canyon Rd
Malibu, CA 90265-4474
(310) 589-3200
ceres.ca.gov/smmc/

Topanga State Park
20825 Entrada Drive
Topanga, CA 90290

(310) 455-2465
cal-parks.ca.gov

Helen's Cycles
2501 Broadway
Santa Monica, CA 90404
(310) 829-1836

Supergo Bike Shops
501 Broadway
Santa Monica, CA 90401
(310) 451-9977

Notes on the trail: From the intersection of Bayliss and Queensferry, go north (uphill) on Bayliss. Turn left on Westridge Road at 0.5 mile. This is by far the toughest climb in the entire trip, so don't be ashamed to walk your bike. At 1.1 miles you'll finally come to a gate marking the end of paved Westridge Road and the beginning of dirt West Mandeville fire Road (though everyone calls the dirt portion Westridge as well). Go around the gate and veer left, climbing gently past several intersections with single-track detours and utility pole access roads. Stay on the main trail and you'll be fine. The only questionable fork comes at 3.7 miles; stay right, climbing toward the radar tower on the ridge ahead of you. Reach San Vicente Mountain Park at 4.8 miles. Jog east, then north through the park to a gate and a T intersection with unpaved Mulholland Drive and a great vista of Encino Reservoir. Turn left. After some washboard terrain, pass your first gate at 5.6 miles and keep going straight. At 5.9 miles, on a small uphill, you'll come to an intersection with two gates. Make a soft left and go around the furthest gate, marked by a spray-painted "Sullivan." You're now on curvy Sullivan Ridge Fire Road. When the knolls on your left drop away, you'll come to a fairly wide trail on your left at 6.4 miles. Turn left here. You'll find a vestige of old pavement as well as dirt that is marked with scores of bike tracks. In a quarter-mile you'll come to an open gate signed "No Trespassing or Loitering." If for some rare reason the gate is closed, you must obey the sign and turn around. But that's almost never the case, and if it's open, you can legally ride here. You'll drop into Sullivan Canyon presently, on terrain that's initially rocky, then buffed. Control your speed; there are numerous hikers and dog-walkers here. Feel free to explore the single-tracks branching off the main trail—as long as they head down-canyon, they'll eventually rejoin the route. After several stream crossings, short drop-offs, and some sycamore gazing, you'll come to a dam and a steep road (Queensferry) going uphill to your left at 10.8 miles. Climb this road, go around the gate, and return to the intersection of Bayliss and Queensferry at 11.1 miles.

RIDE 62 · Sullivan Ridge/Backbone Trail

AT A GLANCE

Length/configuration: 21.3-mile loop on pavement, fire road, and single-track

Aerobic difficulty: Difficult; there are several climbs, some of them long

Technical difficulty: Moderate/difficult; there are some very narrow trail sections

Scenery: Pacific Ocean, Santa Susana Mountains, city views, rugged canyons, oak woodlands, and, sometimes, actress Goldie Hawn

Special comments: A beautiful route along three different ridges, topped with an exquisite single-track

Much of the terrain covered in this 21.3-mile loop constituted a very good ride before the mid-1990s. It was then, however, that a previously off-limits section of the Backbone Trail was opened to bikes. The addition of this sublime single-track makes this one of the jewels of the Santa Monicas.

Starting just off of Sunset Boulevard on Monaco Drive, you'll spin through a celebrity-heavy neighborhood. More than once, I've seen actress Goldie Hawn jogging here. After grunting hello to her (the climb is kind of steep), turn onto Sullivan Ridge fire road which immediately grants views of aptly named Rustic Canyon on the left and Sullivan Canyon on the right. There's some great single-track detours on the way up to unpaved Mulholland Drive. Now you'll experience some more ridge views of the San Fernando Valley on the right and the Los Angeles Basin on the left.

After some roller-coastering, you'll reach the Hub, the nexus of several different rides in the area. A short spin down a third ridge, Temescal, delivers you to the Backbone Trail. The Backbone is a 70-mile treasure that crosses the spine of the Santa Monica Mountains all the way to Point Mugu. You'll only be sampling 6 rolling miles of the Backbone, but it's so regal that afterward you'll feel like a king—which is good, since on weekends you can often take in a polo match at Will Rogers State Historical Park before humping up Sunset back to your car.

General location: In Topanga State Park and Will Rogers State Historical Park north of Pacific Palisades, approximately 3.5 miles west of I-405.

Elevation change: Ride climbs from 500 feet to 2,025 feet with several ups and downs.

Season: Year-round.

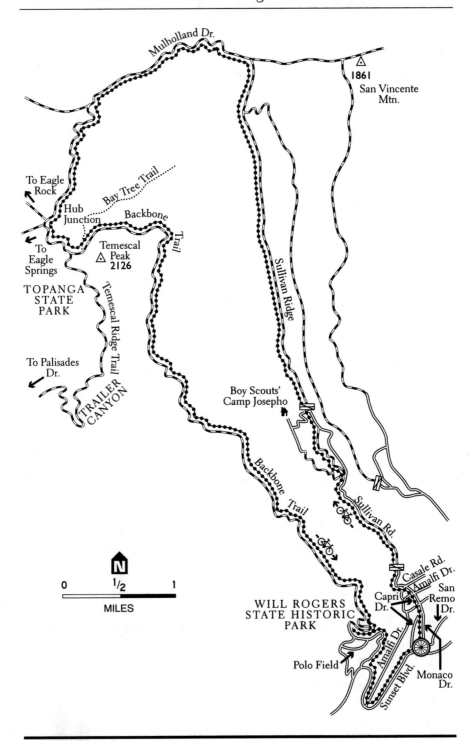

Mulholland Dr.

△ 1861
San Vincente
Mtn.

To Eagle
Rock

Bay Tree Trail

Hub
Junction

Backbone

Trail

To
Eagle
Springs

Temescal
△ Peak
2126

TOPANGA
STATE
PARK

Sullivan Ridge

Temescal Ridge Trail

To Palisades
Dr.

TRAILER
CANYON

Boy Scouts'
Camp Josepho

Backbone

Trail

Sullivan Rd.

N

0   1/2   1

MILES

Casale Rd.

Amalfi Dr.

Capri
Dr.

San
Remo
Dr.

WILL ROGERS
STATE HISTORIC
PARK

Amalfi Dr.

Polo Field

Monaco
Dr.

Sunset Blvd.

Catching early-morning
rays on Sullivan Ridge.

Services: Rest rooms, water, phones, and rangers can be found at the Will Rogers State Historical Park near the ride's end. No services are available elsewhere on the trail. All services are available in Pacific Palisades.

Hazards: Automobile traffic on paved sections, narrow cliffside single-tracks, and rattlesnakes.

Rescue index: Help is available at Will Rogers State Historic Park near the ride's end. Topanga State Park rangers regularly patrol Mulholland Drive. In addition, Sunset Boulevard can often be reached by riding downhill from many points on this ride.

Land status: State park, state historic park, and city streets.

Maps: *The Trail Map of the Santa Monica Mountains East* is available from Tom Harrison Cartography, (800) 265-9090 or (415) 456-7940, www.tom harrisonmaps.com. Also refer to the *Thomas Brothers' Guide to Los Angeles*, (available in bookstores and drugstores throughout Los Angeles). Also, the Topanga State Park map is available by contacting the park itself (see "Sources of additional information" below).

Finding the trail: From I-405, go west on Sunset Boulevard approximately 3.5 miles. After passing the traffic light at Allenford Avenue, make the next right onto San Remo Drive. Take an immediate left at the fork with Monaco Drive and park. Obey all posted regulations.

Sources of additional information:

Will Rogers State Historical Park
1501 Will Rogers State Park Road
Pacific Palisades, CA 90272
(310) 454-8212
cal-parks.ca.gov

Topanga State Park
20825 Entrada Drive
Topanga, CA 90290
(310) 455-2465
cal-parks.ca.gov

Helen's Cycles
2501 Broadway
Santa Monica, CA 90404
(310) 829-1836

Supergo Bike Shops
501 Broadway
Santa Monica, CA 90401
(310) 451-9977

Notes on the trail: Start pedaling north on Monaco Drive (away from Sunset). At 0.4 mile you'll reach a traffic circle. Go around it and take the upper left artery, Capri Drive. Ascend Capri Drive, and stay with Capri as it veers left at the intersection with Casale Road. Capri soon turns into dirt, then turns back into pavement again as it reaches a gate at 1 mile. Go around the gate. You're now in Topanga State Park. Keep going past an abandoned mansion at 2 miles. As the road starts to climb, keep your eyes peeled for a single-track snaking off to the left immediately before a chain-link fence. Turn left on this single-track at 2.3 miles. You'll soon come to two forks: go right at the first, left at the second. You'll get splendid backcountry views of Rustic Canyon before returning to the fire road (paved) at 3.1 miles. Head left and you'll soon come to a gate at 3.2 miles. To the left is the Boy Scouts' Camp Josepho. Go around the gate to the right and onto dirt. It's mellow climbing from here to 4.7 miles, where a big shade tree offers a good rest spot. A steep ascent takes you to the turnoff to Sullivan Canyon (on the right) at 6.3 miles. But keep heading straight and turn left on Mulholland Drive at 6.8 miles. After some roller-coastering, you'll come to a gate on the left at 9.6 miles which provides access to Topanga State Park. Turn here, going around the gate, and stay on the main fire road as it climbs up to the Hub Junction at 11.8 miles. From Hub Junction—where several trails intersect at the top of a hill—veer left toward the Backbone Trail, which you'll reach on your left at 12.3 miles. Drop onto this single-track and prepare for wildlife encounters with rabbits and scores of lizards. At 15.9 miles, after riding through a particularly lush rainforesty section of trail, you'll reach a lone California live oak. This natural vista provides excellent views of the Getty Museum and the whole eastern Santa Monicas. Descending some more, the trail clings to a narrow ridge. At a fork at 17 miles veer right, staying on the Backbone Trail. You'll soon come to a bridge where you're required to walk your bike, and then some technical descending over waterbars. At 18.2 miles, turn left onto the Will Rogers State Historical Park fire road. This trail winds around to a paved road at 19 miles. Go left twice on pavement so that you're heading south and downhill along a straightaway that parallels a large grassy field. Go left once more at the parking lot ringing the Polo field. At 19.3 miles you'll pass a sign reading "Locked Gate Ahead" and descend a crumbling pavement road to the locked gate, which you circumvent to reach Sunset Boulevard at 20 miles. The traffic can be busy here, so be careful while making a left onto Sunset. Turn left a final time at San Remo to reach your car at 21.3 miles.

RIDE 63 · Eagle Rock/Eagle Springs

AT A GLANCE

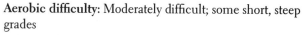

Length/configuration: 6-mile combination; 3-mile out-and-back (1.5 miles each way) and a 3-mile loop

Aerobic difficulty: Moderately difficult; some short, steep grades

Technical difficulty: Difficult; loose rocks and sand complicate ascents and descents

Scenery: Eagle Rock provides a good vantage point for gazing out over Topanga State Park and distant landmarks

Special comments: Pleasant nature trail at Trippet Ranch (hiking only)

This out-and-back, 6-mile round-trip ride (with a loop to Eagle Rock) is moderately difficult. Begin with 3.5 miles of moderately steep climbing interspersed with some steep uphills, level stretches, and rolling terrain. There is a screamer descent just before reaching Eagle Rock, but keep in mind that the park requires riding in a safe manner at all times. It is mostly downhill riding on the return. The route follows four-wheel-drive dirt fire roads in fair to good condition. Some of the steeper sections contain loose rocks and sand. Riding here requires good bike-handling skills.

The view from Eagle Rock is excellent. The canyons and ridges of Topanga State Park stretch out below you. In the distance are Santa Ynez, the San Fernando Valley, and the Pacific Ocean. After your ride, lock your bike and take some time to walk the 1-mile self-guided nature trail at Trippet Ranch.

General location: Begins at Trippet Ranch in Topanga State Park, approximately 10 miles northwest of Santa Monica.

Elevation change: Starts at 1,310 feet and climbs for 1 mile to 1,700 feet. From here it drops to the Eagle Rock/Eagle Springs intersection at 1,600 feet and then climbs to the Hub intersection at 2,000 feet. You reach the ride's high point of 2,100 feet at Eagle Rock. Total elevation gain: 890 feet.

Season: This route can be ridden year-round. The best seasons are the early spring and late fall; temperatures are cooler, the vegetation is greener, and there are fewer hikers using the trails.

Services: Water can be obtained at the rest rooms near the Trippet Ranch parking area. All services are available in the community of Topanga.

RIDE 63 · Eagle Rock/Eagle Springs

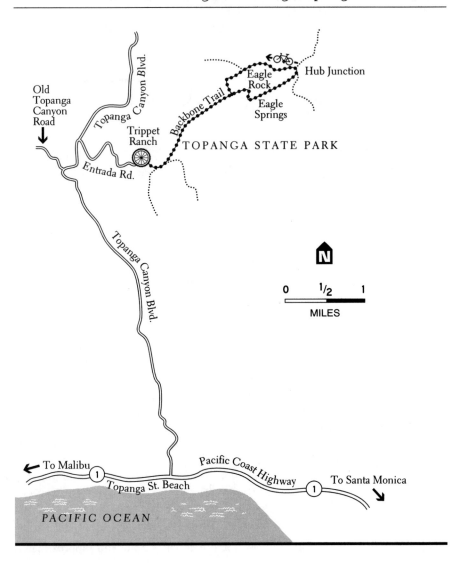

Hazards: Topanga State Park is popular with equestrians, hikers, and cyclists. Rattlesnakes reside in the park. If you encounter one, let it avoid you; they will not attack unless disturbed.

Rescue index: The nearest help in an emergency is available at Trippet Ranch or in the community of Topanga. The closest public phone is at Trippet Ranch.

Land status: State park.

Maps: A map of Topanga State Park may be obtained at the Trippet Ranch Information Center. It is a good guide to this trail.

Eagle Rock.

Finding the trail: The ride begins at the trailhead in the southeast corner of the day-use parking lot at Trippet Ranch in Topanga State Park. From Santa Monica, follow CA 1 Northwest for approximately 6 miles to Topanga Canyon Boulevard (Topanga Canyon Boulevard intersects with CA 1 across from Topanga State Beach). Follow Topanga Canyon Boulevard north for approximately 5 miles to Entrada Road. Turn right (east) onto Entrada Road. Stay left at all intersections to reach the Trippet Ranch day-use parking area. Paid parking is available. Hours of operation are from 8 a.m.–7 p.m. in summer and 8 a.m. –5 p.m. in winter.

Sources of additional information:

California Department of Parks and
   Recreation
Angeles District/Malibu Sector
1925 Los Virgenes Road
Calabasas, CA 91302
(818) 880-0350

Topanga State Park
20825 Entrada Drive
Topanga, CA 90290
(310) 455-2465
cal-parks.ca.gov

Notes on the trail: Start at the trailhead in the southeast corner of the parking lot. Follow the fire road for 0.2 mile to a junction of roads with a sign for Eagle

Rock and other trails. Turn left toward Eagle Rock and proceed to the intersection with a sign for Eagle Rock and Eagle Spring. Turn right toward Eagle Spring and follow the road to the Hub intersection. At the Hub intersection, turn hard to the left and ride uphill. Take this fire road to the sign for North Loop Trail/Eagle Rock. Continue on the main road to Eagle Rock. Go 0.5 mile beyond Eagle Rock to the intersection for Eagle Spring. Continue straight to return the way you came.

RIDE 64 · Paseo Miramar/Topanga Loop

AT A GLANCE

Length/configuration: 18.6-mile loop on pavement and fire road

Aerobic difficulty: Very difficult; one of the most grueling climbs in the Santa Monicas

Technical difficulty: Moderate; some rocky descents

Scenery: Pacific Ocean, wooded canyons, pinkish volcanic boulders, Eagle Rock, and caves

Special comments: A very popular trail, this route serves as an exemplary training ride, a tour of some lovely views, and a long cruise all in one

The thought that always pops into my head during this ride is that if I had shelled out a thousand bucks to fly somewhere for an exotic mountain biking vacation and the outfitter took me on this route, I'd be a very happy customer. But if you live in Los Angeles, you don't have to shell out anything but sweat for this scenic, very accessible loop. So what are you waiting for?

Starting less than a half-mile from Pacific Coast Highway (PCH) in Pacific Palisades, the ride grinds up Paseo Miramar, which is ungodly steep on both its paved and dirt sections. If you ask me, it's the toughest 20 minutes of riding in the Santa Monicas. (In fact, my wife still kicks me when she remembers that I took her here on her second-ever dirt ride.) But once you reach the Parker Mesa Overlook and its gorgeous ocean vistas, the riding gets a lot easier. The views are incredible as you spin by pinkish-colored volcanic boulders high above wooded Santa Ynez Canyon. The trail gets a lot of use, especially on weekends, but everyone is accustomed to seeing other users, so conflicts are rare.

After passing the turnoff to Trippet Ranch (where rest rooms and park rangers can be reached in an emergency), the trail gets a little hairy again as you climb to a sublime rest spot, the jaw-droppingly scenic Eagle Rock. I always have a hard time figuring where to point my camera up here, it's so picturesque. Anyway, after spinning up to the Hub Junction, a fast but controlled descent on Trailer Canyon Road (which sees relatively little use) takes you down to Palisades Drive, where a deli awaits. It's all downhill from there, so if you'd rather snarf some seafood, pass on the deli and head to Gladstone's Seafood right on the beach at

RIDE 64 · Paseo Miramar/Topanga Loop

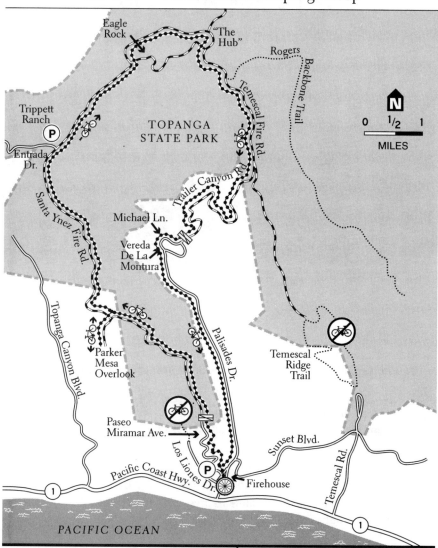

the intersection of Sunset and PCH. The food and service don't quite match the setting, but then, nothing could.

General location: In Topanga State Park, north of Pacific Palisades, less than a mile from the intersection of Sunset and Pacific Coast Highway.

Elevation change: Ride climbs from 75 feet to 2,025 feet with several ups and downs.

Season: Year-round.

Oh yeah, I forgot. That's why we live here!

Services: Rest rooms, water, and a ranger station can be found at Trippet Ranch midway through the ride. You'll also pass a deli near the ride's end.

Hazards: Occasionally crowded trails, and automobile traffic on paved sections.

Rescue index: Help is available at Trippet Ranch midway through the ride. In addition, Sunset Boulevard is easily reached from most points on the ride.

Land status: State park and city streets.

Maps: *Trail Map of the Santa Monica Mountains East* is available from Tom Harrison Cartography, (800) 265-9090 or (415) 456-7940, www.tomharrison-maps.com. Also, the Topanga State Park map is available at the Trippet Ranch entrance station or by contacting the park itself (see "Sources of Additional Information," below).

Finding the trail: From Pacific Palisades, take Sunset Boulevard west past Palisades Drive to Los Liones Drive (just west of a fire station). Turn right on Los Liones. From PCH, head east on Sunset Boulevard and turn left on Los Liones Drive, just west of the fire station. There is some legal street parking on Los Liones Drive, but if you cannot find any, then proceed northwest (away from Sunset) on Los Liones for a few hundred yards, and park in the recently built parking areas on the right.

Sources of additional information:

Topanga State Park
20825 Entrada Drive
Topanga, CA 90290
(310) 455-2465
cal-parks.ca.gov

Helen's Cycles
2501 Broadway

Santa Monica, CA 90404
(310) 829-1836

Supergo Bike Shops
501 Broadway
Santa Monica, CA 90401
(310) 451-9977

Notes on the trail: From Los Liones Drive, stay on the north side of Sunset in front of the fire station and turn immediately left on Paseo Miramar. The street winds around and climbs steeply; follow the yellow lines to prevent turning onto side streets. At 1.3 miles go around a gate at the end of paved Paseo Miramar and start climbing a cruel dirt road. After one teasing downhill, climb up to the Parker Mesa Overlook turnoff at 3.5 miles. Turn left and ride to the vista with great ocean views at 4 miles. Turn around, return to the fire road (which is now called Santa Ynez Fire Road), and turn left. Some occasional tough climbs ensue, but nothing like what you've already endured. At 7.3 miles, reach the turnoff to Trippet Ranch (you will have already noticed a lot more trail users in this area). If you need a rest room or ranger assistance, turn left for a quarter-mile ride to Trippet Ranch. Otherwise, keep going straight, following signs to Eagle Rock and the Hub. At 8.5 miles you'll reach a three-way intersection. Take the middle route toward Eagle Rock, which you'll reach on your right at 9 miles. Get off your bike and explore the rock for a while (it makes a great lunch spot). Afterward, turn right and roller-coaster to the Hub at 9.9 miles. Head right and south on Temescal Fire Road toward Trailer Canyon (make sure not to go sharply right to Eagle Springs). Some roller-coaster hills follow as you pass by Temescal Peak (2,126 feet) and then descend rapidly to the junction with Trailer Canyon at 12.6 miles. Veer right here (the left, Temescal, is soon closed to bikes) and descend to a gate and paved cul-de-sac on Michael Lane at 15.3 miles. Head right on Michael Lane for about a block, then left on Vereda de la Montura. Go right at the big intersection with Palisades Drive (a deli is on the southwest corner). Descend for a spell on Palisades Drive until you reach Sunset Boulevard at 18.5 miles. Turn right toward your car at Los Liones at 18.6 miles.

RIDE 65 · Red Rock Canyon/Calabasas Motorway

AT A GLANCE

Length/configuration: 7.4-mile loop

Aerobic difficulty: Moderate/difficult; some steep sections, but climbing is not prolonged

Technical difficulty: Easy; smooth fire roads and pavement

Scenery: Amazing sandstone rock formations and ridgeline views

Special comments: A short but incredibly scenic ride with some family-friendly detours

This is a short 7.4-mile loop in a little-used canyon flanked with gorgeous sandstone outcroppings. Hard-packed trails climb out of exposed, shadeless Red Rock Canyon to a large saddle offering splendid views of rock formations to the east and family-owned ranches to the west. A steep climb up Calabasas Motorway past more geological wonders leads to even more striking vistas. A descent down twisty fire roads and even some pavement returns riders to quiet Red Rock Canyon.

Since the ride bypasses numerous rock hollows and mini-caves, its first stage in Red Rock Canyon appeals to families with distractible young riders. It can be fun to simply tool around the lower stretches of Red Rock Canyon and skip the climbing altogether. The ride is located between the bohemian/artsy town of Topanga and the ranches of the central Santa Monica Mountains, and it offers a lot of scenery for comparatively little effort.

General location: The park is located outside of Topanga on Santa Monica Mountains Conservancy land, approximately 4 miles south of Mulholland Highway and 7 miles north of PCH.

Elevation change: Approximately 1,100-foot gain.

Season: October through June. (Almost completely unshaded, it's very hot going in summer.)

Services: No water is available on the trail. Most services are available in Topanga.

Hazards: Fast drivers on the paved section of this loop.

Rescue index: The ride is never more than 5 miles from civilization. A pay phone is located in the parking lot at the start of the ride.

Land status: Santa Monica Mountains Conservancy land, open to mountain bikers except where indicated.

Maps: The *Trail Map of the Santa Monica Mountains Central* is available from Tom Harrison Cartography, (800) 265-9090 or (415) 456-7940, www.tom harrisonmaps.com. In addition, a general map of the area is posted at the trailhead. The route is very easy to follow.

Finding the trail: To reach Red Rock Road from the north, take Mulholland Highway to Old Topanga Road. Travel south on Old Topanga for 4 miles. After a bridge, be on the lookout for Red Rock Road on the right. From the south, take PCH to Topanga Canyon Boulevard, travel north for 4.5 miles, and then turn left on Old Topanga Road. After 2 miles, turn left onto Red Rock Road. Once on Red Rock Road, you travel west on a single-lane paved road which gives way to a rutted but passable dirt road. After 0.8 mile, Red Rock Road ends in the Santa Monica Mountains Conservancy's (SMMC) small dirt parking lot. The ride starts here.

RIDE 65 · Red Rock Canyon/Calabasas Motorway

Sources of additional information:

Santa Monica Mountains
  Conservancy
5750 Ramirez Canyon Road
Malibu, CA 90265-4474
(310) 589-3200
ceres.ca.gov/smmc

Helen's Cycles
2501 Broadway

Santa Monica, CA 90404
(310) 829-1836

Supergo Bike Shops
501 Broadway
Santa Monica, CA 90401
(310) 451-9977

Notes on the trail: After looking back at the striking red rocks you've just driven through, jump on your bike and pedal west (the direction you've been driving), past the SMMC buildings on your left and picnic tables on the right. Go around a gate and begin gently climbing Red Rock Canyon Road. If traveling with younger riders, by all means pull off to the left and disembark to explore the hollows and caves in the sandstone escarpments. After passing the Red Rock Hiking Trail, the road ascends more steeply and reaches a low saddle at 1.2 miles. There is a bench here for snacking and viewing. After a quick break, turn right onto Calabasas Peak Motorway and begin the grueling, switchbacking climb to the summit at 2.3 miles. There's a large sandstone cornice here, perfect for lunching, resting, or just taking in the views. When you're ready, descend a generally hard-packed fire road past the Calabasas Cold Creek hiking trail on your left. At 4 miles you'll reach pavement again in the form of Old Topanga Road. Turn right. At 6.8 miles, turn right on Red Rock Road (which you previously drove on) and follow it through the notch in between the red sandstone formations back to your car, at 7.4 miles.

RIDE 66 · Malibu Creek Loop with Beginner Option

AT A GLANCE

Length/configuration: 15.4-mile loop through park, up Bulldog Road to Mesa Peak, and the return on brief single-track, dirt road, and pavement; beginner option is 5.8 miles (2.7 miles each way, plus 0.2-mile spur to Rock Pool) on fire road and brief single-track

Aerobic difficulty: Loop is difficult; fire road climbs are a real grind. Beginner option is fairly flat except for one small hill

Technical difficulty: Full loop is moderate; some rocky, steep and occasionally rutted slopes; beginner option is mostly easy, except for a section that travels through a gravelly streambed

Scenery: Rock Pool, Century Lake, oak woodlands, Pacific Ocean, mountain panoramas, volcanic sandstone rock escarpment

Special comments: This park offers a challenging loop for intermediate and advanced riders, and provides a scenic out-and-back for beginners

This 15.4-mile loop taxes the legs but rewards the eyes. Mile for mile, it is one of the most scenic tours in all of Southern California. Even the much shorter beginner option is bursting with eye candy. (Which also makes it great for families; bring the kids in your Burley trailer and you won't be disappointed.)

After spinning by the mesmerizing Rock Pool, the year-round Century Lake, and burned-out exterior set for the TV show *M*A*S*H*, you come to an intersection with Bulldog Road. Beginners will turn around here, but more experienced cyclists will take a left and ascend a fire road that's often surrounded by surprisingly green grasses. That's because Malibu Creek State Park seems to get more moisture than almost anywhere in the Santa Monica Mountains; there's even a unique freshwater marsh next to Century Lake.

It's nice to know this, because you need to occupy your mind with something as you climb over a frustrating false summit on your way up to Castro Peak Road. An easy coast down to the intersection with Mesa Peak Road delivers you to a massive volcanic sandstone escarpment, where it's mandatory to settle into a hollow for lunch with a view. A little more climbing brings you to a summit with excellent ocean views. Then comes a downhill that seems disproportionately short. But then, don't they all.

General location: In Malibu Creek State Park, 5 miles north of Pacific Coast Highway, 3 miles south of US 101 in Calabasas.

Elevation change: Full loop gains approximately 2,400 feet total, with one main climb of 1,800 feet from 500 feet to 2,300 feet. Beginner option elevation gain is approximately 150 feet.

Season: Year-round, except for immediately after rainstorms. In summer, you don't want to be riding Bulldog Road during the heat of the day.

Services: Water, rest rooms, vending machine available at trailhead. Water, rest rooms, phone available at Visitor Center. All other services available in Malibu and Calabasas.

Hazards: Parts of the beginner option can be very wet, even underwater, after heavy rains. The full loop has near-slickrock riding on volcanic sandstone, rocky trails, steep descents, rattlesnakes, and automobile traffic on paved sections.

Rescue index: This park sees a lot of use and is well-patrolled. Help is available at Visitor Center partway through the ride or at Park Headquarters near start of ride.

Land status: State park and state roads.

Maps: Malibu Creek State Park Map available at Visitor Center and through California Department of Parks. Also, *Trail Map of the Santa Monica Mountains Central* is available from Tom Harrison Cartography, (800) 265-9090, (415)456-7940, www.tomharrisonmaps.com.

Finding the trail: From Pacific Coast Highway in Malibu, drive north 6 miles on Malibu Canyon (which turns into Las Virgenes Road) and turn left into Malibu Creek State Park. From US 101 in Calabasas, exit on Las Virgenes Road and go south 3.3 miles (passing Mulholland) and turn right into Malibu Creek State Park. Park visitors arriving by car must pay a small day use fee; those arriving by bike are admitted free. Continue to the farthest parking lot. The ride starts next to the trailhead kiosk and the rest rooms.

Sources of additional information:

California Dept. of Parks and
   Recreation
Angeles District/Malibu Sector
1925 Las Virgenes Road
Calabasas, CA 91302

(818) 880-0367
www.csp-angeles.com/sites/
   mcsp.html
cal-parks.ca.gov/south/angeles/
   mcsp537.htm

RIDE 66 · Malibu Creek Loop with Beginner Option

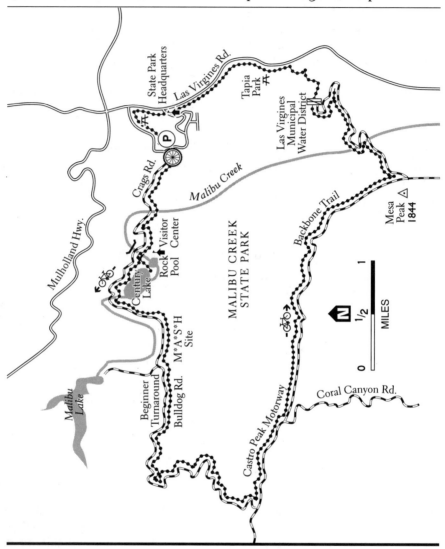

Santa Monica Mountains National
Recreation Area Visitor Center
401 W. Hillcrest Drive
Thousand Oaks, CA 91360

(805) 370-2300
www.nps.gov/samo

Notes on the trail: From the trailhead kiosk, head south on a road marked "Authorized Vehicles Only." You almost immediately take a left so that you can cross over a cement bridge. Turn right immediately after the bridge and head toward the Visitor Center on Crags Road. It winds up to the Visitor Center at 0.7 mile. Stop in for information or a historical display about the area, but otherwise cross a pretty bridge over Malibu Creek. Then take an immediate left and spin 0.2 mile out to the gorgeous, oasis-like Rock Pool. Numerous movies have been shot at the Rock Pool and throughout the park, including early Tarzan films, *How Green Was My Valley*, and the original *Planet of the Apes*.

After you've enjoyed the sights, backtrack to Crags Road and go left, up a small but fairly steep hill. On the other side of the hill, Century Lake comes into view. Though man-made, the lake has naturally silted up and created a unique freshwater marsh—an unusual body of water in a place where it normally doesn't rain for eight months of the year. In this area you'll come to the first of several intersections with small trails. Stay on the main track which becomes a gravely streambed.

At 2.8 miles you reach a familiar-looking area; it was the outdoor set of the television show *M*A*S*H*, which burned in a devastating 1982 fire. Spinning past an immolated jeep, you reach the trailhead for Bulldog Road at 3.1 miles. Beginners should turn around here, and return to the start (avoiding the spur to the Rock Pool) for a ride totaling 5.8 miles.

Fit intermediate to advanced riders, however, should turn left onto Bulldog Road and begin climbing. Ignore intersections with electric tower access roads, and stay on the main road. At 4.1 miles, skeep to your right (uphill) at the fork. At 4.2 miles, go left at a Y intersection. The climbing becomes particularly tough here, but views begin to unfold before you. On a clear winter day, you can see all the way to snow-capped Mount San Antonio in the San Gabriel Mountains.

After grunting past a few false summits, the road crests at 6.7 miles at the intersection with Castro Peak Motorway. Go left and downhill here. At 7.2 miles, veer right, continuing downhill toward paved Coral Canyon parking lot below you, which you reach at 7.5 miles. Just past the gate to the lot, go left on an unsigned dirt road and onto the otherworldly volcanic sandstone outcroppings. The trail here goes east-southeast over the sandstone. Though occasionally it's hard to pick up which trail is yours, continue in the direction you've been going, and you'll eventually find it. In the meantime, explore the wild-looking sandstone formations. This is a great place to enjoy lunch with a view.

From atop the sandstone escarpment, you see Mesa Peak Road heading southeast. Descend to it. This dirt road begins climbing at 8.1 miles. After some ups and downs Mesa Peak Road, you'll come to section of road that—at press time—was buried under a rockslide. If the slide is still there during your ride, don't panic. You can get around it, just go slowly.

Mesa Peak Road ultimately reaches a saddle at 2,049 feet above sea level. You just begin to descend when you reach a Y junction at 10.5 miles. Go left here and veer left again a few hundred feet later. You descend steeply on a rutted, rocky trail, so be careful. At 12.5 miles, you reach an intersection with Tapia Spur Trail, marked only with a sign reading "Tractors Only." You're not a tractor, but go right here anyway. (If you miss this turnoff—which is easy to do—you quickly dead-end at a fenced-off water reclamation facility; simply turn around and take a left on Tapia Spur Trail.) This is a rutted single-track which ends at a gate at Las Virgenes Road at 13.2 miles. Go left on Las Virgenes and climb the paved road to the entrance to Malibu Creek State Park. Go left and return to the start at 15.4 miles.

RIDE 67 · Backbone Trail/Castro Crest

AT A GLANCE

Length/configuration: 12.6-mile combination (3.9 miles each way with a 4.8 mile terminus loop) on single-track and dirt road

Aerobic difficulty: Moderate/difficult; climbs are tough at times, but usually short and broken up by downhills

Technical difficulty: Difficult; trail is very narrow and rocky in places

Scenery: Pacific Ocean, rock formations, valleys, canyons, stream crossings

Special comments: A mostly single-track ride with abundant scenery and minimal grunting

This is a 12.6-mile lollipop-shaped route where the sucker is bigger than the stick, but every part is worth devouring. Much of this ride takes place on the Backbone Trail, a path that snakes across the spine of the Santa Monica Mountains and is primarily closed to bikes. Irresponsible riding could close this section as well, which would be a shame since it offers a great deal of fun and an easily accessible single-track.

From the Kanan-Dume Road parking area, the ride climbs, then drops into a canyon, climbs out of it, then drops into another before climbing back up to Newton Motorway. After crossing the motorway, an especially scenic but rocky single-track falls into a canyon formed by the west fork of Solstice Creek. This loose sandstone section can be dauntingly slick, especially for clueless mountain bike guidebook authors who vainly think they can outrun an approaching Pacific winter storm there.

In any case, the trail soon delivers riders to the canyon floor and several rideable stream crossings before climbing to Castro Crest Motorway. The fire road ascent up to Castro Peak isn't inordinately steep or high, but clouds gather here anyway and it can be very disorienting to ride this section during a fast-moving storm. Luckily, the trail is well marked, and even the aforementioned authors can find their way back to Newton Motorway and the end of the sucker part of the ride. The climbs and drops of the stick section ensue, and they're just as much fun to ride in this direction as the other.

General location: Approximately 8 miles south of Agoura Hills, and 4 miles north of Pacific Coast Highway in Malibu.

Elevation change: Approximately 1,500 feet.

Season: Year-round, but don't ride immediately after rains.

Services: No services on trail; all services in Malibu and Agoura Hills.

Hazards: Technical descents, steep cliffsides, and stream crossings in winter and spring.

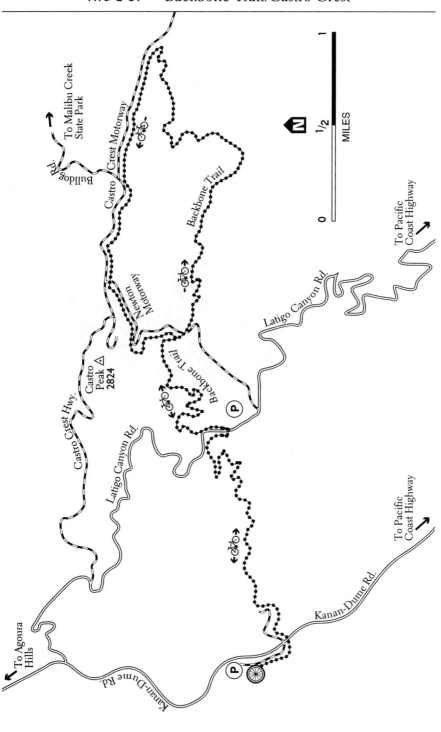

To Malibu Creek State Park

Bulldog Rd.

Castro Crest Motorway

Backbone Trail

N

MILES

0   ½   1

To Pacific Coast Highway

Latigo Canyon Rd.

Newton Motorway

Castro Peak △ 2824

Castro Crest Hwy.

Backbone Trail

Latigo Canyon Rd.

P

Kanan-Dume Rd.

To Pacific Coast Highway

To Agoura Hills

Kanan-Dume Rd.

P

Leaving the mist behind
on the Backbone Trail.

Rescue index: The route is occasionally patrolled by volunteers of the Santa Monica Mountains National Recreation Area's Mountain Bike Unit. Otherwise, help is available in the nearby towns of Malibu and Agoura Hills.

Land status: Federal parkland, National Park Service, Santa Monica Mountains National Recreation Area.

Maps: *Trail Map of the Santa Monica Mountains Central* from Tom Harrison Cartography, (800) 265-9090 or (415) 456-7940, www.tomharrisonmaps.com.

Finding the trail: From US 101 in Agoura Hills, go south on Kanan-Dume Road for almost 8 miles to the third tunnel and park in a small dirt parking area just before the tunnel. From CA 1/PCH, go north on Kanan-Dume Road 4.3 miles to the first tunnel. As you pass through the tunnel, put your left-turn signal on; there are numerous tailgaters in this area. Almost immediately after emerging from the tunnel, go left into the dirt parking area.

Sources of additional information:

Santa Monica Mountains National
   Recreation Area
401 W. Hillcrest Drive
Thousand Oaks, CA 91360
(805) 370-2300
www.nps.gov/sam

Helen's Cycles
2501 Broadway
Santa Monica, CA 90404
(310) 829-1836

Supergo Bike Shops
501 Broadway
Santa Monica, CA 90401
(310) 451-9977

Cycle Design
3900 Cross Creek Road
Malibu, CA 90265
(310) 456-1685

Bicycling America's National Parks:
   California, David Story,
   (Countryman Press, 2000)

Notes on the trail: From the parking area on the west side of Kanan-Dume Road, start riding up the trail that heads south (toward the tunnel). You have about 0.25 mile of steep climbing as you go up and over the tunnel and begin riding east on the single-track. Once the trail crests, you drop down into Newton Canyon on a particularly juicy single-track.

I call this a lollipop ride, since there's a long out-and-back portion (resembling a stick), topped with a terminus loop (the candy circle). However, unlike real lollipops, this stick portion is as delicious as the candy. It's a great deal of fun winding through this lush oak woodland, despite the rugged (but short) climb up to paved Latigo Canyon Road, which ends at 2.4 miles. Cross the road, jog slightly left, and pick up the trail again at the end of a small parking lot.

After a fun descent on the well-marked Backbone Trail over erosion bars, rocks, streams, and roots into a forested canyon, begin climbing. At 3.9 miles, you come to a T-intersection at Newton Motorway. Jog right and quickly turn left onto the Backbone Trail again, marked by a sign reading "Corral Canyon Trailhead 2.8 miles." You're now on the "sucker" part of the lollipop, and will ride counterclockwise in a big circle to return to this spot.

As you drop down the trail, you gain lovely views of the canyon formed by the upper fork of Solstice Creek. But you may never get the chance to appreciate them, because the technical single-track will demand all your attention. If it's wet or foggy, be very careful riding the sandstone in this section. Also, be on the lookout for eroded switchbacks; the drop-offs here are steep.

Next comes a delicious ramble on the canyon floor where you thoroughly splash your Cannondale through countless (but rideable) stream crossings. A moderate ascent brings you to a four-way intersection at 6.2 miles. Going right will take you to the Corral Canyon Trailhead, but you want to take a hard left on Castro Crest Motorway, which sounds as if it's some grand passageway, but is actually just a fire road climbing toward Castro Peak. At the next unmarked but unmistakable T-intersection, go left and up. After a few hundred yards, stay left at the intersection, following the sign marked simply "Backbone." Climb past some gorgeous rock formations and at the next T-intersection veer slightly left, following the arrow on a sign pointing the way to "Latigo Canyon." There are some great vistas around here, and since you're nearly at the top of your ride, feel free to have a snack and enjoy them. At 7.8 miles, turn sharply left at the sign marked "Backbone Trail .8 mi." You're now on Newton Motorway again and the descent soon begins. Gradual at first, it gets steep near the end. At 8.7 miles, turn right on the Backbone Trail again (this is the "stick" portion of the "lollipop", which you've already ridden in the opposite direction). Retrace your route back to the start at 12.6 miles.

RIDE 68 · Paramount Ranch

AT A GLANCE

Length/configuration: 3.6-mile combination (2.4-mile loop with 0.6-mile out-and-back spur) on pavement, dirt road, and single-track

Aerobic difficulty: Easy; any hills are short in duration

Technical difficulty: Easy/moderate; wholly rideable except for a few narrow, rocky sections

Scenery: Mock western town, oak savannas, and Sugarloaf Mountain

Special comments: This is a behind-the-scenes movie set tour and mountain bike ride rolled into one—a must for families

The family rides listed in this book certainly appeal to children interested in wildlife and nature. But what makes this 3.6-mile loop in Paramount Ranch unique is that it also captivates those kids who might also be couch potatoes and movie buffs.

Paramount Pictures bought this land in 1927 for use as a movie ranch, and for 25 years filmed westerns, exotic foreign-set dramas, and even Revolutionary War pictures here. Some people point out that Sugarloaf Peak, in the southwest corner of the park, even looks like the mountain in Paramount's logo. In 1953, after Paramount sold the ranch, an ardent movie fan leased the land and painstakingly built a western town as a tribute to the cowboy movies shot here. Western Town has been busy ever since and served from 1991–1998 as the set for *Dr. Quinn Medicine Woman*. Though film and television production can sometimes shut down access to Western Town, it's surprising how much is open to your examination.

As fun as it is to explore the town, it's even more entertaining to sample the myriad single- and double-track paths weaving through the ranch. Though there are far too many trails here to prescribe a single, conclusive loop, the ride described below offers a good sample of trails in the area. Just be aware that the trail intersections are so numerous that all mileages and descriptions are rough— you can't describe this area on paper, you can only ride it in person.

Two rules: First, obey the instructions of any television or film personnel in the ranch—the production crew's lease on the land pays for its upkeep. Secondly, do

RIDE 68 · Paramount Ranch

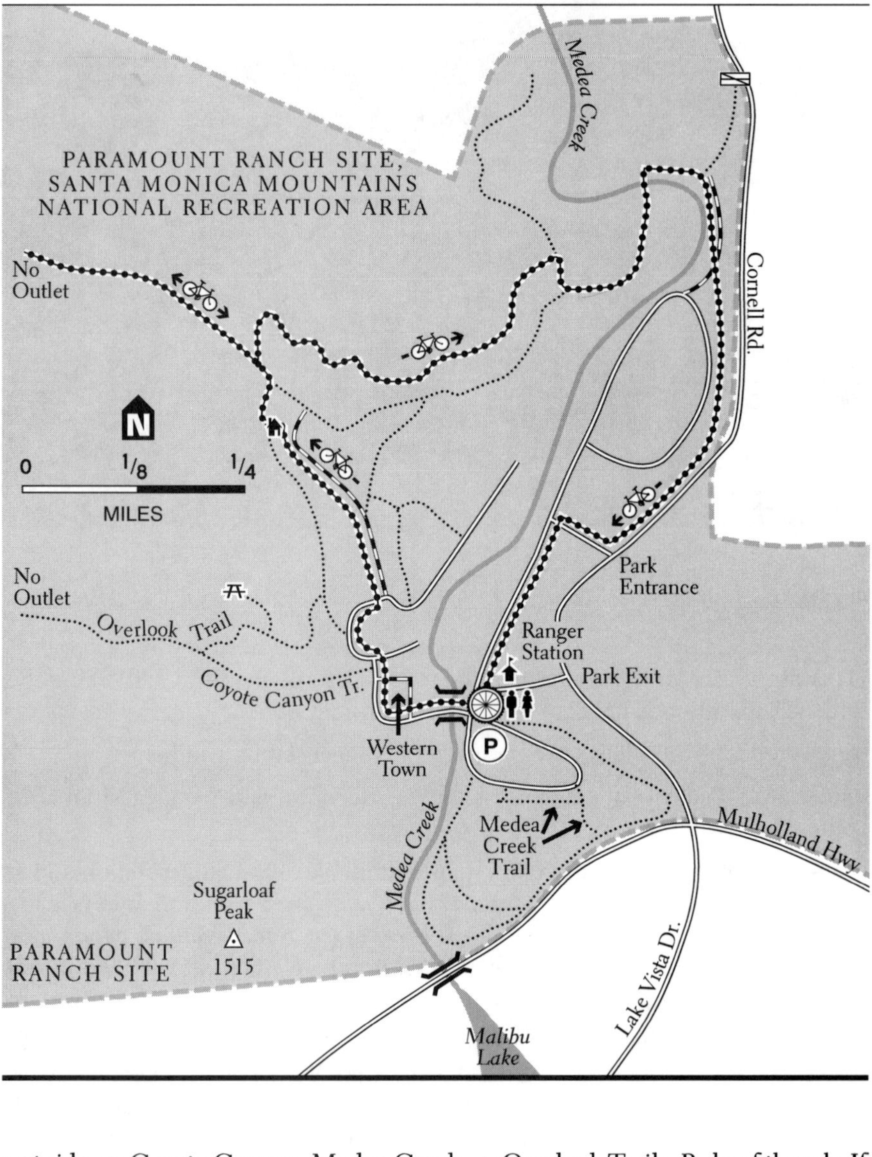

PARAMOUNT RANCH SITE,
SANTA MONICA MOUNTAINS
NATIONAL RECREATION AREA

No
Outlet

Medea Creek

Cornell Rd.

N

0   1/8   1/4

MILES

No
Outlet

Park
Entrance

Overlook Trail

Coyote Canyon Tr.

Ranger
Station

Park Exit

P

Western
Town

Medea
Creek
Trail

Mulholland Hwy

Sugarloaf
Peak

Medea Creek

△
1515

Lake Vista Dr.

PARAMOUNT
RANCH SITE

*Malibu
Lake*

not ride on Coyote Canyon, Medea Creek, or Overlook Trails. Rule of thumb: If a trail is named on a sign, it's probably off-limits to bikes.

General location: In Paramount Ranch, 2 miles south of Agoura Hills and US 101.

Elevation change: Insignificant.

Season: Year-round (but avoid riding during the heat of the day in summer).

Services: Rest rooms, water, a ranger station, and a picnic area are available at the ranch. All other services are available in Agoura Hills.

School's out: time for mountain biking.

Hazards: Watch out for rattlesnakes, as well as some poison oak flanking the trails. Also, wasps and bees are common in summer.

Rescue index: The ride is never far from the ranger station and help.

Land status: Federal parkland, National Park Service, Santa Monica Mountains National Recreation Area.

Maps: The Paramount Ranch Site map is available at the ranger station and at the Santa Monica Mountains National Recreation Area Visitor Center (see the following information). Also, the *Trail Map of the Santa Monica Mountains Central* is available from Tom Harrison Cartography, (800) 265-9090 or (415) 456-7940, www.tomharrisonmaps.com.

Finding the trail: Take US 101 to Kanan Road in Agoura Hills. Proceed south on Kanan past Agoura Road. Turn left on Cornell Way. The road becomes Cornell Road after it takes a bend to the right. Travel on Cornell Road approximately 1.8 miles, and turn right into Paramount Ranch. (If you reach Mulholland Highway, you've gone too far.) From the Cornell Road entrance to Paramount Ranch, drive south and park by the bridge linking the parking lot to Western Town.

Sources of additional information:

Santa Monica Mountains National
    Recreation Area
Visitor Center
401 W. Hillcrest Drive
Thousand Oaks, CA 91360
(805) 370-2300
www.nps.gov/samo

Agoura Cycling Center
29041 Thousand Oaks Boulevard
Agoura, CA 91301
(818) 991-6333

Notes on the trail: The following directions should be taken as a recommendation for one possible ride and not as the definitive ride in the area. It's probably more fun to simply explore here on your own (while keeping off prohibited trails). Families would be better advised to explore according to the child's ability and interest rather than insist on trying to strictly follow any specific route. Furthermore, since the paths in this area intersect frequently, it's somewhat futile to give directions. Regard these directions as a very loose guideline and nothing more.

From the parking lot, ride westbound across the bridge connecting to Western Town. Explore Western Town at your leisure, then circle clockwise through the town. After passing the mock train station, veer left and onto the banked asphalt road. Stay on the asphalt as it curves clockwise to a dirt road heading north. Go north on this dirt road toward a farm building at 0.6 mile. Turn left toward the building, then right alongside a fence paralleling the dirt road you were previously riding. Veer left at the end of the fence and then left again at a Y junction at 0.7 mile. You're now on a dirt single-track spur that climbs past chaparral up to a saddle at 1.3 miles. Enjoy the view of Kanan Road from here, then turn around and return to the Y junction. Turn left on the trail, which goes north, then doubles back to the south, then curves northeast, all in a short span. At 2.5 miles, turn right at a T-intersection, and immediately left (toward Cornell Road). After crossing Medea Creek at 2.6 miles, look for the trail curving right along the north bank of Medea Creek and paralleling Cornell Road. The trail clings to the edge of the park boundary within sight of Cornell Road until it swings right at the park entrance at 3.3 miles. Now meander on the pavement back to the Western Town bridge and your car at 3.6 miles.

RIDE 69 · Cheeseboro/Palo Comado Canyons

AT A GLANCE

Length/configuration: 12.2-mile loop (with short bit of repeated terrain in middle) on dirt road and single-track

Aerobic difficulty: Easy/moderate; the trail is very level in sections, only steep when crossing the ridge between the two canyons

Technical difficulty: Easy/moderate; stream crossings and some sandy terrain

Scenery: Canyons, abundant wildlife, and oak woodlands

Special comments: Just one of many possible trail combinations in this family-friendly area

This 12.2-mile loop is a prime beginner/intermediate ride. It features lots of level riding at first to build confidence, rewards efforts with abundant wildlife views, and then segues into some tough but quick climbs that challenge riders to improve themselves. It's no surprise that this is one of the most family-friendly riding areas in the Santa Monica Mountains National Recreation Area.

Technically speaking, the ride is located in the Simi Hills and not the Santa Monicas, but the scenery is just as beautiful. As you spin slightly uphill on well-signed Cheeseboro Canyon Trail, the oak savannas give way to steeper canyon terrain. You'll likely see ground squirrels, voles (also known as meadow mice), red-tailed hawks, and perhaps even mule deer before the trail narrows. After a series of stream crossings, you'll emerge into rocky Shepherds' Flat, where you turn left for a climb and then descend into Palo Comado Canyon. A fast downhill brings you to another couple of steep ridge climbs, but the sights of vibrantly green mountainsides and spring wildflowers lessen the pain as you glide back to the parking lot.

If for some reason the loop isn't to your liking, feel free to explore. There are dozens of combinations here, and it's possible to ride on mostly level terrain if you're not in the mood for hills.

General location: Cheeseboro Canyon/Palo Comado Canyons in the Simi Hills northeast of Agoura Hills, 1 mile north of the Ventura Freeway (US 101).

Elevation change: Approximately 1,200 feet.

Season: Year-round (but avoid riding in the heat of the day during summer).

Services: Pit toilets and water are available at the trailhead. All other services are available in Agoura Hills.

Hazards: Stream crossings, narrow trails.

Rescue index: The route is regularly (but not always) patrolled by rangers and volunteers with the Santa Monica Mountains National Recreation Area's Mountain Bike Unit (M.B.U.). In an emergency, call 911.

Land status: Federal parkland, National Park Service, Santa Monica Mountains National Recreation Area.

Maps: The Cheeseboro Canyon/Palo Comado Canyon Site map is available through Santa Monica Mountains National Recreation Area Visitor Center (see "Sources of additional information," below).

Finding the trail: From the San Fernando Valley: Take US 101 westbound to the Chesebro Exit (yes, it's spelled differently than the canyon). Turn right at the off ramp on Palo Comado Canyon Road, then immediately right onto Chesebro Road. Turn right into the park just before the Agoura Hills City Limits sign. Park as directed in the lot. From Thousand Oaks: Take US 101 eastbound to the Chesebro Exit. Turn left at the off ramp on Dorothy Drive, then left on Palo Comado Canyon Road, then immediately right onto Chesebro Road. Turn right into the park just before the Agoura Hills City Limits sign. Park as directed in the lot.

RIDE 69 · Cheeseboro/Palo Comado Canyons

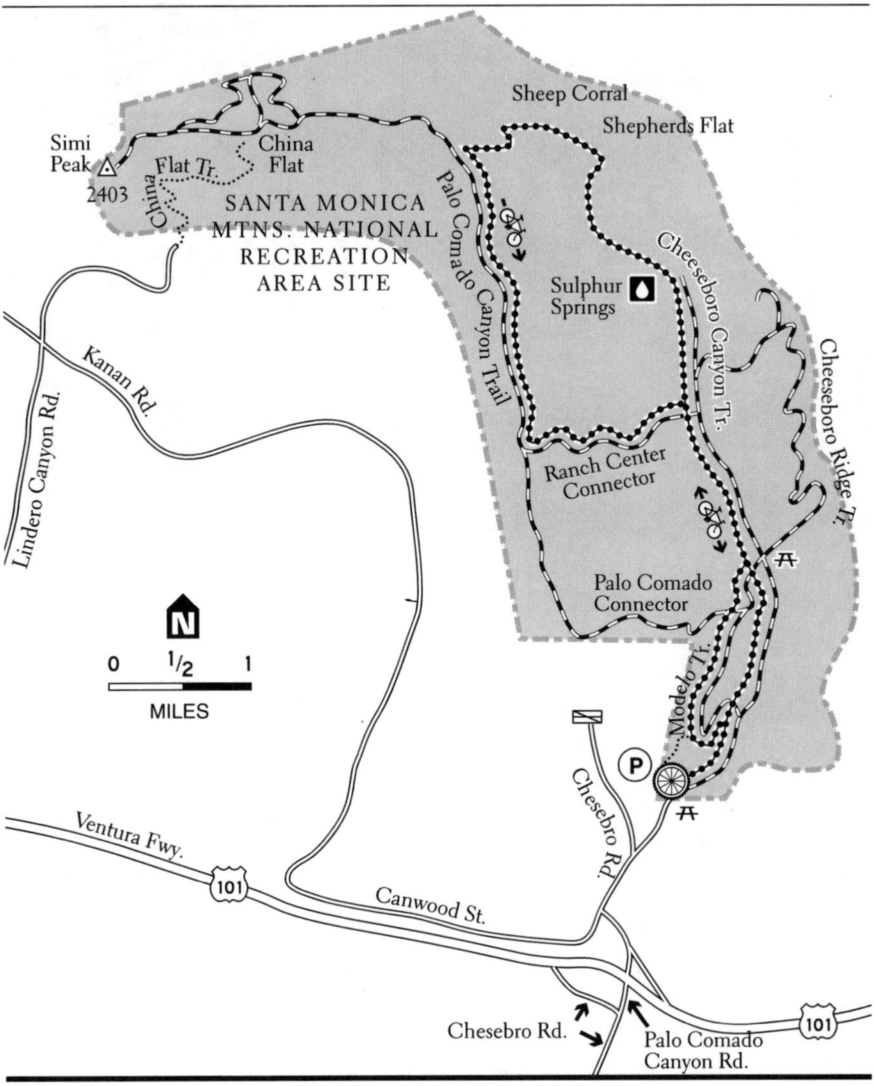

Sheep Corral

Shepherds Flat

Simi Peak △
2403

China Flat Tr.

China Flat

China

Flat Tr.

SANTA MONICA
MTNS. NATIONAL
RECREATION
AREA SITE

Palo Comado Canyon Trail

Sulphur
Springs

Cheeseboro Canyon Tr.

Cheeseboro Ridge Tr.

Kanan Rd.

Ranch Center
Connector

Lindero Canyon Rd.

Palo Comado
Connector

N

| 0 | 1/2 | 1 |

MILES

Model T Rd.

P 🚲

Ventura Fwy.

101

Canwood St.

Chesebro Rd.

Chesebro Rd.

Palo Comado
Canyon Rd.

101

Sources of additional information:

Santa Monica Mountains National
   Recreation Area
Visitor Center
401 W. Hillcrest Drive
Thousand Oaks, CA 91360
(805) 370-2300
www.nps.gov/samo

Agoura Cycling Center
29041 Thousand Oaks Boulevard
Agoura, CA 91301
(818) 991-6333

When it comes to mountain biking terrain, Sulphur Springs is no slouch.

Notes on the trail: From the parking lot, go through the split-rail fence and ride north on well-signed Cheeseboro Canyon Trail through all intersections. At 1.4 miles, you'll reach the intersection with Cheeseboro Ridge Trail on the right and Cheeseboro Canyon/Palo Comado Trail on the left. Go left. Stay right when you reach the junction with Modelo Trail/Palo Comado. Continue north on Cheeseboro Canyon Trail. You'll reach a fork at 2 miles. Either fork is okay as they soon rejoin each other, but head left for a narrower, shadier trail. You'll soon begin crossing streams, especially in winter and spring. At 2.6 miles stay right at another turnoff to Palo Comado. At 3.1 miles, the trail narrows as you reach Sulphur Springs. If you're riding with tired kids or don't want to ride any terrain more hilly than what you've just experienced, you might want to turn around and explore as you make your way back to the parking lot. Otherwise, forge ahead and pass from a riparian oak environment to a coastal scrub sage ecosystem. At 4.5 miles, turn left at the T intersection at Shepherds' at. Try to stay as high and to the right as possible, as it's easy to lose the trail in this section. If you feel like you're off the trail, simply look for a lone rocky knoll in the west and head toward it. More precisely, you're aiming toward a trail on the knoll which switchbacks after climbing off the valley floor. Reaching the switchback at 5.5 miles, turn left and begin climbing the knoll in earnest. You'll pass an unmarked single-track trail at 5.6 miles on your left, then come to a little vista point, and finally pour out onto Palo Comado Canyon Trail (a fire road at this point) at 5.9 miles. Make a sharp left to ride down Palo Comado. It's a fast descent to 7.8 miles, where you'll turn left onto Ranch Center connector. Climb over the chaparral-covered ridge and go right twice—the second time onto Cheeseboro

Canyon Trail at 9 miles. Cruising by the fork in the trail you encountered earlier, go right on the Modelo Trail/Palo Comado Connector at 10.2 miles. Head left at the fork (staying on the Cheeseboro Canyon side of the ridge) at 10.5 miles. Climb to a steep summit and then descend to a T-intersection at 11.2 miles and turn left. Turn right when it ends on Cheeseboro Canyon Trail at 11.6 miles and descend to the parking lot at 12.2 miles.

RIDE 70 · Zuma/Trancas Canyons

AT A GLANCE

CA

Length/configuration: 13.6-mile loop on rocky fire road, double-track, single-track, and pavement

Aerobic difficulty: Difficult; some steep climbing

Technical difficulty: Difficult; some rocky stretches and steep sections

Scenery: Channel Islands, Pacific Ocean, steep canyons, gorges, pools, waterfalls, lush canyon bottoms, and spring wildflowers

Special comments: A scenic, challenging ride that can be capped off by a post-ride dip in the Pacific at nearby Zuma Beach

Taking place at a rarely visited site, this demanding yet gorgeous ride climbs Zuma Ridge then drops into and climbs out of indescribably beautiful Zuma Canyon. It's no surprise that to the native Chumash Indians, the word "zuma" means "abundance." It aptly describes the wildlife, plant life, and views you'll find here; everything, that is, but the number of fellow trail users.

The route climbs up a fairly steep grade along Zuma Ridge Motorway, with some tough switchbacks in parts. If the climb doesn't take your breath away, the views of the Pacific coastline and the Channel Islands out at sea sure will. It's hard to tear yourself away from the views as you turn to descend steeply into Zuma Canyon and sail past its red rock walls. If you're lucky, you might see a bobcat on one of the switchbacks in this area. But even without wildlife, the area doesn't lack for scenery. As you near the canyon bottom, the sycamores, oaks, willows, and black walnut trees become thick. In late fall, they carpet the fire road under your wheels with brilliant yellow leaves.

But the most vibrant color here is green. Visit after a spring rainstorm, and the verdancy of the wild, ubiquitous clover will make you check your calendar to see if it's St. Patrick's Day. Regrettably, your face might also turn green during the sickeningly steep climb out of the canyon. The ascent culminates with a fun but brief single-track on a knife-blade ridge. Afterwards, it's time to head back into civilization on a dirt road that passes through private property, where you must be absolutely sure to honor all signs posted by the landowners. Ultimately, you hit pavement and circle back on some fairly busy roads to the start of the ride.

RIDE 70 · Zuma/Trancas Canyon

General location: Near Zuma Beach, just off Pacific Coast Highway (20 miles northwest of Santa Monica).

Elevation change: Two major climbs on dirt, and a smaller one on pavement result in a total elevation gain of 2,640 feet.

Season: Year-round.

Services: No water available on trail. All services available in Malibu.

Hazards: Some very steep and rocky terrain; rattlesnakes.

Zuma Ridge Motorway and Edison Road.

Rescue index: The route is regularly (but not always) patrolled by rangers and volunteers with the Santa Monica Mountains National Recreation Area's Mountain Bike Unit (M.B.U.). Help is also available in Malibu at the county beaches on CA 1. In an emergency, call 911.

Land status: Federal parkland, National Park Service, Santa Monica Mountains National Recreation Area.

Maps: *Trail Map of the Santa Monica Mountains Central* is available from Tom Harrison Cartography, (800) 265-9090 or (415) 456-7940, www.tomharrison maps.com.

Finding the trail: From Santa Monica, take CA 1/PCH north. After passing Kanan-Dume Road, go another mile and turn right on Busch Drive. Go north on Busch Drive 1.4 miles, and park on the right in a dirt parking area at the Zuma Ridge Trailhead.

Sources of additional information:

Santa Monica Mountains National
Recreation Area Visitor Center
401 W. Hillcrest Drive
Thousand Oaks, CA 91360
(805) 370-2300
www.nps.gov/samo

Bicycling America's National Parks:
California, David Story,
(Countryman Press, 2000)

Notes on the trail: From the trailhead, begin ascending the fire road called Zuma Ridge Trail. After a tough ascent, the road comes to a crest at 2.7 miles.

Turn right here, at the intersection with Zuma Edison Road. A steep descent leads you to Zuma Creek, which you cross. (Beware: after rains, it runs deep— you may get wet trying to ford it.)

A very tough 1.5-mile climb ensues, taking you to the turnoff for Zuma Canyon Connection Trail at 6.6 miles. Go right onto the single-track trail, which clings to the top of a knife-blade ridge, then heads down to a T-intersection with Kanan Edison Road. If you go right, you hook up with the hiking trails of Lower Zuma Canyon where bikes are prohibited, or otherwise come to a dead end in private property some distance from Kanan-Dume Road.

So go left instead. The trail curves sharply downhill and reaches paved Kanan-Dume Road at 7.8 miles. Turn right, heading downhill some more until you reach CA 1/PCH. Go right again, then again in a mile or so onto Busch Drive, and climb back up to the start at 13.6 miles.

RIDE 71 · Big Sycamore Canyon/ Point Mugu State Park

AT A GLANCE

Length/configuration: 15.5-mile loop

Aerobic difficulty: Difficult; longer ride with plenty of moderately difficult climbing; steep, 1.5-mile pull up Hell Hill

Technical difficulty: Moderately difficult; some loose gravel and sand on roads; the single-track includes obstacles

Scenery: Larger deciduous trees in the canyon, wildflowers in the spring, and open hillsides with pleasant coastal views

Special comments: Excellent and varied loop for strong intermediate cyclists; beginners can ride up Big Sycamore Canyon Trail and turn around when they get tired

Contained within Point Mugu State Park are mountain bike routes suited to all abilities. Strength and good bike-handling skills are required of cyclists during this 15.5-mile loop. The first 5.6 miles are a gentle ascent on Big Sycamore Canyon Trail to Ranch Center Road. The pedaling on Ranch Center Road is moderately difficult for 1.5 miles, and then the road drops rapidly for 0.8 mile. Wood Canyon Trail is picked up at this point, and the route continues downhill for 2 miles to Overlook Trail at Deer Camp Junction. On Overlook Trail you climb very steeply for 1.5 miles and tackle the aptly named Hell Hill. The biking gets easier as you ride around the south side of an unnamed peak. The loop ends with an exhilarating 3-mile descent.

The first 4.5 miles are over an unpaved, two-wheel-drive road in good condition. This is followed by 3.2 miles of pavement. The remaining miles are on dirt trails in fair to good condition with some loose gravel and sand.

   This ride has it all: an easy warm-up, lovely scenery, tree-shaded lanes, open roads, single-track trails, a grinding sweat-in-the-eyes climb, exhilarating descents, splendid coastal views, ample water, wildlife, and wildflowers. Who could ask for more?

General location: Starts at the campground in Big Sycamore Canyon at Point Mugu State Park (approximately 30 miles west of Los Angeles).

Elevation change: Big Sycamore Canyon Trail begins at 25 feet and climbs to 400 feet at Ranch Center Road. On Ranch Center Road you'll climb to 700 feet and then drop to 500 feet at the intersection with Wood Canyon Trail. You will then descend on Wood Canyon Trail to Deer Camp Junction at 300 feet, and climb to 1,200 feet on Overlook Trail before descending to the trailhead. Total elevation gain: 1,575 feet.

Season: This trail can be enjoyed year-round. Due to its beautiful trails and proximity to a large urban area, Point Mugu State Park is a popular riding area. Good bets for light-use times are weekday mornings. Trail closure due to high fire danger can occur at any time.

Services: You will find water at the Big Sycamore Canyon Campground and at various locations along the ride. The last place to fill up before climbing on Overlook Trail is at the Ranch Center Maintenance Center. All services are available in Malibu.

Hazards: The park is well used by cyclists, equestrians, hikers, and runners. Care must be taken to watch out for others on the trails. Be especially cautious around blind corners. Watch for motor vehicles on Ranch Center Road.

Rescue index: Help can be obtained at the park headquarters at the park's entrance. There is a pay phone here as well.

Land status: State park.

Maps: A park map can be purchased at the headquarters. It is an excellent guide to this trail.

Finding the trail: The trail begins at the north end of the Big Sycamore Canyon Campground in Point Mugu State Park. The park's entrance is off the PCH (CA 1), 32 miles west of Santa Monica and 12 miles east of Oxnard. There is a day-use fee for parking at the campground or across the highway at the beach. Automobiles may also be parked outside the park in an area off the highway marked "No Parking 10 p.m. to 5 a.m."

Sources of additional information:

California Department of Parks
   and Recreation
Angeles District/Malibu Sector
1925 Los Virgenes Road

Calabasas, CA 91302
(818) 880-0350
cal-parks.ca.gov

Notes on the trail: Follow Big Sycamore Canyon Trail. The road turns to pavement and climbs to an intersection with Ranch Center Road. Turn left and follow Ranch Center Road to Ranch Center and Wood Canyon Trail on the left.

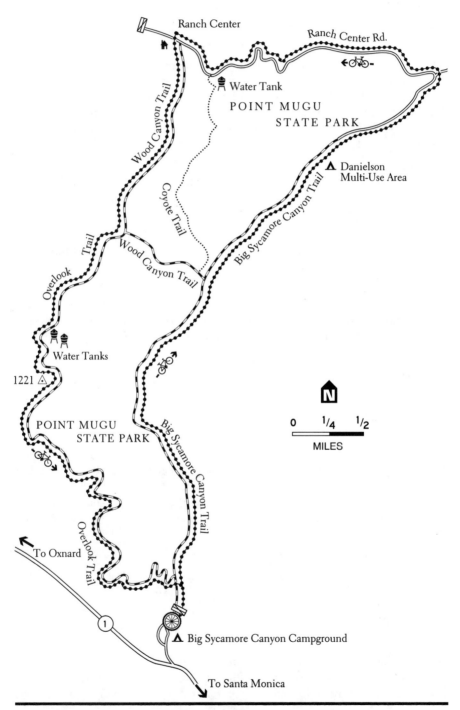

Ranch Center

Ranch Center Rd.

Wood Canyon Trail

Water Tank

POINT MUGU
STATE PARK

▲ Danielson
Multi-Use Area

Coyote Trail

Overlook Trail

Wood Canyon Trail

Big Sycamore Canyon Trail

Water Tanks

1221 △

POINT MUGU
STATE PARK

Big Sycamore Canyon Trail

N

0   1/4   1/2

MILES

To Oxnard

Overlook Trail

Big Sycamore Canyon Trail

1

▲ Big Sycamore Canyon Campground

To Santa Monica

Easy riding in Big Sycamore Canyon.

Take Wood Canyon Trail to Deer Camp Junction. Continue straight onto Overlook Trail as Wood Canyon Trail veers left. Follow Overlook Trail to Big Sycamore Canyon Trail and turn right to return to the trailhead.

Cyclists have damaged portions of the park's trails by skidding their tires. Walk your bike if you cannot descend without skidding.

Bicycles are not permitted on all of the trails in the park. Obey signs indicating closings.

VENTURA COUNTY

Once a sleepy region where farming and fishing were the prime industries, Ventura County is now in flux. As Los Angeles continues to expand, this county is becoming more suburban, especially in its rapidly growing southeastern communities such as Thousand Oaks and Camarillo. The good news is that the various governments operating in Ventura County seem especially concerned about the issues of open space and outdoor recreation. There are superb riding opportunities here, and if things stay on course, mountain bikers will flock here for years to come.

Small in size, Ventura County is big in landscape diversity. Flat plains on its southern edge produce some of the most prolific strawberry harvests in the world. The coast and the outlying Channel Islands are well-suited to both fishing and offshore oil drilling.

The majority of the county, however, is made up of rugged mountains and hills. In the Simi Hills and Conejo Valley, bikers can swoop along awesome single-tracks that rival the best in the state. For more rugged terrain, go to Los Padres National Forest, which occupies a significant portion of the county. Just be aware that the forest contains several wilderness areas that are off-limits to bicycles. Indeed, one of the better rides in the area along Sespe Creek was lost when the Sespe Wilderness was established. Yet the forest is so vast that it's still relatively easy to find a mountain bike route to your liking, especially in and around the city of Ojai (pronounced "Oh, hi"). In short, whatever your riding needs, you'd do well to say "Oh, hi!" to Ventura County yourself.

RIDE 72 · Rocky Peak/Hummingbird Trail

AT A GLANCE

Length/configuration: 6.6-mile loop on fire road, single-track, and pavement

Aerobic difficulty: Difficult; one steep fire road ascent, then a long but gentle pavement climb

Technical difficulty: Difficult; rocky, tight, but fun single-track

Scenery: Otherworldly volcanic rock outcroppings and views of the Santa Monica and Santa Susana Mountains

Special comments: Half pavement, half single-track, this is a choice ride for those cyclists who are seeking to test or improve their single-track skills but who are short on time

One of the most easily accessed rides in this book, this 6.6-mile loop has a lot of pavement riding. But its single-track portion (on land once owned by Bob Hope) is so delicious, it's worth the sacrifice.

Starting mere yards off of CA 118 in the Simi Hills, this trail immediately begins grinding up steep Rocky Peak Road. The builders of this road seem to have known how desperate riders would be for an excuse to take a break from the climb, as there's a bench on a vista and a dark little cave within the first mile. But the real attraction then takes over as you start descending the Hummingbird Trail. You might not see any hummingbirds, but you'll feel like one: bursting with energy and adrenaline, you'll flit back and forth over stoney but rideable terrain. The rock formations are as sweet as sugar water until you leave the hillside behind and ride out into a primitive dirt parking lot.

If you look back, there's a great view of all the switchbacks you took to get where you are now. You can think about all of them during the fairly long but peaceful pavement ride back to your car. After all, "Thanks for the Memories" was former landowner Bob Hope's theme song.

General location: Rocky Peak Park, located in the Simi Hills just inside the Ventura County line, 4 miles east of Simi Valley.

Elevation change: Approximately 1,100 feet elevation gain.

Season: October through May; during the summer it's best to ride early in the morning.

Services: No services are available on the trail. All services are available in Simi Valley.

Hazards: Narrow, rocky trails; mountain lions.

Rescue index: Trail is within 3 miles of major roads at all times, and help is available in Simi Valley from the Ventura County sheriff.

RIDE 72 · Rocky Peak/Hummingbird Trail

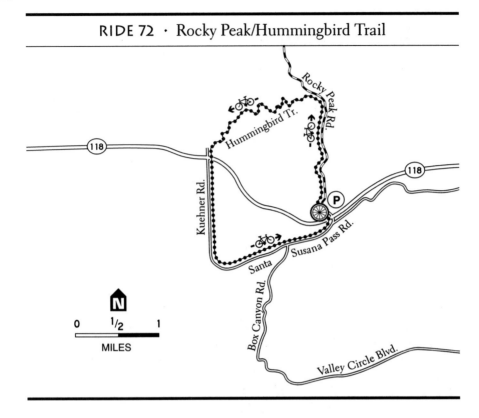

Land status: Parkland belonging to the Mountains Recreation and Conservation Authority (M.R.C.A.) and the Santa Monica Mountains Conservancy.

Maps: USGS 7.5-minute quadrangle map: Simi Valley East.

Finding the trail: From the San Fernando Valley, take CA 118 west to the Rocky Peak turnoff 5 miles east of Simi Valley. From the off ramp turn north for a few hundred feet until the road dead-ends in a dirt parking lot. Park here. From Simi Valley, head east on CA 118 and exit at Kuehner Drive. Go right (south) on Kuehner until it becomes Santa Susana Pass Road. Follow it east as it winds to the top of the pass and intersects with Rocky Peak Road. Turn left, cross the bridge over CA 118, and park in the parking area.

Sources of additional information:

Santa Monica Mountains
  Conservancy
5750 Ramirez Canyon Rd
Malibu, CA 90265-4474
(310) 589-3200
ceres.ca.gov/smmc

Mountains Recreation and
  Conservation Authority

5810 Ramirez Canyon Road
Malibu, CA 90265
(310) 589-3230

Simi Bike Works
2687 Cochran Street
Simi Valley, CA 93065
(805) 583-2124

The Hummingbird Trail, where single-track is the sweetest nectar.

Notes on the trail: From the parking area, ride left (west) past the trailhead sign and begin climbing an exposed slope that tends to be hot and dry. At 0.6 mile, you'll come to a bench on a scenic overlook. Passing the cave at 0.8 mile, you'll come to the well-signed intersection with the Hummingbird Trail at 0.9 mile. Turn left and follow the always obvious trail down. The ride can be a blast if you don't let the rocks bother you. At 2.2 miles, you'll come to a massive stone outcropping that might remind you of Moab—this is as close to slickrock as this area comes. Look downhill for the trail, and take it into a primitive dirt parking lot. Veer left out of the parking lot, and at 3.4 miles head south on paved Kuehner Road. A short while after passing under CA 118, Kuehner turns into Santa Susana Pass Road, which swings to the east as it climbs back level with CA 118. Turn left over Rocky Peak Road bridge at 6.5 miles and return to your car at 6.6 miles.

RIDE 73 · Lynnmere/Wildwood Regional Park

AT A GLANCE

Length/configuration: 4.8-mile loop on pavement and single-track

Aerobic difficulty: Moderate; some short, steep hills—a workout if ridden fast

Technical difficulty: Moderate/difficult; very rideable single-track with a few tricky sections

Scenery: Famous for spring wildflowers and volcanic outcroppings

Special comments: A rollicking roller-coaster of single-track in the middle of suburbia, it seems too good to be true—ride it, then pinch yourself

W hen approaching this 4.8-mile ride, you'll swear the directions must be wrong. However wild this country was once, it has long since been tamed by housing tracts—it couldn't possibly support a great mountain bike ride now, right? Wrong. This ride comes across like nothing less than a sampling of California's greatest mountain biking hits.

Located just 3 miles north of US 101 in Thousand Oaks in Wildwood Regional Park, the ride begins inauspiciously on pavement before veering off onto a single-track. For the first time you'll see that the area does have some open space, and this trail is going to lead you right into it. The landscape is dry and exposed at first, but things change as you plunge into Wildwood Canyon. Oak trees shade you as you meander through the canyon on captivating trails that are so twisty and fun, you'll feel as if you've stumbled into a little boy's backyard refuge. A big climb out of the canyon follows, but a final single-track over a grassland plateau tops off the day nicely—unless, of course, you want to go back and ride it again. And you just might.

General location: 3 miles north of US 101 in Thousand Oaks.

Elevation change: Approximately 300-foot elevation gain.

Season: Year-round, but avoid riding in the heat of a summer day. The park is commonly closed after big rainstorms. If it has rained in the last week, call the park before riding.

Services: Water and rest rooms are available at the Wildwood Regional Park entrance and at the Nature Center two-thirds of the way through the ride. All other services are available in Thousand Oaks.

Hazards: Steep, narrow trails, and water crossings.

Rescue index: The route is always close to the city roads of Thousand Oaks. Help is available from park rangers roaming the park.

Land status: City of Thousand Oaks, Conejo Open Space land, and regional park.

Maps: The free *Wildwood Park Trail Guide* is available at the information kiosk at the parking lot.

Finding the trail: Take US 101 to Lynn Road in Thousand Oaks. Go north on Lynn Road 3.2 miles. Turn left on Avenida De Los Arboles for approximately 1 mile. Avenida De Los Arboles ends just after the park entrance; make a legal U-turn around the median and immediately turn right into the parking lot. Pay heed to all parking lot closure signs.

RIDE 73 · Lynnmere/Wildwood Regional Park

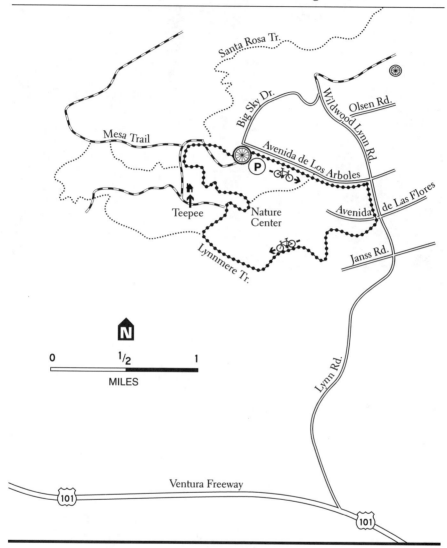

Sources of additional information:

Wildwood Regional Park
Conejo Open Space
  Conservation Agency
2100 Thousand Oaks Boulevard
Thousand Oaks, CA 91362
(805) 449-2340

Simi Bike Works
2687 Cochran Street
Simi Valley, CA 93065
(805) 583-2124

Notes on the trail: Turn right out of the parking lot and head east on Avenida de Los Arboles (the road you just took to the parking lot). At 0.9 mile, turn right

Wildwood Park—where dogs must be leashed, but grins don't have to be.

onto Lynn Road. You'll pass Avenida De Las Flores; then look to your right for a single-track trail leading up to a small knoll (it'll appear just after the fence that parallels Lynn Road gives way to open space). At 1.4 miles, turn right onto the as-yet-unnamed single-track. (If you reach Janss Road, you've gone too far.) The single-track quickly climbs a small knoll and heads west past a sign indicating you're on the Lynnmere Trail. (If you use your common sense, the Lynnmere Trail is usually quite obvious despite all the intersections it has with other dirt paths. And even if you mess up, don't worry. The trails will still deliver you into Wildwood Regional Park at some point.)

At a fork in the trail at 1.7 miles, turn left and cross a stream. Stay left after scrambling up the embankment on the other side of the stream and climb a fairly steep but small hill. Turn right at 1.9 miles and descend. The trail really roller-coasters now past coastal sage scrub. Keep veering right and you'll cross a railroad tie bridge at 2.6 miles. Keep swooping through the hills, and at 3.2 miles turn right onto Wildwood Canyon Trail as you leave the Conejo Open Space and enter Wildwood Park. Stay on the main trail for a sharp descent to a picturesque stream. Veering right some more, you'll arrive at the turnoff to the Nature Center at 3.9 miles. Visit the Nature Center to learn about the area's plants, including bladderpod, whose crushed leaves smell like urine.

Okay. So upon leaving the Nature Center, go right onto Wildwood Mesa Trail, the wide dirt road that climbs up a hill on the northwest side of the creek. Going around a locked gate at 4.3 miles, you'll enter a parking lot. Keep riding the Wildwood Mesa Trail north out of the parking lot until you reach a single-track at 4.6 miles. Head right (east) on this path back to your car at 4.8 miles.

RIDE 74 · Butte Trail/Santa Rosa Trail

AT A GLANCE

CA

Length/configuration: 4.5-mile loop on pavement, single-track, and dirt road

Aerobic difficulty: Moderate/difficult; the single-track uphills can be quite tough

Technical difficulty: Moderate/difficult; mostly rideable single-track with some perilous switchbacks

Scenery: Ridgeline views of Santa Rosa Valley, spring wildflowers, and volcanic outcroppings

Special comments: A short but prime single-track ride with views to spare

If you're a movie or TV buff, you've seen picturesque Mountclef Ridge double as both Peniston Crag in the classic Laurence Olivier film *Wuthering Heights* and as the backdrop to Dodge City in *Gunsmoke*. Now, on this 4.5-mile loop, you're going to see Mountclef Ridge under your tires. It's much prettier there.

Starting from Wildwood Regional Park in Thousand Oaks, this route courses through suburban streets before climbing a ride studded with volcanic outcroppings. The scope of the views is expansive, even if the scenery is limited to houses in some directions. After a quick jaunt on a dirt road, the single-track gets serious. Riders descend Mountclef Ridge via some extraordinarily tight turns known as the Santa Rosa Switchbacks. It's a challenge getting to the valley floor, but once you're there, it's an easy cruise back to the start point.

General location: 3 miles north of US 101 in Thousand Oaks.

Elevation change: Approximately 300 feet in elevation gain.

Season: Year-round, but avoid riding in the heat of a summer day. The park is commonly closed after big rainstorms. If it has rained in the last week, call the park before riding.

Services: Water and rest rooms are available at the Wildwood Regional Park entrance to the southwest of parking lot. All other services are available in Thousand Oaks.

Hazards: Steep, narrow trails, and tight switchbacks.

Rescue index: The route is always close to the city roads of Thousand Oaks. Help is available from rangers roaming the park.

Land status: City of Thousand Oaks, Conejo Open Space land, and regional park.

Maps: A free *Wildwood Park Trail Guide* is available at the information kiosk at the parking lot.

Finding the trail: Take US 101 to Lynn Road in Thousand Oaks. Go north on Lynn Road 3.2 miles. Turn left on Avenida De Los Arboles for approximately 1 mile. Avenida De Los Arboles ends just after the park entrance; make a legal

RIDE 74 · Butte Trail/Santa Rosa Trail

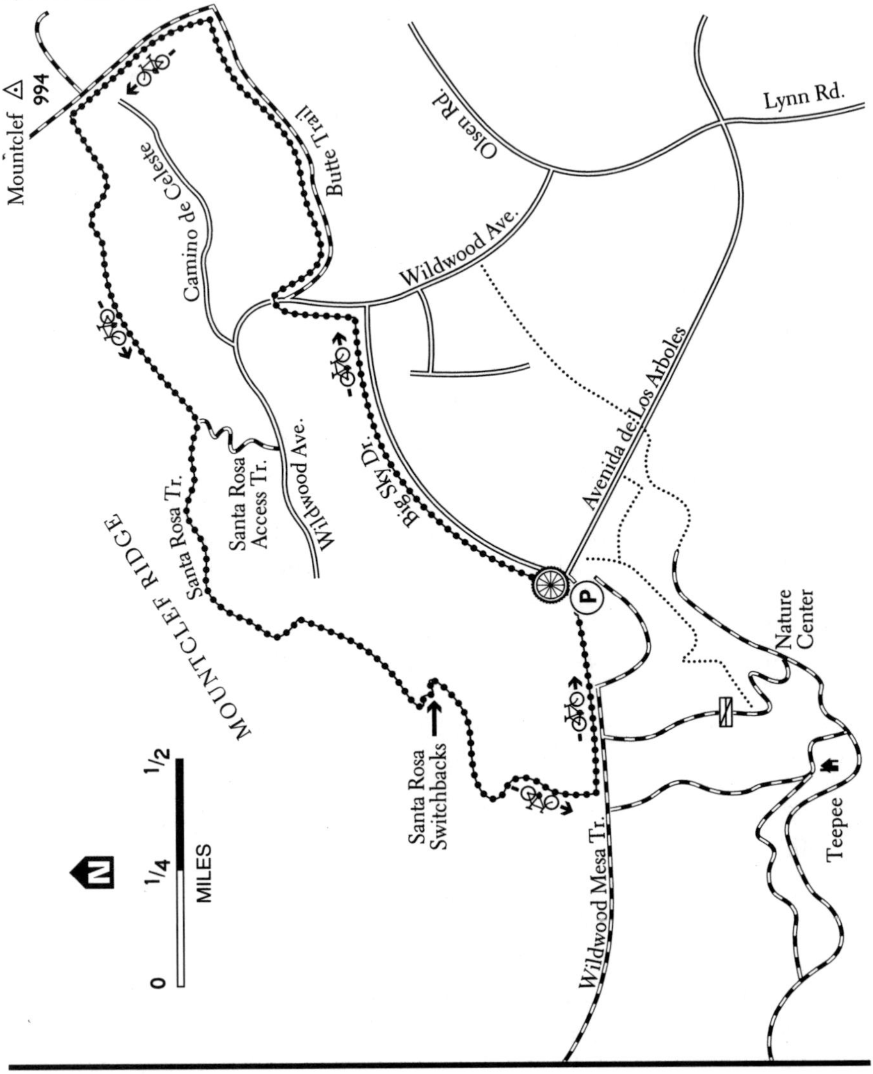

U-turn around the median and immediately turn right into the parking lot. Pay attention to all parking lot closure signs.

Sources of additional information:

Wildwood Regional Park
Conejo Open Space
  Conservation Agency
2100 Thousand Oaks Boulevard
Thousand Oaks, CA 91362
(805) 449-2340

Simi Bike Works
2687 Cochran Street
Simi Valley, CA 93065
(805) 583-2124

Biking through a beaut of
a butte.

Notes on the trail: From the parking lot, go north on Big Sky Drive. At 0.7 mile,
turn left onto Wildwood Avenue. About 175 yards up Wildwood Avenue on your
right is the signed Butte Trail. Go right onto the Butte Trail single-track, which
embarks on a tough climb through thick vegetation up to a saddle overlooking
much of Thousand Oaks. The single-track widens as you reach a dirt service road
at 1.6 miles. Turn left onto the service road which first dips, then climbs. (You're
now circling the end of the Camino Celeste neighborhood.) Turn left again at
1.9 miles onto Santa Rosa Trail, which gradually descends to an intersection
with the Santa Rosa Access Trail at 2.6 miles. (If you need to bail out for any reason, go left here, then left again onto paved Wildwood back the way you came.)
Otherwise, keep riding on the Santa Rosa Trail, which soon climbs steeply up
Mountclef Ridge. It's hard to say for sure, but this seems to be the exact spot
where key scenes in *Wuthering Heights* were filmed. Crossing over Mountclef
Ridge at 3.5 miles, you'll drop into the notorious Santa Rosa switchbacks. Keep
going, and turn left at the T intersection with Wildwood Mesa Trail at 4.2 miles
and return to the parking lot at 4.5 miles.

RIDE 75 · Sulphur Mountain Road

AT A GLANCE

Length/configuration: 18.7-mile out-and-back ride (9.35 miles each way) on dirt road

Aerobic difficulty: Moderate; a gentle but long climb

Technical difficulty: Easy; the road is very smooth except for sections churned up by grazing cattle

Scenery: Lake Casitas, the Pacific Ocean, the Channel Islands, and the Topatopa Mountains

Special comments: Sticking to a ridgeline for most of its length, this ride offers a lot of views and a fun downhill without too much effort

This 18.7-mile out-and-back fire-road ride would likely be a forgettable training ride were it situated anywhere else but this section of Ventura County. But with a location like this, the ride is memorable.

Starting just south of the little town of Oak View, climb up a Ventura County road that travels through private property. Where most counties would probably find a way to bar citizens from utilizing such a road for recreation purposes, Ventura County has done the right thing by opening it up. This policy certainly benefits our sport. It's fun, interesting riding. Not only do views of the Channel Islands to the south and the Topatopa Bluffs to the north reveal themselves, but so do interesting geological phenomena. Early in the climb, you'll pass a natural oil spring that has been active for decades, and later you'll pass the rock vent whose discharge gives the mountain its name. Keep pedaling and you'll encounter coyote, deer, hawks, and especially cattle.

Take care not to startle the cows. If you let them know you're there before slowly riding toward them, you'll have no problems. After more and more views, you'll reach pavement and a lonely mansion perched on a cliffside. Turn around and enjoy a mostly downhill cruise back toward CA 33. From there, immediately proceed north to the Oak Pit Bar-B-Que in Oak View for tasty post-ride vittles.

General location: Just south of the town of Oak View (7.4 miles north of Ventura) on CA 33.

Elevation change: Approximately 2,300 feet from (300 feet to 2,600 feet), though it sure doesn't feel as if the differential is that great.

Season: Year-round, but avoid riding during the heat of a summer day. Also, cattle can really churn up muddy roads—don't ride for 48 hours after rainstorms.

Services: No services are available on the trail. All other services are available in Oak View or a few miles north in Ojai.

Hazards: Cattle on the trail, sometimes in great numbers.

Rescue index: At any point on the trail, it's easy to turn around and return to Oak View, where help can be summoned.

RIDE 75 · Sulphur Mountain Road

Land status: County land. (Note: Riding the road itself is legal; all other usage is considered trespassing.)

Maps: USGS 7.5-minute quadrangle maps: Matilija and Ojai.

Finding the trail: Take CA 33 7.4 miles north of Ventura or 6.5 miles south of Ojai. Turn east on Sulphur Mountain Road, between the two communities of Casitas Springs and Oak View. Proceed 0.3 mile up Sulphur Mountain Road. Park before you come to a gate (you'll see a Girl Scout camp across the road). Pull well to the side of the road; this area gets some truck traffic.

A gentle reminder to ride responsibly.

Source of additional information:

Bicycles of Ojai
108 Canada Street
Ojai, CA 93023
(805) 646-7736

Notes on the trail: From the parking area, go around the gate and head northeast (uphill) on the smooth fire road. As you ride past California live oaks and native grasslands, you'll see sternly worded signs saying, "Abuse it, Lose it: Stay on the Road." Do so. At 3 miles cross over a cattle guard. Not surprisingly, there are a lot of cattle in this area. As a result, the soil is sometimes churned up and difficult to ride. You might have to ride at the edge of the road to find a smooth line. At 5.2 miles, pass over another cattle guard and the road smoothes considerably. The ride is easy the rest of the way to a mansion and the end of the dirt road at 9.3 miles. From here, turn around and simply enjoy the ride downhill back to your car at 18.6 miles.

RIDE 76 · Gridley/Pratt Loop with Novice Option

AT A GLANCE

Length/configuration: 17.5-mile loop on pavement, single-track, and fire road, or a much easier novice option, consisting of a 5.1-mile loop on pavement and fire road

Aerobic difficulty: Full loop is very difficult—initial climb is comprised of 9 fairly unrelenting miles; novice option is moderate, with a mile-long pavement climb

Technical difficulty: Very difficult—extremely narrow trails and boulder-hopping sections; novice option is easy—pavement and dirt road

Scenery: Staggering views of entire Ojai Valley, Lake Casitas, Pacific Ocean, Channel Islands, Sespe Wilderness, and mountain ranges too numerous to mention

Special comments: Launching right in downtown Ojai, both loops serve scenic terrain that's accessible without a car; leave the gas guzzler and squeamish riders at home, and start pedaling

Most visitors to the touristy town of Ojai only know Nordhoff Ridge to be a picturesque green wall that defines the Ojai Valley. This 17.5-mile loop actually allows you to climb the wall and experience a Humpty Dumpty perspective as you gaze over the gorgeous valley. (Or you can embark on the shorter novice option, which only goes partway up before traversing the wall on aptly named Shelf Road.)

Starting from smack dab in the center of downtown Ojai, 750 feet above sea level, this ride spins up past orange and avocado groves. Less experienced riders can bail out on the novice option to ride Shelf Road, which is sometimes called "Ojai's balcony," for a good 5-mile workout. But advanced riders will want to keep going uphill, leaving the pavement and riding into the Los Padres National Forest via Gridley Trail's single-track. Even for accomplished riders, portaging is a necessity at first. But the grade soon eases, and as the trail switches back up to the Nordhoff Summit, your unspoken fears that there's no way you can climb this ridge gradually dissipate. The switchbacks are tight but largely rideable all the way to the ridge. Congratulations! You made it! Now the hard part begins, as you soon grind up to an abandoned lookout tower offering magnificent 360° views of the region. At 4,485 feet, it can be cool here even on the hottest summer days.

Your descent takes you to the Pratt Trail, which is steeper than Gridley. A thrilling, jaw-dropping ride on narrow, mountain-clinging trails brings you back down in a hurry. But unless you have sublime rock-hopping skills, your pace slows as you return to downtown Ojai, where a quick left on Ojai Avenue will bring you to Antonio's for a Mexican feast.

General location: Downtown Ojai.

Elevation change: 3,735 feet from 750 feet to 4,485 feet. On the novice option loop, the change is about 300 feet, climbing from 750 feet to a high point of

RIDE 76 · Gridley/Pratt Loop with Novice Option

1,000 feet, before adding some undulating elevation on Shelf Road.

Season: Year-round, but avoid riding up Gridley in the heat of a summer day.

Services: Water available at Gridley Springs Camp. Collect it at the spring (before the pipe to the horse trough) and treat it first. All other services available in Ojai.

Hazards: Novice option and full loop both take place partly on roads with vehicular traffic. Full loop features an extremely narrow trail with exceedingly steep drop-offs.

Rescue index: At any point on trail, it's simple to go downhill to return to downtown Ojai, but the going is rugged. Help is available through Ojai Ranger District Headquarters on Ojai Avenue.

Land status: Municipal property, national forest.

Maps: Los Padres National Forest map and "Trails of the Ojai Ranger District" are both available through Ojai Ranger District Headquarters on Ojai Avenue.

Finding the trail: From west, north, or south of downtown Ojai, take CA 33 to CA 150/Ojai Avenue and travel east to the intersection with Signal Street. From east of downtown Ojai, go westbound on CA 150/Ojai Avenue to the intersection with Signal Street. Ride begins in front of the Main Post Office on the southeast corner of Signal Street and Ojai Avenue. Parking is available on nearby streets. Make sure to obey posted regulations.

Sources of additional information:

Los Padres National Forest
Ojai Ranger District Headquarters
1190 East Ojai Avenue
Ojai, CA 93023
(805) 646-4348, TTY: (805) 646-3866
www.r5.fs.fed.us/lospadres

Bicycles of Ojai
108 Canada Street
Ojai, CA 93023
(805) 646-7736

Notes on the trail: From the Main Post Office, head east on Ojai Avenue. At 0.8 mile, pass the very helpful Ojai Ranger District Headquarters on your left. Turn left onto Gridley Road at 1 mile. Proceed uphill on Gridley Road past orange groves. At 2.3 miles, you'll reach the intersection with Shelf Road/FS 22W09. (If you're an inexperienced rider, or one who has found the preceding pavement climb to be taxing, then by all means turn left here to take the novice option. Go around the gate and enjoy the pleasant, rolling, vista-providing fire road until it ends at a gate at the top of Signal Street. Then go left on Signal Street all the way back to the start for an amusing 5.1 mile ride.)

Otherwise, keep climbing on Gridley Road, which ends in a cul-de-sac at 2.6 miles. Turn left onto Forest Service 22W05/Gridley Trail, a well-marked single-track. The first half-mile of single-track is tough going with some certain portages. The grade eases as you ride through avocado orchards. At 3.4 miles, there's a intersection with several orchard roads. Go straight and slightly left onto signed FS 22W05/Gridley Trail. The trail is smooth and good to climb. It becomes lush and shaded just before Gridley Springs Camp at 5.5 miles. The camp has a horse trough and a bench—a nice place to take a break.

The trail soon becomes steeper, and you think you're about to reach Nordhoff Ridge long before you actually do. When you finally reach FS FNO8/Nordhoff Ridge at 8.9 miles, the climbing doesn't end; it gets harder. Turn left to begin a steep, gravelly, and tough ascent which brings you to a saddle just below the lookout tower at 10 miles. Go right on the short access road to the lookout tower, reached at 10.2 miles. The steel frame of the lookout tower is all that's intact; the floor is missing, so it's not as perfect a lunch spot as one might hope. Return to the saddle at 10.4 miles and turn right (west) on Nordhoff Ridge. After a fast mile-long descent, make a hairpin left turn onto FS 23W09/Pratt Trail at 11.3 miles. This is a thrilling or harrowing downhill, depending on your mood. At 14.2 miles, make a sharp left turn onto an unsigned fire road. You descend some more, but go slowly; it's easy to miss the next turnoff at 14.9 miles, at which time you leave what seems to be the main road and turn right and downhill on another fire road. (You know you've gone too far and missed your turnoff if you begin climbing.) A few hundred feet after making your turn onto this fire road, you turn right again (onto single-track) at a brown Forest Service sign that's otherwise unmarked (even though it's still FS 23W09/Pratt Trail). You soon enter a residential area, and the trail alternates between well-signed single-track and dirt road portions. It's all well-signed, perhaps because the wealthy landowners want you to stay on the trail (and off their property) even more than you do.

At 16.1 miles you come to a big gulch where the route isn't immediately obvious. Cross the gulch and veer to your right (heading mostly south) and you soon pick up the single-track once more. At 16.4 miles, you reach the Pratt Trail trailhead and a gravel road. Go right and downhill to Signal Street at 16.6 miles. Go right on Signal Street (which temporarily jogs west on Grand Avenue) and return to the start at Ojai Avenue at 17.5 miles.

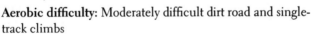

RIDE 77 · Pine Mountain

AT A GLANCE

Length/configuration: 8.3-mile out-and-back (4.15 miles each way)

Aerobic difficulty: Moderately difficult dirt road and single-track climbs

Technical difficulty: Moderate to advanced; some rocks and sand on the single-track and roads

Scenery: Views to the coast from ridge road; wooded trail offers glimpses of Cuyama Valley and Mt. Pinos

Special comments: Good camping along Pine Mountain Road

This ride is an out-and-back, 8.3-mile round-trip. It requires a moderate amount of strength and good bike-handling skills. The first mile is an easy downhill on Pine Mountain Road. This section is a maintained, hardpacked dirt two-wheel-drive road in good condition. Going out-and-back on the single-track Trail 23W04 is more challenging. The condition of the trail is mixed, with some excellent firm surfaces and some sandy and rocky sections. Back on Pine Mountain Road, you'll descend around the south side of Reyes Peak. This portion of the road is in poor condition and is very rocky in places. Finish with a moderately difficult, 2-mile climb.

Pine Mountain is a long ridge that affords visitors a good look at the surrounding countryside. Beyond the forested hills and valleys to the south lie the beaches of Ventura and Oxnard. Trail FS 23W04 winds through a cool, shady, conifer forest with intermittent views of the Cuyama Valley and Mt. Pinos. The roadside camping off Pine Mountain Road is especially inviting—a great place to watch the city lights turn on in the evening.

General location: Begins at the end of the pavement on Pine Mountain Road (FS 6N06), approximately 30 miles north of Ojai.

Elevation change: Total elevation gain: 950 feet, but feels greater due to the altitude and the multitude of short climbs.

Season: Late spring through early fall. The high elevation of this route makes for pleasant summer riding.

Services: No water is available on the ride or on Pine Mountain. Take all the water you will need with you. Water can be obtained at Ozena Ranger Station on CA 33; the station is located approximately 5 miles north of the intersection of Pine Mountain Road and CA 33. All services are available in Ojai. There is excellent car camping along Pine Mountain Road, but there are only roughly 12 sites available.

Hazards: Cars are permitted on the first mile of the ride. Some sections of Trail 23W04 drop off sharply to the side and have been knocked down-slope. Walking your bike will help minimize further damage. You will encounter a washed-out section of road after turning off Trail 23W04 and descending on Pine Mountain Road. Walk your bike through. There is a lot of broken glass on Pine Mountain Road beyond this washed-out section.

Rescue index: Help is available in Ojai. A phone for emergency services can be found at the Wheeler Gorge Ranger Station, about 20 miles south of Pine Mountain Road on CA 33.

Land status: National forest.

Maps: USGS 7.5-minute quadrangle map: Reyes Peak.

Finding the trail: You can reach Pine Mountain Road (FS 6N06) by traveling north on CA 33 from US 101 in Ventura. Pine Mountain Road is not signed from the highway. Keep an eye on the milepost signs along the roadside as you drive north on CA 33. You'll come to Pine Mountain summit (unmarked) near milepost 42.7. The paved Pine Mountain Road goes east from the summit. Pine Mountain Road climbs steeply and is narrow and twisting. Go slowly, watch for oncoming traffic, and sound your horn when approaching corners. The ride begins at a gate at the pavement's end, approximately 6 miles from CA 33. There is room to park a vehicle on the roadside near the gate. Additional parking can be found to the east along Pine Mountain Road. Forest Adventure Pass required.

Sources of additional information:

Los Padres National Forest
Ojai Ranger District Headquarters
1190 East Ojai Avenue

Ojai, CA 93023
(805) 646-4348; TTY: (805) 646-3866
www.r5.fs.fed.us/lospadres

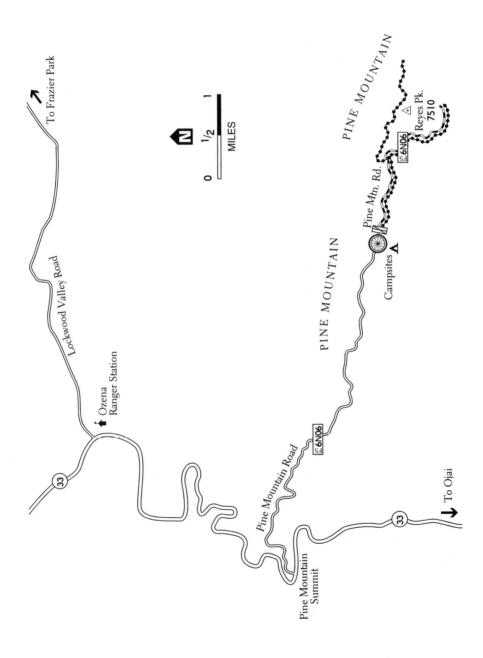

Haddock Mountain from Pine Mountain.

Notes on the trail: Leave the pavement at the gate on Pine Mountain Road. After 1 mile of riding you'll come to a turnaround where the road seems to end. The road does continue, but it is closed to most motor vehicles by means of some tank traps installed across the road. Turn left here onto unmarked Trail 23W04. The trail is not apparent from the road; look to the left (north) for a small dirt hill. Push your bike up the hill and you will see the trail. Stay left and uphill into the woods. After 1.5 miles on Trail 23W04 you will see some viewpoints on the right that you can walk toward. Return the way you came. When you arrive back at Pine Mountain Road, turn left (go through the tank traps) and descend. You will reach the end of the road at a mound of earth. You can continue riding by pushing over the rise to an old road that will take you to a good vantage point. Return the way you came.

SANTA BARBARA COUNTY

It's fitting that Santa Barbara is home to the world-renowned Brooks Institute of Photography; everywhere you look could be the subject of a profitable postcard for one of Brooks's photographers. This is such a breathtakingly beautiful county that it's certain you'll burn through rolls of film like local professionals. The county is made up of several diverse regions, including incredibly steep mountains, undulating hills, starkly eroded canyons, savanna-like grasslands, coastal plains and valleys, and, finally, the longest east-west stretch of Pacific Ocean coastline between Alaska and Cape Horn.

The 50 miles of shoreline between Carpinteria and Pt. Conception comprise the most visited area in Santa Barbara County. Indeed, most visitors to this county rarely go anywhere else. Fortunately, your mountain bike gives you both the tool and the impetus to go exploring in Santa Barbara County, where the inland areas are easily as captivating as the shore.

Though Santa Barbara County is quite large, a sizeable portion of it is off-limits to bikes. In addition to the huge San Rafael and Dick Smith Wilderness Areas within Los Padres National Forest, there's Vandenberg Air Force Base along the coast, and scattered, privately owned oil fields. But the riding opportunities that are available more than make up for it. The Santa Ynez Mountains, which rise steeply from the city of Santa Barbara, are lush, wooded, and full of beguiling trails, such as Romero Canyon. Little Pine Mountain is a popular peak climb in the Los Prietos area of the national forest, and Bates Canyon Road plus Wildhorse/Zaca Peak give riders the chance to view the beauty of the San Rafael Wilderness Area from vantage points just outside of it. Perhaps best of all, many rides take place near wineries. So pack your helmet and a designated driver, and have some fun.

RIDE 78 · Romero Canyon

AT A GLANCE

Length/configuration: 13.8-mile out-and-back (6.9 miles each way)

Aerobic difficulty: Long, moderately difficult climb; first half-mile is steep

Technical difficulty: Climb is moderately difficult with loose and embedded rocks; return descent is demanding due to rough tread, loose conditions, and tight corners

Scenery: Nice views of the ocean while climbing

Special comments: Romero Road is a direct route into the backcountry; longer trips can be made from Romero Saddle

This out-and-back, 13.8-mile round-trip is an uphill workout. The climb to the turnaround point is long and moderately difficult. The road is steep for the first half-mile and then moderate after the second creek crossing. The return is fast and technically demanding. Romero Road is unmaintained and has been closed to motor vehicles since the 1970s. At times it seems like a road, and at other times it narrows to a single-track trail. The single-track sections are generally rough with loose and embedded rocks. The dirt road sections are in fair condition with some loose rocks.

The route climbs through Romero Canyon and deposits you on the Coast Ridge at Romero Saddle. Excellent ocean views are a bonus as you grind it out to reach the top. Romero Road is the most direct path out of Santa Barbara and into the backcountry. Longer day trips and overnighters can be made from Romero Saddle.

General location: Romero Road (FS 5N15) starts from Bella Vista Road in Montecito, approximately 10 miles east of Santa Barbara.

Elevation change: The trip begins at 1,300 feet and climbs to a high point of 3,100 feet at Romero Saddle. Total elevation gain: 1,800 feet.

Season: Year-round. This ride can be a sweaty one, even in winter. Carry a dry shirt and a windbreaker.

Services: There is no water available on this ride. All services are available in Santa Barbara and surrounding communities.

Hazards: Romero Road is a very popular hiking and cycling route. Watch for other trail users. Control your speed while descending and approach corners with care.

Rescue index: Help can be found in Santa Barbara.

Land status: National forest.

Maps: Map 4 of the Santa Barbara County Recreational Map Series—Santa Barbara Mountain Biking Routes—is an excellent guide to this and other trails

RIDE 78 · Romero Canyon

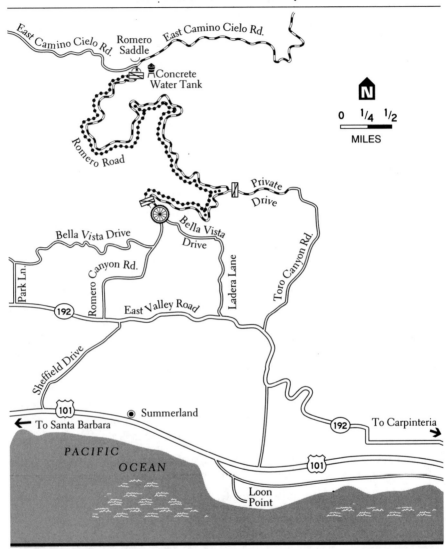

in the area. This map can be purchased at district offices of the Los Padres National Forest or by writing the publisher: McNally and Loftin, 5390 Overpass Road, Santa Barbara, CA 93111.

Finding the trail: From Santa Barbara, follow US 101 south to the exit for Sheffield Drive. Follow Sheffield Drive north for 1.5 miles to East Valley Road. Turn left onto East Valley Road and then immediately turn right onto Romero Canyon Road. Follow Romero Canyon Road north for 1.5 miles and turn right onto Bella Vista Drive. Take Bella Vista Drive 0.3 mile to a red steel gate on the left side of the road. The red gate marks the start of Romero Road. Park your car here. Do not block access to Romero Road. Forest Adventure Pass required when parking in Los Padres National Forest.

Source of additional information:

Los Padres National Forest
   Santa Barbara Ranger District
3505 Paradise Road

Santa Barbara, CA 93105
(805) 967-3481; TTY: (805) 967-7337
www.r5.fs.fed.us/lospadres

Notes on the trail: Begin the ride at the red gate at Romero Road and Bella Vista Drive. After 2 miles stay left, as the road to the right (blocked by a blue gate) leads to a private residence. In approximately 2 more miles you'll come to some signs that indicate you are on your way to Romero Saddle and Camino Cielo Road. There is also a sign that directs hikers on Romero Trail to Oceanview Trail and Blue Canyon Trail. Continue straight on the main road toward Romero Saddle. Two miles beyond the signs you'll reach an open area where there is a shot-up water tank on the hillside to your right. Continue heading straight. Soon you'll arrive at a locked gate that can be ridden around on the left. Just past the gate is Romero Saddle and East Camino Cielo Road at a concrete water tank (6.9 miles into the ride). Return the way you came.

RIDE 79 · Little Pine Mountain

AT A GLANCE

Length/configuration: 23.4-mile out-and-back (11.7 miles each way)

Aerobic difficulty: Strenuous; 10 miles of moderate to steep climbing

Technical difficulty: Easy to moderate; four-wheel-drive road in fair condition—intermittent soft conditions

Scenery: Nice views of surrounding scrubby mountains

Special comments: Fun, exciting descent

This is an excellent ride for the strong cyclist who wants a good workout as well as great views. It is a strenuous out-and-back ride (23.4 miles round-trip). The first 1.5 miles provide a good warm-up with easy to moderate climbing and some shade. From this point you'll face ten miles of moderate to steep climbing toward the road's crest. This long exposed climb is broken up by some easier stretches and some short descents. All of the cycling is on unpaved four-wheel-drive roads in generally good condition. Good bike-handling technique is necessary for climbing and descending over intermittently loose and soft surfaces. Rounding a bend after 5.5 miles you will see the chalk bluffs on Little Pine Mountain and the long, exposed switchbacks that you'll be climbing soon. Riding up the switchbacks provides an outstanding view. Leave your bike at Happy

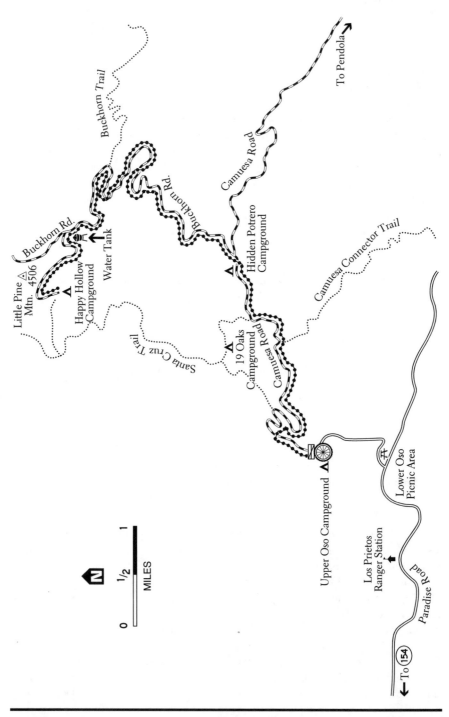

The long and winding road down Little Pine Mountain.

Hollow Camp and follow the hiking trail to the west 0.25 mile for another great vista. The return descent is a thrill.

General location: Begins in the Lower Santa Ynez Recreation Area in the Los Padres National Forest, approximately 15 miles north of Santa Barbara.

Elevation change: The ride begins at 1,200 feet in Upper Oso Campground and climbs to a high point of 4,400 feet near the top of Little Pine Mountain. Undulating terrain adds an estimated 100 feet of additional climbing to the ride. Total elevation gain: 3,300 feet.

Season: Early spring and late fall are the best riding seasons for the Lower Santa Ynez Recreation Area. It is possible to ride throughout the year, though high temperatures in summer and inclement weather in winter are limiting factors.

Services: There is no water available on the ride. Water may be obtained at Upper Oso Campground; take plenty. A general store is located on Paradise Road near CA 154. All services are available in Santa Barbara.

Hazards: The road is shared with off-road vehicles and care must be taken on blind corners. Between miles 1 and 3 along the route, the road is particularly narrow and winding. Control your speed on the descent.

Rescue index: Help is available at the Los Prietos Ranger Station on Paradise Road (approximately 2.8 miles southwest of the start of the ride).

Land status: National forest.

Maps: *The Mountain Bicycle Guide*, available at the Los Prietos Ranger Station, is an excellent guide to this trail.

Finding the trail: Follow CA 154 north from Santa Barbara for approximately 10 miles; turn right onto Paradise Road. Follow it for 5 miles to Lower Oso Picnic Area and turn left; then continue 1.3 miles to Upper Oso Campground. Parking is permitted near the locked gate for the trailhead. Overnight parking is permitted. Forest Adventure Pass required

Sources of additional information:

Los Padres National Forest
Santa Barbara Ranger District
3505 Paradise Road

Santa Barbara, CA 93105
(805) 967-3481; TTY: (805) 967-7337
www.r5.fs.fed.us/lospadres

Notes on the trail: Begin this ride on the unsigned Camuesa Road at the locked gate at the north end of Upper Oso Campground. After 0.7 mile a side trail is signed Santa Cruz Trail. Continue on Camuesa Road as Camuesa Road Connector Trail goes to the right after 2 more miles. Continue past 19 Oaks Trail on the left, and at the intersection 2 miles farther, turn left onto Buckhorn Road toward Little Pine Mountain; Camuesa Road goes right to Pendola. Nine miles into the ride, where the Buckhorn Hiking Trail turns right, you will continue on the main road. Just past a water tank a mile later, turn left into Happy Hollow Camp as Buckhorn Road continues straight. In another 1.5 miles you will reach Happy Hollow Camp, where you will find picnic tables, shade, and ants. Return the way you came.

RIDE 80 · Wildhorse/Zaca Peak

AT A GLANCE

Length/configuration: 18.5-mile out-and-back (9.25 miles each way)

Aerobic difficulty: Difficult; long ride with lots of moderately difficult climbing

Technical difficulty: Moderately difficult gravel roads; portions are great, others are rough and rocky

Scenery: Excellent views into Santa Ynez Valley and San Rafael Wilderness

Special comments: Lovely drive to trailhead; scenic bicycling

Here is a good trip for strong cyclists, or moderately strong cyclists with an excess amount of energy. It is an out-and-back ride and covers 18.5 miles round-trip. There are some long, steep hills and some sections that may bring the words "roller-coaster" to mind. Good bike-handling skills are needed to negotiate rough ascents and descents. Catway and Zaca Ridge Roads are unpaved (hard-packed dirt and rock base) four-wheel-drive roads. They are in good condition, although the steeper hills have some loose rocks and gravel. The road out to Zaca Peak is in fair condition, with loose rocks and ruts.

RIDE 80 · Wildhorse/Zaca Peak

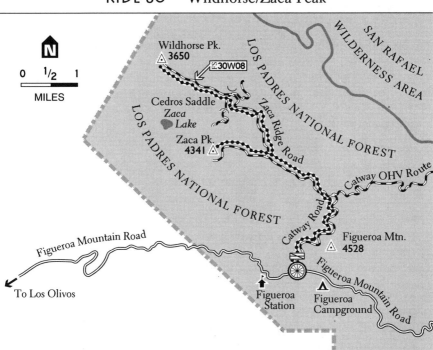

Exceptional views of the Santa Ynez Valley and the San Rafael Wilderness Area, combined with good roads, challenging terrain, and an abundance of wildflowers make this an excellent ride. The drive on Figueroa Mountain Road to the start of the ride is also lovely. The road winds past peaceful ranchlands and gnarled old oak trees before snaking steeply up Figueroa Mountain.

General location: The ride starts on Figueroa Mountain, approximately 10 miles northeast of the Santa Ynez Valley (50 miles southeast of Santa Maria).

Elevation change: A lot of ups and downs result in a total elevation gain of 3,060 feet.

Season: Early spring through fall. The altitude of this ride makes for pleasant riding in the summer.

Services: There is no water available on this ride. Water is available on a seasonal basis at Figueroa Campground (0.5 mile east of Catway Road on Figueroa Mountain Road). All services can be obtained in Los Olivos.

Hazards: There are loose rocks and gravel on the steeper hills. Motor vehicles are permitted on the roads described in this ride. Expect sudden weather changes and carry extra clothing.

Rescue index: Help can be found in Los Olivos. Help may be available at Figueroa Station (1 mile west of the start of the ride on Figueroa Mountain Road).

Land status: National forest.

Maps: USGS 7.5-minute quadrangle maps: Zaca Lake, Bald Mountain, Figueroa Mountain, and Los Olivos.

Finding the trail: From Los Olivos, drive north on Figueroa Mountain Road. Follow Figueroa Mountain Road for 13 miles to Figueroa Station. Continue 1 mile beyond Figueroa Station on Figueroa Mountain Road to Catway Road on the left (north) side of the road. Catway Road is marked by a sign that reads "Gate Temporarily Closed When Road Is Wet." Park here, but do not block the gate or access to the road.

Source of additional information:

Los Padres National Forest   Santa Maria, CA 93454
Santa Lucia Ranger District   (805) 925-9538; TTY: (805) 925-7388
1616 North Carlotti Drive   www.r5.fs.fed.us/lospadres

Notes on the trail: Follow Catway Road for about 2.5 miles to an intersection. Turn left to stay on the main road (now Zaca Ridge Road), as Catway OHV Route goes right toward Davey Brown Campground. After another 2 miles, continue straight as a road goes left to Zaca Peak and Zaca Lake (follow this road to the south side of Zaca Peak on the return). Ride 1.5 miles farther to Cedros Saddle (an intersection of trails). At the saddle, continue straight on the main road. Pedal 2 more miles to the end of the road at unmarked Wildhorse Peak (reached after 8 miles of riding). Return the way you came, passing Cedros Saddle, and turn right at the sign for Zaca Peak. After about 1.5 miles, the road ends at a spot that offers nice views to the south. Return the way you came.

RIDE 81 · Bates Canyon Road/Sierra Madre Road

AT A GLANCE

Length/configuration: 15-mile out-and-back (7.5 miles each way)

Aerobic difficulty: Long, moderately difficult climb; some steep grades

Technical difficulty: Moderately difficult to demanding (depends on proficiency of rider); sections of road are rocky and soft

Scenery: Views from Sierra Madre Road into the mountainous San Rafael Wilderness

Special comments: Relatively remote area; uncrowded mountain biking

This is an out-and-back, 15-mile round-trip ride. Most of the pedaling is only moderately difficult, but there are several very steep sections. Overall, Bates Canyon Road is a long, difficult climb requiring good bike-handling skills.

Sierra Madre Road is less demanding—the climbing is mostly moderate. Both Bates Canyon and Sierra Madre Roads are unpaved, four-wheel-drive roads in fair condition.

Bates Canyon Road, while a challenge to climb, provides access to one of the best mountain bike routes around—Sierra Madre Road. For those seeking remoteness, this is a wonderful region to explore. From the top of the ridge you'll look down on the San Rafael Wilderness and across to the San Rafael Mountains. Those arriving via Santa Maria enjoy an added bonus—a lovely drive along a scenic stretch of CA 166.

General location: The ride begins at Bates Canyon Campground at the end of Cottonwood Canyon Road (approximately 50 miles east of Santa Maria) in the Los Padres National Forest.

Elevation change: Bates Canyon Road starts at 2,900 feet and climbs to 5,200 feet to meet Sierra Madre Road. Sierra Madre Road follows the ridge to the turnaround point of the ride, Hot Peak, at 5,587 feet. Total elevation gain: 2,687 feet.

Season: Spring through fall. High temperatures in the summer can make this an uncomfortable ride, and insects can be bothersome. Rain or snow may make these roads impassable in the winter.

Services: No water is available on the ride. Limited services are present in the small town of New Cuyama, 12 miles east of Cottonwood Canyon Road on CA 166. All services are available in Santa Maria.

Hazards: The road surface may be rough and can cause handling problems. Although this is a relatively remote area, you still must expect others to be around the next bend in the road. Motor vehicles are permitted; take care on blind corners. Be prepared for sudden weather changes; a ridge can be a dangerous place in a thunderstorm. Poison oak is abundant in Bates Canyon.

Rescue index: Help is available in New Cuyama or Santa Maria. Don't ride alone; ride with others who may be able to provide a first response in an emergency.

Land status: National forest.

Maps: USGS 7.5-minute quadrangle maps: Bates Canyon and Peak Mountain.

Finding the trail: From US 101 in Santa Maria, travel east on CA 166 for 40 miles to Cottonwood Canyon Road on the right (south) side of the highway. From New Cuyama, travel 12 miles west on CA 166 to Cottonwood Canyon on the left (south) side of the highway. Signs on both sides of the highway direct you towards White Oak Station (no longer in use) and Bates Canyon Campground. Follow Cottonwood Canyon Road 6.5 miles to White Oak Station, where you can park your car. Bates Canyon Campground and the start of the ride are 0.25 mile farther down the paved road. A Forest Adventure Pass is required to park vehicles in Los Padres National Forest.

Source of additional information:

Los Padres National Forest
Santa Lucia Ranger District
1616 North Carlotti Drive
Santa Maria, CA 93454
(805) 925-9538; TTY: (805) 925-7388
www.r5.fs.fed.us/lospadres

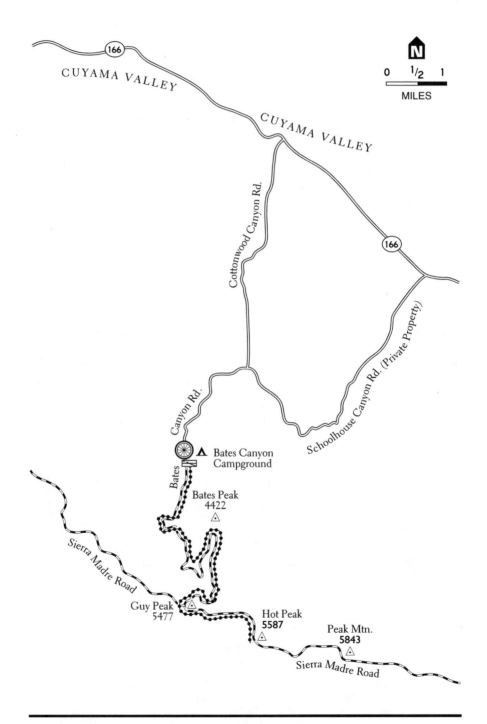

Looking down Bates Canyon.

Notes on the trail: From Bates Canyon Campground, follow the unsigned, paved Bates Canyon Road (FS 11N01) as it passes behind the pit toilets. Follow it to the end of the pavement. You will immediately pass a sign indicating that you are on Bates Canyon Road and will soon ride through an open gate. After approximately 4 miles, the road makes a sweeping right turn as you pass Bates Peak. Turn left after 2 miles onto unmarked Sierra Madre Road (which runs along the top of the ridge). You will reach Hot Peak in 1.5 miles. Turn around and return the way you came.

CENTRAL COAST

California Highway 1, which carves along the coastline between Big Sur and San Luis Obispo, is widely regarded as one of the most scenic roads in the world. Though the sights along the highway itself are spectacular, they're even more incredible off-road. Good thing you've got a mountain bike to explore this gorgeous region.

The bicycle rides along the Central Coast mostly take place between the rugged Santa Lucia Mountain Range and the cliffs abutting the Pacific Coast. Two divisions of the huge Los Padres National Forest can be found in this region, and while much of the national forest land is taken up by wilderness areas in which bicycles are not allowed, there's also great bicycling terrain here.

Andrew Molera State Park, for example, offers views of the gorgeous Big Sur area that most tourists never take the time to see. The Central Coast Ridge Road, on the other hand, treats riders to views of both the Pacific and the rugged interior, most of which is occupied by the Ventana Wilderness Area.

Yet the crown jewel of mountain biking in this area is without a doubt Montana de Oro State Park in San Luis Obispo County. The Bluff and Islay Creek Trails serve as excellent introductions to this magnificent park, especially for riders of beginning and intermediate abilities. Be aware, however, that we've barely tapped the potential of this park. Riders with advanced skills can create fantastic single-track loops here simply by cobbling bits of trails together.

Wherever you choose to ride in this area, you'll understand why newspaper tycoon William Randolph Hearst—who had the means to locate his dream house, La Cuesta Encantada, or "The Enchanted Hill," anywhere in the world—chose San Simeon, on the Central Coast.

RIDE 82 · Bluff Trail/Montana de Oro State Park

AT A GLANCE

Length/configuration: 3.3-mile loop

Aerobic difficulty: Easy; good trail for beginners and families

Technical difficulty: Easy single-track with a couple of ditch crossings

Scenery: Trail parallels a beautiful coastal bluff; lovely wildflowers in the spring

Special comments: Good warm-up for the park's tougher trails

This is an easy 3.3-mile loop. The ride follows a hardpacked dirt trail in good condition and pavement on Pecho Valley Road.

Bluff Trail is a fine spot for beginning mountain bikers to give off-road riding a try. It is also a wonderful warm-up for cyclists intent on riding the more advanced trails in the park. The trail skirts the coast and provides views of tidal pools, cliffs, and arches. Profuse wildflower displays and whale watching are seasonal bonuses.

General location: Montana de Oro State Park is located approximately 20 miles west of San Luis Obispo on Pecho Valley Road.

Elevation change: Bluff Trail begins at 60 feet of elevation and climbs very gently to 100 feet at the trail's end. The paved portion of the loop involves several short climbs and reaches a high point of 200 feet. Total elevation gain: 140 feet.

Season: Year-round. Spring and early summer are especially beautiful, for wildflowers and many kinds of birds are abundant. The wave-swept headlands of the park are a popular whale-watching spot in the winter.

Services: Water may be obtained at the park headquarters. The headquarters and a 50-site campground are located on the east side of Pecho Valley Road, 2.7 miles beyond the entrance sign for the park. All services are available in the community of San Luis Obispo.

Hazards: This trail is heavily used by hikers. Be especially alert when approaching children, for they can be unpredictable. Although the trail is adequately set back from the sheer cliffs of the coast, exercise caution when stopping for a closer look. Heed signs directing trail users to stay back from unstable edges. At mile 1.8, the trail crosses a drainage ditch with very steep sides. Beginners should walk their bikes at this point.

Rescue index: Help is available at the park headquarters.

Land status: State park.

Maps: A good topographic map of the park may be purchased at the park headquarters.

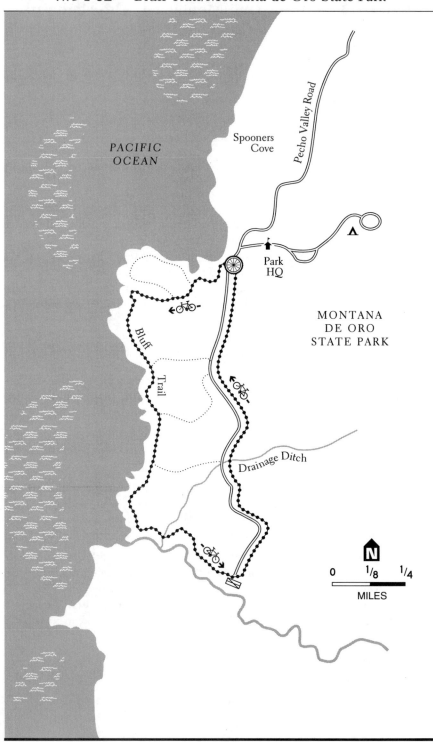

PACIFIC OCEAN

Spooners Cove

Pecho Valley Road

Park HQ

Bluff Trail

MONTANA DE ORO STATE PARK

Drainage Ditch

N

0   1/8   1/4

MILES

Crashing surf from the
bluffs of Montana de Oro
State Park.

Finding the trail: From points north, travel 3 miles south of San Luis Obispo on
US 101 to the Los Osos/Baywood Park exit. From points south, travel 10 miles
north of Grover City on US 101 to the Los Osos/Baywood Park exit. Exit and
travel 12 miles northwest on Los Osos Valley Road. Los Osos Valley Road
becomes Pecho Valley Road and enters the state park. The park headquarters is
2.7 miles past the Montana de Oro State Park entrance sign. The trailhead is
signed on the west side of Pecho Valley Road, 100 yards south of the headquarters. There is a parking lot at the trailhead.

Source of additional information:

Montana de Oro State Park
Los Osos, CA 93402
(805) 528-0513
cal-parks.ca.gov/

Notes on the trail: The ride starts at the trailhead signed as Bluff Trail. After a
little more than 0.5 mile, you'll come to a wooden bridge. Cross the bridge and
stay right. Follow Bluff Trail south as it parallels the coast. After 2 miles you'll
reach a parking lot, picnic tables, and pit toilets. Turn left to return on the paved

road to your vehicle. Should you decide to forego completion of the ride, several trails lead east from Bluff Trail and take you to Pecho Valley Road.

RIDE 83 · Islay Creek Trail/ Montana de Oro State Park

AT A GLANCE

Length/configuration: 8-mile loop

Aerobic difficulty: Difficult climbs on dirt and gravel road; ups and downs on trails

Technical difficulty: Demanding; rocky, sandy single-track; some ditch-like conditions

Scenery: Outstanding views of the coastline from Hazard Peak

Special comments: Beginners and families can enjoy the first 3 miles on Islay Creek Road—turn around at (or before) East Boundary Trail

This 8-mile loop is a relatively short but demanding ride. The first 3 miles on Islay Creek Road climb gently and steadily over several short, easy hills. Beginners should turn around here for a pleasant out-and-back trip, for after this the narrow, single-track East Boundary Trail climbs very steeply. It is rocky and sandy in places and at times more closely resembles a ditch than a trail. On the single-track Ridge Trail you will encounter many ups and downs of varying technical and physical difficulty. Ridge Trail includes a variety of trail conditions. Expect rocky and sandy portions as well as some fine riding surfaces. There is some deep sand on the descent to paved Pecho Valley Road.

The views on this ride are outstanding. Nearing the top of East Boundary Trail, you'll have a good view of Los Oso Valley and the community of Morro Bay. The rock at the bay's entrance is Morro Rock—one of nine volcanic plugs that lie in a line from Morro Bay to San Luis Obispo. You can see many of them from this vantage point. The coastal views from Hazard Peak are tremendous. In spring and early summer the wildflowers are particularly dazzling. Entire hillsides covered in monkey flowers and other yellow, blooming plants inspired the name of this area—Montana de Oro, or "Mountain of Gold."

General location: Approximately 17 miles west of San Luis Obispo.

Elevation change: Total elevation gain: 1,900 feet.

Season: Year-round. The climate is mild in winter and cool in summer with considerable coastal fog and clouds. Whale watching is good from late November through January.

Services: All services are available in the community of Morro Bay. Water may be obtained at the park headquarters, located off Pecho Valley Road 2.7 miles beyond the park entrance sign.

RIDE 83 · Islay Creek Trail/Montana de Oro State Park

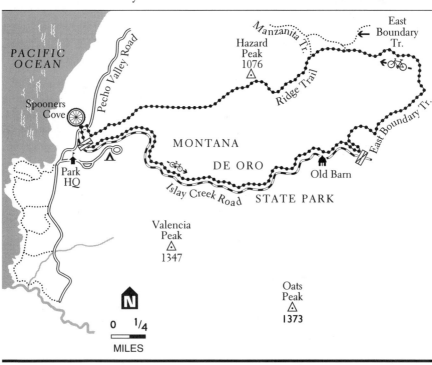

Hazards: Narrow trails that are often flanked with poison oak. Route includes rocky and sandy sections. Trails sometimes travel over rock outcroppings and cliffs. Definitely not the place for beginners or unconfident riders.

Rescue index: Help is available at the park headquarters, 0.2 mile south of the trailhead on Pecho Valley Road. Although this is a popular park, this particular route is not as heavily used as other trails in Montana de Oro State Park. You may not see anyone else on the trail. Park personnel patrol the trails, but not necessarily on a daily basis. Be prepared—carry adequate water, spare parts, and a first-aid kit. Beginners should travel with others.

Land status: State park.

Maps: A good topographic map of the park may be purchased at the state park headquarters.

Finding the trail: From San Luis Obispo, travel south on CA 101 approximately 2 miles and take the Los Oso/Baywood Park exit. Travel northwest for 12 miles on Los Oso Valley Road (Los Oso Valley Road becomes Pecho Valley Road and enters Montana de Oro State Park). Follow Pecho Valley Road 2.5 miles beyond the entrance sign for the park to a parking area on the right (west) side of the road. Park here. Islay Creek Road begins across the road at a gate. Additional parking is available at the park headquarters, 0.2 mile farther south on Pecho Valley Road.

Source of additional information:

> Montana de Oro State Park
> Los Osos, CA 93402
> (805) 528-0513
> cal-parks.ca.gov

Notes on the trail: Begin the ride at the gate at Islay Creek Road. Turn left after 3 miles onto East Boundary Trail. After 5 miles you'll come to a Y intersection and Ridge Trail. Turn left and follow Ridge Trail. Turn left after 0.25 mile to continue on Ridge Trail at an intersection with Manzanita Trail. Follow Ridge Trail to reach Pecho Valley Road. Turn left to return to your vehicle.

You will encounter some tall waterbars set across the route near the end of Ridge Trail. Do not go around them and cut a new trail. This defeats their purpose, which is to curtail erosion and preserve the existing trail. Hop them if you are experienced with this bike handling technique, or stop, dismount, and lift your bicycle over them.

RIDE 84 · Central Coast Ridge Road

AT A GLANCE

Length/configuration: 10.8-mile out-and-back (5.4 miles each way)

Aerobic difficulty: Easy to moderately difficult terrain

Technical difficulty: Easy; smooth dirt road; some loose rocks and ruts

Scenery: Shaded winding road; views of grassy coastal hills and forested slopes

Special comments: Stash your bike and take the 2-mile hike (each way) to Cone Peak Lookout; lovely views of the coast

This is an out-and-back, 10.8-mile round-trip ride. It requires little technical skill, the terrain is generally easy to moderate, and there is plenty of shade. The unpaved, two-wheel-drive road is in good condition. After approximately 4 miles you'll encounter a 0.25-mile steep hill that contains some loose rock and rutting.

Central Coast Ridge Road winds back and forth along the ridge, providing alternate views of the Pacific Ocean to the west and the interior valleys and mountains of the Ventana Wilderness to the east. A 4-mile out-and-back hike from the turnaround point to Cone Peak is well worth the extra time and effort. The hiking trail is basically a long uphill meander, with the steepest section being the last quarter mile. The view of the coastline from the lookout tower is excellent. To the south is Point Sal; to the north is Big Sur.

RIDE 84 · Central Coast Ridge Road

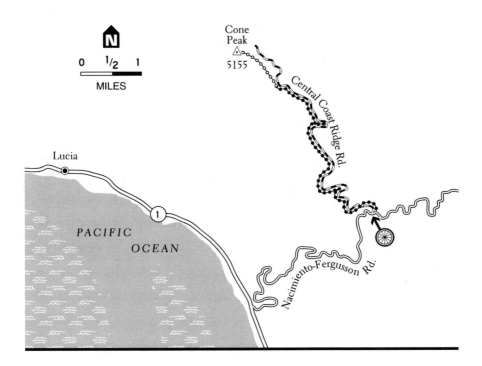

General location: Begins off of Nacimiento-Fergusson Road, 7.5 miles east of California State Highway 1 (approximately 40 miles north of San Simeon).

Elevation change: The ride begins at 2,660 feet, passes San Antonio hiking trail at the 4-mile point at 3,200 feet, and ends at a high point of 4,150 feet at the trail to Cone Peak. The hike tops out at 5,155 feet. Total elevation gain: 1,490 feet (hike not included).

Season: Year-round. Wildflower displays in the spring can be outstanding. Dry conditions can create extreme fire danger and road closures. Winter months can be wet and roads may be closed to minimize erosion. Check with the Forest Service concerning road conditions before setting out for the trailhead.

Services: There is no water available on the ride. There is water available at the intersection of CA 1 and Nacimiento-Fergusson Road at Kirk Creek Campground. There are grocery stores in Gorda and Lucia. All services are available in San Simeon.

Hazards: Speed should be controlled on descents. Motor vehicles use this road, so be alert, especially on blind corners. Poison oak grows next to the trail to Cone Peak.

Chris cruising on the Central Coast Ridge Road.

Rescue index: Help can be found in the town of Lucia.

Land status: National forest.

Maps: USGS 7.5-minute quadrangle map: Cone Peak.

Finding the trail: From points north, drive 4 miles south of Lucia on CA 1 and turn east on Nacimiento-Fergusson Road. From points south, drive 5 miles north of Gorda on CA 1 and turn east on Nacimiento-Fergusson Road. Follow Nacimiento-Fergusson Road for 7.5 miles to the ridge top and Central Coast Ridge Road. The ride begins at the sign indicating Central Coast Ridge Road 20S05. Park your vehicle in the pullout; do not block access to the road. Forest Adventure Pass required.

Source of additional information:

Los Padres National Forest
Santa Lucia Ranger District
1616 Carlotti Drive
Santa Maria, CA 93454-1599
(805) 925-9538
www.r5.fs.fed.us/lospadres

Notes on the trail: Begin on Central Coast Ridge Road (FS 20S05) in a northerly direction; a sign reads "Vincente Flats Trail 4, San Antonio Trail 4, Cone Peak Trail 6." Follow the main road toward Cone Peak Trail on the left. Return the way you came.

The Central Coast Ridge Road runs through the Ventana Wilderness Area. No bicycles are permitted on trails leading off the main road. If you travel on Cone Peak Trail, leave your bike at the trailhead.

RIDE 85 · Ridge Trail/Andrew Molera State Park

AT A GLANCE

Length/configuration: 7.8-mile combination; 2.6-mile loop and a 5.2-mile out-and-back (2.6 miles each way)

Aerobic difficulty: Tough; steep climb to the ridge top

Technical difficulty: Moderate to advanced; some loose, rocky surfaces

Scenery: Clear days provide views of the Big Sur coastline

Special comments: Tough little ride through meadows and across open hillsides

This is a strenuous out-and-back ride with a short loop around Creamery Meadow. It is 7.8 miles long and is fairly technical (due to a loose, rocky surface). All but the strongest riders with the lightest bicycles will do some walking up the ridgeline. The downhill return is also difficult. It is steep and bumpy—a very rough ride. The riding around Creamery Meadow is easy. Ridge Trail is a four-wheel-drive dirt road that varies from fair to good condition. There are loose rocks on the steeper sections.

Cyclists tackling this tough little ride will reap huge rewards. Here, foggy days can be looked upon as wonderful opportunities. You may be able to climb above the coastal layer to sunshine and surreal scenery. On clear days the view down the coast to Big Sur is phenomenal.

General location: Begins at the parking area of Andrew Molera State Park, 22 miles south of Carmel on the Pacific Coast Highway (CA 1).

Elevation change: The ride begins 100 feet above sea level and follows mostly level terrain to mile 1.1, where you'll begin climbing on Ridge Trail. Ridge Trail ends at 1,100 feet at mile 3.9. Rolling terrain adds some 200 feet of additional climbing to the ride. Total elevation gain: 1,200 feet.

Season: Year-round, but the best riding is spring through fall. Due to the park's proximity to the ocean, daytime temperatures can be low and fog is common. Carry extra clothing for sudden changes in the weather. Winter and spring can be rainy.

Services: Drinking water is now available in the Andrew Molera State Park parking lot. All services are available in the community of Big Sur, approximately 3 miles south on CA 1.

Hazards: There is a footbridge over the Big Sur River near the trailhead. The bridge is built out of two wooden planks, so walk or carry your bike across. Control

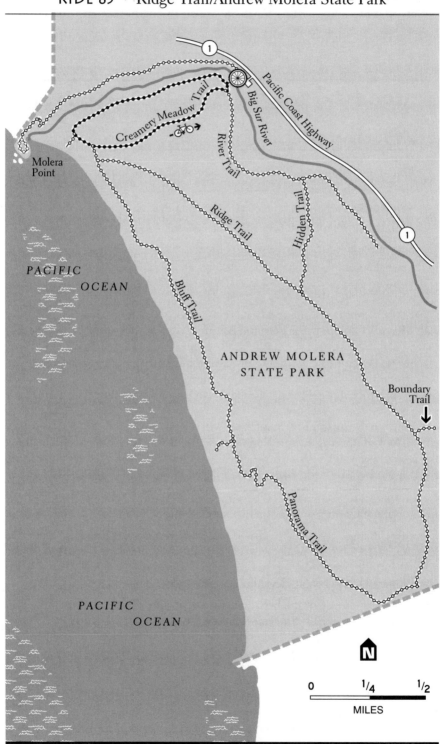

Fog rolling in north of Big Sur.

your speed while descending on Ridge Trail. It is rough and rocky in places. Watch for other trail users.

Rescue index: Help is available in the community of Big Sur.

Land status: State park.

Maps: A good map of the park may be obtained at the entrance station, or at the Big Sur Station 4 miles south of the park.

Finding the trail: From points north, drive 22 miles south of Carmel on CA 1 to Andrew Molera State Park on the right (west) side of the highway. From points south, drive 3 miles north of the community of Big Sur on CA 1 to Andrew Molera State Park on the left (west) side of the highway. Enter and park in the parking lot near the picnic area and trailhead.

Sources of additional information:

Andrew Molera State Park
Big Sur Station 1
Big Sur, CA 93920
(831) 667-2315
cal-parks.ca.gov

Notes on the trail: Begin at the hiking trailhead (not the trailhead for the campground) and cross the wooden bridge. Ride to the main trail at a T-intersection and turn right. Stay right at the next Y-intersection. Just before you've pedaled 1 mile you'll see a sign for Beach Trail; turn left to continue on Creamery Meadow Trail. Soon after, turn right uphill at the sign for Ridge Trail. Continue straight on Ridge Trail as Bluff Trail goes right toward the ocean (no bikes). Continue on Ridge Trail past Hidden Trail to the left (no bikes). Continue straight as North Boundary Trail goes left (no bikes). You will reach the top of the climb and a fence at 3.9 miles—turn around and return the way you came. When you come again to the Creamery Meadow Trail, follow it to the right around the meadow. Turn left at the Y-intersection before the barbed wire fence to continue around the meadow. In 0.1 mile, turn hard right and follow the trail back across the bridge to the parking area and your vehicle.

Another place within the park you may wish to explore is Molera Point. Bicyclists can ride out to the mouth of Big Sur River, but not to Molera Point via Headlands Trail, which is closed to bikes. Reach the point by following Beach Trail from the parking lot. The view from the point is excellent, especially at sunset. This is a fine location for whale watching, which is generally at its best in January.

SEQUOIA NATIONAL FOREST

L ocated in the southern end of the Sierra Nevada, Sequoia National Forest may be one of the most scenic places in an already very scenic state. The forest is best known as home to the world's largest trees, the aptly named *Sequoiadendron giganteum*, or giant sequoias. Also the largest living organisms on this planet, sequoias are amazing to see up close. (You can cycle near them on Ride 90, Converse Basin.) The height (over 200 feet) and diameter (often 40 feet or so) of sequoias are astonishing. But the forest seems to enjoy showing off its granite monoliths, glaciated canyons, roaring rivers, lush meadows, and daunting mountain peaks just as much.

But while the scenery is blatantly visible, other mountain bikers are not. You won't always be alone while riding here, but it sure feels like it. The forest is so big (1.1 million acres) and distant from the metropolises of Southern California, that it's easy to find solitude. Plus, the bike routes are spread out over some of the forest's 1,500 maintained roads, 1,000 miles of jeep roads, and 850 miles of single-track trails.

The above roads and trails wind through untamed country that's notable for its extremes. For instance, some of the routes in this chapter unfold in the meadows near the Kern River, where grasslands can easily waver in 100° heat. On the same day, meanwhile, riders higher up in the Sierra Nevada can be struggling to stay warm on a mountain peak. But while the land is rugged, the bike routes listed in this chapter appeal to a wide variety of abilities. Ride here soon, and experience some *fun giganteum* of your own.

RIDE 86 · Black Gulch Rabbit Ramble/Keysville Road

AT A GLANCE

Length/configuration: 9.7-mile loop on fire road, single-track, and pavement

Aerobic difficulty: Moderate; many short hills—a real workout if you ride it fast

Technical difficulty: Difficult; a narrow trail atop steeply sloping hills

Scenery: Grasslands, spring wildflowers, gushing Kern River, Lake Isabella, mining artifacts, and ubiquitous rabbits

Special comments: Primarily a locals' ride, this route demands (but also rewards) technical riding skills, path-finding ability, and patience

In this part of the Kern River Valley, there's no doubt that mountain biking takes a distant backseat to whitewater rafting. Like a second-born child escaping its big sibling's shadow, this 9.7-mile loop starts inauspiciously but keeps achieving bigger and better things as it makes a name for itself.

Starting near Keysville Road approximately 2 miles from the intersection of CA 178 and CA 155, the ride initially follows a road heavily utilized in the summer by whitewater tour operators. After stopping to pay tribute at the odd, yet touching, homemade Pearl Harbor Survivors Association Living Memorial, you'll join the rafting traffic heading down to a put-in on the Kern River. After some people-watching, you'll start climbing above the river and find yourself on an unmarked, totally unexpected single-track jewel. The path clings to a steep cliffside high above the river, and you'll gain exemplary views of the narrow Kern River Canyon. Just when you're sure the single-track will peter out, it always seems to resurrect itself. Turning away from the river, it gives a tour of beautiful grasslands before yielding to a double-track leading up Black Gulch. A sizeable climb ensues, but the downhill on Keysville Road is worth it as you fly past old mining artifacts back to your car.

General location: 2 miles north/northwest of Lake Isabella.

Elevation change: Several short climbs; the largest is less than 650 feet. Total gain is approximately 1,800 feet.

Season: Year-round. Summer is very hot and dry, and more importantly, the raft operators tend to take over the fire road between Keysville Road and the river. But there's a buzz of outdoor activity then, and it's fun to be part of that.

Services: None available on the trail. All services are available in Lake Isabella.

Hazards: Narrow trail, few trail markers, and loose dirt on trail.

Rescue index: Much of the ride is within view of CA 178, which can almost always be reached by careful portaging. Help is available along CA 178 at Lake Isabella and near the ride's start/finish at Lake Isabella Visitor Center, 0.5 mile south of Keysville Road.

RIDE 86 · Black Gulch Rabbit Ramble/Keysville Road

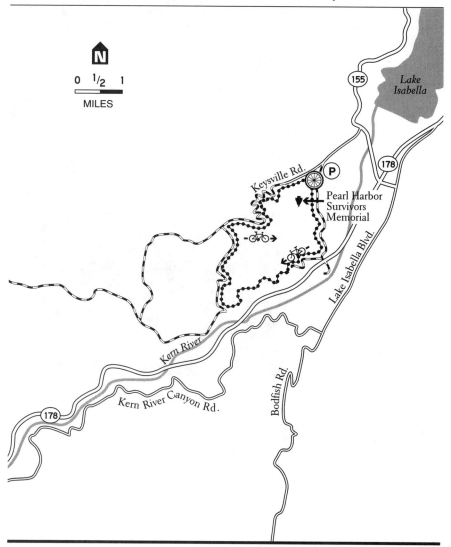

Land status: BLM land; Sequoia National Forest.

Maps: USGS 7.5-minute quadrangle maps: Lake Isabella North, Miracle Hot Springs, and Alta Sierra.

Finding the trail: From the intersection of CA 178 and CA 155 in Lake Isabella, drive north on CA 155. After 1.2 miles (0.5 mile past the entrance to the Lake Isabella Visitor Center), turn left on Keysville Road, marked by signs reading "Keysville Rec. Site." Drive west up a rudimentary paved road for 0.9 mile. Turn left at a dirt road marked with an arrow pointing to Boat Ramp/Pearl Harbor

A ramble past rocks and
rabbits near Black Gulch.

Memorial. After driving 125 yards up this road, turn left into a small unmarked
parking area and park.

Source of additional information:

Sequoia National Forest	P.O. Box 3810
Greenhorn Ranger District	Lake Isabella, CA 93240
Lake Isabella Visitor Center	(760) 379-5646
4875 Ponderosa Drive	www.r5.fs.fed.us/sequoia

Notes on the trail: A cyclometer helps a great deal on this ride, and for this reason more mileage numbers than usual are given. However, common sense, a
knack for knowing your location, and route-finding skills are much more valuable. Since it's usually easy to ascertain your position along the ride relative to CA
178, getting lost is not a big worry. From the parking area, head left (following the
signs pointing to the boat ramp and Pearl Harbor Memorial). The Kern River Valley prides itself on containing five of the six distinct bioregions found in the state.
You're now riding through the California Grasslands region. Staying on the primary dirt road despite numerous intersections, pass the Pearl Harbor Survivors
Association Living Memorial on your right at 0.7 mile. Continue riding in the
same direction, and you'll soon begin a major descent toward the Kern River and

CA 178. Passing under a CA 178 bridge, the road dead-ends next to a popular raft put-in. Have fun people-watching, then turn around, pass back under the bridge, and you'll reach a fire road on your left. (You passed this road a few moments ago while descending.) Now turn left on it at 2.2 miles and begin climbing. Chances are you'll see a lot of bike tracks here. At a three-way junction after a descent, take the middle trail (which, at times in the past, has been flagged with red ribbon). You'll see huge jackrabbits as you crest a quick little hill. Turn left at the crest at 2.4 miles onto your first real single-track of the ride. With CA 178 now on your left, have fun on the single-track, which, again, may be marked by red flags. Stay left past a cairn and more flagging at 2.7 miles. With some climbing under your belt, you'll ascend far above CA 178 and the Kern River before descending toward the highway. At 3.2 miles, you'll reach your nearest brush with CA 178. (If you need to bail out, do so here by going left on CA 178, left on CA 155, left on Keysville Road, and left on Pearl Harbor Road to reach your car.)

Otherwise, stay on the single-track, which climbs away from CA 178 by turning north. (Now that CA 178 is no longer in sight, it's a bit tougher to find your bearings should you get lost. There might be abundant flagging, cairns, and bike tracks showing you the way, but there might not be. So if all else fails, just head northwest until you reach a double-track, and then head right on it.) There now, back to the directions. You're heading west on the single-track, remember? Turn left at a re-road intersection at 3.7 miles (the busier route, judging from the bike tracks). The trail turns to double-track at 3.9 miles and curves a bit northward. At 4.4 miles you'll reach a barbed wire gate reading "Please Close Gate." Do so and keep riding in the same direction. At 4.8 miles, the road forks. According to a sign, if you go left you'll enter the Kern Canyon Trail/FS 31E75. Instead, head right and uphill. You're now on Black Gulch North Road, and it's much easier to find your bearings. At 5.7 miles, stay left at an intersection with another dirt road and keep climbing. At 6 miles, you'll reach a T-intersection with Keysville Road. Turn right and grind up to a summit high above the Kern River valley floor at 7.1 miles. From here, you can see for miles. Keep going the way you've been traveling, and at 8 miles you'll reach an old dilapidated mining storage shed. Keep going downhill and reach pavement again at 8.7 miles. At 9.6 miles, turn right onto Pearl Harbor Avenue, and return to your car at 9.7 miles.

RIDE 87 · Shirley Meadows Shebang

AT A GLANCE

Length/configuration: 25.7-mile loop on single-track, fire road, and pavement (or 16.2-mile point-to-point ride with car shuttle.)

Aerobic difficulty: Very difficult if ridden as loop; moderate if car shuttle is used

Technical difficulty: Moderate/Difficult; some steep, rutted sections and narrow single-track

Scenery: Lake Isabella, incense cedars, ponderosa pines, huge manzanita, wildflowers

Special comments: A spectacular single-track downhill to the shore of Lake Isabella, it can be accessed via a tough paved climb or with a car shuttle

This downhill is one of many fabulous rides in the Lake Isabella area. In an area that can be very hot and dry, this ride seems more cool and refreshing—perhaps because of its invigorating whoosh of a descent. You can access the downhill by riding up to it or driving and leaving a car. If you're in decent shape, consider the climb. The smooth pavement allows you to make good time, and you'll have warmed-up your legs and gained a helpful appreciation for the area's topography before starting on the downhill.

Regardless of how you gain your elevation on this ride, you'll lose it quickly—and blissfully.

General location: In Sequoia National Forest, near Wofford Heights and Lake Isabella.

Elevation change: Loop starts at 2,650 feet, climbs to 6,600 feet (where shuttled riders begin), and returns. With approximately 300 vertical feet on the way down, total elevation gain for this loop is around 4,250 feet.

Season: May to October.

Services: Water, pit toilets, telephone, and information are available at Summit Ranger Station just north of the trailhead. All other services available in Wofford Heights, Kernville, and Lake Isabella.

Hazards: Narrow, sometimes rutted trails, stream crossings.

Rescue index: Help is available at the Forest Service's Summit Ranger Station, located at Greenhorn Summit at the apex of the ride.

Land status: National forest.

Maps: USGS 7.5-minute maps: Alta Sierra, Lake Isabella North.

Finding the trail: From Lake Isabella, head north on CA 155 to Wofford Heights. From Kernville, go south on County Road 495 to Wofford Heights. In the town of Wofford Heights, you will come to Evans Road, where CA 155 swings west from the shore of Lake Isabella. On the east side of CA 155 is Tillie Creek Picnic Area. Turn east to park there, obeying all posted regulations. It is also possible to park on many city streets in Wofford Heights.

Source of additional information:

Sequoia National Forest
Greenhorn Ranger District
Lake Isabella Visitor Center
4875 Ponderosa Drive

P.O. Box 3810
Lake Isabella, CA 93240
(760) 379-5646
www.r5.fs.fed.us/sequoia

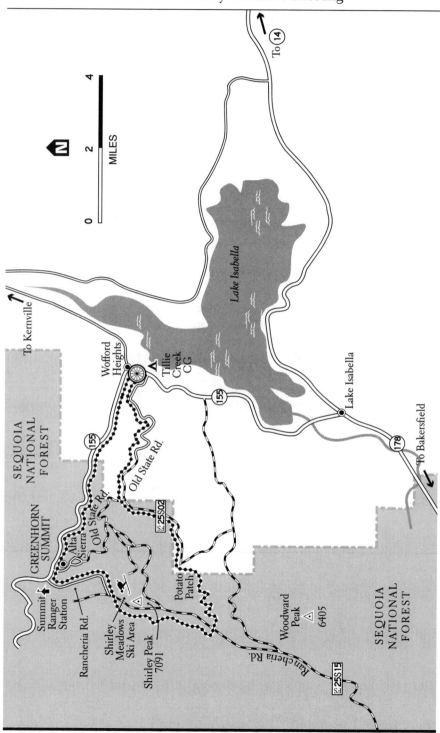

Notes on the trail: If you want to use a car shuttle to access this ride, drive with your bikes in a second car and follow the route directions to the Shirley Meadows Ski Area. Start riding from the ski area, following directions in the paragraph that begins with "Staying on dirt FS 25S15 . . . ". Otherwise, loop riders should turn right out of Tillie Creek Picnic Area and go north on CA 155. It soon turns sharply to the left (west) at Evans Road. Make the sharp turn with CA 155 and begin climbing in earnest. After some relentless ascending, you reach a summit and Rancheria Road/FS 25S15 at 7.3 miles. Go left (south) on Rancheria Road, passing Summit Ranger Station on the right (stop here if you need water, a rest room, information, or a phone). You'll climb some on Rancheria Road as well, but nothing like what you've already done. Around 9.4 miles, you reach the edge of Shirley Meadows Ski Area. Keep heading south past the ski facilities on FS 25S15, which turns to dirt at the far end of the parking area.

Staying on dirt FS 25S15, you'll encounter a nice downhill. You'll be tempted to really fly, but don't; you want to head right on a single-track coming up on the right at 9.8 miles. The trail has previously been marked with a flag, but it may not be when you visit. After a short climb, the single-track heads downhill through fun whoop-de-doos. The conditions are usually perfect: a curvy path that's shady and carpeted with pine needles. Lots of easy-to-follow orange flags were here when I visited, but even if they're gone, the trail is pretty obvious most of the way. After crossing one fire road, the trail seems to come to an end at a T-intersection with a second fire road at 10.8 miles. Jog right on the fire road, and quickly pick up the single-track again on the left.

At 11.9 miles, you again encounter a fire road and go right for a 0.1 mile before heading sharply left on a rutted dirt road. At 12.6 miles, veer right on a trail which leaves the fire road and winds through manzanita before crossing a stream at 13.1 miles. There's an unmarked Y-intersection here where you want to go to the right and downhill.

After another stream crossing, you spin through a pretty meadow and begin the toughest single-track climb of the ride, which comes to a quick and merciful end at 14.6 miles. There is a Y-intersection here as well, and this time you go left. You're now back on a fire road, which climbs past a cattle guard and delivers great views of Lake Isabella around 16.7 miles.

Catch your breath, lower your seat if that's your style, and prepare for a fast and bumpy fire road descent to another Y-intersection at 19.3 miles. Go right here onto Old State Road, which is a lot smoother than what you've been riding. My Cannondale gobbled up the miles so quickly here I worried it might choke. But watch your speed; there's auto traffic at times. You don't want anything to go awry as you glide down on switchbacking fire roads to where Old State Road becomes a paved street at 24.1 miles.

Staying on Old State Road, be wary of traffic as you coast back to the lakeshore-hugging CA 155 at 25.6 miles. Go left and return to the start at 25.7 miles.

RIDE 88 · Unal Trail

AT A GLANCE

Length/configuration: 3.6-mile combination (0.2 mile each way, with a 3.2-mile loop) on single-track

Aerobic difficulty: Easy/moderate; a short climb with occasional tough spots

Technical difficulty: Moderate; the single-track has some tight sections

Scenery: Incense cedars, ponderosa pines, and views of faraway Lake Isabella and the San Joaquin Valley

Special comments: A short but substantial ride with all sorts of features, this route is ideal for both single-track hounds and families that don't mind dismounting during some of the trail's trickier sections

This quick 3.6-mile combination ride delivers a lot of bang for the buck. First, it's entirely comprised of loamy single-track. Second, at 7,000 feet in elevation, if offers bracingly clean air. Furthermore, its ridge-top setting provides unimpeded views in nearly all directions. And if that isn't enough, it contains interpretive stations for exploring Native American history in the area.

Starting at Greenhorn Summit 15 miles northwest of Lake Isabella, the Unal Trail begins at a well-marked trailhead where visitors can pick up the interpretive guide, *Unal Trail: On the Trail of the Bear.* Even if your motives for being on the trail are more single-track-related than ursine, you'll appreciate the effort and care that went into constructing this pathway. Quickly reaching the loop part of the ride, you'll travel in a clockwise direction through streams and over knolls to a vista where Lake Isabella can be spotted through a stand of fragrant incense cedars. If you're riding with children or simply feel like learning something, then make sure to stop at the numbered wooden posts and refer back to the guide for information about how the indigenous Tubatulabal people lived in the area for centuries. Some of the guide's information is intriguing, some is not, but it's always interesting to look closer at the sights you so often hurry by while riding.

By post 22, you'll reach the summit and its 360° view. Though it may be crystal clear up here, to the west you can often see the notorious Tule fog enveloping the San Joaquin Valley cities of Bakersfield and Delano. After taking in all the sights and breathing the clean air, start descending the summit in a northerly direction. The downhill can be a bit tricky at first, but by the time you reach the shade of some sugar pines, it settles into a sweet groove. Cushioned with pine needles but firm underneath, the switchbacks are a delight to ride. Make sure to stop at post 25, where a replica of a typical Tubatulabal dwelling is displayed. If you think you're roughing it by mountain biking, this exhibit will make you rethink your position as you return to the trailhead at the end of the ride.

General location: 15 miles northwest of Lake Isabella at Greenhorn Summit in the Sequoia National Forest.

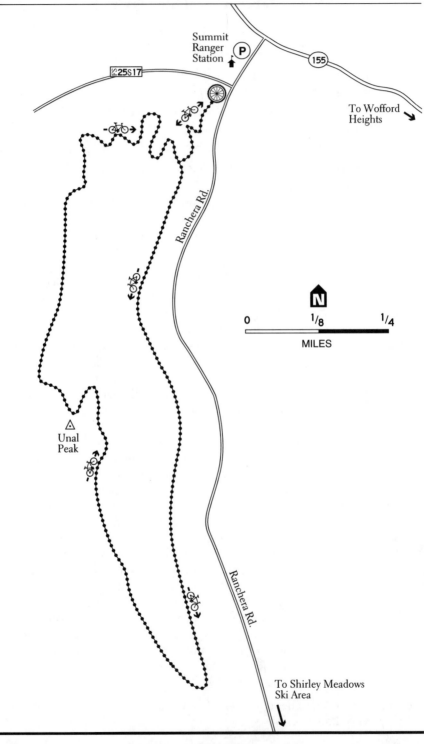

Summit
Ranger
Station

P

155

25S17

To Wofford
Heights

Ranchera Rd.

N

0   1/8   1/4

MILES

Unal
Peak

Ranchera Rd.

To Shirley Meadows
Ski Area

Looking for bears at the summit of the Unal Trail.

Elevation change: Approximately a 275-foot gain.

Season: May through October.

Services: Water, pit toilets, and telephones are available at the Summit Ranger Station just north of the trailhead. All other services are available in Lake Isabella.

Hazards: Narrow trail at times, with some stream crossings.

Rescue index: Help is very close at the Summit Ranger Station just north of the trailhead.

Land status: National forest.

Maps: *The Unal Trail: On the Trail of the Bear* guide and map is available at the trailhead.

Finding the trail: From Lake Isabella, drive 7 miles north on CA 155 to Wofford Heights. CA 155 turns sharply left at Evans Road. Continue on CA 155, which climbs steeply for 7.3 miles to Rancheria Road. Go left (south) at Rancheria Road. (You'll see signs for the Shirley Meadows Ski Area.) One hundred yards up Rancheria Road, park in the small parking lot next to Summit Ranger Station on the right.

Source of additional information:

Sequoia National Forest
Greenhorn Ranger District
Lake Isabella Visitor Center
4875 Ponderosa Drive

P.O. Box 3810
Lake Isabella, CA 93240
(760) 379-5646
www.r5.fs.fed.us/sequoia

Notes on the trail: From the parking area adjacent to Summit Ranger Station, ride south a few hundred yards on Rancheria Road, just past FS 25S17, to the well-marked Unal Trail kiosk. (Mileage readings reflect the distance covered on the Unal Trail only and do not include Rancheria Road yardage.) From the kiosk, start climbing the well-marked trail. At 0.2 mile, turn left when the trail forks so that you're circumnavigating the loop in a clockwise direction. Follow the well-marked trail to the summit at 1.9 miles. Leave the summit by going north on the well-marked trail. At 3.4 miles, you'll reach the end of the loop. Turn left and return to the trailhead at 3.6 miles.

RIDE 89 · Cannell Trail

AT A GLANCE

Length/configuration: 25.5-mile point-to-point ride (with car shuttle) on single-track and fire road.

Aerobic difficulty: Moderate, but the occasional climbs feel more difficult due to high elevation

Technical difficulty: Difficult; some very demanding sections, steep descents, and major drop-offs

Scenery: Giant sequoias, streams, meadows, seasonal wildflowers, mountain peaks, Lake Isabella, and abundant wildlife

Special comments: One of the region's most memorable rides; allot an entire day—or two—for biking, shuttling, and capping the adventure with a meal in Kernville

Perhaps the crown jewel of all Sequoia National Forest rides, this route bumps down through all sorts of regional scenery on a trail that is as breathtaking as the view. The Forest Service recommends spending two days on this trail. It's not a bad suggestion—you don't want to rush through here, and an overnight campout in a beautiful meadow deserves consideration as well. The only problem is that the single-track isn't that conducive to riding with a full stash of camping gear.

The alternatives are compelling, however. If you start early on the full ride, it's easy enough to finish the whole excursion in one day before the sun goes down. Or, you can sign up for a tour with the helpful Mountain and River Adventures outfitters (see "Sources of Additional Information" below), and let them haul everything for you. Regardless of what method is used, advanced bikers will be glad they came to Cannell.

General location: Near the town of Kernville, in the Sequoia National Forest.

Elevation change: Route begins at 9,200 feet and descends all the way to 2,800 feet, but also includes about 800 noticeable vertical feet of climbing.

Season: Early June to early November (but check with Sequoia National Forest for snow conditions during early spring and late fall).

Services: Rest rooms available at campgrounds along route; water is not available on route. All services can be found in Kernville.

Hazards: Narrow, sometimes rocky single-track; riding on precipitous cliffs; possible cattle encounters; high elevation.

Rescue index: Help is sometimes available at Cannell Meadow Ranger Station midway through ride. But this is a long ride, and you may often be miles from help. Carry all first aid and repair supplies, as well as plenty of water.

Land status: National forest.

Maps: USGS 7.5-minute maps: Sirretta Peak, Cannell Peak, and Kernville.

Finding the trail: This ride demands a car shuttle. (If you don't have two cars, you might want to pay for a shuttle from Mountain and River Adventures). Park the first car in Kernville, obeying all posted regulations. In the second car, go north out of Kernville on Sierra Way (FS 99/211) for nearly 18 miles. Go right on Sherman Pass Road for 13 very twisty miles to a summit marked by a sign, "Sherman Pass Vista 9,200 feet". You'll see a cattle guard and a loop-shaped overlook area, where you park the second car. (As of this writing, overnight parking is permitted.)

Sources of additional information:

Sequoia National Forest
Cannell Meadow Ranger District
105 Whitney Road
P.O. Box 9
Kernville, CA, 93238
(760) 376-3781
www.r5.fs.fed.us/sequoia

Mountain and River Adventures
11113 Kernville Road
P.O. Box 858
Kernville, CA 93238
(760) 376-6553
(800) 861-6553
www.mtnriver.com

Notes on the trail: From the overlook parking area, bicycle back to the cattle guard. On your left you will see the Cannell Trail (FS 33E32) trailhead. Go left on the single-track. The trail is loose at times, but you won't mind as you spin through a majestic giant sequoia grove.

Before you know it, the trail intersects with a paved road, which you cross. After picking up the Cannell Trail on the other side, you descend through occasionally steep terrain while crossing a series of dirt roads. (Don't worry; it's easy to pick up the Cannell Trail after each crossing.)

After passing Mosquito Meadows on the right, Cannell Trail begins running alongside a paved road. At 3.3 miles, you cross a small stream and embark on an intense climb. You are now paying for all the vertical feet you've just squandered, as you work your way up to over 9,300 feet—higher than the ride's starting point.

Take a breather at the summit at just over 4 miles, and head downhill on a twisty bit of trail that turns quite technical around 5.5 miles. You'll bounce through a jarring boulder field where rocks and roots conspire to shake your fillings loose. The trail is sometimes narrow, sometimes a double-track as it heads

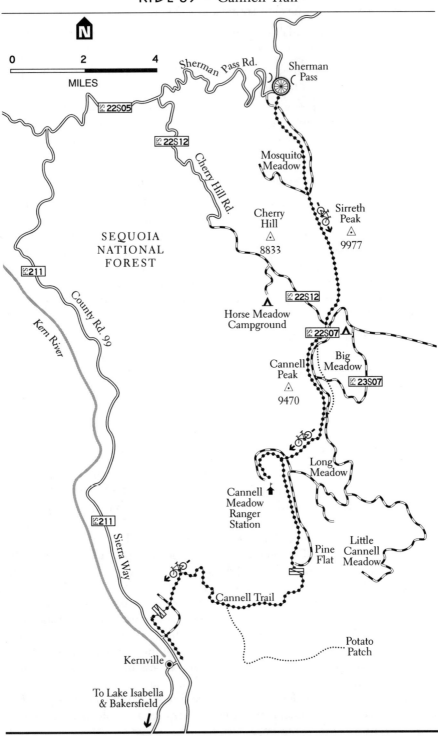

into Big Meadow Campground at 7.2 miles. Continue through the campground on the main dirt road, following signs to Cannell Meadow. You'll come to a signed intersection, where a sign points one way to Cherry Hill Road, the other to Cannell Meadow. Take the latter way.

Stay on the dirt road as you begin climbing around 9.2 miles. You top out at 10.3 miles, then descend for 0.4 mile. Keep your eyes peeled for the Cannell Trail single-track heading off to the right, and begin climbing it. The rocky, step-like trail, thin air, and proximity to steep drop-offs may encourage you to walk parts of this. (Don't worry: you won't be the first to dismount here. The climb isn't that long; less than 0.75 mile.) After topping out, you begin a tricky, technical descent (staying on the main trail) which intersects with a dirt road at 12.7 miles.

The Cannell Trail is directly across the road, but its time for a detour and a little break. For now, go right on the dirt road, bypass a jeep road marked "Horse Camp," and go left when the signed road veers left to Cannell Meadow. You soon come to Cannell Meadow Ranger Station, which was the first ranger station built in the Sequoia National Forest. Take a break here for the lunch you smartly packed. When you're rested and ready for more biking, backtrack to the trailhead for the Cannell Trail and go right, heading toward Pine Flat. At 13.4 miles, you'll begin riding through some meadows where it can be tricky finding the trail. Your intuition will usually guide you the right way, and when things get really questionable, there's usually a trail sign to help.

At 14.3 miles, you come to a road and some thick trees. You can spot the trail (visible through the trees), and you want to turn right to hook up with it. Stay on the main Cannell Trail through some rocky sections and stream crossings on Cannell Creek. Around 16.2 miles, you begin a sequence of dirt road crossings and mergings, where you need to pay attention to trail signs and blazings on pine trees to point you the right way. (It sounds kind of vague, I admit, but it's actually not too difficult to find the right way to go. Rule of thumb: if you have ridden for more than five minutes on a dirt road without seeing a trail sign or blazed tree, you've probably gone too far and should backtrack.)

After passing through the Pine Flat area, you arrive at a cattle gate at 16.7 miles. Open the gate and pass through it, as you ride on a tight cliff-top single-track. The somewhat alpine environment gives way to a typical Southern California yucca, manzanita, and chaparral landscape. The views open up as well, and you catch some amazing glimpses of Lake Isabella and the Kern River Valley while winding along a narrow, totally captivating single-track. You are now on the Cannell Plunge, and it's an apt term. But when you pass the Potato Patch Trail turnoff at 19 miles, the steep Cannell Trail descent is interrupted by a brief but dismount-demanding climb/hike.

After the climb tops out, some very steep descending ensues. Continue downhill past an intersection with a trail heading uphill, and you'll come to a gate at 22 miles. Pass through it and ride a bit on a gentler pitch to a T-intersection with a dirt road. Go left, climb for a short bit, and pick up the trail on the right at 22.8 miles. Head down it while passing dirt roads that branch off to the left. You want to veer right, following trail signs and passing through a gate. You're now almost at the bottom. At 24.1 miles, you'll reach the lower Cannell Trail trailhead on Sierra Way. Turn left, and ride for 1.4 miles back to downtown Kernville and celebrate an exhilarating 25.5-mile ride.

RIDE 90 · Converse Basin

AT A GLANCE

Length/configuration: 10.3-mile loop (from Cherry Gap, past Chicago Tree, spur to Boole Tree, and return) on dirt road and pavement

Aerobic difficulty: Moderate; some climbs are occasionally steep

Technical difficulty: Easy/moderate; roads are usually in good shape, but can become rough

Scenery: Huge sequoia stumps, meadows, wildflowers, grand Boole Tree

Special comments: A scenic ride and hike combination that brings you to an isolated giant sequoia tree

Located just outside of the boundary of Kings Canyon National Park, this popular ride showcases both the stateliness of the giant sequoia trees as well as the thoroughness with which they were cut down.

A fun ride on forest service roads brings you past the Chicago Stump. This is all that remains of a, well, gigantic giant sequoia that was cut down, trucked away, sent around the Panama Canal and delivered to Chicago's famous Colombian Exposition in 1893. You can only imagine how impressed fairgoers were when they saw the tree in Chicago.

Afterward, the ride takes you through Converse Basin, one of the largest sequoia groves before it was thoroughly logged in the 1800s. Finally, you reach a hiking trail to the Boole Tree, the 8th largest tree in the world. In short, a pleasant excursion for tree huggers and bikers alike.

General location: In the Sequoia National Forest, a few miles from Grant Grove, approximately 65 miles east of Fresno.

Elevation change: The route starts at 6,800 feet, eventually drops to 5,900 feet and returns (with some undulations). Total elevation gain is approximately 1,000 feet.

Season: May to October (wildflowers are most prevalent in early summer).

Services: No services on trail. Food, water, basic supplies, lodging, rest rooms, and telephones available in Grant Grove.

Hazards: Vehicular traffic on roads.

Rescue index: Both the National Park Service and National Forest Service have rangers stationed nearby, in Grant Grove and Hume Lake respectively. Both agencies request that trail users call 911 in an emergency.

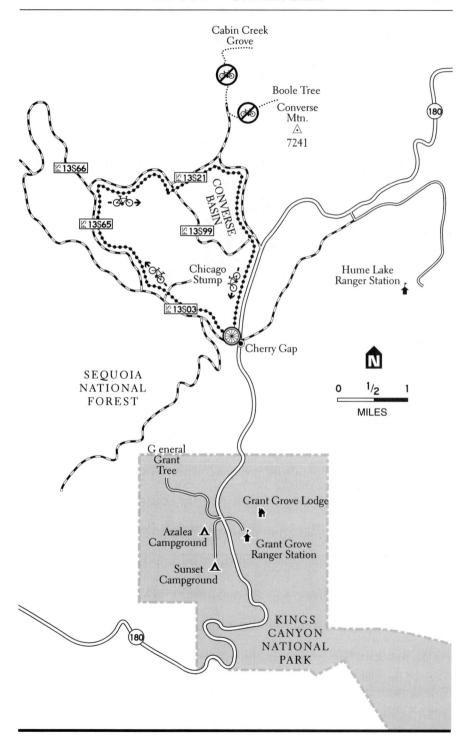

Cabin Creek Grove

Boole Tree
Converse Mtn.
7241

13S66

13S21

CONVERSE BASIN

13S65

13S99

Chicago Stump

Hume Lake Ranger Station

13S03

Cherry Gap

SEQUOIA NATIONAL FOREST

N

0   1/2   1
MILES

180

G eneral Grant Tree

Grant Grove Lodge

Azalea Campground

Grant Grove Ranger Station

Sunset Campground

KINGS CANYON NATIONAL PARK

180

A forest imp frolics in front of a giant sequoia.

Land status: National forest.

Maps: *Sequoia and Kings Canyon National Parks Recreation Map* from Tom Harrison Cartography, (800) 265-9090 or (415) 456-7940, www.tomharrison maps.com.

Finding the trail: From the Grant Grove Visitor Center in Kings Canyon National Park, drive north on CA 180. After leaving the park boundary, you drive up to a saddle at 3.4 miles from the Visitor Center. This is Cherry Gap. Turn left on the dirt road (signs indicate the way to Chicago Stump) and immediately park on the side of the dirt road so that you're not blocking traffic.

Sources of additional information:

Sequoia National Forest
Hume Lake Ranger District
35860 East Kings Canyon Road
Dunlap, CA 93261
(559) 338-2251
www.r5.fs.fed.us/sequoia.

Sequoia and Kings Canyon
    National Parks
47050 Generals Highway

Three Rivers, CA 93271-9651
(559) 565-3341
www.nps.gov/seki

Bicycling America's National Parks:
    California, David Story,
    (Countryman Press, 2000).

Notes on the trail: Following the signs to Chicago Stump, pedal northwest (away from CA 180) on a mellow dirt road, FS 13S03, for 1.3 miles to a turnoff on the right for the Chicago Stump. Follow the turnoff and view the stump. After you've finished gaping, backtrack a few pedal strokes and go right, so that you're riding westbound on FS 13S03 again.

At 1.8 miles, you reach an intersection with FS 13S65. Turn right here. FS 13S65 zigzags on a pleasant descent before arriving at a meadow. It seems like you should go left, but stay to the right of the meadow. You pass a creek, hit some dirt, and may see some cows as you ride through Converse Basin, home to perhaps the largest giant sequoia grove in existence before it was plundered in the late 1800s.

At 5.6 miles you reach a T-intersection with FS 13S55. Go left, through the aptly named Stump Meadow, to the Boole Tree trailhead. It's a 1-mile hike to Boole Tree. The tree was once considered the largest in the world, but it's actually eighth largest. Yet its isolation and position make it seem easily as grand as any other. Hike a bit further to gain superb views of Kings Canyon or return to your bike. Turn left down FS 13S55 the way you came in, but go left at the intersection (staying on FS 13S55), which climbs gradually for almost 2 miles to CA 180, 9.1 miles into your trip. Go right on the pavement of CA 180 to Cherry Gap saddle, and return to the start at 10.3 miles.

RIDE 91 · River Road Loop

AT A GLANCE

Length/configuration: 6.3-mile loop on dirt road and pavement

Aerobic difficulty: Easy; inclines are very modest

Technical difficulty: Easy; dirt portion can be rugged in spots

Scenery: Roaring River Falls, South Fork of Kings River, rock formations, wildlife, forests

Special comments: A ride where the terrain is easy on the thighs, and the scenery is easy on the eyes

This ride doesn't actually take place in Sequoia National Forest itself, but rather the forest's picturesque neighbor, Kings Canyon National Park. Kings Canyon enthusiasts boast that it's the deepest canyon in the United States, with a 8,200-foot elevation differential between Kings River and the 10,051-foot peak of Spanish Mountain. What's more, no less a naturalist than John Muir called the Cedar Grove area of Kings Canyon "a yet grander valley" than Yosemite. It's a strikingly beautiful place, and this ride shows it off.

Recommended for cyclists by Kings Canyon National Park, this loop on dirt and pavement travels along what used to be known as the "Motor Nature Trail." But the park has come to realize that such a name is something of an oxymoron; so—besides changing the route's name to River Road—it is looking into the process of opening this dirt portion only to bikers and hikers. At present, cars are still

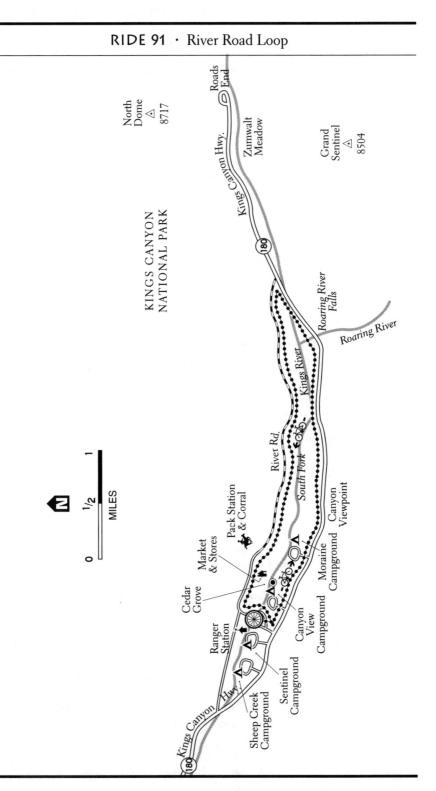

KINGS CANYON
NATIONAL PARK

North
Dome
△
8717

Zumwalt
Meadow

Grand
Sentinel
△
8504

Roads
End

Kings Canyon Hwy.

180

Roaring River
Falls

Roaring River

Kings River

River Rd.

South Fork

Canyon
Viewpoint

Pack Station
& Corral

Market
& Stores

Cedar
Grove

Ranger
Station

Canyon View
Campground

Moraine
Campground

Sentinel
Campground

Sheep Creek
Campground

Kings Canyon Hwy.

180

N

0   ½   1

MILES

Forest in Kings Canyon
National Park.

allowed, and you might occasionally share the dirt road with them. With or without cars, the views are bountiful enough to go around.

General location: Near Cedar Grove Village, in Kings Canyon National Park.

Elevation change: Insignificant; ride hovers near 4,600 feet most of the time.

Season: May to October.

Services: No services on route. Food, water, rest rooms, information, and basic supplies available at Cedar Grove Village.

Hazards: Automobile traffic on paved portions.

Rescue index: Route is never far from Cedar Grove Ranger Station.

Land status: National park.

Maps: The National Park Service's "Sequoia and Kings Canyon National Parks" map comes with admission to the park and depicts the River Road route.

Finding the trail: From the main Kings Canyon Visitor Center at Grant Grove, go northeast approximately 28 miles on winding Kings Canyon Highway/ CA 180 to Cedar Grove. Turn left, following signs to Cedar Grove Ranger Station, which is located 0.2 mile from Kings Canyon Highway.

Sources of additional information:

Sequoia and Kings Canyon
National Parks
47050 Generals Highway
Three Rivers, CA 93271-9651
(559) 565-3341
www.nps.gov/seki

Bicycling America's National Parks:
California, David Story,
(Countryman Press, 2000)

Notes on the trail: Pedal away from the Ranger Station, back to the main road, Kings Canyon Highway/CA 180, and turn left. The road rolls a bit as you spin past Moraine Campground and toward the imposing Sierra Nevada Mountains ahead of you. At 2.7 miles, stop at the trailhead to Roaring River Falls on your right. It's an easy 200-yard paved trail to a viewing point where you can watch water soaring over 80-foot falls. Returning to your bike, be on the lookout for a bridge that comes up in 0.25 mile. Almost immediately after crossing the bridge, take your next left turn (at 3 miles) onto a dirt road. This is the beginning of River Road, formerly known as the "Motor Nature Trail."

You are now circling back toward Cedar Grove, this time heading west along the north bank of the river. The route is certainly more bucolic than its former name, and you're likely to see wildlife skittering through the forest as you approach. This area is very popular with anglers, perhaps because of the silence and quietude of the place. There are also several exhibits along the way which show how the valley was formed by retreating glaciers. At 5.3 miles, you leave the dirt and ride onto pavement. After spinning past the Cedar Grove Pack Station, where groups on horseback depart for High Sierra destinations, you reach a turnoff on your left at 6 miles. Go left here to return to the Ranger Station at 6.3 miles.

EASTERN SIERRA AND
OWENS VALLEY

One of the biggest crimes that Southern California mountain bikers commit is speeding through the Owens Valley and Eastern Sierra regions on their way to ride the trails of Mammoth Mountain Ski Area. Granted, Mammoth is a superb place to ride and has enjoyed a big impact on mountain bike racing. However, this region is home to so many other tantalizing mountain biking experiences, it should be felony to bypass them.

The Owens Valley is a strip of land less than 20 miles wide. It cuts between the massive Sierra Nevada mountains on the west and the imposing but much drier Inyo mountains on the east. In between the two are the scenic Alabama Hills and the Los Angeles Aqueduct, which have delivered, respectively, westerns and water to the megalopolis of Los Angeles. While it's amusing to imagine yourself riding your steed (i.e., your bike) in the same hills where Roy Rogers once rode Trigger, it's even more fun to forget about the big city to the south. It's also easy to do here, with scenery-intense rides such as Movie Road and Mazourka Canyon showcasing the unique geography and geology of the area.

A little farther north, you can ride amidst an ancient bristlecone forest, the only one of its kind in the world. More than 4,000 years old, bristlecone pines are among the oldest living things on earth. Just think about it; while some equestrians call mountain biking a novelty sport, bristlecone pines are so old, horses are a novelty to them (at least in this country).

Without leaving your bike, you can also explore areas of historic volcanic activity near Mammoth Lakes, wander through narrow canyons along Lower Rock Creek, gaze at waterfalls in Buttermilk Country, and check out Native American petroglyphs in Chidago Canyon. In short, you can do just about everything you bought your mountain bike to do.

If that weren't enough, the towns of Bishop and Mammoth Lakes offer all the resources a cyclist could want, from informative rangers to skilled bike shops, cheap taverns, and taquerias. It's not easy to ride here in winter due to the high elevation and snow, but three seasons in this region feel like four anywhere else.

RIDE 92 · Movie Road

AT A GLANCE

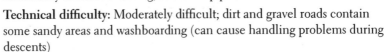

Length/configuration: 17.5-mile loop

Aerobic difficulty: Difficult; longer ride with plenty of moderately difficult climbing; some steep pitches

Technical difficulty: Moderately difficult; dirt and gravel roads contain some sandy areas and washboarding (can cause handling problems during descents)

Scenery: Breathtaking views of Mt. Whitney and Lone Pine Peak from Whitney Portal Road; big rock formations on Movie Road

Special comments: Numerous westerns and television shows were filmed on Movie Road

Strong cyclists with intermediate bike-handling skills will enjoy this scenic 17.5-mile loop. The 5.6-mile climb on paved Whitney Portal Road is moderately difficult, with some steep sections in the last two miles. Hogback Road is mostly downhill and level to the intersection with Movie Road. Movie Road climbs moderately for about 2 miles and then rolls up and down, steeply at times, to the end of the ride. Hogback and Movie Roads are unpaved two-wheel-drive roads in fair to good condition; both contain washboarded and sandy areas.

The view of Mt. Whitney and Lone Pine Peak from Whitney Portal Road is outstanding. A close look may reveal hang gliders skimming the mountain tops. The descent on Hogback Road is invigorating; it starts out fast and then mellows into a cruise that goes on and on. Surrounded by the huge red rocks that line Movie Road, you'll see why this was a choice location for the filming of television and movie westerns.

General location: Begins at the intersection of Whitney Portal Road and Movie Road, 2.7 miles west of Lone Pine.

Elevation change: Total elevation gain is 2,600 feet.

Season: Late fall through spring. It is possible to ride here year-round, but high summer temperatures can make riding unpleasant and even dangerous. The weather can be unpredictable; carry sunscreen, raingear, and extra clothing.

Services: There is no water available on this ride, so fill up in town. If you need more water, a side trip into the Lone Pine Campground is recommended. About 4 miles into the ride, turn left off of Whitney Portal Road and follow an entrance road for about 1 mile to the Lone Pine Campground and piped water. All services are available in Lone Pine.

Hazards: Whitney Portal Road sees a moderate amount of traffic, and vehicles travel at high speeds. There is no shoulder, so watch yourself. There are some sandy sections on Hogback and Movie Roads. After riding on Movie Road for 3

RIDE 92 · Movie Road

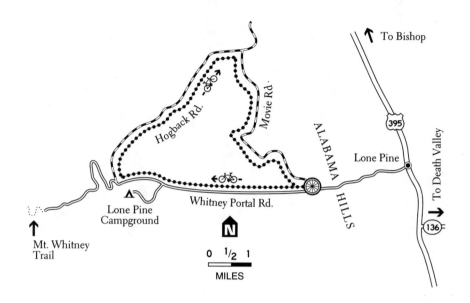

miles you will encounter a steep descent with loose material at the bottom—control your speed.

Rescue index: Help can be found in Lone Pine.

Land status: National forest and BLM lands.

Maps: USGS 7.5-minute quadrangle maps: Lone Pine, Independence, and Mt. Pinchot.

Finding the trail: From the stoplight on US 395 in Lone Pine, head west on Whitney Portal Road and follow it 2.7 miles to the intersection with Movie Road. Park in the large dirt parking area on the right.

Sources of additional information:

Inyo National Forest
Mt. Whitney Ranger District
640 South Main Street
P.O. Box 8
Lone Pine, CA 93545
(760) 878-6200
www.r5.fs.fed.us/inyo

InterAgency Visitor Center
Jct. of US 395 and CA 136
P.O. Box R
Lone Pine, CA 93545-2017
(760) 876-6222
TDD (760) 876-6223

The Sierra Mountains and Whitney Portal Road.

Notes on the trail: Pedal west on the paved Whitney Portal Road. After cycling for 5.6 miles, turn right onto the unsigned Hogback Road before the first major switchback on Whitney Portal Road and just before a sign reading "Trailers Not Recommended." Hogback Road is paved at first but soon turns to dirt and curves around to the right as you begin a long descent. Follow the main road for 6 miles to a T-intersection at signed Movie Road. Turn right onto Movie Road. Three and a half miles of riding on Movie Road will bring you to a narrow outcropping of rocks near some willows. The route passes between the rocks. About 0.5 mile beyond the outcropping, the main road curves hard to the left and a side road continues straight. Follow the main road left. Reach your parked vehicle after another 1.6 miles.

RIDE 93 · Mazourka Canyon

AT A GLANCE

Length/configuration: 22.2-mile combination; a 6-mile loop and a 16.2-mile out-and-back (8.1 miles each way)

Aerobic difficulty: Difficult; long, moderately difficult climb is made more difficult by soft conditions

CA

Technical difficulty: Moderately difficult; long descent is complicated by loose conditions, washboarding, and rocks

Scenery: Dry, barren canyon; views across Owens Valley to the Sierras at the high point of the ride

Special comments: Quiet roads, nice views, good workout

This 22.2-mile ride through Mazourka Canyon is an out-and-back trip with a short loop around Santa Rita Flat. Although the ascent is moderately steep, the cycling is made more difficult due to the length of the climb (9 miles!) and the condition of the road surface. Mazourka Canyon Road is a two-wheel-drive gravel road in fair condition, with some washboarding and loose rocks. The road around Santa Rita Flat is in better condition, but you will cross some sandy washes and rocky areas. This road is nearly level as it winds around the flat.

Mazourka Canyon is barren and dry, but the scenery improves as you gain altitude. At Santa Rita Flat you'll get a beautiful view across the Owens Valley to the rugged peaks of the Sierras. Santa Rita Flat is a well-used cattle grazing area, as evidenced by a corral, a hoof-muddied spring, and an abundance of cow pies in the road. This ride is a good workout if you're looking for an extended moderate climb. The descent is fast and long, but the fun factor is diminished by the bumpiness of the road.

General location: The ride begins east of the community of Independence, at the end of the pavement on Mazourka Canyon Road (approximately 40 miles south of Bishop).

Elevation change: You'll start at 4,000 feet and climb to a high point of 6,800 feet at Santa Rita Flat. Total elevation gain: 2,800 feet.

Season: Spring is the most beautiful time of year to ride in the Inyo Mountains. Summer temperatures can soar, so ride in the early morning. Snow is common in the winter at higher elevations.

Services: There is no water available on this ride. All services are available in Independence.

Hazards: Stay alert for cattleguards, sand, rocks, and washboarding on the return descent.

Rescue index: Help can be found in Independence.

Land status: National forest and BLM lands.

Maps: USGS 7.5-minute quadrangle map: Independence.

Finding the trail: Follow US 395 south from Bishop for approximately 40 miles to Independence. Turn left (east) onto Mazourka Canyon Road and follow it for 4.4 miles to the end of the pavement. Park your vehicle on the right side of the road.

Sources of additional information:

Inyo National Forest
White Mountain Ranger District
798 North Main Street

Bishop, CA 93514
(760) 873-2500
www.r5.fs.fed.us/inyo

RIDE 93 · Mazourka Canyon

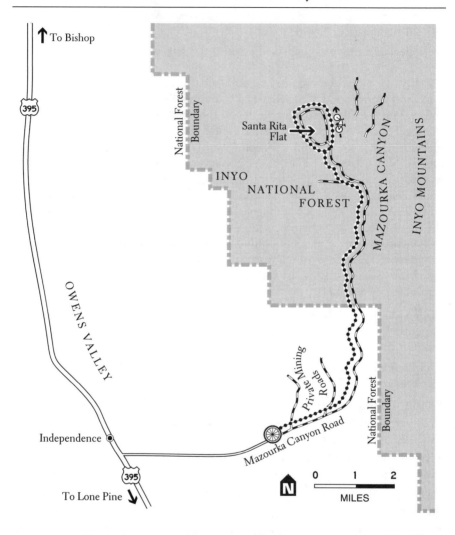

InterAgency Visitor Center
Jct. of US 395 and CA 136
P.O. Box R

Lone Pine, CA 93545-2017
(760) 876-6222
TDD (760) 876-6223

Notes on the trail: Begin this trip at the end of the pavement on Mazourka Canyon Road. Follow Mazourka Canyon Road as it swings north and passes a mining road on the left. You will pass an Inyo National Forest Boundary sign after 4.6 miles of riding. Continue up the canyon for another 3.4 miles to a **Y**-intersection at a sign for Santa Rita Flat/Badger Flat. Turn left toward Santa Rita Flat. Stay to the right as the road circles Santa Rita Flat. Pursue the main road and pedal past a corral. About 1 mile beyond the corral you will reach a **T**-intersection. Turn left at this intersection and proceed downhill toward Santa Rita Spring. As you approach the spring you will pass through a sandy wash. Immediately after climbing out of the wash, you'll arrive at an intersection of trails. Turn left (south) here onto a double-track road and ride past the cattle watering hole that is Santa Rita Spring. Follow this double-track to meet the road you came in on. Return the way you came.

RIDE 94 · Ancient Bristlecone

AT A GLANCE

Length/configuration: 26-mile out-and-back (13 miles each way)

Aerobic difficulty: Difficult; extreme elevation, hard climbs, long trip

Technical difficulty: Difficult; condition of two-wheel-drive gravel road varies from poor to good; rocky, rough, steep descents

Scenery: Incredibly beautiful alpine environment; breathtaking views of the Sierras

Special comments: Twisted, wind-whipped, ancient bristlecone pines; some have lived for over 4,500 years

This 26-mile out-and-back is long, hard, and technically demanding. Grades that would seem easy at sea level will leave you gasping at 10,000 feet. There are several long, steep grinds in both directions, and the road surface is rocky and washboarded. The condition of the unpaved, two-wheel-drive road varies from poor to good. There are even some dangerously rocky and bumpy sections.

At this elevation, the White Mountains are stark and desolate. The forest is composed of pockets of wind-battered trees and expansive alpine meadows. Its harsh and barren character is extremely beautiful. The feeling is one of openness; the air is clean and clear, the sunlight intense. After approximately four miles of riding you'll reach a viewpoint. Here you can see west into the interior of the Sierras to glaciers, meadows, and snowcapped peaks.

In this part of the Inyo National Forest you can walk among the oldest living things on earth—bristlecone pines. Some of these trees have been alive for more than 45 centuries! There is an information center and two self-guided trails at the Schulman Grove. The Patriarch Grove, the turnaround point, also has a self-guided trail.

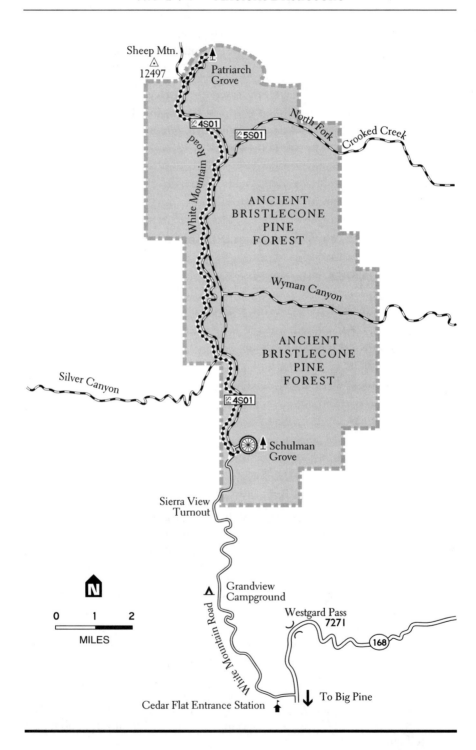

Sheep Mtn.
12497

Patriarch Grove

North Fork Crooked Creek

4S01

5S01

White Mountain Road

ANCIENT BRISTLECONE PINE FOREST

Wyman Canyon

ANCIENT BRISTLECONE PINE FOREST

Silver Canyon

4S01

Schulman Grove

Sierra View Turnout

N

0   1   2
MILES

Grandview Campground

Westgard Pass
7271

168

White Mountain Road

Cedar Flat Entrance Station

To Big Pine

General location: Begins at the Schulman Grove in the Ancient Bristlecone Pine Forest, approximately 25 miles northeast of Big Pine.

Elevation change: The ride starts at 10,100 feet and climbs to a high point of 11,200 feet at the Patriarch Grove. Add an estimated 1,000 feet of additional climbing in each direction for the undulating nature of this ride. Total elevation gain: 3,100 feet.

Season: Late spring through early fall. The Ancient Bristlecone Pine Forest is normally open from June through October; call the Forest Service to check on closings. Be prepared for unpredictable weather. Thunderstorms can occur without warning, and snow is a threat in the spring and fall.

Services: There is no water to be found east of Big Pine; bring all that you will need. There are no gas stations east of Big Pine. All services can be obtained in Big Pine and Bishop.

Hazards: This ride takes place at high altitude on occasionally rough roads. Be prepared for sudden drops in temperature, high winds, thunderstorms, and the possibility of altitude sickness. Bring plenty of water and drink often. If you become severely fatigued, turn around.

Rescue index: Help may be available at the Information Center at Schulman Grove. This center is staffed by rangers during regular business hours. Stop in before embarking on the ride and check on the hours of operation. The next closest help is in Big Pine. Traffic is light. Plan on being completely self-sufficient.

Land status: National forest.

Maps: *The Inyo National Forest Map*, available at ranger stations, is a good guide to this ride. The Information Center at Schulman Grove has several useful maps for sale.

Finding the trail: From US 395 in Big Pine, travel east on CA 168. Drive for 13 miles on CA 168 and turn left on White Mountain Road at a sign for the White Mountain Bristlecone Forest. Follow White Mountain Road in a northerly direction past the Cedar Flats Entrance Station, the Grandview Campground, and the Sierra View Turnout. Go 2 miles beyond the Sierra View Turnout to Schulman Grove on the right. Park your vehicle in the Schulman Grove parking lot.

Source of additional information:

Inyo National Forest
White Mountain Ranger District
798 North Main Street
Bishop, CA 93514

(760) 873-2500
TDD: (760) 873-2501
www.r5.fs.fed.us/inyo

Notes on the trail: From the Schulman Grove parking lot, turn right onto White Mountain Road (FS 4S01). The pavement ends almost immediately, and you'll pass a sign that reads "Patriarch Grove—12 miles." (We found it to be closer to 13 miles.) After 3 miles, you'll pass an intersection and a road that leads left to Silver Canyon Laws and right to Wyman Canyon Deep Spring. There are two mileage signs here; one points to Patriarch Grove and reads "7 miles" (wrong again; it's more like 10 miles). The other points back to Schulman Grove and reads "2 miles" (wrong a third time; it's more like 3 miles). Continue straight toward the Patriarch Grove. In 1 mile you'll reach a parking area with views to the west. From this viewpoint, it's about 3 miles to an intersection where a road goes hard to the right, to Wyman Canyon. Stay to the left toward the Patriarch Grove. Ride 2.6 miles to another intersection where FS 5S01 goes right toward Crooked Creek Station and Cottonwood Creek. Continue straight toward Patriarch Grove; the sign reads "Patriarch Grove — 3.5 miles" (correct!). Cycle 2.5 miles to a Y-intersection and a sign directing you right toward Patriarch Grove. Travel 1 more mile to reach the Patriarch Grove parking area. Bicycles are not permitted on the nature trail. Return the way you came.

RIDE 95 · Buttermilk Country Loop

AT A GLANCE

Length/configuration: 17.8-mile loop on jeep roads and pavement

Aerobic difficulty: Moderate; long and fairly high in elevation

Technical difficulty: Easy/moderate; a few stream crossings and a rocky descent near ride's end

Scenery: Waterfalls, Sierra Nevadas, gnarled foothills, and abundant wildlife

Special comments: A long but moderate ride through beautiful subalpine country where picturesque views are revealed one after another

This 17.8-mile loop ride is named for the prized buttermilk made at a dairy that operated here during the late 1800s. Just as buttermilk enhances the taste of whatever ingredients it touches, this loop has a way of making the already spectacular surroundings that much more delicious.

After you commence the day with a coffee from Kava Coffeehouse in downtown Bishop (phone (760) 872-1010), you'll head 7 miles west of Bishop on CA 168, where the ride starts. Rising through the foothills of the Sierra Nevadas, you'll course through meadows and past granite formations that appear as if the gods were playing with candle wax after dinner. As you approach a massive granite monolith alongside McGee Creek next to a steadily climbing dirt road, an almost negligible detour leads to amazing views of an unexpected waterfall. After more climbing, aspen trees begin to appear and the trip becomes more alpine as you enter the Buttermilk Country Wildlife Area/Winter Deer Range Habitat. Chances are you've already seen a lot of wildlife up to this point, including jackrabbits and lizards. Now be on the lookout for deer as the trail becomes marshier and shady.

Alternating pine and aspen groves carpet the road with needles and leaves as you prepare to traverse McGee Creek (which can be a challenging obstacle during early summer run-off). Soon you'll finish climbing and begin a nice descent

RIDE 95 · Buttermilk Country Loop

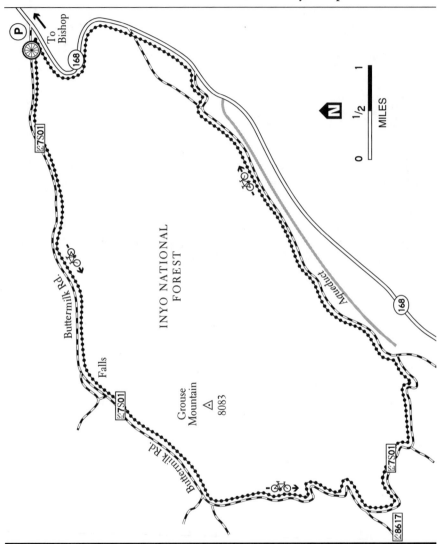

broken up by some small uphills. While you parallel an aqueduct delivering water to hydroelectric stations, stunning views of the north Owens Valley open up on your left. Take a break here before the fastest part of the descent, marred only slightly by some sand and rocks here and there. Reaching the National Forest Service's Bishop Creek Campground at CA 168, you'll turn left for an easy glide on pavement back to your car. Now it's time to return to Bishop for a Mexican feast at Amigo's, 285 North Main Street, (760) 872-2189.

A view as rich as buttermilk itself.

General location: 7 miles west of Bishop on CA 168 in the Inyo National Forest.

Elevation change: Approximately 3,100-foot gain, from 5,100 feet to 8,200 feet.

Season: May through October, snow level permitting. If you do this ride in June after a winter of especially heavy snowfall, it's a good idea to first inquire about the passability of McGee Creek.

Services: No services on trail. All services available in Bishop.

Hazards: Crossing a possibly fast-running stream, and rocky descents in places. Also, watch for cars on the paved section and on the first 4 miles of the route (between the falls and CA 168).

Rescue index: All points on the ride are within 8 downhill miles of CA 168. Help is available at the Inyo County Sheriff's Substation at the intersection of CA 168 and US 395.

Land status: National forest.

Maps: USGS 7.5-minute quadrangle: Tungsten Hills.

Finding the trail: From intersection of CA 168 and US 395 in downtown Bishop, go west on CA 168 for 7.2 miles. Turn right at Buttermilk Road and immediately park in the small gravel area off to the side. Be sure not to block any possible traffic.

Sources of additional information:

Bikes of Bishop
651 North Main Street

Bishop, CA 93514
(760) 872-3829

Inyo National Forest
White Mountain Ranger District
798 North Main Street
Bishop, CA 93514

(760) 873-2500
TDD: (760) 873-2501
www.r5.fs.fed.us/inyo

Notes on the trail: From the parking area, go west over a cattleguard and onto dirt Buttermilk Road. It's a good steady climb, though the road is soft in spots. Keep pedaling past intersections with numerous dirt roads as you climb. At 3.7 miles, you'll cross over another cattleguard and note that you're getting closer to a massive granite outcropping on your left. At 4.1 miles, veer left on a double-track that brings you even closer to the granite, which serves as one side of a massive gorge carved out by McGee Creek. In less than a quarter mile, you can really hear water rushing. Dismount and carefully walk up onto the granite for a splendid view of a waterfall coursing through the gorge's narrows. In contrast to the terrain you've been riding, the gorge is stuffed with colorful birch, willow, and sycamore trees. Returning to your bike, keep going west on the double-track you've been riding, which soon intersects with Buttermilk Road at 4.3 miles. Turn left and head mildly uphill. As you climb, you'll gradually pass striking Grouse Mountain on your left. Stay straight through intersections with jeep roads. After passing an aspen grove, veer left at 6 miles as Buttermilk Road turns to the south. You'll soon pass a sign welcoming you to the deer habitat. The climb levels a bit as aspens and pines take turns shading the trail. At 7.7 miles, stay left as the road forks. You'll pass a primitive campground on your left and come to the intersection with McGee Creek at 7.8 miles. If the creek is running especially high, you might need to scramble up- or downstream to find a better place to cross. After the creek, the trail veers left and then switches back steeply before reaching the intersection of FS 8S17 and FS 7S01 at 8.5 miles. Turn left onto FS 7S01. After an easy climb through birch trees you'll pass a green shack on your right and begin descending except for one small uphill. At 10.9 miles, you'll reach an intersection with a fire road marked with a sign reading "Notice: Locked Gate .7 Miles Ahead." (If you need to bail out for time, health, or equipment reasons, turn right here to quickly get back to CA 168 and a left turn/pavement cruise back to your car.) Otherwise, veer left.

On a ridgeline now, you'll see an aqueduct and CA 168 paralleling you on the right. At 13.2 miles, the road moves to the left side of the ridge, thereby revealing amazing Owens Valley views. At a junction at the bottom of a hill at 14.5 miles, turn right up a small hill. You'll now have a rocky descent in front of you, and you don't need me to tell you it's smoother on the right. At 15.1 miles, you'll reach CA 168. Turn left and head downhill on CA 168 and return to the parking area at 17.8 miles.

RIDE 96 · Red Canyon/Chidago Canyon

AT A GLANCE

Length/configuration: 18-mile out-and-back (9 miles each way)

Aerobic difficulty: Easy to moderately difficult; a longer ride with some brief, moderately difficult climbing

Technical difficulty: Easy; good dirt road

Scenery: Dry, sparse, open landscape

Special comments: Turnaround point at Chidago Canyon Petroglyphs; abundant, tightly spaced pictographs—nicknamed "Newspaper Rock"

This is a relatively easy, 18-mile out-and-back ride. The route follows a good two-wheel-drive dirt road. One and one-half miles into the trip there is a short, moderately steep hill; then it's mostly downhill to the turnaround point. The return is an easy to moderately difficult ascent.

Forefathers of the Paiute Indians once roamed here. They left behind many carvings on nearby rock outcroppings. The Red Rock Petroglyphs can be explored 3.5 miles into the ride. This group is known for its many examples of human hand- and footprints and large animal tracks. At Chidago Canyon you will find the Chidago Canyon Petroglyphs. This group's nickname, "Newspaper Rock," is derived from the pictures, which are numerous and crowded together.

General location: Begins on Chidago Canyon Road, approximately 19 miles north of Bishop on US 6.

Elevation change: The ride starts at 4,500 feet, climbs to 4,600 feet in 2.2 miles, and then descends gradually to 4,200 feet at the Chidago Canyon Petroglyphs. Total elevation gain: 500 feet.

Season: The riding here is best in the spring, fall, and winter. Set out in the early morning if you are planning on a summer visit.

Services: There is no water available on this ride. All services can be obtained in Bishop.

Hazards: Control your speed on the moderately steep descent near the end of the ride. The road surface contains some loose gravel here, and there are deep, silty patches at the bottom of the hill. This is an exposed ride through the desert; be prepared to help yourself out of any trouble that might arise. Travel with others and carry plenty of water.

Rescue index: Help is available in Bishop.

Land status: BLM lands.

Maps: The Inyo National Forest map that can be purchased at ranger stations is a good guide to this route. You may wish to pick up the Petroglyph Loop Trip

RIDE 96 · Red Canyon/Chidago Canyon

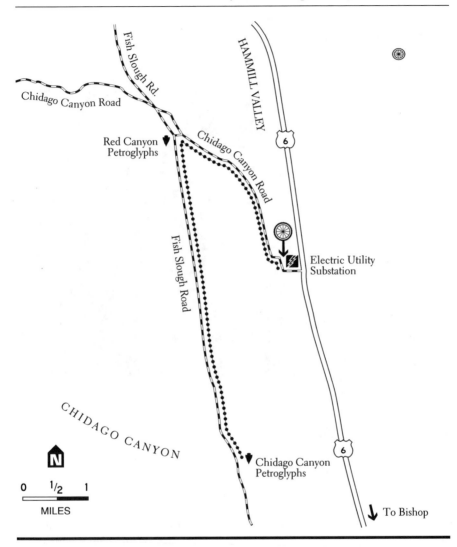

handout that is available at the White Mountain Ranger District Office in Bishop.

Finding the trail: In Bishop, at the intersection of US 395 and US 6, travel north on US 6. Drive for 19 miles to Chidago Canyon Road on the left (west) side of the highway. Turn left and follow the gravel road past the electric utility substation. Continue downhill as the road curves right (north) and park on the right side of the road. There is a fee to park at the Schulman Grove Visitor Center.

Chidago Canyon
petroglyphs.

Sources of additional information:

Inyo National Forest
White Mountain Ranger District
798 North Main Street
Bishop, CA 93514

(760) 873-2500
TDD: (760) 873-2501
www.r5.fs.fed.us/inyo

Notes on the trail: Begin the ride on Chidago Canyon Road and follow it in a northerly direction. After 3.2 miles, you'll come to an intersection; turn left toward a rock outcropping. In .2 miles you'll reach another intersection that is directly across from the rock outcropping (Red Canyon Petroglyphs). Turn left here onto unsigned Fish Slough Road. Ride for approximately 5.5 miles on Fish Slough Road to reach the Chidago Canyon Petroglyphs on the left at a chain-link fence. Return the way you came.

RIDE 97 · Lower Rock Creek

AT A GLANCE

Length/configuration: 16.3-mile loop on pavement and single-track

Aerobic difficulty: Difficult; a long, sometimes strenuous pavement climb

Technical difficulty: Difficult; the lower single-track section is extremely rocky in places

Scenery: Pink-rock volcanic canyons, heavily wooded creekbed, and summit views of Owens Valley

Special comments: A long pavement climb grants access to a spectacular single-track marred only by excessively rocky stretches in its lower section—though not for beginners, it's possible for intermediates to bail out of the ride before things get tough

Located 15 miles north of Bishop, this 16.3-mile loop is a classic "eat your vegetables, then you can have dessert" type of ride. You pay dues during a long pavement climb before cashing in with a wonderful single-track.

This trip may start in a community called Paradise, but the initial ascent is infernal. As it climbs above its namesake stream, paved Old Rock Creek Road seems to get steeper and steeper. Fortunately, this road only sees light traffic, so if you occasionally wobble as you grind up the hill, you're not likely to be in any danger. Voyaging from BLM jurisdiction into Inyo National Forest land, you'll eventually arrive at a summit. A brief but welcome descent ensues, and though you'll climb another 3 miles, the steepness dissipates somewhat.

Just before the road (now called Lower Rock Creek Road) ends at a junction with US 395, you'll finally reach the turnoff for the trip's single-track portion. Be prepared for a shock: The path is officially named the Lower Rock Creek Mt. Bike Trail. Needless to say, bikers are rarely singled out for acceptance like this, and the welcome only becomes more sincere as the single-track unfolds under you. Simply put, this is one of the most fun rides anywhere. Flanked by massive pine trees, aspens, and gurgling Lower Rock Creek, the trail is wild, untamed, and challenging but never frustrating. It seems made for biking.

By the time the route crosses Lower Rock Creek Road for a second time and plunges into Lower Rock Creek Canyon, you'll start making plans to move to Paradise full time. Unfortunately, that's where things get ugly. Hindered by an infinite amount of rocks, the trail is still scenic and remote, but its melodic rhythm has vanished. Though the trail does get better, you'll never quite recapture the magic of the upper section. Nonetheless, by the time you return to Paradise, you certainly can understand where the community got its name. For post-ride refreshments, head into the Paradise Lodge convenience store (open 8 a.m.–3 p.m.) or restaurant (open evenings after 5:30 p.m.).

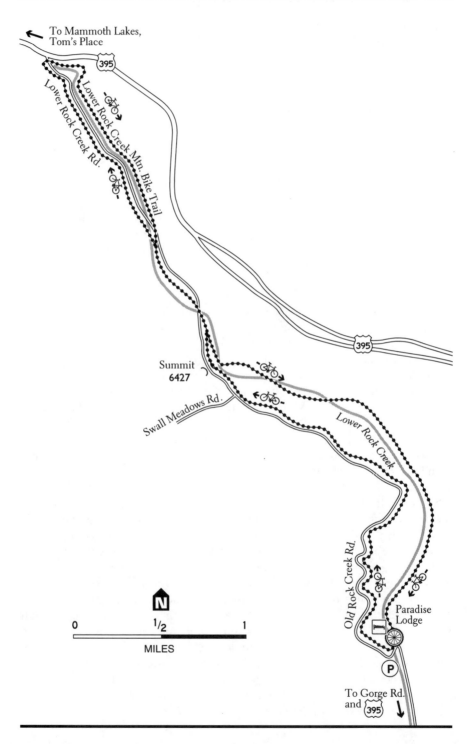

To Mammoth Lakes,
Tom's Place

395

Lower Rock Creek Mtn. Bike Trail

Lower Rock Creek Rd.

Summit
6427

Swall Meadows Rd.

Lower Rock Creek

395

Old Rock Creek Rd.

Paradise
Lodge

P

To Gorge Rd.
and 395

N

0   1/2   1

MILES

Rockin' through Lower
Rock Creek.

General location: Beginning of ride 15 miles from Bishop in the small community of Paradise.

Elevation change: Approximately 2,000 feet, from 4,900 feet to 6,900 feet.

Season: April through November, snow level permitting.

Services: No services are available on the trail. Food, phones, and rest rooms are available during business hours at the Paradise Lodge at the ride's start/finish. All other services are available 1 mile north of Rock Creek Road's single-track turnoff at Tom's Place off of US 395.

Hazards: Very rocky descent in parts, narrow trail, narrow bridges, and automobile traffic on Rock Creek Road.

Rescue index: Most of the trail is within easy access of the phones at Tom's Place and Paradise Lodge. The only troublesome section is the lower single-track, which doesn't see much use and runs along the bottom of a 600-foot-deep canyon. If you have trouble here, you'll likely have to make it out by yourself.

Land status: State, BLM, and national forest land.

Maps: USGS 7.5-minute quadrangle maps: Tom's Place, Casa Diablo Mountain, and Rovana.

Finding the trail: If you're coming from the south, drive 11 miles north of downtown Bishop on US 395 to Gorge Road. If you're coming from the north, drive 12.5 miles south of Tom's Place on US 395 to Gorge Road. Go west on Gorge Road. At a T-intersection just west of US 395, turn right (north) on Old Rock Creek Road for 4 miles to the community of Paradise. Park in the creekside gravel lot on your left, directly opposite Paradise Lodge.

Sources of additional information:

Inyo National Forest
White Mountain Ranger District
798 North Main Street
Bishop, CA 93514
(760) 873-2500
TDD (760) 873-2501
www.r5.fs.fed.us/inyo

Bikes of Bishop
651 North Main Street
Bishop, CA 93514
(760) 872-3829

Paradise Lodge
(760) 387-2370

Brian's Bicycles and
    Cross Country Skis
3059 Chateau Road

Mammoth Lakes, CA 93546
(760) 924-8566

Footloose Sports
3069 Main
Mammoth Lakes, CA 93546
(760) 934-2400

High Sierra Cycle Center
123 Commerce Drive
Mammoth Lakes, CA 93546
(760) 924-3723

Sandy's Ski and Sports
3325 Main Street
Mammoth Lakes, CA 93546
(760) 934-7518

Notes on the trail: Turn left on Old Rock Creek Road and begin climbing. You'll pass a fire station on your right and later a BLM sign that reads "Entering Public Lands." At 3.2 miles the road enters Inyo National Forest. Keep climbing. At 4.4 miles, you'll finally reach a summit, with good views of Lower Rock Creek Canyon on your right. A brief descent takes you into Lower Rock Creek Day Recreation Area and the first of two intersections with the single-track you'll eventually be riding. But for now, stay on the pavement. Just before the 8-mile mark, US 395 comes into view. Keep your eyes peeled on the right for the Lower Rock Creek Mountain Bike Trail at 8.1 miles. Turn right onto the trail and begin a blissful descent, save for a little sand and some occasional rocks. At 10.4 miles, at the intersection with Lower Rock Creek Road, jog right on the pavement for 150 feet and go left onto the trail once more. (You're now on the west side of the creek.) The only blemish to this section is that there are more washboards than one would expect, created by inexperienced riders who shuttle this ride and apply their brakes at inappropriate times. At 11.5 miles, intersect with the road once more. Go diagonally across the road to pick up the trail as it drops into the canyon. (But if you're an intermediate and not comfortable with rocks, it might be wise to bail out by turning right on Lower Rock Creek Road, climbing for a bit, then descending back to your car. The same goes for riders racing against darkness: Bail out now, for darkness will win and this canyon isn't a place to be in the dark without a light.) For those wanting more single-track, drop into the canyon as directed and cross over Lower Rock Creek on a picturesque bridge at

12.1 miles. The trail cozies up to a sheer, 600-foot granite wall cradling gorgeous pink boulders. (The pink color is caused by the way volcanic materials were released into the rocks.) In any case, it's nice on the eyes but hard on the bike. It's slow going until the 14-mile mark, at which point the trail opens up. After numerous stream crossings, you'll gain views of snowcapped Mt. Tom. At 15.8 miles, you'll reach a trailhead register and information kiosk. The single-track gives way to a fire road, and you'll cruise down easily to Paradise Lodge and return to the start at 16.3 miles.

RIDE 98 · Knolls Trail

AT A GLANCE

Length/configuration: 9.8-mile combination (9.3-mile loop with 0.25-mile out-and-back spur)

Aerobic difficulty: Moderate/difficult; the climbs aren't inordinately grueling, but surfaces are sometimes loose

Technical difficulty: Easy/moderate; obstacle-free but loose dirt roads

Scenery: Pine forests, outstanding vistas overlooking Mammoth Lakes and Owens Valley

Special comments: A superb introductory ride to mountain biking at Mammoth, this trail continually staggers its climbs and descents—you'll never fall into a rut on this route

Unlike rides you'd expect in an area as mountainous as Mammoth, this 9.8-mile combination trip isn't comprised of a single, long, grinding ascent capped by a clattering, numbing downhill. Rather, it links several smaller hills (the knolls it's named for) in a ride that showcases Mammoth's unique terrain and surroundings.

Beginning a mere mile from Mammoth Lakes' main business artery on CA 203, the Knolls Trail takes you on a winding tour of thick pine forest as it switch-backs up to a clearing. A short spur to a vista confirms that you've already climbed quite a bit and that this is dang beautiful country. A little later, a slog of a climb takes your breath away—nothing to be ashamed of, since the elevation is near 8,400 feet. A fun descent follows, and if you do it in the late afternoon you'll be chasing your shadow. If you crash while trying to catch your shadow, you can bail out on a road that leads back to your starting point.

But more likely you'll keep going, a decision that rewards you with numerous ridge-top vistas plus boulder formations from which to enjoy them. A perfect downhill straightaway with excellent visibility allows you to ride at your own speed limit. Finally, you'll circle by Shady Rest Municipal Park, where you can indeed recline in the shade and take in a baseball game before winding through some more pine trees back to your car.

RIDE 98 · Knolls Trail

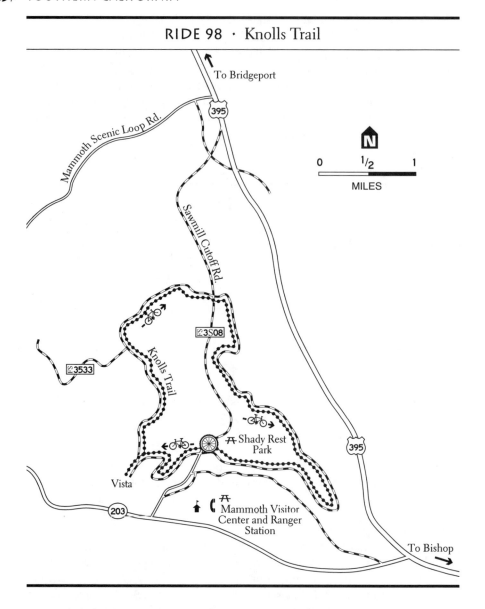

General location: Approximately 1 mile north of CA 203 in Mammoth Lakes in the Inyo National Forest.

Elevation change: An 800-foot differential between the highest (at 8,400 feet) and lowest (at 7,600 feet) points on the trail, with substantial roller-coaster terrain between the two. Approximate elevation gain: 1,200 feet.

Season: May through October, snow level permitting.

Choices, choices.

Services: Water and rest rooms are available in Shady Rest Municipal Park; all other services are available in Mammoth Lakes.

Hazards: Steep drop-offs from scenic overlooks and some very fast downhill stretches.

Rescue index: This ride is never far from the town of Mammoth Lakes, and Sawmill Cutoff Road provides a bail-out opportunity at the north end of the loop. Help is available at the U.S. Forest Service Ranger Station just east of Sawmill Cutoff on CA 203.

Land status: National forest.

Maps: "Mammoth Lakes Off-Highway Vehicle and Mountain Biking Map," available from Mammoth Ranger Station and Visitor Center.

Finding the trail: From downtown Mammoth Lakes, take CA 203 to the intersection with Sawmill Cutoff Road just west of the Mammoth Visitor Center and Ranger Station. Turn north on Sawmill Cutoff Road. Go about a mile, passing Old Shady Rest Campground on your left and Shady Rest Municipal Park on your right. A quarter mile past the municipal park driveway on your right, look for a waist-high Knolls Trail sign on your left. Turn left into a primitive, informal, wooded parking area. Park here, being careful not to block any possible traffic.

Sources of additional information:

Inyo National Forest
Mammoth Ranger Station and
  Visitor Center
CA 203 and Sawmill Cutoff Road
P.O. Box 148
Mammoth Lakes, CA 93546
(760) 924-5500
TDD (760) 924-5531
www.r5.fs.fed.us/inyo

Brian's Bicycles and Cross Country
  Skis
3059 Chateau Road
Mammoth Lakes, CA 93546
(760) 924-8566

Footloose Sports
3069 Main
Mammoth Lakes, CA 93546
(760) 934-2400

High Sierra Cycle Center
123 Commerce Drive
Mammoth Lakes, CA 93546
(760) 924-3723

Sandy's Ski and Sports
3325 Main Street
Mammoth Lakes, CA 93546
(760) 934-7518

Notes on the trail: With your back to Sawmill Cutoff Road, leave the parking area by angling left on well-signed Knolls Trail. (The signs are waist high and brown, depict a mountain bike, and read simply "Knolls.") At 0.3 mile you'll begin cruising past intersections with innumerable dirt roads. Just stay straight on the main road, which is sometimes marked with the Knolls signs, and sometimes with blue diamonds nailed into trees adjoining the trail. If there's ever a stretch where things get confusing, just look up and you're almost certain to see a blue diamond or Knolls sign. A good climb brings you to an intersection with a trail marked "Vista" at 1.3 miles. Turn left on this spur. It's a steep climb that you may have to portage, but the overlook at 1.5 miles is well worth it, offering excellent views of Crowley Lake. Return from the vista, and turn left on Knolls Trail again for a climb through a meadow and a saddle at 2.8 miles. A fun, modest descent takes you to an intersection with another dirt road at 3.3 miles, where you'll veer right, again following a Knolls sign. The blue diamonds are soon replaced by orange diamonds, but don't worry. The fast, shadow-chasing descent brings you to the junction with Sawmill Cutoff Road at 4.8 miles. Turn right here to bail out back to your car; otherwise go straight across the road and uphill. To your left is a ridgeline topped with striking rock formations. Offering wide vistas, the ridge is well worth a stopover, but any mileage incurred in exploring up there is not reflected here. At 5.5 miles, follow the signs and turn sharply right at an intersection and then left a short bit later at 5.6 miles. The trees retreat to grant you another expansive view. Continuing to follow the Knolls signs, you'll turn left at 6.7 miles for the last climb of the trip and then reach a saddle at 7.3 miles. This is a great place to stop and relax while taking in the scenery. Turn left from the saddle down a long, fast straightaway, making sure to head sharply right at 8.1 miles as indicated by the signs. Soon, Shady Rest Municipal Park appears on your left. You can explore a little here by taking some of the single-tracks through the woods on your right, but again, that mileage isn't reflected here. After staying on the northeast side of Shady Rest Park, the Knolls Trail crosses Sawmill Cutoff Road again at 9.7 miles and returns you to the start at 9.8 miles.

RIDE 99 · Inyo Craters

AT A GLANCE

Length/configuration: 7.9-mile combination (7-mile out-and-back (3.5 miles each way) plus 10.5-mile loop and 0.2-mile spur to Inyo Craters Trailhead) on single-track and dirt roads

Aerobic difficulty: Moderate; climbs take place in high altitude, but are not too grueling

Technical difficulty: Moderate; some occasionally technical sections in both single-track and fire road portions

Scenery: Jeffrey pines, Inyo Craters, mountain peaks, wildlife

Special comments: A fun ride with just enough challenges to test—but not dismay—intermediate riders. Bring a lock so that you can cap the ride with a short hike to Inyo Craters

This ride combines a fun single-track leaving from a Mammoth Lakes neighborhood with a satisfying loop around the mesmerizing Inyo Craters. Easier than the neighboring Knolls Trail, it's an ideal ride to enjoy when you first arrive on a mountain biking vacation in the area. You can acclimate yourself to the altitude, get a taste of the region's amazing volcanic legacy, and work up a sweat all in one fun ride. Afterward, you can spin into Mammoth Lakes for a post-ride meal.

General location: Outside of the town of Mammoth Lakes.

Elevation change: Approximately 700 feet.

Season: May to October, but it's possible that early or late season snow may cover trail. Weather can change rapidly; dress accordingly.

Services: No services on trail. All services in town of Mammoth Lakes.

Hazards: Stream crossings; vehicular traffic on the roads near Inyo Craters; high altitude.

Rescue index: Area sees a lot of use, and route is close to town of Mammoth Lakes, where help is available at Mammoth Ranger Station and Visitor Center.

Land status: National forest.

Maps: "Mammoth Lakes Off-Highway Vehicle and Mountain Biking Map" available from Mammoth Ranger Station and Visitor Center.

Finding the trail: From Mammoth Ranger Station and Visitor Center, go west on CA 203. Turn right on Knolls Drive, then take the first left. Go up a steep hill, around a corner and to a Water District pumphouse. Park here, obeying all posted regulations. The trail begins behind a gate near the small stone building.

RIDE 99 · Inyo Craters
RIDE 100 · Horseshoe Lake Loop
RIDE 101 · San Joaquin Ridge/Mountain View Trails

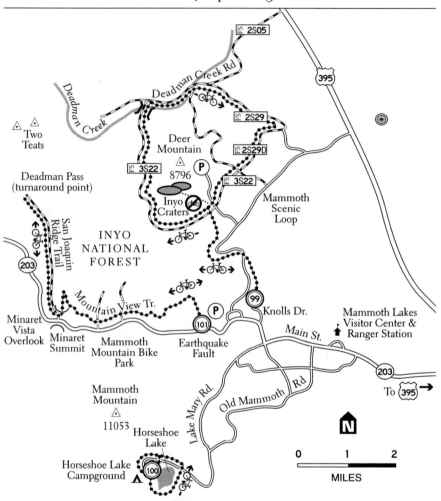

Sources of additional information:

Inyo National Forest
Mammoth Ranger Station and
  Visitor Center
CA 203 and Sawmill Cutoff Road
P.O. Box 148

Mammoth Lakes, CA 93546
(760) 924-5500
TDD (760) 924-5531
www.r5.fs.fed.us/inyo

The volcanic Inyo Craters.

Brian's Bicycles and
    Cross Country Skis
3059 Chateau Road
Mammoth Lakes, CA 93546
(760) 924-8566

Footloose Sports
3069 Main
Mammoth Lakes, CA 93546
(760) 934-2400

High Sierra Cycle Center
123 Commerce Drive
Mammoth Lakes, CA 93546
(760) 924-3723

Sandy's Ski and Sports
3325 Main Street
Mammoth Lakes, CA 93546
(760) 934-7518

Notes on the trail: Begin riding on the single-track behind the gate next to the stone building. You're heading north and will soon begin paralleling nearby Mammoth Scenic Loop, a paved road. A little past the 1.5-mile mark, you cross over Mammoth Scenic Loop just before it drops down a hill. The single-track is very fun to cruise on as you descend to the intersection with FS 3S22 at 3.5 miles.

You're now very close to the parking area and trailhead for the Inyo Craters hiking trail. You'll come back here later to view the craters, but for now, go left on FS 3S22. You spin along on mostly flat fire roads, and the route is well-signed. After one small creek crossing, you go over deeper Deadman Creek on a bridge, and turn right at the junction with FS 2S05 at 7.5 miles. (This stretch is also called "Deadman Creek Road.")

You're now heading east on a slight decline. Turn right at 9.3 miles on well-signed FS 2S29. Then, at 11.1 miles, go right on FS 2S29D, which turns into FS 3S22 and takes you to the turnoff for the parking area and trailhead for the Inyo Craters hike. Go right for 0.2 mile, lock up your bike in the parking area, and take the short hike. Spend a while looking at the 600-year-old craters and reading the interpretive displays about their creation, then remount your bike. You'll have a nice climb as you return to the start via the single-track you originally rode, for a ride totaling 17.9 miles.

RIDE 100 · Horseshoe Lake Loop

AT A GLANCE

Length/configuration: 7-mile loop around Horseshoe Lake on single-track and pavement

CA

Aerobic difficulty: Easy; route is mostly level, but with numerous dips

Technical difficulty: Easy/moderate; a multitude of stream crossings (many bridged, some not) and dips demand your constant attention

Scenery: Horseshoe Lake; panoramic views of snow-capped backcountry peaks; lodgepole pine forest.

Special comments: One of the easier rides in the area; a great intro to the Mammoth Lakes region.

This route offers views of backcountry peaks and a picturesque mountain lake—as well as picnic opportunities and some fun stream crossings—all in a ride that the whole family can enjoy. Plus, it's a loop, which means you won't repeat any terrain. This is one of those rides that justifies getting that mountain bike in the first place.

General location: Approximately 5 miles (driving distance) southwest of town of Mammoth Lakes.

Elevation change: Insignificant; route is essentially flat.

Season: June to October.

Services: Rest rooms and water available at start of ride in Horseshoe Lake Campground. Basic supplies available at stores at Twin Lakes and Lake Mary. All services in Mammoth Lakes.

Hazards: Stream crossings, narrow bridges.

Rescue index: Route is never far from Lake Mary Road. Inyo National Forest Rangers commonly patrol this area.

Land status: Inyo National Forest.

Maps: Mammoth Lakes Off-Highway Vehicle and Mountain Biking Map, available at Mammoth Ranger Station and Visitor Center. (Note: the map lists this ride as an out-and-back single-track instead of a loop.)

Finding the trail: From town center of Mammoth Lakes, head west on curvy Lake Mary Road for approximately 5.5 twisting miles. The road will take you past Lake Mary and Lake Mamie, after which the pavement ends. Stay on the dirt until reaching Horseshoe Lake Campground. Obey all posted regulations, and park near Group Campsite #4, where the trail begins.

Sources of additional information:

Inyo National Forest
Mammoth Ranger Station and
    Visitor Center
CA 203 and Sawmill Cutoff Road
P.O. Box 148
Mammoth Lakes, CA 93546
(760) 924-5500
TDD (760) 924-5531
www.www.r5.fs.fed.us/inyo

Brian's Bicycles and
    Cross Country Skis
3059 Chateau RD
Mammoth Lakes, CA 93546
(760) 924-8566

Footloose Sports
3069 Main
Mammoth Lakes, CA 93546
(760) 934-2400

High Sierra Cycle Center
123 Commerce Drive
Mammoth Lakes, CA 93546
(760) 924-3723

Sandy's Ski and Sports
3325 Main Street
Mammoth Lakes, CA 93546
(760) 934-7518

Notes on the trail: First, locate the trail near Group Campsite #4 on the west side of the lake. Start pedaling along this trail, which soon enters a lodgepole pine forest. The pines make it shady and sweet smelling, but also block your view of the lake for long stretches. If riding with small children, make sure they're comfortable crossing the bridges over the many inlets that you'll encounter. There are also some stream crossings that demand either skill or portaging. At just past 1.4 miles, you reach paved Lake Mary Road. Turn left here, and ride back to the campground, over the paved and dirt sections, to the start at 1.7 miles.

RIDE 101 · San Joaquin Ridge/Mountain View Trails

AT A GLANCE

Length/configuration: 4.2-mile combination ride (9.4-mile loop, plus 2.4-mile spur to Deadman Pass); a shorter—but still strenuous—option is possible

Aerobic difficulty: Strenuously difficult; steep climbs and high altitude

Technical difficulty: Difficult; single-track has soft pumice sections and some off-camber turns, and the dirt road is rocky

Scenery: Lodgepole pine forest, wildlife, and outstanding views of the Minarets, Ansel Adams Wilderness, Mammoth Mountain, Long Valley, and Reds Meadow

Special comments: A tough ride that showcases striking scenery—dress warmly so you can enjoy it

This ride busts your lungs and knocks you to your knees, but it also knows how to release the endorphins, and in the end, that's all that counts. Starting at Earthquake Fault, the route climbs through a landscape that shows off the region's volcanic legacy. Because of abundant pumice (which is a lot more fun to descend than ascend) on Mountain View Trail, I recommend climbing the pavement to Minaret Vista, where a very demanding dirt road climb leaves for Deadman Pass. You might fret about how rocky and steep the road is, but the views here demand that you look past petty worries such as those. Just make sure you are prepared (it can be very cold and windy up here, even on hot summer days). Return via the superlative downhill single-track Mountain View Trail, and you'll forget the route was ever anything but a joy ride.

General location: Just northwest of the town of Mammoth Lakes, between the town and Mammoth Mountain Ski Area.

Elevation change: 1,900 feet elevation gain.

Season: June to October, depending on snow level.

Services: The route passes by Mammoth Mountain Bike Park, where all services are available.

Hazards: Traffic on paved portions, rocky dirt roads, off-camber turns on single-track portions.

Rescue index: You're never far from CA 203 and civilization. Help is available at Mammoth Ranger Station and Visitor Center.

Land status: National forest.

Maps: Mammoth Lakes Off-Highway Vehicle and Mountain Biking Map, available from Mammoth Ranger Station and Visitor Center.

Finding the trail: From the town of Mammoth Lakes, go west on CA 203, toward Mammoth Mountain. Turn right at the well-marked Earthquake Fault, and park in the designated parking area.

Sources of additional information:

Inyo National Forest
Mammoth Ranger Station and
   Visitor Center
CA 203 and Sawmill Cutoff Road
P.O. Box 148
Mammoth Lakes, CA 93546
(760) 924-5500
TDD (760) 924-5531
www.r5.fs.fed.us/inyo

Brian's Bicycles and
   Cross Country Skis
3059 Chateau Road
Mammoth Lakes, CA 93546
(760) 924-8566

Footloose Sports
3069 Main
Mammoth Lakes, CA 93546
(760) 934-2400

This is why they call it the Mountain View Trail.

High Sierra Cycle Center
123 Commerce Drive
Mammoth Lakes, CA 93546
(760) 924-3723

Sandy's Ski and Sports
3325 Main Street
Mammoth Lakes, CA 93546
(760) 934-7518

Notes on the trail: From the parking area at Earthquake Fault, return to CA 203, and go right, or uphill. You'll encounter some automobile traffic, but fortunately, everyone here seems accustomed to bikers. The climb takes you through the Mammoth Mountain resort area, where you'll encounter the Mammoth Mountain Bike Park in summer. When the bike park is in operation, there are numerous facilities open should you need them.

After 3.8 miles of riding (including one brutal final climb), you reach a summit where you'll find the Reds Meadow Entrance Kiosk and signs pointing to the Minaret Vista Overlook. Go right here, and stay right so that (at 3.9 miles) you begin riding on San Joaquin Ridge Trail. Despite the "trail" part of its name, this route is open to four-wheel-drive traffic, so be alert as you ride.

The road clings near the top of San Joaquin Ridge as it heads up toward the distant, aptly named landmark, Two Teats. Stay on the main road at all times, which begins climbing even more steeply at the 2-mile mark. This ascent puts you on the ridge itself, which is often very windy. If you need to get off the bike at times, you're not alone. After 6.3 miles of riding, stop when the jeep portion of the road peters out at Deadman Pass. Enjoy the 360° view from here, then turn around and retrace your way back to Minaret Vista at 8.7 miles.

On the left (before you get to CA 203), you'll see the well-marked Mountain View Trail. Go left on it. It's a beautiful ride, descending through lodgepole pine forest on a tight trail that has some powdery pumice in sections. The pumice makes a much better surface for descents than climbs, and my Cannondale swooped through here as if it were on automatic pilot.

Though the trail is well-signed, there are two occasions where you come to unmarked intersections with dirt roads. At both times, jog right on the roads, then turn left on the single-track when the Mountain View Trail resumes. The trail brings you all the way back to Earthquake Fault, where you'll end a euphoric ride at 14.2 miles.

GLOSSARY

This short list of terms does not contain all the words used by mountain bike enthusiasts when discussing their sport. But it should serve as an introduction to the lingo you'll hear on the trails.

ATB	all-terrain bike; this, like "fat-tire bike," is another name for a mountain bike
ATV	all-terrain vehicle; this usually refers to the loud, fume-spewing three- or four-wheeled motorized vehicles you will not enjoy meeting on the trail—except, of course, if you crash and have to hitch a ride out on one
blaze	a mark on a tree made by chipping away a piece of the bark, usually done to designate a trail; such trails are sometimes described as "blazed"
blind corner	a curve in the road or trail that conceals bikers, hikers, equestrians, and other traffic
blowdown	see "windfall"
buffed	used to describe a very smooth trail
catching air	taking a jump in such a way that both wheels of the bike are off the ground at the same time
clean	while this may describe what you and your bike won't be after following many trails, the term is most often used as a verb to denote the action of pedaling a tough section of trail successfully
combination	this type of route may combine two or more configurations; for example, a point-to-point route may integrate a scenic loop or an out-and-back spur midway through the ride; likewise, an out-and-back may have a loop at its farthest point (this configuration looks like a cherry with a stem attached;

the stem is the out-and-back, the fruit is the terminus loop); or a loop route may have multiple out-and-back spurs and/or loops to the side; mileage for a combination route is for the total distance to complete the ride

cupped a concave trail; higher on the sides than in the middle; often caused by motorcycles

dab touching the ground with a foot or hand

deadfall a tangled mass of fallen trees or branches

diversion ditch a usually narrow, shallow ditch dug across or around a trail; funneling the water in this manner keeps it from destroying the trail

double-track the dual tracks made by a jeep or other vehicle, with grass or weeds or rocks between; mountain bikers can ride in either of the tracks, but you will of course find that whichever one you choose, and no matter how many times you change back and forth, the other track will appear to offer smoother travel

dugway a steep, unpaved, switchbacked descent

endo flipping end over end

feathering using a light touch on the brake lever, hitting it lightly many times rather than very hard or locking the brake

four-wheel-drive this refers to any vehicle with drive-wheel capability on all four wheels (a jeep, for instance, has four-wheel drive as compared with a two-wheel-drive passenger car), or to a rough road or trail that requires four-wheel-drive capability (or a one-wheel-drive mountain bike!) to negotiate it

game trail the usually narrow trail made by deer, elk, or other game

gated everyone knows what a gate is, and how many variations exist upon this theme; well, if a trail is described as "gated" it simply has a gate across it; don't forget that the rule is if you find a gate closed, close it behind you; if you find one open, leave it that way

Giardia shorthand for Giardia lamblia, and known as the "backpacker's bane" until we mountain bikers expropriated it; this is a water-borne parasite that begins its life cycle when swallowed, and one to four weeks later has its host (you) bloated, vomiting, shivering with chills, and living in the bathroom; the disease can be avoided by "treating" (purifying) the water you acquire along the trail (see "Hitting the Trail" in the Introduction)

gnarly	a term thankfully used less and less these days, it refers to tough trails
grated	refers to a dirt road that has been smoothed out by the use of a wide blade on earth-moving equipment; "blading" gets rid of the teeth-chattering, much-cursed washboards found on so many dirt roads after heavy vehicle use
hammer	to ride very hard
hammerhead	one who rides hard and fast
hardpack	a trail in which the dirt surface is packed down hard; such trails make for good and fast riding, and very painful landings; bikers most often use "hardpack" as both a noun and adjective, and "hard-packed" as an adjective only (the grammar lesson will help you when diagramming sentences in camp)
hike-a-bike	what you do when the road or trail becomes too steep or rough to remain in the saddle
jeep road, jeep trail	a rough road or trail passable only with four-wheel-drive capability (or a horse or mountain bike)
kamikaze	while this once referred primarily to those Japanese fliers who quaffed a glass of sake, then flew off as human bombs in suicide missions against U.S. naval vessels, it has more recently been applied to the idiot mountain bikers who, far less honorably, scream down hiking trails, endangering the physical and mental safety of the walking, biking, and equestrian traffic they meet; deck guns were necessary to stop the Japanese kamikaze pilots, but a bike pump or walking staff in the spokes is sufficient for the current-day kamikazes who threaten to get us all kicked off the trails
loop	this route configuration is characterized by riding from the designated trailhead to a distant point, then returning to the trailhead via a different route (or simply continuing on the same in a circle route) without doubling back; you always move forward across new terrain but return to the starting point when finished; mileage is for the entire loop from the trailhead back to trailhead
off-camber	a trail that slopes in the opposite direction than one would prefer for safety's sake; for example, on a side-cut trail the slope is away from the hill—the inside of the trail is higher, so it helps you fall downhill if your balance isn't perfect

ORV	a motorized off-road vehicle
out-and-back	a ride where you will return on the same trail you pedaled out; while this might sound far more boring than a loop route, many trails look very different when pedaled in the opposite direction
point-to-point	a vehicle shuttle (or similar assistance) is required for this type of route, which is ridden from the designated trailhead to a distant location, or endpoint, where the route ends; total mileage is for the one-way trip from the trailhead to endpoint
portage	to carry your bike on your person
quads	bikers use this term to refer both to the extensor muscle in the front of the thigh (which is separated into four parts) and to USGS maps; the expression "Nice quads!" refers always to the former, however, except in those instances when the speaker is an engineer
runoff	rainwater or snowmelt
scree	an accumulation of loose stones or rocky debris lying on a slope or at the base of a hill or cliff
side-cut trail	a trail cut on the side of a hill
signed	a "signed" trail has signs in place of blazes
single-track	a single, narrow path through grass or brush or over rocky terrain, often created by deer, elk, or backpackers; single-track riding is some of the best fun around
slickrock	the rock-hard, compacted sandstone that is great to ride and even prettier to look at; you'll appreciate it even more if you think of it as a petrified sand dune or seabed (which it is), and if the rider before you hasn't left tire marks (from unnecessary skidding) or granola bar wrappers behind
snowmelt	runoff produced by the melting of snow
snowpack	unmelted snow accumulated over weeks or months of winter—or over years in high-mountain terrain
spur	a road or trail that intersects the main trail you're following
stair-step climb	a climb punctuated by a series of level or near-level sections
switchback	a zigzagging road or trail designed to assist in traversing steep terrain; mountain bikers should not skid through switchbacks

technical	terrain that is difficult to ride due not to its grade (steepness) but to its obstacles—rocks, roots, logs, ledges, loose soil . . .
topo	short for topographical map, the kind that shows both linear distance and elevation gain and loss; "topo" is pronounced with both vowels long
trashed	a trail that has been destroyed (same term used no matter what has destroyed it . . . cattle, horses, or even mountain bikers riding when the ground was too wet)
two-wheel-drive	this refers to any vehicle with drive-wheel capability on only two wheels (a passenger car, for instance, has two-wheel drive); a two-wheel-drive road is a road or trail easily traveled by an ordinary car
waterbar	an earth, rock, or wooden structure that funnels water off trails to reduce erosion
washboarded	a road that is surfaced with many ridges spaced closely together, like the ripples on a washboard; these make for very rough riding, and even worse driving in a car or jeep
whoop-de-doo	closely spaced dips or undulations in a trail; these are often encountered in areas traveled heavily by ORVs
wilderness area	land that is officially set aside by the federal government to remain natural—pure, pristine, and untrammeled by any vehicle, including mountain bikes; though mountain bikes had not been born in 1964 (when the United States Congress passed the Wilderness Act, establishing the National Wilderness Preservation system), they are considered a "form of mechanical transport" and are thereby excluded; in short, stay out
windchill	a reference to the wind's cooling effect upon exposed flesh; for example, if the temperature is 10 degrees Fahrenheit and the wind is blowing at 20 miles per hour, the windchill (that is, the actual temperature to which your skin reacts) is minus 32 degrees; if you are riding in wet conditions things are even worse, for the windchill would then be minus 74 degrees!
windfall	anything (trees, limbs, brush, fellow bikers . . .) blown down by the wind

INDEX

DAVID STORY was born in Kansas City, Missouri, educated in New Hampshire, and first fell in love with mountain biking in Colorado, where he pro-

moted mountain bike races in the mid-1980s. Wisely getting out of race promotion before it became profitable, he turned to writing and now mainly works in the television and motion picture business. In addition to devoting his time to his wife and two children, David contributes articles to a variety of biking and travel magazines from his home in Santa Monica, California.

LAURIE LEMAN was born in Vancouver, British Columbia. There she grew to love Elvis, ice hockey, and Canadian beer. CHRIS LEMAN grew up in Detroit,

Michigan. His early youth was spent playing army, eating mud pies, and running down passersby with his tricycle. They met while working as bicycle tour leaders in Canada and now live in Ketchum, Idaho. When not writing bestselling mountain bike guides Laurie works as a pasta slinger at a local restaurant and helps coach the community's cross-country ski team. Chris is an apprentice carpenter and spends his free time trying to keep up with his wife on the trails.